The Devil Wins

The Devil Wins

A HISTORY OF LYING
from the
GARDEN OF EDEN
to the
ENLIGHTENMENT

DALLAS G. DENERY II

Princeton University Press
Princeton and Oxford

Library of Congress Cataloging-in-Publication Data

Denery, Dallas G. (Dallas George), 1964–
    The devil wins : a history of lying from the Garden of Eden to the
Enlightenment / Dallas G. Denery II.
        pages cm
    Includes bibliographical references and index.
    ISBN 978-0-691-16321-5 (alk. paper)
    1. Truthfulness and falsehood.   I. Title.
BJ1421.D46 2014
177′.309–dc23   2014006311

British Library Cataloging-in-Publication Data is available

This book has been composed in 10/13.5 Sabon.

Printed on acid-free paper. ∞

Printed in the United States of America

10 9 8 7 6 5 4 3 2 1

FOR LORRY

Contents

Part Two: Courtiers and Women Ask the Question

Acknowledgments

This book was a long time in the making and, before that, an even longer time in the putting off. Most of the doing and delaying occurred in three places, and I want to thank people from each of them.

Cambridge University has become a sort of home away from home. I owe a real debt of gratitude to Richard Newhauser, a great supporter and friend, who led an NEH seminar on the vices in medieval society at Darwin College during the summer of 2004. I began the preliminary research for this book that summer and profited from numerous conversations with Dwight Allman, Stan Benfell, Susan Dudash, Holly Johnson, Tom Parisi, and Derrick Pitard. In 2009, Nicolette Zeeman, along with Kantik Ghosh, Mishtooni Bose, and Rita Copeland, invited me to help organize a conference at King's College on doubt and skepticism in the Middle Ages. The event allowed me to discuss my work with them, as well as with Hester Gelber, Christophe Grellard, Dominik Perler, and, especially, Eileen Sweeney, who has read various chapters with great care over the years. Two years later, Nicolette invited me back to present several chapters of my book at a three-day work-in-progress seminar during which I had very useful conversations with her, Bill Burwinkle, and Emily Corran. William D. Wood was kind enough to meet me for a beer in Oxford.

During the 2012–2013 academic year, I was a Laurance S. Rockefeller Fellow at the University Center for Human Values, Princeton University. Under Alan Patten's leadership, the Center was a convivial and lively place, and between the fellows and faculty at the Center, various other Princeton faculty, and an extraordinary number of visiting speakers, I incurred debts too many to recall. At the Center, I benefited particularly from numerous mobile conversations with Alexander Voorhoeve, as well as with Renate Blumenfeld-Kosinski, Kimberly Ferzan, Samuel Goldman, Christopher Heathwood, Bennet Helm, Nannerl Keohane, and the late, much beloved, Paul Sigmund. In addition, I had the pleasure to meet and talk things historical with Moshe Shluvosky and Sophie Lunn-Rockwell, both of whom were in residence at the Davis Center. I want to thank Rob Tempio at Princeton University Press for his early and continued enthusiasm for this book and books in general.

At Bowdoin College, a number of colleagues and friends have read and discussed various versions and stages of this book over the years, including Margaret Boyle, Mary Agnes Edsell, Paul Franco, Paul Friedland, Kristen Ghodsee, Page Herrlinger, Ann Kibbie, Aaron Kitch, Robert Morrison, Steve Perkinson, Patrick Rael, Meghan Roberts, Arielle Saiber, and Scott Sehon. It goes without saying that without our superb library staff this book would have been much more difficult to complete, but I must single out Guy Saldanha and everyone at Interlibrary Loan for their amazing facility at quickly tracking down even the most obscure material. Part of the research for this book was funded through a Kenan Family Research Grant, sponsored by the college. Georgia Whitaker and Maya Little helped construct the bibliography on very little notice. I must also thank seven years worth of seminar students who patiently and, hopefully, enjoyably, worked through a litany of biblical commentaries, court treatises, and theological quagmires as I struggled to figure out what this book would be about.

I want to thank Steven Justice and Stephen Lahey for commenting on early drafts, as well as Lisa Bitel, David Luscombe, Cary Nederman, Daniel Smail, and Nicholas Watson for their various kindnesses. I owe a real debt of gratitude to Jonathan Sheehan for his meticulous reading of the entire manuscript, the anonymous readers who reviewed the book for Princeton University Press, and Will Hively for his expert and attentive copyediting.

I dedicate this book to my wife Lorry.

A Note on the Text

I have incorporated parts of the following previously published essays into this book: "From Sacred Mystery to Divine Deception: Robert Holkot, John Wyclif and the Transformation of Fourteenth Century Eucharistic Discourse," *Journal of Religious History*, June 2005, 129–44; "Biblical Liars and Medieval Theologians," in *The Seven Deadly Sins: From Individuals to Communities*, ed. Richard Newhauser (Leiden: E. J. Brill, 2007), 111–28; "Christine de Pizan against the Theologians: The Virtue of Lies in *The Book of the Three Virtues*," *Viator: Medieval and Renaissance Studies* 39:1 (2008): 229–47; "Christine de Pizan on Misogyny, Gossip and Possibility," in *The Middle Ages in Texts and Texture*, ed. Jason Glenn (Toronto: University of Toronto Press, 2011): 309–21; and "Uncertainty and Deception in the Medieval and Early Modern Court," in *Uncertain Knowledge in the Middle Ages*, ed. Dallas G. Denery II, Kantik Ghosh, and Nicolette Zeeman (Turnhout: Brepols, 2014): 13–36.

The Devil Wins

Is It Ever
Acceptable to Lie?

Punishment awaits those who lie.

Dante had little doubt about this, little doubt that unrepentant liars would suffer an eternity of pain, and he devoted much of his early fourteenth-century masterpiece, the *Inferno*, to describing their torments. As the pilgrim Dante and his guide, the revered Roman poet Virgil, enter the eighth circle of hell, a place called Malebolge, the final, painful residence for the fraudulent and every type of falsifier, they witness flatterers stewing in dung "that might well have been flushed from our latrines" and seducers condemned for eternity to walk naked in endless circles as "horned demons with enormous whips" beat them from behind. Pausing for a moment, Virgil asks his companion to look at one of the figures, a disheveled woman wallowing in excrement, squatting then standing then squatting again, forever scratching herself raw with filth-encrusted fingernails. "It is Thaïs," Virgil explains, "the whore who gave this answer to her lover when he asked, 'Am I very worthy of your thanks?': 'Very, nay, incredibly so!'" Disgusted, Virgil urges his companion to hurry on: "I think our eyes have had their fill of this."[1] Perhaps they have seen more than enough seducers and flatterers, but the variety of deceivers and falsifiers proves limitless. As the two continue farther into the depths of Malebolge, they discover hypocrites struggling under the weight of gold-gilded iron robes, false counselors transformed into heatless flame, a frozen lake filled with traitors submerged to their bellies, their teeth chattering "notes like storks' beaks snapping shut."[2]

A journey through hell, Dante's *Inferno* maps a geography of sin. Though all in hell are guilty, all are not equally punished. The gravity of sin increases the deeper Virgil and the pilgrim descend. Sinners guilty of lust and gluttony, avarice and prodigality, wrath and sullenness, give way to the violent, to murderers and suicides. But worst of all are the fraudulent, all those liars, deceivers, and traitors that fill hell's final two circles. "Since fraud belongs exclusively to man," Virgil explains, "God hates it more and, therefore, far below, the fraudulent are placed and suffer most."[3] Those guilty of lust allowed their passions to overwhelm them, like the winds that batter them in hell's upper reaches, catching them in storms of desire that lay waste to reason. Though their crimes were worse, the same is true of the malicious, of murderers condemned to cook in boiling rivers of blood as fitting justice for the burning rage and greed they let go unchecked, clouding all sense of charity as it drove them toward homicide. Traitors are different. Condemned to suffer forevermore in the arctic depths of hell, they composed their deceitful words with cold calculation, sundering every bond of love and friendship, like Judas before Jesus. When asked if he was the one who would betray the Son of Man, Judas calmly replied, "Surely, not I?"[4]

The denizens of hell not only suffer, their suffering poses a challenge to the two travelers. Forever trapped in forms and punishments emblematic of their crimes, the damned are forever doomed to repeat them. Well inside the eighth circle of hell, Virgil and the pilgrim discover that a bridge they had hoped to cross now lies in rubble. When Virgil questions a nearby demon, the creature promises that there are other bridges still standing farther along the path. Although the pilgrim warns his leader to be wary of this information, Virgil accepts it as true, only to discover later that every bridge has collapsed. "Once, in Bologna, I heard discussed the devil's many vices," a nearby hypocrite snidely comments. "[O]ne of them is that he tells lies and is the father of all lies." Virgil stalks off, angry with himself for having been fooled.[5]

If Virgil proves occasionally too trusting, the pilgrim responds differently to hell's challenges. Now in the ninth and final circle of hell, the abode of traitors, Virgil and the pilgrim come across a soul who refuses to name himself, frozen in place, his head bent back with tears turned to pools of ice so that "weeping puts an end to weeping, and the grief that finds no outlet from the eyes turns inward to intensify the anguish." Blinded and believing the pilgrim to be dead and damned just like himself, the frozen figure cries out, "O wicked souls, so wicked that you have been assigned the ultimate post, break off these hard veils covering my eyes and give relief from the pain that swells my heart—at least until the new tears freeze again." The pilgrim, doing nothing to correct the suffering soul's mistake, makes a promise: "If you wish me to help you, tell me who you are, and if I do not extricate you, may I have to go down to the bottom of the ice." These are misleading words at best, no doubt deceitful, perhaps even dishonest. With Virgil as his guide, the pilgrim knows he will soon descend to the bottom of the ice, the very pit and nadir of hell, fulfilling in some sense the strict letter of his promise, if not its spirit, and certainly not the promise as the soul understands it. Deceived, the soul immediately reveals himself to be Alberigo, a man whose treachery is so great his soul already suffers in hell while his body remains on earth inhabited by a shade. His crime? Under the false pretense of a reconciliation with relatives, he invited them to dine at his house, where he gleefully watched hired hands slaughter them as they ate. "But now extend your hand and open my eyes for me," the soul cries out. "I did not open them," the pilgrim reports. "To be mean to him was a generous reward."[6]

If cruelty can become generosity, can lies ever become virtuous?

∞

This is a book about the history of lying from the Garden of Eden to the Enlightenment. With one notable exception, it is not a history of specific lies, of who said what to whom, but a history of responses to a very fundamental, if straightforward, question: *Is it ever acceptable to lie?* A perennial question, one that remains with us to this day, it no longer means for us what it meant for people who lived during the Middle Ages, the Renaissance, and the Reformation. Contemporary behavioral psychologists and evolutionary biologists tell us that deception is woven into the very fabric of nature. Plants have evolved to look like insects and insects to look like plants. The bolas spider can emit a scent so similar to that of a female moth that it lures males to their death. For their part, different sorts of baboons, gorillas, and chimpanzees engage in what can best be described as intentional acts of deception, purposefully leading their fellows away from banana-laden trees only to scurry back unseen to gorge themselves, alone and in peace.[7] We humans are little different, and evolution seems to have favored those of us who deceive better than others. If we don't lie constantly, we certainly lie frequently. One study suggests that during every ten minutes of conversation, we lie three times and even more frequently when we use e-mail and text messaging.[8] Contemporary philosophers may debate whether it is ethical to lie, whether the standards and expectations of human society and conduct allow for or prohibit dishonesty, but these debates simply assume that lying is one of many questionable things we do.[9]

No one living before the eighteenth century would ever have claimed that our penchant for lying was simply natural. Scripture may have famously proclaimed "Every man is a liar," but that was an observation rooted in much more than mere empirical analysis. Near the beginning of his meditative treatise *On Humility and Pride*, Bernard of Clairvaux, perhaps the most famous religious figure of the twelfth century, writes that we can understand what it means to be a liar only if we humble and humiliate ourselves before God's truth and in that humiliation experience how wretched we really are. Reflecting on the book of Psalms, Bernard writes: "The prophet has humbled himself [. . .] as he says in another Psalm, 'And in your truth you have humbled me.' He has been thinking about himself. Now he looks from his own wretchedness to that of others, and so passes to the second step, saying in his ecstasy, 'Every man is a liar.' " But what does it mean to say "Every man is a liar?" It means, Bernard continues, that "every man is weak, powerless, unable to save himself or others." It means that anyone "who trusts his own strength deceives himself . . . [for] . . . he cannot hope for salvation from himself, nor can anyone else hope for salvation from him."[10] To assert that every man is a liar is to say something profound about who we are and how we got to be this way, about our relationship to God and ourselves, to those around us and to the world itself. Every man is a liar because every man is fallen, cast out of paradise, full of pride and utterly at God's mercy.

While Bernard's deeply monastic and religiously severe assessment of human depravity and helplessness may have been more extreme than those of his nonreligious peers, Christian writers from the earliest days of the Church to the seventeenth-century writings of Blaise Pascal, John Milton, and beyond would have agreed with him that the problem of the lie, of lying, was the problem of human existence itself. Its roots dug deep into the ground of ontology, metaphysics, and theology, and reached as far back as the very first moments of human history, a history blasphemed into existence beneath a tree in a garden, in the serpent's lying words to a woman who would soon be named Eve. For this tradition, human history, the history of fallen man, began with the serpent's lie, and that lie shaped and marked us, deformed and weakened us. It transformed us into sons of the Devil, liars and sinners both, even as it entangled us ever more tightly in the misery of a life lived in exile from the earthly paradise that God had created for us. Given this history, with all it entailed, the question *Is it ever acceptable to lie?* was always more than a question about acceptable or unacceptable behavior. It rephrased in the most trenchant form possible a much broader question: *How should we live in a fallen world?* Should the faithful Christian, when need be, adapt to the ways of a corrupt and deceitful world, lie to the liars, or is such accommodation the very hallmark and sign, root cause and continuing symptom, of our miserable lives as sinners? This account of the human penchant for perversity would begin to unravel, perhaps already in the seventeenth century but certainly in the next, a

development most obvious in the writings of the French *philoso-*
phe Jean-Jacques Rousseau, who would look to society as the entirely this-worldly source of human corruption and deceit.

From the Garden of Eden to the Enlightenment, from the serpent to society, at least one of the questions this book hopes to
answer is how lying became a natural phenomenon, how religiously inspired accounts of human mendacity slowly gave way to
accounts that had nothing to do with either God or the Devil.
Human beings would remain liars forever after, but there would
no longer be anything divine or damned in that fact. The Devil's
greatest victory, even if it meant his own self-annihilation, was to
set in motion the long slow process that would one day make a
corrupted world seem like the world God had meant to create all
along.

∞ ∞

More often than not, when historians tell the history of lying and
deception, it is a history of early modern Europe, of the sixteenth
and seventeenth centuries, "the Age of Dissimulation."[11] Both religious controversies and the centralization of power in the various
European states during this period leant particular urgency to
questions about the morality of lying and deception. Protestants in
Catholic lands and Catholics in Protestant lands had to ask themselves if it was acceptable to lie, conceal, or dissimulate their true
beliefs in order to avoid jail, torture, and death at the hands of
their persecutors, whether they could lie to protect friends and
family from similar fates.[12] Members of the aristocracy felt similar
pressures as they vied with one another to secure positions in the
increasingly centralized and politically absolutist European states.
Whether engaged in diplomatic missions or managing life in the
competitive, often capricious and conspiratorial world of the
court, the courtier needed to manage his self-presentation with utmost care, knowing what to say and what not to say, when to
mislead and when to lie. Machiavelli, who not only wrote the most
infamous book of political advice of the Renaissance but also
served as a diplomat for the Republic of Florence, described the

personal consequences of this predicament in a famous letter he wrote to Francesco Guicciardini: "For a long time I have not said what I believed, nor do I even believe what I say, and if indeed I do happen to tell the truth, I hide it among so many lies that it is hard to find."[13] A tad hyperbolic perhaps, but certainly fitting for an era whose most oft-repeated maxim may well have been "A man does not know how to live, who does not know how to dissimulate."[14]

The question of deception was seemingly everywhere during these centuries, in conduct manuals and ethical treatises, in plays and novels, touched on directly or implicitly, at length or in passing. Baldassare Castiglione's *Book of the Courtier*, first published in 1528, was reprinted 108 times by 1616 and translated into most every European language. After Castiglione, Giovanni della Casa's *Galateo: Or, the Rules of Polite Behavior* appeared in 1558, Torquato Tasso's dialogue *Malpiglio, or the Court* in 1587. The Spanish Jesuit Baltesar Gracián's *Art of Worldly Prudence* proved an overnight sensation on publication in 1647. In France, both Pierre Charon's early seventeenth-century treatise *On Wisdom* and Madeleine de Scudéry's *On Lying* (part of her popular late-century work *Conversations on Diverse Subjects*) achieved wide readership, while, a century earlier, Philbert de Vienne's satirical *Philosopher of the Court* hit close enough to home that more than a few readers took it for the real thing. No one missed the point when the renowned playwright Molière parodied both the self-interested religious hypocrite and the insufferably vain truth-teller in two of his greatest comedies, *Tartuffe* and *The Misanthrope*. Meanwhile, in England, Nathaniel Walker translated della Casa's treatise as *The Refin'd Courtier*, while John Taylor would strike a blow for truth-telling in *A Satyre against, Equivocation, Mentall Reservation and Detestable Simulation*.

All this early modern interest in deception must mean something, and historians have often argued that its significance becomes clear only when contrasted with medieval attitudes about lying, and especially those of the early fifth-century North African bishop Augustine of Hippo, who famously and categorically prohibited all lies. Every lie is a sin, Augustine would argue, and we must never choose to sin, never mind our reasons, never mind the consequences. Augustine's opinion soon became every theologian's opinion, repeated over the centuries, throughout the Middle Ages, the Renaissance, and long after as a truism never to be doubted. "Is every lie a sin?" the Dominican Sylvester Prierias would ask late in the fifteenth century. "I answer that it is not even licit to lie for the sake of saving someone's life, as Augustine, St. Thomas and all the theologians and canon lawyers teach."[15] A difficult standard to live up to and one that almost every subsequent theologian would try to work around, but certainly one that contrasts profoundly with what would soon be common, if never uncontroversial, advice in the sixteenth century. In Dante's *Inferno*, for example, Guido de Montefeltro suffers eternally among the false counselors for having so often played the part "not of a lion, but of a fox," advising acts of cunning and fraud, telling lies and making false promises.[16] When Machiavelli takes up the metaphor in *The Prince* several centuries later, he famously advises his readers that "it is necessary to be a fox in order to recognize the traps and a lion in order to frighten the wolves. Those who play only the part of the lion do not understand matters. A wise ruler, therefore, cannot and should not keep his word when such an observance of faith would be to his disadvantage and when the reasons which made him promise are removed."[17] His stratagems may have been successful, but Guido languishes in hell all the same, while Machiavelli, in *The Prince* at least, seems simply not to care at all about the spiritual consequences of his advice.

While these contrasts are stark, they are a bit misleading. Too often, historians imagine that the difference between medieval and early modern Europe can be captured in the differences between medieval monks, priests, and theologians, on the one hand, and Renaissance humanists and courtiers, on the other. Through a sleight of hand, even if unintentional, "Scholastic" comes to stand in for "medieval," as if the writings of university-trained theologians speak transparently for all medieval men and women.[18] Compared with medieval religious writings, the early modern emphasis on deception looks new indeed, as if people had suddenly become less concerned about faith and more concerned about the world. Hand in hand with this new worldliness, people similarly seem to turn inward. As any number of historians have argued, the promotion of techniques of concealment and dishonesty among early modern writers allegedly provides evidence for new conceptions of the individual, rooted in clearer (or more complicated or more ambiguous) divisions between the exterior and interior self. While there might be something to these claims, there is not as much as historians think. Is it really all that surprising that Scholastic theologians and theologically inspired poets had different views about lying, about how to live in the world, than did Renaissance humanists and courtiers? Even the attitudes of medieval humanists and courtiers differed from those of their Scholastic peers.[19]

This is not another example of the historian's trick of arguing that everything new is old again, of the medievalist's cry that "so-called" Renaissance discoveries are little more than thefts from the closet of the past. Rather, it is to suggest that if we hope to understand what changed as Europe moved from a premodern to an early modern society, we need to be careful about how we put that story together. We must not unduly smooth it over, nor mismatch its narrative parts to create startling, though not entirely accurate, contrasts. There was not one medieval response to the question *Is it ever acceptable to lie?*—there were many. If theologians achieved a fair degree of consensus when specifically addressing the question, they disagreed, often significantly, in the fine points of their analyses. When questions about lying came up in other theological contexts, in biblical passages in which the patriarchs or demons or even God seem to lie, or when mulling the many mysteries of the Eucharist or Christ's incarnation, theological analyses of lying were often stretched near to the breaking point. Outside the rooms and walls of the medieval university, there were entirely different attitudes about lying. In both medieval court manuals and vernacular romances, those ever-popular stories of knightly chivalry and clandestine love, writers understood lying to be an unfortunate, but completely legitimate, response to a fallen and confusing world. Even Dante's pilgrim in the ninth circle of hell is not above misleading and deceiving, making promises that he knows his interlocutor cannot possibly understand and then confidently justifying his deceptions by claiming his ice-blinded victim deserves whatever mistreatment he receives.

To attempt to do justice to these many historical strands, this book does not offer a single monolithic and chronological account of the history of lying. Rather, it presents the history of lying through five separate narratives, each one beginning in the early days of the Catholic Church or the Middle Ages and ending sometime late in the seventeenth or early in the eighteenth century. The book's organizing question, *Is it ever acceptable to lie?* is well suited to this project of multiple retellings because it begs us to ask an additional question, a question about who it is that can or cannot sometimes justifiably lie. While theologians, at least when specifically addressing the question of lying in their commentaries on Peter Lombard's *Sentences*, did not believe specifying the speaker mattered (that is, they believed that the same response applied identically to one and all alike), this was not the case when the question slipped into other sorts of theological discussions or when nontheologians asked the question.[20] Is it ever okay *for whom* to lie? makes it possible to explore the different facets of this history.

This is at least one reason why it can be useful to do history, at least this history, in terms of an enduring and perennial question whose answer will differ depending on who does the asking and when. It allows us to perceive the fragmentations, the differences and debates, that exist in any culture at any one time, while simultaneously allowing us to trace how similarly situated people responded to the same question over time.[21] And people were similarly situated when they pondered this question from the early days of the Christian church until the eighteenth century, not least because they agreed about the origin of human mendacity and its consequences. The narrative of the Fall—of the serpent's lying deception of Eve, Adam's decision to disobey God, and the first couple's exile from Eden—provided something like the bare bones of a tradition within which Christians would ask and answer this question until well into the eighteenth century. Seventeenth-century natural scientists may have understood parts of that narrative differently than sixteenth-century reformers, and medieval theologians would understand it in yet other ways, but that tradition, transmitted from one generation to the next—some elements remaining unchanged, others evolving, disappearing, then reappearing, or taking on changed significance—set the stage within which Christians formed their beliefs about lies and lying.[22]

If the narrative of the Fall set the stage for over a millennium of reflection on lies, it was a stage whose borders were porous and shifting, first decorated one way, then another. Simply put, even while accepting much the same narrative, different people brought different sets of concerns to it, interpreted it differently, drew varied conclusions from it. This has at least two consequences for how the history of lying will be presented in this book. First, there are elements of this narrative that writers will assert again and again over the centuries, beliefs that fifth-century bishops hold in common with sixteenth-century reformers. To stress these continuities and to elaborate on them more fully, there will be moments when it will be useful, for example, to bring Augustine into dialogue with Martin Luther, to use Luther's writings to make sense of and give added nuance to Augustine's writings, to look to the Franciscan Nicholas of Lyra's monumental fourteenth-century biblical commentaries as a way into the challenges that the seventeenth-century scientist and philosopher René Descartes faced as he worried about the problem of divine deception. Second, precisely because different writers told the story of the Fall differently, stressing different elements, integrating them with other sets of traditions, concerns, and ideas, it will be necessary to return to that story more than once in order to clarify how various writers drew on it, even as they used it to differentiate themselves from their peers and predecessors as they repeatedly asked the question *Is it ever acceptable to lie?*

In order to accomplish these various tasks, the following chapters, divided into two parts, tell the history of lying as a response to this question when posed to five different types of speakers in the medieval and early modern world. The first part considers how theologians addressed the problem of lying, the second how non-theologians addressed the problem. Since one of the claims this book makes is that theological attitudes about lying were much more varied than often realized, the first half of the book examines how theologians analyzed lying in three different contexts: in their attempts to understand the nature of the Devil's deceitful words in the Garden of Eden, when they asked whether God could lie, and, finally, when they asked if it was ever licit for human beings to lie. Since another claim this book makes is that the opinion of professional theologians did not entirely define medieval attitudes about lying, the second half of the book shifts from the opinions of theologians to the opinions of two very different types of speakers: courtiers, on the one hand, and women, on the other.

The first chapters frame the ontological and metaphysical issues that will shape the rest of the book, but also seek to reveal how diverse the theological discussion of deception really was. To discuss lying and the Devil is to ask what precisely he did in the Garden of Eden, how did his words so quickly convince the Woman and, after her, Adam to sin against God's commandment not to eat from the Tree of the Knowledge of Good and Evil. From very early on, the Church fathers asserted that the serpent's words were lies precisely because they altered and misinterpreted God's sacred Word. Genesis made the danger of misinterpretation obvious, as it spread contagion-like to the Woman, who, responding to the serpent's lying question, proceeded to alter God's command yet again. As a result, the Devil came to stand for the prototypical sophist swaying his audience with self-serving lies, the heretical teacher leading his flock away from the clear and inspired holy words of scripture. To misinterpret scripture was, in a very real sense, to lie about God, and we lie about God whenever we deviate from the truth of his Word. But as fallen creatures, our intellects dimmed, no longer able to see God face to face and easily confused, how do we know if we have deviated? This question took on renewed significance in the aftermath of Martin Luther's break with the Catholic Church as reformed theologians and believers

endlessly divided and subdivided into exegetically cantankerous
sects, each claiming to be the sole keepers of God's literal word
while accusing everyone else of colluding with the Devil. An impossible situation, and one that could be surmounted, according to
the sixteenth-century Italian Protestant convert Jacobus Acontius,
only if we turned our attention from the Devil, as the source of
lies, to our diminished faculties, as the continuing cause of our inability to reach complete interpretive clarity and agreement. In his
treatise *Satans Strategems* Acontius would urge his fellow reformers to treat interpretive disagreement not as a sign of demonic possession but rather as the consequence of our fallen and finite state.
Misinterpretation, the cause of our exile from Eden, becomes the
possible precondition for our peaceful coexistence with others.

The second chapter turns from the Devil's lie to ask the troubling question *Can God lie?* Considered in his essence, most theologians had no doubt that not only could God not lie, he could not
even deceive. Beginning with Augustine (who, in part at least, drew
on Platonic and Neoplatonic ideas concerning divinity), theologians understood God to be eternal and unchanging, immutable,
just, and wise. It was inconceivable for such a being, incompatible
with its very essence, to act so imperfectly as to deceive. Unfortunately, theologians had a rather difficult time squaring this philosophically inspired conception of God with the God described in
scripture, a God who speaks, punishes, deceives, lies, and orders
others to lie for him. How, for example, were they to explain away
the fact that the entire possibility of human salvation depended on
an apparent act of deception? A long line of theologians, poets,
and artists, from Gregory of Nyssa in the fourth century to Martin
Luther in the sixteenth, believed that Christ had intentionally concealed his divinity from the Devil, hiding it within human flesh so
the Devil would not know the true identity of the man he sought
to crucify. The ritual consecration of the Eucharist posed a related
problem. After the consecration of the host, the Church taught
that the body of Christ was really and truly present, hidden within
or behind the appearance of a simple piece of bread. Theologians
attempted to justify these apparent deceptions through the lan-

guage and tools of rhetoric. Just as the Devil was the corrupt rhetorician, the evil sophist, God was the morally upright orator, perfectly fitting his words and deeds to the moment, countering evil
with goodness, cunning with prudence. Whether this tactic successfully rescued God from charges of lying and deception is not
entirely clear, but it highlights just how at odds the biblical and
narrative conceptions of God as involved and interacting with the
world were with philosophical conceptions of God as omnipotent,
unchanging, and transcendent. Throughout the Reformation and
the Scientific Revolution of the seventeenth century, the tension
between these two conceptions would prove completely incompatible, compelling the French philosopher René Descartes to argue
that we can learn next to nothing about God from the Bible. God
would be forever freed from charges of lying, but at the cost of no
longer playing any active part in the world.

Taken together, the first two chapters describe the changing
relations between the supernatural and the natural, between the
Devil, God, and the world. In both cases, the history of lying reveals a gradual process of clarification and separation as the lines
between the natural and supernatural become more distinct, more
difficult to cross, as what once were divinely inspired features of
the world become mere features of the world, ever more loosely
tied to divine origins. The third chapter concludes the discussion of
theological opinions about lying. Writing early in the fifth century,
Augustine rooted his prohibition against lies in the nature of the
Trinity and in the incarnation of Christ as the Word made flesh.
When we lie, we undo our image and likeness to God. Every lie is
a sin because with every lie we turn away from God. Scholastic
theologians accepted Augustine's prohibition as authoritative but
grounded it, not in God, but in conceptions of justice, that is, in
terms of our obligations to ourselves and others. A crucial reorien-
tation, this move offered a basis for considering the possible benefits of our lies while simultaneously asserting that no lie can ever
be justified in terms of its outcomes. From this point forward, the
history of theological debate about the legitimacy of lying becomes
the history of unending efforts to expand the range of misleading,

but nonmendacious, speech, an effort culminating in the sixteenth-
and seventeenth-century writings of Dominican and Jesuit casuists with their advocacy of such practices as equivocation and
mental reservation. Blaise Pascal would lampoon these practices
in his *Provincial Letters*, accusing the casuists of the most base
and despicable sort of accommodation to the world. In response,
he called for the good Christian to stand apart from worldly values, but even his writings evince some of the very adaptation he
condemns.

The fourth and fifth chapters take up the problem of lying as it
appeared to people whose relationship to the world made the
problem of lying appear distinctly different than it did to theologians. The fourth chapter considers attitudes about lying among
the members of Europe's ecclesiastical and secular courts. A long
tradition, dating back to Rome, consistently depicted the court as
a place of deception and mendacity gone wild as status-seeking
courtiers did everything in their power to win the notice of their
superiors, mislead their equals, and quash their inferiors. In the
Middle Ages, especially in the writings of John of Salisbury, the
court came to represent most clearly the conditions of life in a
fallen world. The response of courtiers to this situation, in the
Middle Ages and throughout the sixteenth and seventeenth centuries, remained much the same: we must be skeptical, we must employ the tools of rhetoric and the faculty of prudence to determine
how we should act and what we should say and, when necessary,
when we must lie. We have no choice but to adapt to the ways of a
fallen and deceitful world, to lie to the liars. Medieval, no less than
early modern, works stress the difference between our inner
thoughts and our outward appearance, and the need to regulate
our self-presentation to fool and please and deceive those around
us. Simply put, the alleged differences between medieval and early
modern conceptions of the self are overstated and, when it comes
to the history of lying, a distraction from a much more significant
development. John of Salisbury in the twelfth century, Christine de
Pizan at the beginning of the fifteenth, and Castiglione in the sixteenth century all stress that we must lie to counteract the lies of

others. Lies are the regrettable tools we must employ in our own self-defense and for the good of the community. Over the course of the sixteenth century, but especially in the seventeenth, writers such as Giovanni della Casa, François La Rochefoucauld, and Pierre Nicole will contend that lies are not simply weapons deployed in our self-defense. Rather, lies constitute the very foundation of society itself. Without all forms of deception and flattery, society would rend itself irrevocably as our most base and inescapable passions would be revealed for one and all to see. Early in the eighteenth century, Bernard Mandeville would push this line of thought one step further, arguing that lies do more than help us endure one another's narcissistic pride: they are necessary if society is to progress and flourish.

The problem and fact of lying affected women differently than men. While we all might be liars, only women were thought to be inveterate liars. Greek medical ideas propounding the inferiority of women merged easily with a tradition of biblically based misogyny rooted in the story of the Fall, together forming the notion that all women were feebleminded and inconstant, lacking in both prudence and judgment, and always under the sway of their desires with no qualms about lying to satisfy them. Women were to men, so the analogy went, as the body was to the soul. In other words, women were associated with deceptive coverings, false surfaces, and seductive adornment. Endlessly repeated, these ideas passed down from the third-century writings of Tertullian and other Church fathers to the Middle Ages, and from there to succeeding generations. The challenge women faced was not simply whether or not it was licit to lie, but how to respond to a situation in which they were thought to be—indeed, taught that they were—the very embodiment of dishonesty. Confronted with this oppressive and institutionalized ideology, women writers responded with a two-pronged critique. On the one hand, they revealed the misogynist tradition for the fabric of lies it was. On the other, they rehabilitated the function of adornment, decoration, and deception. Christine de Pizan, writing at the beginning of the fifteenth century, took up the first task, correcting slanderous accounts of famous women and pointing out the implausibility of biologically based misogyny. Some two centuries later, two Venetian women, Lucrezia Marinella and Moderata Fonte, would argue that men, no less than women, depend on style and adornment to make themselves known, while contending that the lies of men are infinitely more harmful than any lie a woman could tell. Madeleine de Scudéry, the most popular author of the seventeenth century, would bring this line of thought to its conclusion. For Scudéry, style and adornment become the very mark and basis of the ideal society. If our self-interested passions and desires pose the greatest threat to social harmony, then we must conceal, even repress, them behind false and insincere adornments of speech, little lies and social niceties. Societal relations may well become utterly superficial, with people more interested in amicability than truth, but at least in such a society women, finally, can coexist in peace with men.

Decomposing the history of lying into five separate narratives raises questions, not only about the interrelations between and among those narratives, but also about the movement from medieval to early modern conceptions of lying. While each chapter can be read on its own, independently of the others, taken together they do tell a larger story about the domestication and naturalization of mendacity as it moves from being a devastating demonic disruption of the orderly world of paradise to being the source of worldly order itself. These movements seem gradual rather than sudden, beginning sometime in the High Middle Ages and generally reaching their conclusion sometime in the mid-seventeenth or even eighteenth century. At least when it comes to the history of lying, sharp divisions between the medieval and the early modern seem to be more hindrance than aid to understanding these developments, rendering differences sharper and more radical than they really are. If there is a moment that seems to divide the past from the present, these narrative histories suggest it can be found sometime in the eighteenth century, when it became possible to ask the question *Is it ever acceptable to lie?* outside the tradition of the Fall.

No doubt some readers will be surprised that certain topics or writers are barely discussed or not discussed at all. There is nothing on politics and lying, on Renaissance debates about "the reason of state," nor anything about the truth status of fiction and history. In response, I can only point out that the history of lying is immense, and no book could provide anything approaching a comprehensive account of it. Hopefully the book itself, its aims and logic, will justify what is included and what has been quietly passed over. This is a book about the problem of lying as it appeared to people from the fourth until the eighteenth century, that is, as a problem deeply connected to the tragic events in the Garden of Eden and how, finally, it became possible to imagine it as a problem having nothing to do with those events. In other words, it is a book about how the problem of lying became our problem, the problem as we know it today. At the same time, it is a book that hopes to upset a popular narrative that contrasts the medieval and the early modern in terms of diametrically opposed attitudes about lying and the easy contrasts that flow from that opposition. In order to accomplish these joint goals, this book examines the historical response to one question from a variety of perspectives, the theological and the secular, the uncreated and the created, the masculine and the feminine, revealing, if not the total diversity of opinions, a much greater diversity than historians have previously recognized. No doubt other perspectives could have been included, but it is difficult to imagine this history without these five perspectives, and certainly these five seem adequate to fulfill this book's goals. Augustine may have had some sympathy for the predicament of having more to say than one should or has the time to say. "Hence it is not a lie when truth is passed over in silence," he writes in his early fifth-century treatise *Against Lying*, "but when falsehood is brought forth in speech."[23] And hopefully, if it is not a lie to pass over the truth in silence, neither will it be misleading, at least in what follows.

PART ONE

Theologians Ask the Question

CHAPTER ONE

The Devil

SIX DAYS AND TWO SENTENCES LATER

It took God six days to create the world and the Devil two sentences to undo it.

Until sometime in the seventeenth century, most every European, Catholic and Protestant alike, agreed that Moses had recorded these events in the first three chapters of Genesis. They also agreed on the general outline of Moses's narrative, filling in missing details to transform it into the first step in the increasingly drawn-out history of human salvation. According to this story, God speaks the world into existence. "And God said, 'Let there be light,'" we read at Genesis 1:3, "and there was light." On the sixth day, after creating Adam and placing him in the Garden of Eden, God sets forth one final command, a rule to be followed. "You may freely eat of every tree in the garden," he tells Adam, "but of the tree of the knowledge of good and evil you shall not eat, for in the day that you eat of it you shall die." God's words are powerful, they are creative, and they are absolute. The Devil's words are by no means as powerful as God's, but they are efficient, and their efficiency carries its own type of unsettling power. If God's words create order and goodness out of nothingness, the Devil's words create disorder out of what is good. Appearing in the guise of a serpent before the Woman in the Garden of Eden, the Devil asks, "Did God say, 'You shall not eat from any tree in the Garden?'" The Woman responds, "We may eat of the fruit of the trees in the garden; but God said, 'You shall not eat of the fruit of the tree that is in the middle of garden, nor shall you touch it, or you shall die.'" Moses never explains how the Woman learned this command, nor does he tell us why she adds the prohibition against touching the tree. With a maximum of narrative simplicity, he simply records the Devil's second sentence: "You will not die; for God knows that when you eat of it your eyes will be opened, and you will be like God, knowing good and evil."

After this everything changes. The Woman sees that the tree is "good for food and a delight to the eyes." She eats some of its fruit, offers it to Adam, who is "with her," and he eats as well. Suddenly, their eyes opened, they recognize their nakedness and cover themselves with fig leaves. When God calls for them, they hide, fearful because they are not dressed. There follow more words—questions, answers, defenses, curses, punishments. Adam blames the Woman for giving him the fruit to eat. The Woman blames the serpent. These words engender further transformations. God announces that the Woman will suffer pains in childbirth and that her husband will rule over her. Adam will now toil for his food, gathering plants from the fields of a newly cursed earth that will bring forth little more than "thorns and thistles." Adam names the woman "Eve," and God drives the two of them out of Eden, placing angels and a flaming sword at its entrance to prevent them from ever approaching the Tree of Life.

Throughout all this, the serpent, now condemned to crawl on its belly, to live on dust and in constant enmity with the Woman, remains silent. Of course, the Devil, having achieved everything he had hoped to achieve, has no reason to say anything else. And he did it all with a few simple words, one or two sentences, a question and a statement. "Did God say, 'You shall not eat from any tree in the garden?'" he asks. "You will not die; for God knows that when you eat of it your eyes will be opened, and you will be like God, knowing good and evil," he states.

THE DEVIL AND THE LIE

Surprisingly, especially given their prominent role in the opening chapters of Genesis, Adam and Eve soon vanish from the Hebrew

Bible, never to be mentioned again after Genesis 5:3–5, when we learn that Adam lived for 800 years after the birth of his son Seth, dying, finally, at the age of 930.[1] By contrast, Adam is mentioned several times in the New Testament. While Luke traces Jesus's lineage, albeit through Joseph, all the way back to "Seth, son of Adam, son of God,"[2] it is in Paul's epistles to the Romans and Corinthians that Adam achieves his singular importance for Christian theology as "a type of the one who was to come."[3] "[S]in," Paul writes, "came into the world through one man, and death came from sin." He immediately puts names to deeds when he adds, "Yet death exercised dominion from Adam to Moses, even over those whose sins were not like the transgression of Adam."[4] For Paul, Jesus's crucifixion makes sense only in the light of Adam's violation of God's prohibition against eating from the Tree of Knowledge. "Therefore just as one man's trespass led to condemnation for all," he adds, "so one man's act of righteousness leads to justification and life for all." And, just in case the notion of trespass might prove too subtle and vague a specification of the crime committed, Paul clarifies: "For just as by one man's disobedience the many were made sinners, so by the one man's obedience the many will be made righteous."[5]

Given the weight Paul placed on Adam's sin, it is hardly surprising that subsequent Christian writers would return again and again to the frustratingly brief story of the Temptation, to Adam and to Eve and, especially, to the serpent.[6] Already in the early fifth century, the North African bishop Augustine, summarizing a tradition that had built up around Paul's letters while giving it a form that would influence every subsequent religious writer, would lament the catastrophic consequences of the Fall. "For because of [Adam and Eve's] sin," he writes in *The City of God*, "human nature was made subject to all the great corruption that we see and feel, and so to death also . . . and so [mankind] became very different from what he had been when he dwelt in Paradise before his sin."[7] Alcimus Ecdicius Avitus, the early sixth-century bishop of Gaul and the first Christian to rewrite the Creation story as a pastoral poem, was, if anything, more blunt and certainly more to the

point. "To you Adam, our first father," he writes at the very beginning of his poem *The Beginning of the World*, "I shall attribute the
cause of mankind's various sufferings, to you the reason why our
mortal life possesses so brief a span."[8] Things looked no better
nearly a millennium later. When Martin Luther, during the decade
leading up to his death in 1545, considered the Temptation and
Fall in his *Lectures on Genesis*, he stressed their enormous and
continuing consequences, consequences that can be appreciated
only if "we look back at that image of the state of innocence . . . in
which the will was upright and the reason was sound." We must, in
other words, return to the first chapters of Genesis and compare
what life was like for Adam and Eve before the Fall with what it is
like now. Luther assured his readers that it was a contrast horrible
in its implications. As a result of the Fall, we had lost "a most
beautifully enlightened reason," and our will had lost its natural
concord with God. The Fall had extinguished the body's glory "so
that now it is a matter of the utmost disgrace to be seen naked,"
and left our flesh burning with passions that have turned us into
enemies of God.[9] None of this had been the case when Adam and
Eve lived in innocence, when they were naked together without
shame, without lust.

Genesis not only explained what we had been, what we had
become, and what we continue to be, it also explained how that
transformation occurred. It placed our current state of misery
within the context of God's Creation of the universe, while tracing
it to a specific series of events. A grand cosmological narrative set
the stage for a seemingly simple story involving a tree, a snake, two
human beings, and God, a story that began with the prohibition
against eating from the Tree of Knowledge, and from there proceeded as if inexorably to the serpent's temptation of the Woman,
to the eating of the forbidden fruit and, finally, to human exile
from paradise. For early Christian, medieval, and Reformation
writers, the specific details of how the first couple fell were no less
important than knowledge of what that Fall had cost the human
race. Those details may have been even more important, more relevant. Eve may have been the first person to be tempted, but she

certainly was not the last. "Some people are puzzled by this temptation of the first man," Augustine writes in his extended commentary, *The Literal Meaning of Genesis*, a work he began in 401,
"wondering why God allowed it to happen, as if they do not see
that in our days the whole human race is unceasingly tempted by
the snares of the devil."[10] The first temptation offered Christians
something like a prototype and modus operandi for all future
temptations, what the sixteenth-century Italian Protestant convert
and religious exile Jacobus Acontius referred to as the *stratage-
matum satanae*, an alliteration that found its way into the 1648
English translation of his book *Satans Strategems or the Devils
Cabinet-Counsel Discovered.*[11]

Predictably, it was the apostle Paul who had set the stage for
the continuing relevance of these details. In his second letter to the
faithful at Corinth, he warned, "But I am afraid that as the serpent
deceived Eve by its cunning, your thoughts will be led astray from
a sincere and pure devotion to Christ."[12] What the Devil had first
done to Eve, he continues to do to each and every one of us, and
what he continues to do is lie. The Gospels made it clear that lying
was, for all intents and purposes, the Devil's unique contribution
to God's Creation. The Gospel of John records a confrontation "in
the treasury of the temple" between Jesus and the Pharisees, in
which Jesus accuses them of having strayed from the faith of Abraham, from faith in God. "Why do you not understand what I say?"
Jesus asks them. "It is because you cannot accept my word. You
are from your father the devil, and you choose to do your father's
desires. He was a murderer from the beginning and does not stand
in truth, because there is no truth in him. When he lies, he speaks
according to his own nature, for he is a liar and the father of lies."[13]
An important passage: it not only would provide the Devil with his
most famous sobriquet, it also cemented a number of defining contrasts between God and the Devil, between God's creative truth
and the Devil's destructive falsehoods. Luther captured these contrasts succinctly when, commenting on Genesis, he noted that
"Moses expresses himself very carefully and says: 'The serpent
said,' that is, with a word it attacks the Word."[14]

The Devil is a liar, and he is the father of lies. He uses words as traps and snares, as weapons to lure and to harm, to attack and to murder his victims. There was never any doubt about this, never any question about the very real connection between falsehood and violence. In his *Commentary on John*, the thirteenth-century Franciscan theologian Bonaventure wrote: "*He was a murderer from the beginning*, that is after the beginning of the human race; because he led the first man to death by promising life and denying death. 'You will not die,' he said at Genesis 3."[15] Just as there was universal agreement that the Devil had lied to Eve when he said "You will not die," religious writers were convinced that deception even tainted his initial question. John Chrysostom, who died in A.D. 407, had already noted this in his sixteenth homily on Genesis. "So [the Devil] employs this irrational animal for laying his plan," Chrysostom preached, "and by means of it he speaks to the woman in these words: 'Why is it that God said, Do not eat of any tree in the Garden?' Notice in this case the extreme subtlety of his malice: in the unfolding of his planning and inquiry he introduces words not spoken by God and acts as though motivated by care."[16] Falsehood, deception, and lies permeate every aspect of the two sentences the Devil speaks to Eve, and they permeate more than just his words. Chrysostom suggests that the Devil planned this line of discussion in advance, put on a costume and staged a performance in order to convince Eve that he had her best interests at heart. Nicholas of Lyra, perhaps the most revered biblical commentator of the Middle Ages, had precisely these sorts of considerations in mind when he explained what it means to call the Devil "the father of lies." "That he is called a liar and the father of lies does not only refer to [spoken] lies," Nicholas writes, "but to those things he pretends. For this reason the Devil is called the father of lies because he invents the first lie when he said to the woman, 'You will not die.' "[17]

The Devil invented the lie, and it is an invention that defines and mars his very essence and existence. More, it is an invention whose effects seem to define and mar Creation itself, a creation God cursed and punished, that God transformed because the Devil's lie had proven so successful. The sixteenth-century reformer John Calvin stressed the damage done when he noted that the Devil "knew that with the ruin of man the most dreadful confusion would be produced throughout the world."[18] And the Devil's strategy was no less popular than it was harmful, at least according to Psalm 116, which announced that "[e]veryman is a liar," a sentiment concerning the universal dissemination of evil that Paul was more than happy to pass on to the Romans as being at the very heart of our sad distance from God.[19] "Although everyman is a liar," Paul writes, "let God be proved true."[20] Proving God true, not to mention specifying the exact dogmatic details of that truth, no doubt motivated religious writers as they burrowed into the details of the Temptation narrative, but they were no less concerned with uncovering the precise nature of the Devil's weapon, the lie, a weapon whose secrets were hidden in the text of Moses's story. In fact, given the Temptation's place within the broader narrative of divine Creation beginning at Genesis 1:1 and, even more broadly, as the starting point for Christian providential and eschatological histories, the Devil's first two sentences were crucial to uncovering God's truth. Making sense of the Devil's actions required fitting them into more general conceptions of God and Christ and the nature of a true Christian faith. If we were to understand our own earthly predicament, the Devil's lie had to have its place as part of the very fabric of creation. Augustine's spiritual mentor Ambrose, writing in Milan late in the fourth century, stressed the practical necessity of this knowledge: "We read in the oracular words of Scripture of the wiles of the Devil, so that we learn how we can escape his arts. We should be aware of his temptations, not that we may follow his lead, but that by instruction we may avoid these pitfalls."[21]

From Augustine to Luther, and from Luther to the Italian Protestant-in-exile Jacobus Acontius, theologians had no doubt that the Devil's greatest ploy was to tempt man away from God's Word. If God's prohibition against eating from the Tree of Knowledge was clear, the Devil's lie could be nothing except an intentional misinterpretation of God's command. As a result, the Devil's lie would become the very emblem of heresy and false preaching. The Devil changes God's Word to tempt our pride, and our only defense against such malignant exegesis is to cling to the original in all its purity. Sound advice when there was one official Church and at least some, if not complete, agreement about the meaning of God's Word, perhaps still sound when there were only two churches, as during those first brief years of the Reformation, each accusing the other of having colluded with Antichrist, but what if there are many churches, each claiming to possess its own unique and perfect interpretation of scripture? The Devil may have been the first exegete, but in deceiving Adam and Eve, he transformed them and all their descendants into exegetes. Fallen, with crippled wills and weakened faculties, he left them to make sense of a world made confusing, in which disagreements could only proliferate and finding a way to tolerate disagreement the only way to undo Satan's stratagems.

MAKING SENSE OF GENESIS 1, 2, AND 3

The Temptation story is brief, even absurdly so. It is also problematic, raising as many questions as it answers. The story as most every Christian from at least the late fourth century knew it, indeed, the story as most people know it even today, is really an attempt to resolve those questions into some sort of coherent narrative. In other words, it is an interpretation, a gloss on the biblical story. The original narrative, for example, offers no explanation for why the serpent approaches the Woman, nor how it could speak and, most significantly, it makes no mention at all of the Devil. These were expansions to the story that found nearly universal approval among all Christians, not only in the early Church but throughout the Middle Ages and even across the ever-multiplying confessional divides of the Reformation. Complicating matters even further, the narrative challenges posed in the first chapters of Genesis were not limited to the Temptation story. When that story was set within the broader context of the first three chapters of Genesis, biblical exegetes needed to exert a fair amount of effort to fit everything together.

The most striking challenge that readers faced was the apparent presence of two Creation narratives within the first three chapters of Genesis. The seven-day Creation narrative, the one in which God announces, "Let us make humankind in our image according to our likeness," runs from Genesis 1:1 to 2:3. A second narrative immediately follows, beginning at Genesis 2:4 with the words "These are the generations of the heavens and the earth when they were created." This second narrative includes the creation of the Garden of Eden, the fabrication of Adam out of dust, of the Woman out of Adam's rib and, of course, the story of the Temptation, the Fall, and the Exile. Although religious writers had long noted this curiously twice-told telling of the Creation, the French Protestant-turned-Catholic professor of medicine Jean Astruc was the first to argue seriously that these two narratives derived from distinct sources. In 1753, he anonymously published his *Conjectures on the Original Notes which It Seems Moses Used to Compose the Book of Genesis*, in which he argued that Moses did not write these stories. Rather, Moses acted as an editor who stitched the two stories together from preexisting sources.[22] Modern scholarly consensus now assumes these two stories are truly distinct, the product of different authors, composed at different times, deriving from different Jewish traditions. The seven-day story derives from a priestly tradition dating somewhere between 550 and 450 B.C. The second narrative, beginning at Genesis 2:4, dates from some four hundred years earlier, having been composed sometime between 960 and 930 B.C., during the "Davidic/Solomon kingdom."[23] Before Astruc (and long after him, for that matter), Moses was almost universally accepted as the author of the Torah, the first five books of the Bible. Since one author implied one coherent narrative, it was believed that these two Creation stories must somehow constitute a single narrative, a single account of the world's Creation. If this solved one problem, it raised others. Specifically, how did they fit together to form one story, the story of a single Creation?

Theologians would offer a wide variety of answers to this question. At one extreme, Augustine suspected that the second Creation story made it clear that God did not create the world in six days. Rejecting the idea that the second Creation story was a mere recapitulation and retelling of the first, he stressed the final words of Genesis 2:4, "when day was made" ("This is the story of the creation of heaven and earth when day was made"), and argued that God had created the world in a single day, in a single instant, as a sort of embryonic whole full of the seeds of its future development. The first Creation story presented that single instant as a series of discrete temporal steps so that human beings could better understand the structure and complexity of God's work.[24] The second Creation story, including Adam's formation from dust and the Woman's formation from Adam's rib, represented the later blossoming and divinely ordered maturation of these primordial seeds. Not surprisingly, Reformation writers stood at the other extreme. Calvin had little patience for what he took to be the North African bishop's byzantine interpretive maneuvers. Although God could have created the world in an instant, Calvin countered, he chose to create it over the course of six days so that men could appreciate the structure and complexity of his work.[25] In his 1554 commentary on Genesis, he argued that Moses doubled up his narratives in order to stress God's creation of the world out of nothingness, repetition serving to hammer this point into the recalcitrant reader's mind. "For there have always been ungrateful and malignant men," Calvin wrote, "who either by feigning that the world was eternal or by obliterating the memory of the creation would attempt to obscure the glory of God."[26]

Despite these differences over time and across the religious spectrum, Augustine and most every subsequent Catholic commentator, as well as every Reformation theologian, argued that, insofar as possible, the events described in the second Creation narrative needed to be taken seriously and understood as real events. If there were any place for allegory (and, of course, Reformation writers doubted there was much room for it), it must be reined in, rooted to and built upon a foundation of literal and historical interpretation. More to the point, both Catholic and Protestant writers agreed that the second Creation narrative told a story that formed a historical sequence of events that must be respected, no matter how strange that story might seem. And the story certainly could seem strange. The influential first-century Jewish exegete Philo of Alexandria, for example, argued that little or nothing in the second Creation story could be literally true. Assuming the likeness of past and present as a basic interpretive approach, Philo contended that "no trees of life or understanding have ever appeared on earth in the past or are ever likely to appear in the future." He likewise found it difficult to believe "that the venomous and earthborn reptile, the snake, could project a human voice." Of course, he quickly added that Moses is no liar and these things "are not the fabrications of myth, in which the race of poets and sophists rejoice, but indications of character types which invite allegorical interpretation through the explanation of hidden meanings." Given these peculiarities, Philo believed the entire temptation scene had to be read as a sort of psychological drama played out within the human soul symbolized by the Garden of Eden itself, the actors in the Temptation drama representing the soul's basic powers or inner forces. The serpent was a symbol for base desire, the Woman a symbol for the senses, and the man, naturally enough, filling in for reason.[27] Philo's allegorical reading influenced a number of early Christians, including Origen and Ambrose of Milan, and would continue to shape Catholic allegorical readings throughout the Middle Ages.

Augustine understood the challenges that could motivate such allegorical readings. He was also absolutely clear it was a tendency that needed to be held in check. "[I]n Genesis, since there are matters beyond the ken of readers who focus their gaze on the familiar course of nature, they are unwilling to have these matters taken in the literal sense," he wrote in his own commentary, "but prefer to understand them in a figurative sense."[28] At least one advantage of allegorical readings was their ability to explain away the more fantastic elements in the Creation narrative, like talking snakes and magical trees, elements that, taken literally, might seem unworthy to serve as the basis for a real religion. The third-century theologian Origen noted that pagan critics of Christianity, such as Celsus, made fun of just these fairy-tale-like aspects of the story, suggesting it read like the sort of legend "told to old women."[29] As far as Augustine was concerned, resorting to allegory to counter such critics created more problems than it solved. If we interpret Adam and Eve allegorically, Augustine asks, then "who begot Cain, Abel and Seth?" More important, the standard of interpreting the past in terms of the present would undermine the literal truth of both Creation accounts. Genesis describes the creation of a new world and new creatures. "Surely," Augustine asks, "we are not to believe that God did not make the world because He does not make worlds today?"[30] Luther, who complained frequently about what he perceived as Augustine's own allegorical flights of fancy and needless probing of problematic passages better left alone, put the matter simply near the very beginning of his commentary: "[L]et us turn to Moses," he advised, "as the better teacher. We can follow him with greater safety than the philosophers, who, without benefit of the Word, debate about unknown matters."[31]

Even for those exegetes ready to tackle the story of the Temptation literally, there was no shortage of problems to resolve. When, for example, did the Fall occur? While combining the two Creation stories into a single narrative provided some chronological clues, even here there was room for disagreement. Augustine suggested that it had occurred on the sixth day, no more than six hours after the creation of Adam and Eve. Luther extended the first couple's paradisiacal stay another twenty-four hours, arguing it had occurred on the seventh day. He had little difficulty imagining something of the day's events leading up to the Fall. "Early on the following Sabbath," he writes, "Adam preached to Eve concerning God's will," told her about the glories of paradise and about the Tree of Life, "through the use of which the powers of the body would be refreshed and perpetual youth would be maintained." He also told her about "the tree of the knowledge of good and evil, from which it was not permitted to eat—was forbidden; and that in this respect they should obey so gracious a creator." Luther described Adam leading Eve on a brief tour of paradise, highlighting its beauties and pointing out the two trees. "But then, alas," Luther finishes, "Satan interfered and within a few hours ruined all this."[32] In "The Second Week," the second part of the sixteenth-century French writer Guillaume de Saluste Sieur du Bartas's lengthy verse account of Creation's earliest days and weeks, *The Divine Weeks*, Adam and Eve enjoy the seventh day in peace. According to Du Bartas, the Fall occurred on the eighth day, the first day of the second week.[33] Of course, Du Bartas's 1584 poem eventually found itself eclipsed when John Milton published *Paradise Lost* in 1667, narrating a Temptation and Fall that began on the morning of the seventh day, soon after Adam and Eve (at Eve's urging) had separated for the day to ensure they did not waste time staring into each other's eyes, whispering sweet nothings into each other's ears. As Eve warns her husband: "For while so near each other thus all day/Our task we choose, what if so near/Looks intervene and smile, or object new/Casual discourse draw on, which intermits/Our day's work brought to little, though begun/Early, and th' hour of Supper comes unearn'd."[34]

As it turned out, issues of importance hinged on correctly identifying the day Adam and Eve ate the forbidden fruit, but an even more pressing problem faced anyone who hoped to make sense of the story. The story narrated in Genesis 3 makes no mention whatsoever of the Devil. It refers only to the "serpent" and does so with a minimum of background: "Now the serpent was more crafty than any other wild animal that the Lord God had made."[35] Between the excesses of hyperbolic allegory and a literalism that verged on transforming the story into an overly terse Aesop's fable, Jewish exegetes first and then early Christian writers gradually came to invoke the Devil as the real behind-the-scene actor.[36] John Chrysostom seems to have been the first to identify precisely the relation between the serpent and the Devil, and he did so recognizing that animals do not now, and did not then, have the power of speech. Noting, and noting something that would exercise much attention among future exegetes, that Eve did not fear a talking serpent, Chrysostom writes: "Consider from this . . . how in the beginning none of the wild beasts then existing caused fear either to the man or the woman; on the contrary, they recognized human direction and dominion. . . . But perhaps in this case some may raise a difficulty and seek to find out if the wild animals also shared the power of speech. Not so—perish the thought; rather people, following Scripture, need to consider the fact that the words came from the devil, who was spurred to this deception by his own ill-will."[37] The Devil used the serpent as a tool, a costume, speaking through it as he tempted Eve. "This serpent," Augustine would write, condensing and passing on what would become accepted as indisputable, "could be called the wisest of all the beasts not by reason of its irrational soul, but rather because of another spirit—that of the Devil—dwelling in it."[38]

Accepted or not, commentators readily admitted it was a confusing narrative tack for Moses to have taken in what, for Christians at least, was a decidedly crucial moment in human history. Calvin found the suppression of Satan's role in this episode to be "scarcely consonant with reason." Still, he agreed it was an interpretation that could not be denied. "The testimonies of Scripture are sufficiently numerous," he writes, "in which it is plainly asserted that the serpent was only the mouth of the devil; for not the serpent but the devil is declared to be the 'father of lies,' the fabricator or imposture and the author of death." Moses's oblique storytelling, "his homely and uncultivated" style, were suited to his primitive audience, "for not only had he to instruct an untaught race of men, but the existing age of the Church was so puerile, that it was unable to receive higher instruction."[39]

It was through these sorts of interpretive accommodations and cross-referencings, not to mention fudgings and blurrings, that religious writers across the centuries, as well as across a multitude of theological and denominational divides, reached a fair degree of unanimity on the general narrative outline of the Temptation, and how it fit within the larger narrative of Creation and Salvation. The mainstream of interpreters understood it to be a literal story, a narrative of events that had really happened, and that had most likely happened on either the sixth or seventh day of Creation. It was a story crucial for understanding the world's current lamentable condition, but it was a story so slimly told that questions about it could only multiply. Potential solutions to those questions multiplied even more quickly, solutions whose ever-changing details reveal something like a history of the Devil, his lie, and the world he transformed.

THE DEVIL'S LIE FROM LATE ANTIQUITY TO THE MIDDLE AGES

No other biblical commentary from the later Middle Ages achieved greater popularity than Nicholas of Lyra's *Postilla super totam bibliam*. Born in Vieille-Lyre, Normandy, around 1270, Nicholas had joined the Franciscan Order by the time he was about thirty. He became Franciscan provincial master of France no later than 1319 and of Burgundy in 1324. He died in 1349. Educated at the Sorbonne, he became interested in Jewish sources, especially Jewish postbiblical interpretations of scripture, and it was his use of them that differentiated his commentary from most of its medieval competitors. Perhaps Jews, as standard Christian teaching held, were blind to the deeper secrets hidden within what Christians had come to call the Old Testament, blind to its moral, mystical, and allegorical senses, but they could certainly shed light on its all-important literal interpretation. Nicholas's knowledge of Hebrew and his use of rabbinic sources was unparalleled, earning him the nickname "The Second Jerome" to go along with another that made his intellectual virtues clear, "The Plain and Useful Doctor."[40] His influence remained great even beyond the Middle Ages. Martin Luther relied heavily on Nicholas's commentary when he composed his own, sometimes agreeing, often disagreeing, but reminding his readers nonetheless that he had no doubt Nicolas was a good man.[41] Precisely because of its vast popularity and continuing influence, its clarity and emphasis on the literal sense of scripture, Nicholas's commentary on Genesis provides a particularly valuable way into the specific questions that religious writers asked themselves when considering the Devil's sudden appearance in the Garden on the sixth or seventh day of Creation.

In typical Scholastic fashion, Nicholas approaches the story of the Temptation with a kind of analytical mania, searching for meaning in its most discrete narrative moments. "After [Moses] describes the formation and state of the first man," Nicholas writes, "he goes on to describe his transgression or fall. First, he describes the transgression, second the infliction of the penalty and third the spread of their misery." In a process that seeks something like the atomic and indivisible elements that make up the story, it is hardly surprising that he subjects these three divisions to still further subdivision. "Concerning the first division," Nicholas continues, "he first describes the tempter, second he describes the stages of the temptation, and third the act of the transgression." Having isolated the story's most basic elements, Nicholas asks a series of questions designed to illuminate each of those elements. Beginning with the tempter, for example, Nicholas will consider whether it was reasonable for God, who must have known in advance what would happen, to have allowed it to occur at all, and what sorts of powers over mankind the Devil possessed during those brief hours of human innocence. Similarly, when Nicholas moves to his second subdivision concerning the Temptation itself, he will consider why the Devil approached Eve first, why the Devil selected the words he did, Eve's response with its curious addition concerning the prohibition against touch, and how this conversation worked to move Eve against God.[42]

These questions were hardly original with Nicholas. They had been asked for centuries and would continue to be asked for centuries to come. While the story's dramatic tension could easily slip through the cracks of these divisions and subdivisions that so appealed to medieval scholars, the story's importance was never far from their mind. Certainly the need, in short order, to address the punishments God would level against the drama's three (or four) actors would force this recognition. But the contrast between the Devil's powers then and now needed always to be kept in mind.

"During the time of innocence," Nicholas notes, "the Devil did not have the power to tempt man from within, by directly stirring up his passions with forbidden yearnings or by imposing illicit images directly upon his intellect." These sorts of limits on the Devil's powers had much to do with the first couple's uncorrupt nature, a nature in which the body was not yet at war with reason, in which the flesh did not yet have its own eruptive motions and guilty pleasures. In the state of innocence, "nothing disorderly could happen to man's inferior parts, unless something were first to upset his reason," and so, Nicholas reasons, "man could only be tempted from without, by things presented to his senses."[43] The Devil had little choice, in other words, than to tempt Adam and Eve in some sensible guise, with appearances and sounds, with touch and odors, entering through the senses and, finally, beguiling and deceiving the intellect.

The distinction between exterior and interior temptation went at least as far back as the early twelfth-century Augustinian canon Hugh of St. Victor and was assured universal Scholastic dissemination when Peter Lombard invoked it in his twelfth-century theology textbook, *The Sentences*. "Exterior temptation," Peter writes, "occurs when evil is visibly suggested to us from without in words or any sort of sign in order that it bends a person towards consent to sin."[44] This twelfth-century distinction merely formalized ideas that had dominated interpretations of the Devil's actions in the Garden of Eden for centuries. In his homily on the Temptation, John Chrysostom had already made it clear that the Devil used both words and signs, questions and costumes, to lead Eve astray. "[The Devil] made use of the [serpent] like some instrument," Chrysostom writes, "and through it inveigled that naive and weaker vessel, namely, woman, into his deception by means of conversation."[45] In Chrysostom's reading of the story, the Devil selects the serpent because its cunning and supremacy over the other animals makes it the ideal weapon to use against the woman. Had the Devil appeared as himself, he would have been easily identified, his original beauty now utterly ruined beneath a facade seething with moral depravity. Of course, the use of the serpent also provided powerful metaphorical associations that Chrysostom quickly exploited. The Devil's words were like a serpent's venom. "Do you see how he uses the words like a bait to inject his poison?" Chrysostom asks.[46]

If the Devil's disguise allows him to approach Eve, his words constitute the exterior temptation that will ultimately bring her down. And he chooses his words with care. The Devil knows about the prohibition against eating from the tree, Chrysostom suggests, but he does not know why God has instituted it, nor does he know the penalty for violating it. Believing that this could be valuable knowledge, knowledge that, if acquired, could be used against the first couple, the Devil's initial verbal assault seeks to pry it from the unsuspecting woman.[47] He begins by incorrectly quoting God's prohibition, pretending that he cares for the woman's well-being, expressing concern that not being allowed to eat from any of the trees of the Garden must be a harsh rule to follow. "Why is it that God said, Do not eat of any tree in the Garden?" Chrysostom explains, "As if the evil demon were saying, Why did he deprive you of such enjoyment?"[48]

Included in the *Glossa Ordinaria*, Chrysostom's analysis of the serpent's opening question would become quite influential. No less influential and no less effective is the serpent's question itself. Evidently its small fraction of false concern is enough to convince Eve of the serpent's good intentions. She becomes "involved in conversation with the serpent and through him as through an instrument she took in the devil's deadly words," Chrysostom writes, "[and] so it ensued that she learnt from the devil's speech the very opposite of the words' real sense, and that whereas the Creator gave one set of directions, the devil said the opposite to the Creator about avoiding them."[49] Hearing God quoted falsely, she should have fled. Instead, she is enticed into conversation. She corrects the serpent, after which the serpent contradicts God's warning, telling her she will not die, that God knows she and Adam will be like gods knowing good and evil should they eat it. "See all the bait he offered," Chrysostom writes. "[H]e filled the cup with a harmful drug and gave it to the woman, who did not want to recognize its deadly character. She could have known from the outset, had she wanted; instead she listened to his words, that God forbade their tasting the fruit for that reason—'He knows that your eyes will be opened and you will be like gods, knowing good from evil'—puffed up as she was with the hope of being equal to God and evidently dreaming of greatness."[50] Caught between God's command and the Devil's lies, Eve allows herself to be persuaded.

When Augustine pondered her predicament, he imagined Eve confronting a choice between two different kinds of perception. Perhaps we don't possess the ability to determine what we perceive, Augustine argues, but we do have it in our power to accept or reject those perceptions. "Thus we must grant," he writes, "that the spirit is affected by higher and lower perceptions. Hence it is that the rational substance selects from both classes what it wills, and by virtue of its selection achieves misery or blessedness. In the Garden of Eden, for example, the command of God was visible in the higher goods; the suggestion of the serpent through the lower."[51] God had offered one sort of good, the Devil another, and Eve, forced to choose, chooses the Devil because she stayed to listen to his lies, lies that somehow convinced her to make the wrong choice. Hugh of St. Victor captured this moment in a saying that would find itself endlessly repeated throughout the later Middle Ages: "God affirmed, woman doubted, the devil denied."[52] God affirmed that should they violate the prohibition, they would die. The Devil denies this punishment, suggests there are other reasons why God has prohibited them from eating from the tree. And Eve expresses doubt. At least this is how virtually every commentator would come to understand what happened next. Repeating God's prohibition to the serpent, Eve adds a critical pause, a moment's hesitation. "Concerning the fruit of the tree which is in the middle of Garden," she responds, "God has commanded us not to eat, nor to touch, *lest perhaps* we will die [*ne forte moriamur*]." This doubt became crucial for understanding the Devil's strategy. Initially fearful of directly contradicting God, Hugh writes, it was Eve's expression of doubt that emboldened the Devil to lie.[53] Nicholas of Lyra would also highlight this moment in his commentary, writing that Eve "inserts *forte* on her own, an adverb expressing doubt, although God had simply asserted his prohibition."[54]

While Chrysostom points to false concern, a feigned empathy for the woman's well-being as key to the Devil's success in finally convincing her to violate God's prohibition, Augustine is less clear about how the Temptation succeeds. Ignoring, as does Chrysostom, the additional prohibition against touch, Augustine contends that her initial response to the serpent's questions simply demonstrates that she knew and understood the command. "The serpent, then, first asked the question, and the woman replied, so that her transgression would be inexcusable . . . the sin is more evident when the command is retained in memory and God as present in his command is despised."[55] In the *City of God*, Augustine would repeat and extend this line of reasoning and argue that Adam and Eve's disobedience was all the worse given the simplicity of God's command, how easy it was to follow given the abundance of food in the Garden and especially because human nature itself was not, at that time, corrupt. All of which simply returns Augustine to the problem of how Eve and then Adam were so easily deceived into trespass. In both his *Literal Meaning of Genesis* and *The City of God*, Augustine pushes that first key moment of disobedience back into some undisclosed and hidden past. "It was in secret," he writes, "that Adam and Eve began to be evil; and it was because of this that they were able to fall into overt disobedience."[56] The sheer blasphemy of the serpent's words could convince, he argues, only if there were already in Eve's "heart a love of her own independence and proud presumption of self."[57] Pride was at the root of the Fall. Here Augustine agreed with Chrysostom, but for the North African bishop when and how those initial stirrings of self-love developed were not at all clear. For Augustine, the Devil's lie operates like the final argument and justification for transforming a private pride into public action.

Whatever the reason, the Devil's words were effective in moving Eve's will toward sin. Augustine's mentor, the bishop Ambrose of Milan, had already, around 389, imagined a basis for these initial stirrings of pride in Eve's soul when he composed his own series of homilies on the events in paradise. A fallen Devil, filled with rage and hate and envy, plots to bring man down. "Will this inferior acquire what I was unable to keep?" the Devil thinks to himself and reflecting on his own experience realizes that he has "many ways and means by which to deceive man. . . . Although of superior nature, [man's] soul is nevertheless subject to temptation, since it exists in the prison house of the body—witness my own experience in being unable to avoid sin." The Devil contrives a two-step strategy for deceiving and ruining the first couple. First, he will deceive them, exploiting the tension inherent in their mixed condition, arousing their ambition to be better than they are. Second, he will tempt the flesh with promises to sate their newly awakened pride. "How else can I appear wiser than all men," the Devil concludes, "if not by the exercise of cunning and fraud in my warfare of entrenchment against all men."[58]

If our mixed nature reveals the weakness in our defenses, Ambrose suggests there was something else that gave the Devil's attack its peculiar advantage. Religious writers often asked why the serpent first approached Eve instead of Adam. In the mid-thirteenth century, the Franciscan theologian Bonaventure summed up this bit of puzzlement when he pointed out that there really isn't all that much glory to be gained in conquering a woman. If the Devil sought to recover some of his lost majesty, it would have made more sense first to deceive and conquer the man.[59] God had decreed and allowed things to proceed otherwise, and so it was that explanations for this order of temptation had to be found. Ambrose had already offered at least one answer to this question when he observed that the Devil does not accost the man, who had received the prohibition from God, but rather "her who had learned of it from her husband. . . . There is no statement that God spoke to the woman. We know that he spoke to Adam. Hence we must conclude that the command was communicated through Adam to the woman."[60] There is a lesson to be learned from this, Ambrose suggests, and he immediately compares Eve's conversation with the serpent to someone recently converted to the faith, full of newfound enthusiasm and eager for a "greater fullness of doctrine." The new catechumen must always beware of allowing his desire for a more robust faith to lead him into error, sin, and heresy. The catechumen must beware, Ambrose notes, that he does not hand himself over to heretics like Photinus, Arius, or Sabellus, teachers "who would attract him by their airs of authority, so that his untrained mind, impressed by the weight of such august prestige, will be unable to discriminate right from wrong."[61] Like Ambrose's imagined catechumen, Eve desires something more. She signals this in her response to the serpent when she adds an additional prohibition to God's command. She tells the serpent they are allowed neither to eat from, nor even to touch, the tree. Both Eve and the catechumen are guilty of a superficial understanding of God's Word. They do not stop to consider why God had not included a prohibition against touch, why scripture does not include something seemingly more robust and demanding. They do not ask what they could learn about God's commands "if they had first touched and handled it, as it were, with the hands of the mind." Instead, they seek to add to it, to make it say more than it does. Comparing this behavior to testimony given in court, Ambrose adds, "It frequently happens that a witness adds something of himself to a relation of facts. In this way, by the injection of an untruth, confidence in his testimony is shattered."[62] No additions to scripture are ever called for, and Ambrose recalls the warnings concerning the sanctity of God's Word from the book of Revelation: "If anyone shall add to them, God will add unto him the plagues that are written in this book. And if anyone shall take away from these words of the book of this prophecy, God will take away his portion from the tree of life."[63]

Unfortunately, neither Eve nor the catechumen heed this advice. Desiring something more, a desire that itself signals the first stirrings of pride, they listen to voices that claim to offer it. Both the Devil and the heretical teacher present themselves as possessing a secret reservoir of knowledge. They present themselves as authorities more trustworthy than scripture itself. Ambrose stresses the line of communication that allows false authority to assume a legitimacy it should never possess. Adam received his instruction from God, whereas Eve only received it from Adam, never herself speaking directly with God, and this allows the Devil to present himself as someone who knows things Adam does not. Moving from the scene in the Garden to our continuing tribulations in this post-Edenic world, Ambrose offers an even more vivid picture of the Devil's deceits, presenting him in the classic guise of the sophist, the morally bankrupt rhetorician. "In addition to this," he warns his audience, "there are other occasions when many other kinds of temptations are in store for us. Some of these come from the Prince of this world, who has vomited into this world what might be called poisonous wisdom, so that men believe the false to be true and are emotionally carried away by mere appearance." Matching character to disguise, Ambrose adds, "The temptations of the Devil, then, are manifold. For that reason he is believed to be a deadly, double-tongued serpent, doing the Devil's work by saying one thing with the tongue and by harboring other thoughts in his mind."[64]

Ambrose had no doubt the Devil's every word was a lie. For example, the serpent promised the woman that she would not die. "Here we have one falsehood," Ambrose writes, "for man, who followed the promises of the serpent is subject to death." Even the serpent's claim that the Woman's eyes would be open if she ate the fruit was full of guile and dishonesty. Yes, Ambrose admits, her eyes and then Adam's were opened, but this was not the good thing the serpent made it out to be: "the truth is that as a result of this act harm followed." Just as damning, the serpent immediately followed this ill-intentioned truth with another lie when he next promised that "they would be like gods, knowing good from evil."[65] More significant than the lies themselves were their sudden effect on the Woman. Already afflicted with the stirrings of pride, wanting to believe the false promises of the serpent, the Woman turned to the tree, looked at it, and decided "that the tree was good for food, pleasing to the eyes and beautiful to gaze upon." The Devil's words confuse the Woman, playing on her desires and inherent weaknesses, causing her "to pass judgment on what she had not tasted."[66] Augustine would build on this scenario, suggesting that the Devil's words awaken a desire that prompts the Woman to look at the tree. "Not content with the words of the serpent, she also gazed on the tree and saw that 'it was good for food and a delight to behold.'" Like Ambrose, Augustine suggests that the Devil's words had confused the Woman, leading her to make false judgments. "Since she did not believe that eating it could bring about her death, I think she assumed that God was using figurative language when he said, 'If you eat of it, you shall die.'"[67]

While Ambrose and Augustine both present the Devil as a corrupt and corrupting rhetorician, they are equally clear that he uses his rhetorical skills to corrupt God's Word, offering tendentious and false interpretations of God's commands. Ambrose explicitly compares the Devil to a heretical spiritual guide. For his part, Augustine stresses how Eve, after listening to the Devil, begins to doubt the literal truth of God's words, wonders if they contain some hidden and deeper meaning, a figurative meaning. Eve was not alone in hoping to find such meanings in the biblical text. Ambrose, influenced by earlier exegetes such as Philo and Origen, was quite partial to figurative and symbolic readings of Genesis, and even Augustine had written a book in which he advanced symbolic interpretations of the Creation story. For all that, Augustine stressed the literal and historical nature of the story, giving it prominence over any other form of interpretation. Augustine believed this stress on literal interpretation provided him with something like a paradigm for proper religious behavior. Straightforward literal interpretation went hand in hand with an obedience to the strict letter of God's commands. The prohibition was straightforward. If nothing else, the Temptation narrative made it clear that Adam and Eve both understood the command and understood that God, who had given them everything, deserved obedience or, as Ambrose put it, Adam was "conscious of the fact that deference should be paid to the person of the Commander."[68] For his part, Augustine modeled all right religious practice on obedience to this rule, suggesting that obedience is the virtue by which we please God. "I can truthfully say," Augustine concluded, "that [obedience] is the only virtue of every rational creature who lives his life under God's rule, and that the fundamental and greatest vice is the overweening pride by which one wishes to have independence to his ruin, and the name of this vice is disobedience."[69]

The Devil succeeds through a perverse eloquence, adding and subtracting words from God's commands, turning assertions into questions, and lies into assertions. If God offers his Word, the Devil offers words, and words can only obscure, seduce, proliferate. After the Devil's first question, Eve amends God's command, adding the prohibition against touch. The Devil speaks more words. After Eve eats from the apple, she seduces Adam into disobedience. While Genesis does not indicate what Eve did or said to convince Adam to eat the apple, theologians were clear she must have done something. Aware of both her sin and that it would be wrong to condemn her husband to a similar fate, Ambrose contends that Eve "sinned . . . with forethought and knowingly made her husband a participant in her own wrong-doing."[70] Augustine, writing with an overt sense of disgust, adds, "And so she took some of the fruit and ate and gave some to her husband who was with her, using perhaps some persuasive words, which Scripture does not record but leaves to our intelligence to supply."[71] Having fallen to the Devil's linguistic seductions, Eve suddenly finds herself able to make use of them, turning the Devil's stratagems against Adam.

While both Ambrose and Augustine assumed the Woman's words seduced Adam to sin, scripture made this somewhat difficult to explain. Nicholas of Lyra agreed, for example, that Adam assented to the Woman's persuasive words, but he found it inconceivable that Adam believed either her words or the Devil's lies. Citing Paul's first letter to Timothy—"For Adam was formed first, then Eve; and Adam was not deceived, but the woman was deceived and became a transgressor"[72]—he asserts that only the woman was deceived.[73] Hugh of St. Victor suggested that Adam assented "lest by resisting [the woman's will] and petition he might offend the heart of the woman who had been associated with him through the affection of love." Indeed, Hugh suspects, Adam may well have done his own amending of scripture, adding his own words, thinking "that he could both yield to the woman and afterwards through repentance and supplication for pardon please the Creator."[74] Bonaventure picked up on this line of thought later in the thirteenth century, noting that Adam and the Woman both broke God's law, but for different reasons. The Woman hoped to be like God, something Adam could never believe would happen. For his part, Adam fell victim to pride, avarice, and a sort of virginal yearning. Pride convinced him that God would punish him lightly. Avarice manifested itself in a curiosity to know what would happen if he ate the fruit. Lasciviousness—felt not so much as carnal desire, for there was none in paradise, but as a certain amicable affection for the Woman—impelled him not to scold and upset her but to follow her lead. Whatever the precise reasons for Adam's own transgression, the Woman's words played a central role. God himself made this clear, Bonaventure noted, citing Genesis 3:17: Adam "listened to the woman's voice and through this had been led into disobedience and transgression of God's mandate."[75]

The first lie traveled from the serpent's mouth to Eve's ear, and from there it multiplied and spread, from Eve to Adam and from their union to all of their descendants. It infected not only everything they would say but everything they would do, everything they would make. Whereas the first couple once enjoyed the fruit of the trees, after their lies and transgressions they now make use of leaves to cover themselves. Ambrose was quick to highlight the deceptive nature of any covering, verbal or vegetal. "Whoever, therefore, violates the command of God has become naked and despoiled, a reproach to himself," he writes. "He wants to cover himself and hide his genitals with fig leaves, make use, as it were of empty and idle talk which the sinner interweaves word after word with fallacies for the purpose of shielding himself from the awareness of his guilty deed."[76]

We cover ourselves with dissembling clothes and our souls with lying words.

THE DEVIL'S LIE FROM THE MIDDLE AGES
TO THE REFORMATION

"At long last we have passed over that expanse of text on which all expositors have toiled exceedingly," Luther writes, having just completed his own commentary on the Temptation and Fall, "and to some degree so have we ourselves, although its entire content was rather clear to us because we did not concern ourselves with allegories, but adhered to the historical and strict meaning." Of course, clarity need not imply brevity, and adherence to the strict letter of the text did little to keep Luther's commentary on Adam and Eve's misadventure with the serpent from doubling the length of Augustine's own commentary on those same passages. Lengthy or not, Luther had no doubt that he had steered clear of the allegorical shoals that had sunk "the majority of interpreters," all those who had attached greater importance to "Origen, Dionysius, and others than to Moses himself."[77] While not an entirely fair characterization of his exegetical forebears, Luther's brief reflection certainly highlights his own interpretive predilections. More important, his reading of Genesis, of the serpent's temptation of Eve, underwrites and validates his focus on the literal and the historic meaning of the text. For Luther, and for any number of reformed commentators who followed him, the story of the Temptation and Fall is a story about the perils of failing to interpret literally God's Word, of amending and adding to his Word, of listening to the Devil's lies and succumbing to the seductions of misinterpretation.[78]

The temptation to misinterpret is everywhere, Luther assures his readers, and it is ever present. The serpent impugns God's good will when it speaks to Eve. "With a word," Luther writes, "it attacks the Word." The serpent questions, misstates, rephrases, asserts, contradicts, and lies. Eve listens and in listening wavers and in wavering departs from God's Word. "For when the Gospel is preached in its purity," Luther observes, "men have a sure guide for their faith and are able to avoid adultery. But then Satan makes various efforts and trials in an effort either to draw away men from the Word or to corrupt it."[79] Heresies arose early on in the Greek Church, Luther notes, when people strayed from the letter of the text, when, for example, Basil denied that the Holy Spirit was God. What happened in the past, Luther then adds while specifically citing the Anabaptists, serves as warning for the present that "our age, too, has instances like these before its eyes, when, after the purer doctrine of the Gospel came to light, several kinds of assailers of the works and the Word of God arose." Luther is quick to admit that Satan has many weapons in his arsenal, inciting us to "fornication, adultery, and similar infamous deeds. But this temptation—when Satan attacks the Word and the works of God—is far more serious and more dangerous."[80]

Luther was hardly the first person to warn against adding to, subtracting from, or misinterpreting scripture. It had been a constant refrain throughout the history of the Church. Concerning these very passages in Genesis, Ambrose had made similar warnings and predicted similarly dire consequences for those who strayed from God's word. Nicholas of Lyra, whose commentary Luther returned to again and again, almost always let the strict letter of the text guide his interpretation. For example, when considering why the Woman included the prohibition against touch when responding to the serpent, Nicholas rejects those who claim that God had probably included this along with the prohibition against eating from the tree. Why? Because it is not found in the text.[81] For all that, Luther's attention to the strict letter of the text went beyond anything even the most literal of Catholic commentators had proposed. If this is hardly surprising given Luther's proud proclamations concerning *sola scriptura*, it nonetheless profoundly shaped the sorts of questions Luther posed and the answers he found when reading the text, especially when he considers the nature of Satan's assault on the first couple.

The consequences of Luther's literalism show up clearly when he considers a problem that had long bothered interpreters. How was it that the Woman was so easily swayed? Eve's sudden willingness to touch and eat the fruit of the tree confounded Augustine who, as we have seen, found it inconceivable that a mere question could turn her against God and everything he had promised and given to her and Adam. The stirrings of pride must already have made themselves felt within her soul, Augustine concluded, making her susceptible to such bogus questioning. It was a dangerous position to take, verging on a sort of Manichaeism, suggesting that the Woman possessed an inner inclination toward sin even before the serpent's well-timed arrival. Although Augustine had labored over this problem, subsequent writers made sure to elaborate on his concerns in ways that exonerated God from having instilled destructive and rebellious impulses in his creations. Citing Augustine's assertion, the thirteenth-century Dominican theologian Thomas Aquinas categorically denied that "pride preceded the promptings of the serpent." The serpent's words—and Thomas asserts that this was Augustine's real point, however ambiguously put—were the source of the Woman's first prideful feelings. "As soon as the serpent had spoken his words of persuasion, her mind was puffed up, the result being that she believed the demon to have spoken truly."[82] Nicholas of Lyra would stress this same interpretation of Augustine's words some fifty years later when he wrote that Augustine by no means had meant to imply that "pride preceded the serpent's persuasions."[83]

The psychological intricacies of the Fall fascinated interpreters prior to Luther. Medieval theologians believed that the various cardinal sins, beginning with pride, could be invoked to explain the hidden workings of a soul that, having heard the serpent's initial words, gradually came to accept and then act on them. According to Hugh of St. Victor the initial swellings of pride were followed in quick succession by avarice and gluttony, each building on the other, finally moving Eve to eat the fruit. "For first she sought the promised excellence through pride," Hugh writes, "then through avarice she desired to possess that promised wealth and all the excellent things that went along with it." Finally, she fell to gluttony and "consented to eat the forbidden fruit." Hugh's analysis of these inner movements, borrowed from Gregory the Great and included in Peter Lombard's *Sentences*, shaped later accounts of this process. The serpent's words stirred up desires that were finally unleashed when the Woman, looking at the tree and seeing that it was good and beautiful, that its fruit was sweet, began to burn "with the desire of gluttony; lastly overcome by desire she took and ate."[84] Bonaventure gave precision to this multifaceted account when he explicitly linked the Devil's sophistry, his "sophistical persuasions," with the temptations of the flesh.[85]

For Luther, all this subtle reasoning and investigation amounted to a thousand years of ingenuity wasted and rebellion redoubled. "The sophists," Luther writes, and by sophists he means everyone who had written about these matters before himself, "discuss the nature of this temptation, namely, what sort it was. Was [the first couple's] sin idolatry, pride, unconcern or just the simple eating of the fruit?" Seeking something more from the text, amending it and altering it, adding to Moses's simple narrative, inventing explanations and psychological theories to fit their own passing intellectual fancies, these interpreters mimic the serpent himself, mimic the Woman's transgression. They assault God's Word just as the serpent did when it improperly rephrased God's prohibition as a question, just as Eve did when she added the prohibition against touch, just as all heretics do when "under the appearance of something good they rob men of God and of His Word . . . and fabricate for them another, new god, who exists nowhere." Satan's assault begins with imitation, with speech. Just as God preached to Adam, Satan preaches to Eve. But it is a very different kind of preaching, for "just as from the true word of God salvation results, so also from the corrupt word of God damnation results." Everything hinges on language, whether spoken or merely thought. Any doubt that occurs within the soul, any inner conviction or opinion that departs from God's Word, is a sign of corruption and future damnation.[86]

The temptation in the Garden, Luther contends, begins and ends with the demands of obedience. Luther imagines the prohibition against eating from the Tree of Knowledge of Good and Evil as the only precept of Adam's religion. "For Adam this Word was Gospel and Law; it was his worship; it was his service and the obedience he could offer God in this state of innocence." Right wor-

ship required only one thing, strict adherence and "outward obedience" to the letter of this one command.[87] Satan's attack was "the
greatest and severest of all temptations," he adds, because he
"makes it his business to prove from the prohibition of the tree
that God's will towards man is not good."[88] Luther simply sidesteps the subtle psychological ponderings of his Scholastic predecessors and reduces everything to language and to the doubt that
corrupt language creates in the soul of the person who listens and
begins to think and ask, Why? Luther is very clear about this and
makes it the centerpiece of Satan's rhetorical strategy. Satan recognizes that Adam and Eve are incapable of understanding why God
has prohibited them from eating the fruit of the Tree of Knowledge. He recognizes that their one duty is to believe and to obey
what God tells them. Exploiting this gap between knowledge and
faith, Satan confuses Eve with an incorrect restatement of God's
prohibition, practically forcing her to respond to and to correct his
error. "For the first and foremost temptation occurs when God's
counsels are discussed," Luther warns. Satan begins that discussion
with his well-chosen question, "Did God say: 'You shall not eat
from every tree of garden?'" Evidently ignorant of the irony, Luther amply embellishes on the words of scripture, drawing out the
hidden power of the serpent's "satanic oratory." "It is as if Satan
were saying: 'Surely you are very silly if you think God did not
want you to eat from this tree, you whom he appointed lords over
all the trees of Paradise."[89] As Eve is drawn into conversation and
drawn away from the Word, simple faith transforms into doubt,
and doubt quickly becomes rejection.

Calvin would follow Luther, stressing the snares latent in the
simple question Why? He contends that it is the greatest of temptations to believe that God should be obeyed only if "the reason of
his command is apparent to us. The true rule of obedience," Calvin
states, "is that we being content with a bare command, should persuade ourselves that whatever he enjoins is just and right."[90] And
just as Luther did before him, as Catholic theologians had done
before Luther, Calvin notes how quickly false language proliferates
once the mind is seduced into interpretation. Both have no doubt

that Eve entangles Adam in sin through the very same language that entangled her, repeating her prior conversation with the serpent, reasserting its fallacies. Luther suggests she had, in those few short sentences, become Satan's pupil, and soon Adam becomes his pupil as well, lying to God as he defends himself.[91] Like Ambrose before them, Luther and Calvin draw analogies between the first couple's shame, their newfound desire to cover themselves with fig leaves, and the lying excuses they use to cover their disobedience. "Nor is it here to be omitted," Calvin notes, "that he, who had found a few leaves to be unavailing, fled to whole trees; for so we are accustomed, when shut out from frivolous cavils, to frame new excuses, which may hide us as under a denser shade."[92] Reviewing the language of Adam's self-defense, Luther compares it to the "well-known teaching in the schools of the rhetoricians that if one has been charged with a crime, he should either deny it or defend it as having been committed legally. Adam does both."[93] Sin and lies multiply endlessly, and we must not think, Luther adds, "that this happened to Adam alone. We, each one of us, do the same thing, our nature does not permit us to act otherwise after we have become guilty of sin."[94]

And we are all guilty of sin.

THE PRINCE OF THIS WORLD

If God created the world in six days and the Devil undid it with two sentences, in whose world do we live now?

At John 14:30, Jesus famously calls the Devil the "prince of this world." Certainly the world bears the Devil's imprint. Luther looked around him and saw signs and indications everywhere of the Devil's dominion. The Devil's lies were propounded in every book of the Catholic Church, in nearly every word spoken by every Catholic priest, by every monk and every mendicant, by every bishop and every cardinal, in every word spoken by the pope himself. And the Devil didn't limit his mouthpieces to Catholics. He spoke through all those reformers who dared disagree with Luther, through Thomas Müntzer, Andreas Carlstadt, Huldrych

Zwingli, through Anabaptists and peasant protesters.[95] Luther's rejection of allegorical interpretation, his emphasis on the literal and historical sense of scripture, had the potential to transform the simplest of exegetical disagreements into confrontations between good and evil, between truth and falsehood, into a confrontation with the Devil himself. The proliferation of treatises on the Devil and Antichrist throughout the sixteenth and well into the seventeenth century testified to his ubiquity and the deafening cacophony of his lies. The Puritan preacher George Gyfford had little doubt that "wicked and abominable errors" were proof enough that the Devil or some demon was speaking. If anyone were to dare doubt that a "devil" could talk, Gyfford warned in his 1587 treatise, *A Discourse on the subtill Practices of Devilles by Witches and Sorcerers*, they should look to Genesis, where Moses shows how the Devil used a serpent to lie to Eve. "If he could then immediately after his fall use speech, shall we doubt he cannot now?" Gyfford asks his readers. "I conclude therefore out of these places of Scripture that Devils can take a bodily shape, and use speech."[96]

The implications terrified. Luther would return again and again to Paul's second letter to the Corinthians, where the apostle "warns us most earnestly to beware of the appearance of goodness, so that the satanic angel, *disguised as an angel of light* does not seduce us by his cunning."[97] Distinguishing the true Word of God from its heretical imposter was no easy feat, because the imposter often appears bathed in a false glow of sanctity as it mimics, apes, and competes with the Word. "Wherever the light of truth arises," Luther warns, "the devil is present and raises up new teachers."[98] If God builds a church, the Devil builds "a chapel or a tabernacle" right next to it and populates it with men who "give such a beautiful impression and appearance that no one can say anything except that they are true, pious preachers, interested in everyone's salvation."[99] Surrounded by illusions, Luther often compared himself to Noah, the lone righteous man in a world unable to perceive its own depravity, in the Devil's world in which evil paraded beneath the appearance of the good and God's will remained hidden and incomprehensible.[100]

In certain respects, Luther's reading of the Temptation differed
very little from those that had come before him. Ambrose and Augustine had explicitly linked the Devil's lying conversation to the
seductive and self-serving babble of sophists and the false wisdom
and pompous posturing of heretical teachers. Likewise, Luther
traced contemporary rhetorical practice and the insane rants of the
Anabaptists and "Papists" to the Devil's oratorical skills. All par-
ties agreed that Eve's fatal mistake occurred when she responded
to the Devil's opening gambit, when she allowed herself to be
drawn into conversation about the meaning of God's words and
by stages came to stray from the precise strictures of God's simple
command. Misleading questions, false speech, and verbosity were
at the heart of the first couple's Fall and, therefore, were the very
source of our current deplorable condition. Death and disease, violence and theft, hunger, old age, despair, everything that characterized our current state of painful exile from God found its origin
in the possibility of the lie, in the possibility that interpretations
could misrepresent the truth, misrepresent reality, misrepresent
God himself. But Luther narrowed his focus on Satan's lie like no
one before him, and in narrowing that focus he sharpened it,
achieving a clarity that necessarily revealed any and all disagreement to be diabolical.

While the Temptation story made clear the tragic consequences
of straying from the exact Word of God, the controversialist position of the reformers also demanded that interpretation of scripture be literal and that those literal interpretations be clear and
self-evident expositions of the text. In debates with Catholics and
fellow reformers, no other evidence could compel one's opponents
except the explicit and unambiguous text of the Bible itself.[101] As a
result, reformed exegetical practice found itself intensified under
the necessities of religious polemic. The logic of *sola scriptura* suggested a world in which there was only one proper, correct, and
holy interpretation of scripture, beyond which lay an entire universe of damning heretical and demonically inspired error. If scripture were clear, then only obstinacy, a refusal to accept a truth that
was plain for one and all to see, could explain exegetical discord.

Of course, discord is exactly what the Devil desired and seemed
to have secured. As the Calvinist minister John Dury put it in a letter appended to the front of Jacobus Acontius's *Satans Strategems
or the Devils Cabinet-Council Discovered*: "As it was then, so it
is now, at every *Period* of our *Reformation*; he doth make every
Truth a Matter of Strife; and what he cannot suppress by the
power of ignorance, he endeavors to pervert by the evil use that
men make of knowledge, to disappoint them of the end for which
God has given it." And it was Acontius, Dury believed, who had
uncovered not only "the grand adversary's design" against the
faithful but also the remedy for it.[102]

FROM SATAN'S STRATAGEMS
TO HUMAN NATURE

"The best way to find out the devil's stratagems," writes Acontius
in *Satans Strategems*, "is to take into serious consideration, what is
the end at which all his consultations aim, which is not very hard
to tell. For seeing that he is defined in Scripture A MAN-SLAYER
from the very beginning, what can we think he should rather aim
at than the death of MAN and that ETERNAL."[103] While hardly a surprising assertion taken on its own, the first sentences of Acontius's
treatise assume added meaning when framed against his personal
biography. Born Catholic in 1500, he fled Italy for Basle in 1557,
a Protestant convert. In Basle, and then Zurich, Acontius associated with a number of Italian Protestant exiles, freethinkers, and
humanists, as well as the great early proponent of religious toleration Sebastien Castellio. Acontius, again under pressure of religious persecution for his views on the Trinity, left Switzerland in
1559, arriving later that same year in England, where he would
spend the remainder of his life. It was in England that he finally
felt safe enough to publish *Satans Strategems*, a work he had composed while still in Italy. The book, which first appeared in 1565 in
Basle, was reprinted numerous times on the Continent and eventually translated into English in 1648.[104] In its very first pages, Acontius assures his readers that Satan's stratagems are as straightfor-

ward as they are effective. Salvation depends on obeying God, and
the Devil knows this. The Devil targets and exploits our weaknesses, using fallen human nature against itself in order to foster
disobedience.

Given our current deplorable condition, Acontius doubts the
Devil's work is all that difficult. "Though MAN at first was created
of a good, right and every ways perfect Nature and disposition," he
writes, "yet breaking the command of God, he became of another
NATURE quite contrary, exceedingly corrupt and liable to all manner of vice." As a result, we love ourselves immoderately, and this
causes us to forget our true nature and dependence on God. Like
our "first parents," we easily imagine ourselves to be "little deities"
as we lust after carnal and temporal pleasures with the "strange
weakness of mind that made the Sovereignty of the whole world
seem too-too little for *Alexander* the great." Worst of all, these
flaws turn us from God and blind us to the truth. Our judgment
corrupted, we take "truth for falsehood, and falsehood for truth
itself." Not only do we find it difficult to discover the truth, even
when we do find it, it is almost impossible for us to maintain it in
its purity. While we are quick to notice these flaws in others, we are
utterly blind to them in ourselves. In fact, should anyone disagree
with us, we are "exceeding prone to wrath and hatred," ready to
attack our opponents with cruel violence and bloody persecutions.
"In a word," Acontius contends, "the nature of man, such as now
it is, is not much unlike the Nature of the unclean spirits."[105]

Human nature has become so corrupt, Acontius adds, that
even the literal interpretation of scripture can become a source of
discord, error, and sin. "It may fall out," he warns, "that while you
think to express that Doctrine which you hold for truth, with more
significant and clear expressions, than it is in Scripture expressed,
and better to shun occasion of cavil (for the wit of man will ever be
more wary and wiser than God) thou wilt use such words or forms
of expression, as from whence another less true and godly tenet
may sometimes be collected."[106] Opponents attack each other with
scripture, distorting it and themselves in the process. Outraged
pride grabs hold of every disagreement, every perceived insult and

injury, magnifying them so that "new controversies arise, and new errors in like manner without end."[107] Nowhere, Acontius contends, has Satan's success at manipulating man's fallen nature been so spectacularly successful than in the "long and very Tragical controversy about the interpretation of those words, *Take, this is my Body*," the sacrament of the Eucharist.[108] While it cannot be denied that what appears "plain and clear" to one person in this debate appears differently to another, Acontius reminds his readers that all who are involved profess themselves to be good Christians. No one doubts the truth of Christ's words, no one ever imagines Christ to be a liar, and yet, Acontius adds, "how far doth hatred, springing from our differences, transport us?" For Acontius, this situation reveals a distinction that is central to overcoming Satan's schemes. "Wherefore of necessity thus much must be granted," Acontius writes, "that the difference is only about the meaning, not the Truth of the words."[109]

All Christians accept the Bible as the true Word of God, even if they do not all agree on how God's Word should be interpreted. Satan exploits the difference between meaning and truth, between different interpretations of scripture and scripture's true, if hidden, revelation, in order to swell each man's pride, and through pride, Satan sows discord. Unlike Luther, unlike so many of the reformers and Catholics engaged in religious debate, Acontius is suspicious of any claim to exegetical certainty. Perhaps Luther could claim a divinely and subjectively inspired justification for his interpretations of scripture, but Acontius is too aware of our fallen state—a state that has left our reason dimmed, our will broken, and our pride burning—to have much confidence in our individual ability to understand each and every one of scripture's intricacies. Corrupt reason and prideful passion too easily deceive us into thinking our personal interpretations of scripture coincide with its actual truth. If the Devil exploits our passions, we must do everything possible to quell them, to set them aside when attempting to discriminate between God's truth and human interpretation. As a result, much of *Satans Strategems* reads like a rhetorical manual, offering advice to those engaged in religious debate. Since people cling to their beliefs and take offense when told they are wrong, we must not absurdly simplify our opponents' positions, angering them even as we misrepresent their ideas. We must understand them, take them seriously, and refute them with the appropriate arguments. Of course, we are no different from our opponents, and Acontius advises us to be wary of our own pride, our own passions, even our own propensity to error: "Forasmuch as for the most part, those that are judged to excel others in wisdom, are at difference among themselves; it must be concluded that many also of those who are accounted wise, do err." Only the most arrogant think they are free from arrogance, and everyone, Acontius advises, ought to heed Solomon, who observed, "A fool is pleased with his own reasoning, but a wise man seeks councel."[110]

If Acontius is too much the realist, too much the victim of religious persecution, to trust entirely in human reason, he is too much the humanist to despair of it completely. Doubt, as the first stage in the intellectual pursuit of truth, plays a foundational role in the individual's quest for faith. Even those few principles that every Christian must accept should be subjected to temporary scrutiny and skeptical inquiry. Beyond those truths, disagreement is no sign of obstinacy, much less of heresy. "Those who accept the necessary things," Acontius adds, "[should] forbear one another and discuss their controversies lovingly and kindly as brothers."[111] Perhaps we cannot help having a personal stake in what we believe to be true, but we must always attempt to contain our passions through an awareness that others can have good reasons to disagree with us. We can accomplish this only through rational discourse and calm discussion. Where disagreements become irresolvable, we continue to discuss, or we leave things be. To do otherwise is to allow the unclean spirit we are to become the Devil we fear.

But who needs the Devil if we ourselves are already unclean? Reducing Satan's stratagems to manipulations of the mostly manageable play of human emotion effectively reduces Satan himself to little more than those emotions. It is impossible to know whether Acontius intended to blur so fully the division between ourselves and the Devil, to blur the division between our own intemperate passions and those the Devil inspires within us, but blur them he does. Acontius's own recommended techniques for tamping down human pride are the same regardless of their cause, and this, functionally at least, renders the Devil entirely superfluous in explanations of human discord.[112] For all intents and purposes, Acontius's account of Satan's efforts to ruin mankind returns us to the problem that so concerned Augustine, precisely because it calls into question the Devil's role in man's Fall. How was Eve so easily deceived into disobedience? Augustine thought there was nothing for it but to imagine that some sort of propensity toward pride was in her already, ripe for the serpent's exploitation. Thomas Aquinas, Nicholas of Lyra, and Luther all rejected this possibility, as it suggested that God's creatures were less than good, perhaps even predisposed to evil. But, of course, our original propensity to sin is already presupposed in the writings of every exegete who claimed that the first Temptation is a model for all future temptations and that every subsequent one is a replay of the first. For the first to be a model for the rest, it must already contain the structural elements, the forces and leanings, of every future transgression.

All of which suggests something different about the Fall, about the serpent and the Temptation. In *Paradise Lost*, first published in 1667, John Milton sets the Temptation and Fall on the seventh day of Creation. An important narrative decision, this means that Adam and Eve have already spent much of the sixth day together, all of that night, and the beginning of the next day before Eve makes her fateful decision. They have eaten together and spoken to each other, wandered through paradise together, and spent a night in each other's arms and, it would seem, they have fallen. Adam already adores his wife too much, claiming her to be the "fairest of Creation, last and best/Of all God's Works," and this despite the angel Raphael's warning that he must not attribute "overmuch to things/less excellent." There are dangers, Raphael adds, if he should subject himself to his inferior.[113] Of course, this is exactly what Adam does, not only when he eats the fruit Eve hands him on the seventh day, but even earlier on the morning of that same day, when Eve disagrees with him. Eve asks to work at some distance from Adam, who at first refuses, pointing out the dangers of separation given the rumored existence of a possibly lurking "malicious Foe."[114] After lengthy discussion, Adam succumbs to her request against his better judgment. "Seek not temptation then," he tells her, "which to avoid/Were better, and most likely if from me/Though sever not: Trial will come unsought."[115] For her part, Eve knowingly lays herself open to this temptation, disagreeing with Adam whom, only the previous day, she had promised never to question in obedience to God's will. "Unargu'd I obey," she had vowed to Adam, "so God ordains,/God is thy law, thou mine: to know no more/Is woman's happiest knowledge and her praise."[116] But on the morning of the seventh day, in response to Adam's initial entreaties to remain by his side, Eve complains, "If this be our condition, thus to dwell/In narrow circuit strait'n'd by a Foe/Subtle or violent, we not endu'd/Single with like defence, wherever met/How are we happy, still in fear of harm?"[117]

In Milton's grand concluding contribution to the interpretation of the Fall, it takes less than a day for the first couple, left to themselves, to begin to question and interpret God's Word, as they naturally acquire the subtle skill of accommodating God's commands to their own desires. Milton makes explicit a line of thought implicit in Acontius's treatise. The Devil was never needed for the Fall, and the Fall was something always imminent, if not always already accomplished. Perhaps the Devil's lie led Eve down one path of false interpretation, but Adam had already charted its contours when he allowed her to go off on her own, rationalizing his decision to let the inferior dictate to the superior with what would become forever after one of love's great laments: "Go; for thy stay, not free, absents thee more."[118] Eve is little different from Adam at this point, and even before meeting the serpent, she has rebelled against the strictures of her superiors, reinterpreting her state, while desiring something new and dangerous in the groves of paradise.

Milton's rendering of Genesis 3 suggests that the Devil did not so much cause the Fall as perform a service. He made a hidden fallen nature visible for all to see, and visibility, as it turns out, has its uses. "And I venture to say," Augustine had long before written in the *City of God*, "that it is of benefit to the proud that they should fall into some open and manifest sin, which can cause them to be displeased with themselves even after they have already fallen through being pleased with themselves."[119] Useful, no doubt, as both Acontius and Milton would agree, because it set in motion the redemption of fallen man through Christ. But it was useful for another reason as well. As Augustine suggests, Adam and Eve, caught up in their own desires, their own prideful interpretations, were unaware that they had deviated from God's Word. Milton depicts them no differently. Adam blithely ignores Raphael's warnings, and Eve unreflectively convinces herself to give up perfect obedience. The Devil strips them of this ignorance about themselves and their nature. The Devil's lie is the gift of self-knowledge, and this is the real insight hidden within Acontius's treatise. Forever caught between truth and meaning, too often mistaking the lie for the truth, we are forever caught up in interpretation.

Interpretation may well be the source of our bondage. It is also the source of our freedom and, more, our peaceful coexistence.

CHAPTER TWO

God

CAN GOD LIE?

What if God, like the Devil, could lie?

In his *Sermon on the Creed*, Augustine rejects the very possibility that God could lie. Speaking to an audience of religious novices, Augustine draws their attention to the Nicean Creed's opening words: "We believe in God the Father Almighty." These are words, Augustine tells them, that every Christian must accept, understand, and hold fast. "Since God is omnipotent," he explains, "he is not able to die, he is not able to be deceived, nor is he able to lie for as the Apostle says, 'He cannot deny himself.'" While it may seem surprising that there are things an all-powerful being cannot do, Augustine argues that these sorts of actions would be proof of impotence, not omnipotence. A being that can die is not all-powerful, nor for that matter is a being that can be deceived. But why can't an omnipotent being lie? Augustine offers a different sort of reason to account for this divine inability, one rooted in something like God's moral standing and dignity. "If God could lie or be deceived, if he could deceive or act in any sort of unkind way, God would not be omnipotent because this sort of behavior is not worthy of an omnipotent being." In fact, Augustine continues, God cannot sin, cannot even wish to do evil things. Everything God does God does well, and whatever God does well he does justly.[1]

Some twelve hundred years later, the French philosopher René Descartes would reach a seemingly similar conclusion. "There is fixed in my mind the idea of a God who can do all things," Des-

62

cartes writes in the first of his *Meditations on First Philosophy*, "and by whom I, such as I exist, have been created." Well and good, but Descartes famously raises an unsettling, if rather extreme, possibility. What if God had never created the earth or the heavens, had never created any of the things I see or think about and "yet all these things would seem to me to exist no differently than they do now?"[2] Simply put, what if God has deceived and tricked me into believing that a nonexistent world really exists? Later, in the "Third Meditation," Descartes will reject the possibility that God is a deceiver and liar for reasons that bear at least a superficial resemblance to Augustine's reasons. If God really is all-powerful, if God possesses all possible perfections, then it is impossible for God to be a deceiver. "For it is clear by the natural light," Descartes argues, "that all fraud and deception depend on some defect."[3] Like Augustine, Descartes contends that deceptive, fraudulent, and mendacious actions are utterly incompatible with an all-powerful being. A truly omnipotent being not only would never do such things, it would not even be capable of doing such things. God cannot lie, because God is God.

And so the matter might seem settled except, of course, that Descartes would have agreed with Augustine on something else as well. Nothing happens in this world without God's direct involvement, without God's approval and control. As Augustine put it just a few lines later in his *Sermon on the Creed*, "There is no resisting the omnipotent, such that what he wishes does not happen."[4] Nothing that God wishes to happen fails to happen and, it follows, nothing happens that God does not wish to happen. For theologians who thought about the early chapters of Genesis, about the story of Adam and Eve and their exile from Eden, God's wishes and power raised a very specific type of problem, a problem that did not sit comfortably with Augustine's and Descartes's confident conclusions about what God can and cannot do.

The revered late medieval biblical scholar Nicholas of Lyra broaches this problem at the very beginning of his commentary on the Temptation. "And first," he writes, "we must consider whether it was appropriate for God to allow man to be tempted, especially since He knew what would happen."[5] Nicholas's question depends on an absolutely central assumption, an assumption that might well seem to involve God directly in the deception of Adam and Eve and the Fall, not to mention the entire subsequent history of human suffering. Nicholas's question assumes that the Devil, for all the trouble and havoc he causes, does nothing that God does not allow him to do. Not only does God know forever in advance what the Devil will do in Eden, it is God himself who orchestrates and stages the entire scene. It is God who decides that the Devil, in the false guise of a serpent, will first approach Eve, just as it is God who composes the lying words with which the Devil seduces her. For medieval and Reformation theologians, these were entirely obvious, if potentially troubling, ideas. Perhaps the Devil occupied center stage in those all too brief and tragic moments leading up to the Fall, but God had ordained everything that had transpired. It was God who wrote the script, staged the scene, directed the actors. Given all that, who really is the father of lies?

For all his confidence before the novices, Augustine himself had experienced the power of these problems firsthand. Before his conversion to Catholicism, Augustine had accepted the spiritual teachings of Faustus and the Manicheans precisely because they seemed to offer a theology that liberated God from the responsibility of having created evil, of lying to and deceiving the very creatures he had created in his image and likeness. "Commentators are accustomed to consider very carefully the nature of the Devil," Augustine would write many years after he had turned his back on the Manicheans, "since certain heretics, scandalized by his evil will, want to remove him entirely from the creatures made by the true sovereign God and to attribute him to another principle which in their account is opposed to God." Having raised the possibility that the Devil exists independently of God, Augustine wastes no time rejecting it out of hand. Everything that exists depends on God for its existence, he reminds his readers.[6] This might seem to make things all the worse for God, hinting as it does at his immediate involvement in the Devil's deceptions and lies. Augustine, however, invokes a subtle distinction to free God from personal involvement in sin. "God is not the author of the malice or wickedness of sinners," he argues. Rather, God knows in advance, before he even creates them, which creatures are "going to be wicked by their own perverse will." He allows them to sin, permits them to sin, because their evil actions somehow contribute to the salvation of the good.[7] Writing in the twelfth century, Peter Lombard did his part to ensure the longevity of Augustine's distinction when he included it in his *Sentences*. "Evil things are not done with God willing or unwilling, but with him not willing," Peter writes, "because it is not subject to God's will that an evil be done or not done, but that he allows it to be done, because it is good to allow evil things to be done; and he allows it entirely willingly, not willing evil things, but willing to allow that they be done, because evil things are not good, nor is it good for them to be or be done."[8]

Whether or not the metaphysical, moral, and psychological intricacies among what God wills, willingly allows, or inactively permits could bear the conceptual weight these constructs were meant to support, they comprise a solution that clearly demonstrates the challenges theologians faced. No one wanted to deny that God was all-powerful, that God was good and just, but there was evidence, seemingly irrefutable and scattered throughout the Bible, that God did more than merely permit evil things to transpire. In the sixteenth century, Calvin rejected Augustine's subtle distinction. Invoking the Manicheans (who had long since become a favorite theological whipping post), Calvin writes, "[Some people] have imagined that Satan, not being in subjection to God, laid snares for man in opposition to the divine will, and was superior not to man only, but also to God himself." Any pious and reverent person, Calvin immediately adds, would recognize the folly of this belief and would have to admit that evil does not occur except "by God's permission." Pausing to reflect on the word "permission," Calvin adds, "It offends the ears of some, when it is said God willed the Fall, but what else, I pray, is the permission of Him, who has the power of preventing, and in whose hand the whole matter was placed, but his will?"[9]

Calvin would return to this problem in his *Institutes*, his great summa of reformed theology, refuting all attempts to absolve God from direct oversight of and involvement in the evil that men do. Running through a litany of Old Testament witnesses, Calvin argues that scripture speaks with one voice on the subject. God directs Satan to drive Job to despair and madness, and it is God who "wills that the false king Ahab be deceived," sending the Devil to fulfill this wish "with a definite command to be a lying spirit in the mouth of all the prophets." Perhaps God acts through Satan, Calvin concludes, but there can be no doubt "that Satan performs his part by God's impulsion." Confronted with this unequivocal biblical evidence, one might be tempted to think that "God has two contrary wills," violating secretly the laws he openly commands. God may well have proclaimed through Moses that all lies are strictly prohibited, but this does little to prevent God from instructing others to lie for him. Calvin's response both acknowledges and accepts this apparent contradiction because God's ways are mysterious and unknowable to sinners like us. "When we do not grasp how God wills to take place what he forbids to be done," Calvin writes, "let us recall our mental incapacity, and at the same time consider that the light in which God dwells is not without reason called unapproachable."[10]

The history of God's lies is the history of the unbearable tension between two different ways of conceiving God, one rooted in philosophy, the other rooted in the unfolding narrative of scripture. Philosophers, not to mention theologians when thinking philosophically, asserted an honest, just, infinitely wise, and utterly transcendent God, perfect and immutable. By contrast, the God of scripture is a historical figure, involved with and interacting in the world, mutable, prone to anger, and seemingly all too willing to lie and deceive should the circumstances demand it. Something had to give, and when it did, scripture gave way to philosophy, and God would find himself exiled from the Bible.

ON LIONS, FISHHOOKS, AND MOUSETRAPS

Medieval bestiaries have quite a lot to say about lions. While the lion is a mighty and courageous beast, unwilling to back down from even the most terrifying of foes, it fears the sound of rumbling wheels and the flames of fire even more. The lion is a noble creature and "disdains the company of large numbers." It is also clever. When it discovers that hunters are chasing it, when it picks up their scent among the mountain heights where it loves to roam, the lion uses its tail to sweep away its tracks, obliterating any clues to its presence.[11]

These facts about the lion could be found in ancient and venerable sources. Pliny's *Natural Histories* provided a rich source of information on the lion, and the sixth-century encyclopedist Isidore of Seville had passed on the information about the lion's devious tail.[12] Bestiaries were not simply compendia of data drawn from natural historians. Taking inspiration and content from the *Physiologus*, a second-century Christian treatise that went on to become one of the most popular and influential books of the Middle Ages, bestiaries were primarily concerned with uncovering the allegorical mysteries hidden within the book of nature. And there were powerful mysteries hidden within the brave form of the lion, the king of the animals, the first to be described in the *Physiologus*.[13] Just as a lion, pursued by hunters, erases its tracks, so it is that "our savior, a spiritual lion of the tribe of Judah, the root of Jesse, the son of David, concealed the traces of his love in heaven until, sent by his father, he descended into the womb of the Virgin and redeemed mankind that was lost." As it turns out, his love was not the only thing the savior chose to hide. "Not knowing of his divine nature," the bestiary continues, "the Devil, the enemy of mankind, dared to tempt him like an ordinary man. Even the angels on high did not know of his divinity and said to those who were with them when he ascended to his father, 'Who is this king of glory?'"[14]

The idea that Christ concealed his divinity from the Devil was hardly limited to the bestiary tradition. Augustine had done much to popularize the idea, mentioning it in any number of works, in any number of contexts. "How was the Devil conquered?" Augustine asks in *On the Trinity*. "Because, although he found nothing in Christ worthy of death, yet he slew Him."[15] According to Augustine, the story of Christ's incarnation, life, and crucifixion is that of an extended ruse, a well-thought-out plot to trick the Devil into abusing his power and dominion over mankind. Perhaps the Devil had rightful possession over Adam's sinful descendants, but he lost that right when he overreached and crucified a manifestly guiltless Jesus. As Augustine made clear in a sermon preached for the Feast of Ascension, the Devil would never have abused his power if Christ had not concealed his divinity, " 'For had they known,' " Augustine writes, quoting and then glossing the apostle Paul, " 'they would never have crucified the Lord of Glory.' But if he had not been put to death, death would not have died." Christ's spotless and holy life, his divinity hidden beneath an all too human exterior, was the bait that lured the Devil to his own self-destruction. "The Devil exulted when Christ died," Augustine adds, "and by that very death of Christ the Devil was overcome: he took food, as it were, from a trap. He gloated over the death as if he were appointed a deputy of death; that in which he rejoiced became a prison for him. The cross of the Lord became a trap for the Devil; the death of the Lord was the food by which he was ensnared."[16] Augustine put it even more succinctly in another sermon when he stated, "The Lord's cross was the devil's mousetrap: the bait which caught him was the death of the Lord Christ."[17]

Augustine's older contemporary, Gregory of Nyssa, used different imagery to similar effect to describe Christ's deception of the Devil. "The divine nature," Gregory writes, "was concealed under the veil of our human nature so that, as with a greedy fish, the hook of divinity might be swallowed along with the bait of flesh." According to Gregory, this sort of deception was perfectly fitting, perfectly just, for human beings themselves had long since fallen prey to a different sort of allegorically baited false food. "The heathen fable," Gregory writes, "tells of a dog who caught sight of the reflection in the water of the food he was carrying in his mouth. He opened his mouth wide to swallow the reflection, and dropped the real food; and so went hungry." Likewise, the Devil, "that advocate and inventor of wickedness," had persuaded mankind to "the good with its opposite." He covered the "hook of his wickedness" with "the false semblance of good," and mankind, deceived and caught, became the captives of their worst enemy.[18]

Adam and Eve, as Gregory relates the story of our Fall, had sold themselves into bondage. They had handed over their freedom and willingly become Satan's slaves in exchange for his false promises. God's response to Satan's double-dealing, Gregory contends, makes sense only within this dramatic narrative. We know that God is good and wise, that he is just and powerful. God feels pity for our fallen state, and through his wisdom he knows how best to rescue us. God could simply liberate mankind, but this would be an action fitting only for a tyrant. Justice requires that man's freedom be purchased or ransomed from its current owner. Christ's incarnation, his wondrous birth, and his miraculous life are all aspects of an extended charade to convince the Devil that the value of a sinless Christ exceeds that of all other sinful men combined. Christ's excellent life is the bait, while Christ's divinity, the hook, is hidden within the bait of his human flesh. As Gregory puts it, "It was beyond the Devil's power to look upon the unveiled appearance of God; he would see only in Christ a part of the fleshly nature which he had of old subdued through wickedness." This was, Gregory assures his readers, the only way the Devil would have handed over mankind. Had Christ appeared in his divinity, had he not hid himself behind a veil of flesh, the Devil would have been too fearful to make the exchange. Summarizing the story, Gregory praises each and every aspect of God's plan, especially the deceptive ruse on which everything hinges. "His choosing to save man," Gregory writes, "is evidence of his goodness; his making the ransoming of the captive a matter of exchange displays his justice; while his pre-eminent wisdom is demonstrated by the device by which something was accessible to the Enemy which had been beyond his grasp."[19]

Whatever differences might exist between Augustine's mouse-trap and Gregory's fishhook, both writers treat Christ's incarnation, life, and crucifixion as part of a decades-long exchange, even dialogue, with the Devil.[20] When God deceives the Devil, God is justified because both the specific circumstances of man's Fall and God's intentions warrant and justify such deception. Like an immoral sophist, the Devil convinced Eve willingly to give up her freedom, persuading her that evil was good and good was evil. Reciprocity, fairness, even justice, demand that mankind's freedom be secured in some similar manner, and so it is that Christ engages in a series of negotiations with the Devil as he attempts to persuade the Devil to accept his life in exchange for the rest of mankind's freedom. Christ can succeed in this drawn out exchange only if he conceals key facts. And so Christ, just like the sophist, must make a bad deal appear good, must make himself appear incomparably better than all other human beings combined, and yet conceal the divinity that makes this absolute superiority possible.[21]

Christ's deceptions may well have extended beyond a good disguise and entered into the realm acting. At one point during Christ's forty days of fasting in the desert, the Devil tempts him: "If you are the Son of God, bid this stone to become bread." Cyril, the Patriarch of Alexandria who died in 444, avoiding all talk of deception, praises the Lord's honest response. "And therefore it was that Christ, knowing the monster's artifice, neither made the change nor said that he was either unable or unwilling to make it, but rather shakes him off as importunate and officious, saying, 'Man shall not live by bread alone.' "[22] Augustine's mentor Ambrose, by contrast, suggested the entire forty days constituted a sort of pious fraud. Christ's apparent hunger, his weakness and thirst, were all part of a plot to convince the Devil that the fragile and sickly looking creature before him was a mere man. How else could the Devil be lured into making his fatal deal? Christ's response to the Devil is purposefully deceptive, even if not exactly false. "The devil tempts that he may test," Ambrose explains. "He tests that he may tempt. In contrast, the Lord deceives that he may conquer. He conquers that he may deceive. For if he had changed his nature, he would have betrayed its creator. Thus he responded neutrally, saying, 'It is written, "That man does not live by bread alone, but by every word of God." ' "[23]

From the Church fathers and allegorical works like the *Physiologus*, the narrative of Christ's deception of the Devil, including the imagery of secretive lions and divinely baited hooks and mousetraps, passed on to later generations of the faithful. It appears in commentaries on the Apostles' Creed that were taught in churches as well as in the widely disseminated writings of both Leo and Gregory the Great.[24] Even after Anselm reconceived the entire nature of Christ's sacrifice, rejecting the notion that Christ ransomed or purchased human freedom from a Devil who claimed right of possession over mankind, basic tenets of this narrative of divine deception survived and flourished in both popular and learned religious works. It made its way into sermon handbooks and from there into sermons themselves.[25] It would even become a ubiquitous feature in both German and English Corpus Christi plays. The Chester plays, for example, which were performed throughout the fifteenth century, include a telling summary reflection concerning Christ's victory over the Devil in the desert. Adam fell through his trespass, we are told, but Jesus withstood his tempter through grace and, as a result, Satan was "completely deceived" regarding his "godhead."[26]

If medieval theologians proved a bit less enthusiastic about Christ's various deceptions than did the playwrights, they still discussed and accepted them. For example, Thomas Aquinas interpreted the story of Christ's desert temptations as examples for the holy to follow. Even when directly quoting from Ambrose's decidedly fraud-friendly reading of those same events, he explicitly removed all hints that Christ had engaged in any sort of false, misleading, or deceptive behavior.[27] Still, in other places, Thomas has no problem claiming that it was necessary for Christ to conceal his true identity from the demons. "For had they fully known that he was the Son of God and the effect of His passion," Thomas writes, "they would never have procured the crucifixion of the Lord in Glory."[28]

Thomas includes yet another trick played on the Devil that enjoyed wide currency in popular religious literature. Why did Jesus's virgin mother need to marry? Thomas offers up a variety of reasons, reasons having to do with the insurmountable social and cultural challenges that an unwed mother would have faced in turn-of-the-millennium Palestine and with the need for young boys to have father figures, but he offers another one as well. Citing the church father Ignatius, Thomas argues that Joseph, Mary's husband, was a decoy, a beard, employed so "that the manner of our Lord's birth might be hidden from the devil." Eventually, Thomas contends, the Devil and his minions would know full well just who and what Christ was, but during his infancy and childhood, "it behooved the malice of the devil to be withheld, lest he should persecute Him too severely: for Christ did not wish to suffer such things then, nor to make His power known, but to show himself to be in all things like other infants."[29] Early in the fifteenth century, the chancellor of the University of Paris, Jean Gerson, would support Joseph's role in this divine plot, adding for good measure that this is how we know that Joseph, contrary to popular opinion, must have been young and virile. Had the ancient enemy recognized in Joseph an impotent old man, he would all to easily have uncovered the true "mystery of the incarnation."[30] Many of these ideas come together in the Flemish painter Roger Campin's famous *Merode Altarpiece*. Completed in the late 1420s, the triptych depicts the Annunciation, the moment when the angel announces to Mary that she will be the virgin mother of God. On the center panel, Mary, not yet aware of the angel's presence, leans against a bench, her attention entirely given over to the religious book in her hands. On the right panel, two people, most likely the painting's donors, stare across this scene to the left panel, where an admittedly older Joseph sits on a bench, working a piece of wood. On the table near him sits a mousetrap.[31]

Whether deceptive or misleading, there was no question in anyone's mind, no doubt whatsoever, that Christ's behavior was of a wholly different moral standing than the Devil's deceptive and misleading behavior. The thirteenth-century Franciscan theologian

Bonaventure frames this difference with great clarity. As part of his *Sentences* commentary, he offers four reasons why Christ's offering on the cross was the ideal means for humanity to render satisfaction to God. First, Bonaventure explains, it was the most acceptable form of satisfaction to God because a man can offer nothing greater than his very life. Second, it was the most harmonious form of satisfaction because it undid the tangle of sins at the root of the first couple's Fall. Just as Adam and Eve fell through pride, gluttony, and disobedience, Christ on the cross cured those sins through their contraries, through abasement, humiliation, and obedience to the divine will. Third, it was the most effective form of satisfaction because it was the best means of uplifting the human race. God asks for nothing but our love, and there is no better way of attracting the beloved than by demonstrating your own love, and so Christ willingly endured the gibbet of the cross for mankind. Finally, Bonaventure concludes, it was the most prudent form of satisfaction. "It is fitting that Christ conquered the devil with his prudence [*prudentia*]," he explains, "for the devil deceived the first man with his cunning [*astutia*]." Prudence, Bonaventure remarks, beats back pride, and then, as if exemplifying the truth of that maxim, he quotes Peter Lombard, himself harking back to Augustine: "The Redeemer arrives and the deceiver is destroyed, he stretches himself across the mousetrap of the cross, and sets out for the deceiver the food of his blood."[32] Between Christ and the Devil stands the difference between prudence and cunning.

As Bonaventure explains in his *Collations on the Six Days*, prudence is one of the four cardinal virtues, along with temperance, justice, and fortitude. In the *Collations*, Bonaventure weaves together ideas from a variety of classic authorities, both pagan and Christian, to define the nature of these virtues, and of prudence in particular. "A virtue is so called," Bonaventure writes, drawing from Cicero's popular definition, "because it is the strength of the mind for the performance of good and the avoidance of evil." Doing good and avoiding evil requires that a person avoid extremes, that a person's actions exemplify what Aristotle refers to as "the quality of intermediateness." Bonaventure certainly does not mean that the virtuous act is perfectly situated between emotional extremes, the sort of numb emotionless center between passionate alternatives. It is the act that best fits the demands of the moment, the right balance between sweetness and severity, leniency and justice, given the particular circumstances. "Virtue," Bonaventure adds, now borrowing from Augustine, "is nothing else than a proper measure." The virtuous act, in other words, is measured to fit the situation, and it is prudence that makes these all-important evaluations. In this sense, prudence is an intellectual virtue rooted in a "knowledge of good and evil things and the distinctions between them." It is dependent on memory, intelligence, and providence, refined through reflection on experience. The goal of prudence is not speculative truth but practical knowledge geared toward the present moment and its unique, singular demands. "Prudence," Bonaventure explains, "finds this proper measure, so that you do not go too far in anything, but remain close to the center. Hence prudence is the driver of the virtues. Wherefore prudence says: I have found the proper measure; and temperance acts as a watchman and says: I too wanted this; and justice acts as a distributor, willing not only for itself, but also for the other; and because many adversities occur after that, fortitude acts as a defender, lest the proper measure be lost."[33]

Craftiness or cunning, *astutia*, by contrast, almost always refers to inappropriate, even malicious behavior and is a constant feature in Bonaventure's description of the fallen angels. For example, in a discussion about how demons sometimes intentionally deceive astrologers, Bonaventure observes that "so great is the craftiness of demons, that they know how to hide their fraud, making it clear that they did not err, but rather that it was the astronomer who was guilty of the error or defect in the prognostication."[34] Bonaventure's contemporary Thomas Aquinas offers a more delineated account of craftiness. According to Aquinas, the essence of craftiness resides in the use of unfit means to achieve one's desires. A person commits the sin of craftiness, Aquinas explains, "when, in order to obtain a certain end, whether good or evil, one uses means that are not true but fictitious and counterfeit." The emphasis on means, not ends, is crucial. Just as prudence is an intellectual virtue concerned with properly fitting and measuring our actions to their contexts, so craftiness, the sin "opposed to prudence," is characterized by actions that willfully disregard this proper fit and measure, actions that are false and fictitious. Ends do not absolve means, and Aquinas is very clear that craftiness is a sin even if it is directed toward a good end.[35]

So far so good, except Aquinas does little in this section of his *Summa of Theology* to offer much in the way of guidance concerning what makes some, but not all, deceptive actions false and counterfeit, nor for that matter does Bonaventure. Of course, there is the rough-and-ready, not to mention absolute and unquestionable, guidance to be found in the examples of Christ and the Devil. Christ's actions, no matter how described, are most prudent, most fitting, and completely sinless, even if it is occasionally difficult to reconcile them with the vague standards encompassed in Aquinas's definition of craftiness. As we have seen, while Gregory of Nyssa stressed that God's actions manifested the perfect blend of wisdom, justice, and goodness, Ambrose often resorted to the very worrisome ends-justify-the-means style of reasoning that Aquinas would later condemn. Ambrose is more blunt than most prior or subsequent theologians, happy as he is to describe Christ's actions as holy deceptions and pious frauds. Still, Ambrose, more often than not, invokes the same sorts of justifications for Christ's actions that Gregory and Augustine invoke, that Bonaventure would continue to invoke centuries later. Christ's actions are prudent, justified, and sinless because they perfectly counter the Devil's actions: deception counters deception, fraud counters fraud and, for all that, prudence counters cunning.

Most important, most obvious, and therefore all too easy to overlook, everyone agreed that Christ's actions needed to be understood and interpreted in the context of the biblical stories themselves, in the context of the grand outline of human history beginning with the Fall and culminating in the Christ's resurrection from the dead and ascension into heaven. Christ's actions were most prudent and just because they achieved their ends in the most fitting and appropriate manner possible. Given the specific circumstances of mankind's first transgression and the unique problems to which it gave rise—and this holds whether Christ's work was understood as a form of purchasing man from the Devil or as atonement to an offended God—certain sorts of potentially and sometimes intentionally misleading actions, disguises, and statements were acceptable, even necessary, and never less than good. Implicit in this approach to Christ's work is the idea that quite similar types of actions or behavior can, in different circumstances, take on very different moral qualities. Satan, when he disguises himself as a serpent to deceive Eve, commits an act of guile and craftiness, but when Christ disguises himself as a mere man to deceive Satan, he acts with justice and prudence. William Langland, the fourteenth-century author of *Piers Plowman*, sums up this idea nicely when he writes, "And just as man was beguiled by the guiler's guile, so shall grace from which all began finally succeed and beguile the guiler, and that's a good trick, Art to deceive art."[36]

The idea that circumstances could define or even make the sin was a truism of pastoral literature. Writing in the twelfth century, Alan of Lille notes that the gravity of a sin often depends on its origins and causes. "He sins more gravely," Alan notes, "who is seduced by the smell of lucre or sweet caresses, than if he is deceived through drunkenness."[37] Thomas Chobham concurred in his influential early thirteenth-century penitential treatise, the *Summa confessorum*, in which he offers detailed analyses of how the circumstances surrounding and defining our actions can transform venial sins into mortal sins. Who committed the sin? When and where did the sinner commit it, and for what reasons? As Chobham puts it, "a person sins less who steals in order to feed his father, than he who steals so that he may live lavishly."[38] Sometimes circumstances could determine whether an action was sinful at all. The fourteenth-century Spanish curate Guido of Monte Rocherii explains that a sin can be mortal in two ways, because the deed itself is sinful (and here he cites fornication) or because of the intention governing the deed. "To sing in church," he offers by way of an entirely noncontroversial example, "is not a mortal sin, indeed it can be meritorious. But to sing in church in order to please a woman and entice her to sin is a mortal sin."[39]

Just as the circumstances define our actions, so it seems, they define God's actions, and from the earliest Christian centuries until at least the fifteenth century a great many people believed God could deceive, could commit fraud, perhaps could lie. Theologians who in some places loudly proclaim that God's perfection makes it impossible for him to be a deceiver, in other places praise God's deceptions. Theologians who claim God merely allows or permits evil actions to occur, who argue that God never directly deceives, invoke gripping and memorable metaphors in honor of Christ's duping the Devil. Admittedly, the circumstances demanded this response and, given those circumstances, theologians contended that God's actions were prudent, fair, and perfectly in keeping with the nature of an all-powerful being. Extreme situations, after all, call for extreme measures. Jacobus de Voragine, the Dominican author of one the most popular religious works of the entire Middle Ages, *The Golden Legend*, makes this abundantly clear in his description of Christ's passion. In words not so different from those Bonaventure had used in his *Sentences* commentary, and invoking the language of debts, fishhooks, and mousetraps, Jacobus describes how "our redemption was best adapted to accomplish the defeat of man's enemy." The timing of Christ's actions, their place, and their nature were all perfectly suited to their goal, to the circumstances.[40]

Of course, all this left open another, more troubling question. Could God deceive other types of creatures, not merely sinners, demons, and the Devil, but even the faithful? Could God deceive those who love him?

DIVINE DECEPTION AND THE SACRAMENT OF TRUTH

At the center of medieval religious life was the mass, and at the very center of the mass was the celebration of the Eucharist. "Take away this sacrament from the Church," explains Bonaventure in

On Preparing for the Mass, a training manual he wrote for Franciscan novices in the 1250s, "and only error and faithlessness would remain in this world. The Christian people, like a herd of swine, would be dispersed, consigned to idolatry like all those other infidels. But through this sacrament the Church stands firm, faith is strengthened, the Christian religion and divine worship thrive. It is for all these reasons that Christ said, 'Behold, I am with you always to the end of time.' "[41] The entire mass proclaimed the truth of Christ's promise and the faith he inspired, but it was the consecration of the host that transformed this promise into reality. Facing the altar with his back to the parishioners, the priest would shield the host from their view as he began to intone the words of institution, the words Christ had spoken at the Last Supper: "This is my body." Incense, wafted from the wings, from the altar, would slowly fill the church as the priest reached the end of the consecration with Christ's command "Do this in memory of me." Suddenly, the ringing of bells would alert everyone to the miraculous transformation that had taken place. Only then would the priest raise his arms above his head, revealing to an eager audience the sacramental bread now transformed into the very body and blood of Christ.[42]

Precisely because the truth of the entire religion rested in this sacramental miracle, most theological treatises, pastoral manuals, and popular devotional works would at some point assert that there could be no room for deception, no falsity, in it. As the Parisian-trained theologian William of Auxerre would put it in the 1240s, "deception [*simulatio*] has no place where the truth of the body of Christ is concerned."[43] For his part, William was drawing on an idea that dated at least as far back as the 830s, to the writings of the German monk Paschasius Radbertus. In a treatise originally written for a monastic audience and subsequently presented to Charles the Bald in 844, Radbertus reminds his readers that it was Christ himself who celebrated the Last Supper, that it was Christ himself who stated, as he held bread in his hands, "This is my body." How are we to make sense of this statement? Radbertus assures his readers that Christ cannot lie. Invoking 1 John 6, he writes, "Christ is truth and the truth is God. And if God is the truth, then whatever Christ promised in this mystery must necessarily be true."[44] What Christ promised, Radbertus argues, and what the Church would eventually confirm as official dogma, was that his very body, the body to which Mary gave birth and then nurtured, the body that suffered, died, and was buried only to rise again in three days, was really and truly present within the consecrated bread. Only the true presence of Christ's body in the bread could render his words true, could prevent him from having lied to the apostles.

There would continue to be debates and disagreements about how best to account for this remarkable transformation. Even after the Fourth Lateran Council formally settled the issue in 1215 when it decreed that the transformation of bread into body occurred through a process known as "transubstantiation," theologians continued to voice their displeasure with this particular solution.[45] Doctrinal intricacies aside, almost everyone would have agreed with Thomas Aquinas who, writing in the 1270s, asserted that even though it remains invisible to our senses, we must accept that "the true body and blood of Christ is present in the sacrament. . . . You must not doubt whether this is true, but rather must faithfully accept the Savior's words, since he is the Truth, he does not lie."[46]

No matter who stated it, it was all too easy for some people to doubt this alleged truth. When John Pecham, the Franciscan theologian and soon to be archbishop of Canterbury looked into the matter in the late 1270s, he counted fifty separate miracles that must regularly occur every time any priest, anywhere in the world, says a mass and in so doing transforms the host, which never ceases to look like anything but a piece of bread, into the very body of Christ.[47] Thirteenth- and fourteenth-century religious works are peppered with stories of laymen, laywomen, priests, and friars who find it impossible to accept that all these miraculous changes actually occur. Their skepticism is all too easy to understand. Unlike popular medieval wonder stories in which the consecrated host suddenly appears as a baby boy or a hunk of bloody flesh in the priest's hands, in which it heals deadly illnesses and sends heretical preachers to their watery demise, the official miracle of the Eucharist, like the lion chased by hunters, leaves no tangible traces.[48] In the early 1320s, the English Franciscan William Ockham put the matter this way: "[I]t is clear that the body of Christ is not seen in the sacrament of the altar, it is only understood, only the appearance of the bread is really seen." He then adds for good measure, "No one would hold that the body of Christ really is contained under the appearance of the bread were it not for the authority of the Savior and of the Church."[49] Ockham's observation is hardly original, echoing as it does a sentiment present in every orthodox writer since Radbertus. We believe this happens, Ockham asserts, all empirical evidence to the contrary, simply because Christ tells us that it happens and Christ cannot lie.

While Ockham's observation may lack originality, it resonated in novel ways with significant early fourteenth-century theological discussions concerning the nature of vision, cognition, and the status of human claims to knowledge. These debates themselves were ultimately connected to ongoing controversies about the nature of divine omnipotence that had received a decided jump start with the infamous Condemnation of 1277, in which theologians representing the bishop of Paris, Etienne Tempier, condemned 219 propositions, many of which were deemed to have placed undue restrictions and limits on what God can do. The Franciscan theologian Peter Aureol set the stage for much of this discussion concerning the nature of vision in his commentary on Peter Lombard's *Sentences*. Unhappy with the epistemological theories of his predecessor, John Duns Scotus, Aureol points to a number of familiar experiences of visual error and illusion, experiences in which things appear differently than they really are, in which we see things that don't exist. Large castles look tiny from great distances, and straight sticks appear broken or bent when partly submerged in water. Often after staring at the sun we continue to perceive patches of light even though we have averted our gaze or closed our eyes. Reflecting on experiences like these, Aureol concludes that if they can happen naturally, they can certainly happen through God's direct intervention.[50] William Ockham himself would become the most famous player in these debates when he framed the possibility of this sort of divine deception in a simple thought experiment. Imagine you are looking at a star. Now imagine that God, who can do anything, destroys the star while conserving your vision of it. What you now see is a nonexistent star. There is no necessary connection between what you see and what exists.[51]

The Eucharistic miracle could hardly have seemed that much different from Ockham's mischievous star-destroying God. In both cases, the viewer sees something, either a star or a piece of bread, that no longer exists. In both cases, it is God who is responsible for this sudden and imperceptible interruption in the natural order. Given these similarities, what does it mean to claim "Christ cannot lie" or "There is no room for falsity in the miracle of Eucharist"?

In the 1330s, the English Dominican Robert Holkot offered shockingly new answers to these questions. During his life, Holkot was a well-known figure whose commentary on the Book of Wisdom would remain popular for centuries. Holkot's analysis of the Eucharist, like Ockham's discussion of the star, begins with a recognition of God's omnipotence and human weakness. God can do more than the intellect can understand, Holkot asserts, and if God wishes, he can hide the entire world under the appearance of a mouse, the substance of an ass under the appearance of a man, even a thousand asses under the appearance of a single man.[52] For Holkot, the possibility of this sort of divine activity does nothing to impugn God's goodness. It simply reveals the limits of human knowledge, and he readily admits that we can have no absolute certitude when it comes to knowledge about singular things, of mice and men and stars.[53] For all that, when we see something, we do not normally feel compelled to doubt its existence, and Holkot believes this response is reasonable. "I am sufficiently persuaded," he concludes, "that God would not work such transmutations because he has not revealed such things to anyone, nor does it appear that he would do such things unless great utility would result."[54]

Holkot's willingness to frame his discussion of the Eucharist in terms of deception sets him somewhat apart from most everyone else who had written on the topic. In order to explain away any possible deception and falsity in the very sacrament of truth, earlier theologians had made recourse to the language of figures and mysteries, to the fittingness of what appears in relation to the sacrament's deeper and ultimate truths. The anonymous author of the early fourteenth-century preaching manual the *Fasciculus Morum* argues that the Eucharist's perceptual discrepancies, far from being deceptions or illusions, are actually paradoxes whose meaning, if properly understood, can deepen the believer's faith. The whiteness of the consecrated host, for example, indicates that we ought "to be pure and white in the chastity and purity of our life."[55] On a more visceral level, the appearance of bread served a quite useful purpose. Imagine the disgust we might experience were the reality of what we were eating not hidden from us behind the appearance of simple bread, wrote Ambrose, and a chorus of subsequent theologians pronounced their agreement.[56] While Holkot accepts these sorts of explanations, it is telling that in his actual analysis of the sacrament he leaves the entire discussion at the level of sensory awareness. He never redefines the Eucharist's perceptual challenges as figurative paradoxes, and this means that he never shifts the analysis from the level of empirical to spiritual experience. Holkot opts to define the believer's position with respect to the Eucharist entirely in terms of its deceptive qualities. Just like Ockham's thought experiment with the star, Holkot treats the Eucharist as an example of seeing something that no longer exists.

Holkot returns to the problem of divine deception repeatedly in his commentary, constantly expanding the extent of God's potentially misleading behavior. During an analysis of God's knowledge, he asks whether God could promise or reveal something to someone knowing all the while that he has no intention of keeping that promise. Citing Augustine's *On Lying* (a book we will discuss in the next chapter), Holkot notes, "A lie is to say something false with the intention of deceiving." Augustine had in fact written this, but Holkot provides an illuminating gloss. "[Augustine's] opinion ought to be explained like this: A lie is to say something false with an inordinate intention to deceive." Since God cannot act inordinately, that is, since God cannot do anything that is not suitable to his nature, it follows that by definition God cannot lie. From our perspective this may seem like little more than mere wordplay, leaving us at a loss to know when God is or is not telling the truth. Holkot simply accepts this possibility. There is no reason, he adds, why God cannot fittingly, yet "knowingly, assert something false and with the intention of deceiving a creature." And so it is, Holkot explains, that God rightfully deceived the Egyptians and continues to deceive demons, not to mention various and sundry sinners. Invoking the central idea behind the Devil's mousetrap, Holkot adds that Christ intentionally concealed the nature of his birth from the Devil.[57]

Rummaging through both the Old and New Testaments, Holkot finds numerous examples in which God personally deceives not only evil men but also the good. Among other examples, he reminds his readers of how God famously deceived Abraham when he ordered the old man to sacrifice his only son Isaac. Even Christ was not above misleading his parents. When he was twelve, as his parents left Jerusalem with a crowd of festivalgoers, Christ deceived Mary, causing her to think he was with Joseph and the other men when he had actually hidden himself away, only to be found three days later speaking with the priests of the temple. Scripture, Holkot notes, is replete with stories of good people blamelessly lying to other good people. Rebecca and Jacob, to name but one of the many examples he offers, deceive Isaac when Jacob pretends to be his brother Esau. "Therefore," Holkot adds, "God deceives a good man through good men."[58] None of this much worries Holkot, who distinguishes between appropriate and inappropriate deceptions. "To deceive" simply means to cause a person to have a false belief. While false beliefs can be instilled for entirely unworthy, malicious, disordered, and unjust reasons, they can also be instilled for entirely appropriate, useful, and beneficial reasons.[59] Needless to say, God's deceptions of the good, just like his deceptions of the evil, by definition can never be disordered or unjust. Whenever and whomever he deceives, God has his reasons, even if they remain forever beyond our capacity to understand, and those reasons are appropriate, useful, and entirely just.

Holkot's expansive conception of God's deceptive powers also helps to explain his fascination with illusions, substitutions, and false copies. In the third book of his commentary on the *Sentences*, when he takes up the topic of Christ's incarnation, for example, he orients the entire discussion around the problem of hidden identity. He begins the discussion with a question: "Was it possible for the son of God to have been incarnated?" and immediately offers a reason why it was not possible. Imagine that the incarnate Christ looked so much like Jacob that "no one could look at them and tell them apart." Now imagine that Peter sees Jacob, believes him to be Christ, and begins to worship him as God. Would Peter's adoration be meritorious or damning? Holkot is quick to reject this as any sort of argument against the incarnation, an event that the entire Church accepts as true. It does, however, set the stage for a wide-ranging discussion concerning the moral status of human conduct in what might be described as situations of extreme duress, misinformation, and misperception. Is a person excused from the sin of idolatry who worships the Devil transfigured into the likeness of Christ? Can someone win merit through false faith? Did Abraham absolutely believe that he should sacrifice Isaac as God had commanded?[60]

Holkot's answer to these sorts of questions is simple and straightforward. Just as God's actions (no matter how confusing they are from our perspective) are never disordered or irrational, neither are his judgments of our actions. We can only be judged based on our capacities, on our ability or inability to discern the truth in any given set of circumstances. Imagine the case of John who sees the Devil transfigured into the image of Christ. The illusion is perfect, and it is entirely beyond anyone's power to see through it. In such a situation can the individual be blamed for believing the Devil is Christ, for worshipping the Devil as Christ? "A person is excused from sin," Holkot writes, "when it arises out of invincible ignorance." As Holkot reads the situation, this person's actions would not only be blameless, they would be meritorious. It is impossible for John to discern the terrible truth of the vision that confronts him. Given what he cannot help but see, he believes and behaves as he should. Nothing more can be asked of people.[61] Or as Holkot would put it in a different context, in words that would come to define much of Catholic thought even as they outraged sixteenth-century reformers, if man does what he can, he will not be damned.[62]

Holkot's analysis of the Eucharist as an example of divine deception would profoundly influence even those who found his ideas appalling. Writing in 1379, some thirty-two years after Holkot had fallen victim to the plague, another English theologian, John Wyclif, a committed pastor, fiery preacher, and future heretic, challenged Catholic orthodoxy and denounced the very notion that Christ's body was somehow present behind or within the host. "Since God chose to give us so great a gift," Wyclif writes, "it hardly seems fitting with the splendor of his truth, that he would deliver himself to us to honor in a veil." As far as Wyclif is concerned, God would have to behave like the Devil himself were he to work the sort of miraculous, yet invisible, transformation in the host that would create such a radical rift between what appears and what exists. For all intents and purposes, Wyclif accepts Holkot's analysis of the Eucharist as an example of supernatural deception. Unlike Holkot, Wyclif finds such miraculous interventions entirely antithetical to the nature of God. "Every such deception is evil," Wyclif argues, "for man naturally seeks to know the truth," and since our senses "judge that the very substance of bread and wine remain after consecration, and not just their appearance, it does not seem appropriate for the Lord of Truth to introduce such an illusion when graciously communicating so worthy a gift."[63]

Wyclif had many reasons for rejecting the dogma of the bodily presence of Christ in the Eucharist, reasons related to his own rather singular physical and metaphysical theories, as well as to his reading of scripture and the decisions of Church councils.[64] Even the nature of Eucharistic adoration among the laity throughout the thirteenth and fourteenth centuries, the ever-intensifying and passionate desire to see the host during mass, the explosion of miracle tales, reliquaries, and the popularity of Corpus Christi festi-

vals played a part in convincing him that the religious beliefs and
practices of his fellow Christians had gone seriously offtrack.[65] Im-
plicated in all these reasons is something even more fundamental,
a logical and moral imperative that for Wyclif defines God's very
nature and essence. Given that God made us to be creatures who
"naturally seek to know the truth," who make inferences about
what exists based on what we see, God would be violating his own
wishes, entangling himself in self-contradictions were he to lead
our senses astray, especially in something so important as the celebration of the Last Supper.[66] The epistemological consequences of
such deception would be devastating. It would undermine every
system of knowledge and render our every certitude about the
world worthless. Appearances would have no necessary connection to reality, and the evidence of our senses would be rendered
meaningless.[67] We would find ourselves like the ancient skeptics,
affirming that nothing can be known, asserting nothing but affirmations of our own ignorance. From our perspective, the world
would become nothing but a "ball of accidents," all surface and no
depth, forever misleading, deceiving, damning. We would be unable to know the truth of our vows, of our faith, of our sanctity, of
scripture itself.

"I am horrified," Wyclif writes suddenly and without warning
in the middle of a sermon on the importance of charity, "at the
very idea that a quality or any sort of accident could exist on its
own and not inhere in a substance."[68] Wyclif's horror at this moment certainly has something to do with the nightmare of a world
made unknowable, but its emotional register derives from a related and much more ominous possibility. If illusory appearances
can exist in the world, then why can't they also exist within our
own souls? What if we could perceive the presence of charity
within ourselves and yet still be damned? God's deceptions, no
longer limited to the external world, would infiltrate our souls,
would render us invisible to ourselves. But none of this is possible,
or so Wyclif claims, because God is all-powerful and deception is
incompatible with omnipotence. A litany of Catholic thinkers from
Augustine in the fourth century to Aquinas in the thirteenth cen-

tury would have agreed with this assertion, but then again, as we have seen, many of those same Catholic thinkers also believed the Bible offered evidence of some very significant divinely instigated deceptions. Wyclif simply refused to accept this apparent or potential lapse between divine nature and divine conduct.

Think what one will of this drive for utter consistency, Wyclif's was a lonely road leading to a future in which Church authorities would one day disinter his corpse only to rebury it in unhallowed ground. While much of his vehement rhetoric takes shape against a Church that he believes has been co-opted by Antichrist and now teaches the Devil's heresies, his anger extends to his fourteenth-century peers, to theologians such as Ockham and Holkot who had played a central role in developing and disseminating those lies. For these thinkers, Wyclif complains, omnipotence is no guarantee of divine honesty but rather an excuse to indulge in the most sophistical of inquiries. Rather than search for necessary truths, for actual truths, rather than investigate the world as God created it, Wyclif believes that all too many of his predecessors had become obsessed with their own fantasies, imagining all the various things an omnipotent God could do, not what he had actually done, accepting the fiction that God could deceive as truth rather than accepting the God of Truth.[69] When Wyclif argues that it makes no sense to worry about everything that God could do, that we must limit ourselves to "the order actually imposed," he is doing nothing other than stabilizing the natural order by exiling the possibility of miracles and divine intervention.[70] To imagine anything else, to imagine a world in which God could randomly intervene to create accidents without substances, appearances without reality, is to imagine a world of absurdities in which human reason could no longer function as God himself had designed it to. Wyclif purchases the possibility of human knowledge at the expense of God's unbridled interference in the world.

At the risk of oversimplification, it is entirely possible that the difference between Holkot and Wyclif comes down to the problem of starting points and perspective. Holkot's discussion assumes the perspective of divine omnipotence and finds a way for human beings to accommodate themselves to God's ever mysterious, if ever rational, ways. Perhaps we have to give up the guarantee of certainty and intelligibility, but we gain the confidence that God will judge our best efforts to be enough. Wyclif, by contrast, frames his discussion of omnipotence in terms of the natural order. God's actions must conform themselves to the world, which is the necessary expression of his just and perfect creative power. Whereas Holkot offers a more expansive vision of God's range of actions, in which whatever God does will be just and appropriate by definition, Wyclif at moments seems to restrict God's actions in terms of their consequences, in terms of the impact they will have on human beings.

Holkot and Wyclif offer diametrically opposed responses to the threat of divine deception, and each in his own way points to the future, to the hidden and inscrutable God of the reformers and to the infinitely rational God of the scientists.

LUTHER, CALVIN, AND THE HIDDEN GOD

Luther tells a familiar story that leaves us with a familiar paradox.

"A fisherman deceives a fish by enticing it with bait," Luther writes, "and it is not unreasonable on the part of the [Church] fathers to apply this to Christ." Drawing on the imagery that Gregory of Nyssa had bequeathed to the Church, Luther describes how Christ "came into the world clothed in flesh and was cast into the water like a hook. The bait of his humanity concealed his "eternal and unconquerable majesty." Fooled, "the devil struck at the hook of his divinity and by it all his power as well as the power of death and hell was overcome." Luther has no doubt that Christ "shamefully deluded and deceived" Satan, who "thought that he would kill a man and was himself being killed after being decoyed by Him into a trick." So much the worse for Satan as far as Luther is concerned, and he happily attributes the entire charade to God's "wonderful counsel," a glorious example of the adage "that cunning might deceive cunning."[71]

Luther again invokes the classic image of the fishhook in the course of discussing another famous bit of biblically based deception. Genesis 27 tells of how Isaac, now old, near death, and practically blind, asks Esau, the firstborn of his twin sons, to bring him a meal of freshly slaughtered game so that he may bless him before he dies. Isaac's wife Rebecca overhears this discussion and wishing that the younger son Jacob receive the blessing instead, orders him to impersonate his older brother. Esau is a notably hairy man, so Rebecca advises Jacob to cover his hands and neck with goatskin (should Isaac wish to touch his son) and to bring his father a meal of freshly butchered farm animals. When Isaac asks, "Are you really my son Esau?" Jacob answers, "I am," and receives Isaac's blessing. Luther freely admits, as he did when making sense of Christ's human disguise, that "in the sight of men" there can be no question that Jacob's behavior reeks of "fraud and deceit," but then again, what men think hardly matters in a case like this. "When the saints perpetrate a fraud," Luther explains, "and have a command of God in regard to it, then, although it is a fraud in the sight of men, yet it is a saintly, legitimate and pious fraud." The Israelites were in the right when they defrauded and despoiled the Egyptians because God had commanded that they do these things, just as Jacob is justified because God's prophecy had already granted him the rights of primogeniture. As Luther succinctly puts it, "To contrive a plot and to take away from another by deceit what God has given to you is not a sin."[72] Evidently what applies to the saints applies to the divine as well, and God's use of lies, deceit, and fraud against the Devil to recover his own is no less justified than Jacob's hirsute costume and lying self-identification. Luther seals this interpretation with a lengthy nod to the divine fishhook.

In the writings of Luther and Calvin, the language of truth and falsity, honesty and deception, becomes hopelessly entangled within the inscrutable mystery of God. If Luther happily and graphically draws on the image of the fraudulent fishhook, he also proclaims God as the God of truth, the God who cannot lie. Catholic theologians, of course, had been struggling to overcome, resolve, or at least lessen the tensions of this apparent paradox for over a thousand years. Augustine had introduced the popular distinction between what God wills as opposed to what he merely permits, but since this solution seemed ill suited to deal with Christ's personal deceptions of the Devil, theologians developed other responses to remove any apparent blasphemy from God's actions. Christ's deeds were prudent, appropriate, and justified given the circumstances and his own intentions. Even Holkot, who did so much to expand the range of God's potentially mischievous actions, arguing that whatever God does, deceptive or otherwise, is good and fitting by definition, sought to lessen the apparent contrast between appearance and reality when he suggested that God creates such deceptions infrequently and only if they entail some great benefit. Beneficial deceptions, Holkot notes, are not lies at all.

Luther sidesteps all these philosophical intricacies and roots everything in the will and Word of God. What God wills he wills immutably, and what he promises he promises eternally. Abraham was promised that his descendants would one day be as numberless as the stars, but today God commands him to sacrifice his only son. "Even though there is a clear contradiction here," Luther writes, "for there is nothing between death and life, Abraham nevertheless does not turn away from the promise but believes that his son will have descendants even if he dies." Luther simply accepts the mystery at the very core of our relationship with God. Often it will seem as if God has forgotten us and the promises he has made to us, that he has gone back on them, revoked them. "This trial cannot be overcome," Luther explains, "and is far too great to be understood by us. For there is a contradiction with which God contradicts Himself. It is impossible for the flesh to understand this; for it inevitably concludes either that God is lying—and this is blasphemy—or that God hates me—and this leads to despair." For Abraham, for all of us, during moments like these when God seems to have deceived us, we "should hold fast to this comfort that what has once been declared, this He does not change." Luther then adds for good measure, "For the fact that God cannot lie is sure and dependable."[73]

Perhaps God cannot lie, but how his actions are not evil, deceitful, and wrathful remains forever beyond our comprehension. Whereas medieval theologians had sought ways of making sense of God's actions even while recognizing his omnipotence, Luther denies the very possibility of such understanding. God's omnipotence renders him unknowable to us, hidden from us. Luther rejects entirely the notion that there can be anything like a similarity between human conceptions of justice and truth and God's conceptions of those terms.[74] God's wrath hides his love, and his love takes the shape of Satan's lying speech that urges us to flee the saving Word. Commenting on Psalm 177, Luther raises these paradoxes to dizzying heights: "God's faithfulness and truth always must first become a great lie before it becomes truth. The world calls this truth heresy. And we, too, are constantly tempted to believe that God would abandon us and not keep his Word; and in our hearts He begins to become a liar," Luther writes. "In short, God cannot be God unless He first becomes the Devil."[75] Everything depends on the distinction between "God preached and God hidden, that is, between the Word of God and God himself," Luther writes against Dutch humanist Erasmus in *The Bondage of the Will*. "God does many things that he does not disclose to us in his word; he also wills many things which he does not disclose himself as willing in his word. Thus he does not will the death of a sinner according to his word; but he wills it according to his inscrutable will."[76]

From our perspective inscrutability may well seem like schizophrenia as God appears to be of two wills. Calvin, no less than Luther, stresses that God's providential designs remain hidden from us in this life. It is impossible for us to know why the good suffer as the evil thrive and why, by his "horrible decree," some are predestined to eternal torment. "But let us always remember," Calvin writes in his *Commentaries on Ezekiel*, "that God's judgments are not without reason called a profound abyss (Psalm 36:6), that when we see rebellious men acting as they do in these times, we should not wish to comprehend what far surpassed even the sense of the angels."[77] We should never doubt that whatever God does, he does for the sake of his church, even though it will remain impossible for us to understand. For Calvin, as it was for Luther, this extends to God's apparent lies and deceptions. Calvin asks his readers to consider Ezekiel 14:9: "And if the prophet be deceived when he had spoken a thing, I the LORD have deceived that prophet." Calvin assures his readers that "God does not delight in such deception," and even if "the cause is not always manifest . . . this is fixed, that God punishes men justly, when true religion is so rent asunder by division, and truth is obscured by falsehood."[78]

Calvin locates the possibility of divine deception in God's omnipotence. Nothing happens in this world without God's consent, and this extends from the actions of the angels to those of the demons, for just as the angels "dispense to us God's benefits for our salvation," so too do demons "execute his wrath."[79] And wrath can encompass deception. "Whatever be the explanation," Calvin writes as he continues reflecting on the passage from Ezekiel, God "pronounces *that he deceived the false prophets*, because Satan could not order a single word unless he were permitted, and not only so, but even ordered." Calvin then turns to the story of Micah who, alone of all the prophets, predicted the evil king Ahab's demise. "I saw God sitting on his throne," Micah tells Ahab, "and when all the armies of heaven were collected before him, God inquired, 'Who shall deceive Ahab?' And a spirit offered himself, namely, a devil, and said, I will deceive him, because I will be a lying spirit in the mouth of all his prophets. God answers, 'Depart, thus it shall be.' "[80] Nothing can be clearer than passages like these, Calvin contends. God does not merely permit his creatures to lie, he orders and commands them to lie, and such orders cannot be ignored, put aside or left incomplete.

Having made clear that God can deceive, Calvin, again like Luther, retreats, if only a little. He recognizes that some people might object "that nothing is more remote from God's nature than to deceive." Terms that describe human actions, Calvin responds, can only be metaphorically ascribed to God. There are scriptural passages in which God ridicules his creatures, in which he laughs, sees, and even sleeps. "But we know," Calvin adds, "that it is not agreeable to his nature to ridicule, to laugh, to see, and to sleep." Nor is it agreeable to his nature to deceive. God is immutable in his judgments, passionless in his being, and unchanging in his essence. Providence unfolds with inexorable necessity, but the Bible often describes God's will and work in simpler, less stern and abstract ways. Scripture, Calvin frequently notes, was written for a cruder people, less sophisticated and less educated. "And so in this place," he writes, "there is an improper form of speaking but the sense is not doubtful—that all impostures are scattered abroad by God—since, Satan, as I have said, can never utter the slightest word unless commanded by God." The story of Micah and Ahab makes clear how an eternal and unchanging God effects his deceptions. "God," Calvin explains, "does not deceive, so to speak, without an agency, but uses Satan and imposters as organs of his vengeance."[81]

Whether God deceives personally or through agents, Calvin is unwilling to place responsibility for divinely inspired deception on anyone or anything except God. The Scholastic distinction between what God commands and what God allows cannot stand when confronted with these passages from scripture. "For that cannot be called mere permission when God willingly seeks for someone to deceive Ahab and then he himself orders Satan to go forth and do so."[82] Calvin is thrown back against the inscrutable nature of God's judgment and providence. Occasionally God's actions will appear to contradict his commands, and he will seem for all the world to be a liar. These are harsh realities, and Calvin realizes that "some people find difficulty in what we are now saying, namely, that there is no agreement between God and man, where man does by God's just impulsion what he ought not to do." For these people, for everyone really—they must simply accept God's judgment. At this moment, Calvin looks to Augustine for support. "Who does not tremble at these judgments," he writes, quoting from the bishop's treatise *On Grace and Free Will*, "where God works even in evil men's hearts whatever he wills, yet renders to them according their deserts?" If God chooses to reveal truths that exceed "our mental capacity," there is nothing for it but to accept them. God has his reasons, and we must believe them with humility. "Those who too insolently scoff," Calvin concludes, "even though it is clear enough that they are prating against God, are not worthy of a longer refutation."[83]

RENÉ DESCARTES, PIERRE BAYLE, AND THE END OF DIVINE DECEPTION

To hear Pierre Bayle tell it, Descartes should have known his Bible better. If he had, Bayle informs the readers of his *Historical and Critical Dictionary*, a multivolume work that proved to be among the most popular books of the eighteenth century, Descartes would not have made "so weak a resistance" when critics pointed to scriptural evidence that God deceives.[84] More, he would have recognized that the narrative of scripture teaches us almost nothing whatsoever about God.

Bayle makes these claims in the *Dictionary*'s entry for "Gregory (of Rimini)," in which he casts Rimini, an Augustinian canon who lectured at length on Peter Lombard's *Sentences* during the 1340s, in the role of the villainous proponent of the thesis that God can lie and, therefore, as Descartes's intellectual antagonist. Bayle, sadly, is simply wrong about Rimini, though perhaps his confusion here is excusable. He draws his information concerning Rimini from Marin Mersenne, the Jesuit-educated Minim friar and Descartes's closest correspondent. In the "Second Set of Objections and Replies" to Descartes's *Meditations on First Philosophy*, Mersenne raises a possible objection to Descartes's claim that "God cannot lie or deceive." Mersenne writes, "There are schoolmen who say he can. Gabriel, for example, and Arimenensis, among others, think that in the absolute sense God does lie, that is, communicate to men things which are opposed to his intentions and decrees."[85] While no one, except perhaps Luther in his most desperate moments, had asserted that God could lie, there was no shortage of Scholastic and Reformation theologians who believed God could deceive. Neither Gabriel Biel nor Gregory of Rimini should be numbered among their ranks. As Rimini would put it, "God cannot say something false to someone, willing that the person to whom he speaks will assent to the falsehood."[86]

Without raising any of the concerns about divine omnipotence that compelled medieval thinkers to ponder the possibility of a deceiving God, Mersenne (and Bayle, for the most part, is happy to quote Mersenne almost verbatim) briefly confronts Descartes with two instances of apparent scriptural divine dishonesty. The Lord sends Jonah to proclaim Nineveh's allegedly imminent destruction, and he hardens Pharaoh's heart against Moses's divine message. "Cannot God," Mersenne then concludes, "treat men as a doctor treats the sick, or a father his children? In both these cases there is frequent deception though it is always employed beneficially and with wisdom. For if God were to show us the pure truth, what eye, what mental vision, could endure it?"[87]

Descartes's initial response to these objections willfully misinterprets the entire theological tradition in support of his own philosophical agenda. "In saying that God does not lie, and is not a deceiver," Descartes argues, "I think I am in agreement with all metaphysicians and theologians past and future." This is simply not true concerning the past, and as for future metaphysicians and theologians, Descartes could only surmise (although events may well have proven him right). With this blanket denial of divine deception in hand, Descartes contends that Mersenne's two biblical anecdotes are not examples of deception at all. He finesses his way around Jonah's false prophecy as so many had before him by claiming that God's pronouncement was conditional. He would destroy Nineveh if its inhabitants failed to mend their ways. They did, so he didn't. As for Pharaoh, God "merely hardened Pharaoh's heart in a negative sense, by not bestowing on him the grace which would have brought about his change of heart." On this reading, Pharaoh was simply allowed to be Pharaoh, and devastation for the Egyptians ensued. In neither case could God be accused of nefarious action.[88]

Surprisingly, and this no doubt is the initial source of Bayle's dissatisfaction, Descartes then adds "that through the mouths of the prophets God can produce verbal untruths." God's deceptions in these cases, "like the lies of doctors who deceive patients in order to cure them, are free of any malicious intent to deceive."[89] And so it may well appear that confident assertions of divine veracity to the contrary, Descartes trails along in lockstep after a tradition that moves through most all the great theologians, from Gregory of Nyssa and Augustine to Bonaventure and Aquinas, to Luther and Calvin, proclaiming in unison with them that God is no deceiver, except when he is, and when he is, his deceptions are never malicious, always beneficial, never inordinate, always fitting and always just. Most likely this is true so far as it goes, only it does not go all that far, as Descartes makes clear in his replies to the "Sixth Set of Objections," when he finds himself confronted with yet another selection of biblical passages. Although he agrees to respond to them so that no one thinks they somehow offer proof against his philosophy, Descartes clearly considers the endeavor a bit of a sidetrack. He claims never to have been involved in theological studies "except insofar as they have contributed to [his] private instruction," and that he has never felt much of "a vocation for such sacred studies." He concludes this preamble with a resolution that, in its brevity, implicitly asserts the general irrelevance of biblical narrative for the sort of metaphysics he hopes to establish. "So I hereby declare," he writes, "that in the future I will refuse to comment on questions of this kind."[90]

Descartes had already indicated this attitude toward scripture in his dedicatory letter to the theologians at the Sorbonne, appended to the beginning of the *Meditations*. Descartes informs "those most learned and distinguished men, the Dean and Doctors of the sacred Faculty of Theology," that he has "always thought that two topics—namely God and the soul—are prime examples of subjects where demonstrative proofs ought to be given with the aid of philosophy rather than theology." As believers, Descartes notes, it is enough to accept the doctrines of religion and the veracity of holy scripture on faith, but this will do nothing to convince nonbelievers. Only proofs from natural reason will convince them of these most important truths on which all hope and good morals rest. Scripture itself, he adds, supports this entirely nonscriptural philosophical endeavor. There are numerous passages in the Bible indicating that "knowledge of God is easier to acquire than the knowledge we have of many created things." In his letter to the Romans, for example, Paul writes "that which is known of God is manifest in them," which suggests "that everything that may be known of God can be demonstrated by reasoning which has no other source but our own mind." Descartes sets this challenge for himself in the *Meditations* and promises the members of the Sorbonne that he will demonstrate how God may be "more certainly known than the things of this world."[91]

Descartes's approach to the question of divine deception exploits this distinction between biblical revelation and natural reason. Claiming that God can deceive, Descartes argues, is no different from claiming that God experiences anger or any other human emotion. While the Bible certainly describes God as if he has emotions, Descartes claims, like Calvin, that we must not interpret such expressions literally. Calvin, despite his own warnings against anthropomorphizing God, could never really relinquish such language, sanctioned as it was so clearly and forcefully in scripture. Descartes, by contrast, endeavors to break scripture's hold over our conception of God. Descartes notes that there are two ways of talking about and describing God. The first way "is appropriate for ordinary understanding" and, while it "contains some truth," its truth is "relative to human beings." This way of speaking is common in the Bible. "The second way of speaking," he continues, "comes closer to expressing the naked truth—which truth is not relative to human beings, it is this way of speaking that everyone ought to use when philosophizing." Descartes utilizes this nonscriptural approach in the *Meditations*. In fact, this approach is methodologically necessary. In these investigations, he does not consider himself as one person among others, a mind embodied. Rather, he considers himself as if in isolation and "solely as mind." The very application of this method undercuts the possibility of thinking about God in human terms precisely because it puts in question everything we naturally assume about human nature, and this applies to any normal conception of deception.[92] "It is very clear from this that my remarks in the *Meditations* were concerned not with the verbal expression of lies," Descartes explains to Mersenne, "but only with malice in the formal sense, the internal malice which is involved in deception."[93]

Bayle runs out of patience at this point with Descartes's attempts to distinguish between beneficial and malicious deceptions. So far as he can make out, Descartes has done nothing but entangle himself in the very net he is trying to escape as he seemingly reaffirms the contradiction that God is a nondeceiving deceiver. "When a man is forced to confess that a general maxim," Bayle explains, "which he had lain down as the foundation of a certain and demonstrative doctrine, admits many exceptions, he shakes it to that degree, that it can no longer fix our uncertainties." Once we allow for any divine deception, we open the floodgates to more. A skeptic, Bayle adds, can now argue that our most certain intuitions of things are nothing more than beneficially arranged deceptions. Bayle offers a tellingly implausible biographical explanation for Descartes's backslide. The last thing Descartes expected, Bayle writes, was for theologians to use passages from scripture against him to defend the existence of a lying God, "and yet the storm fell upon him from that very quarter; and it was so violent he was forced to yield."[94]

The pity of it all, Bayle believes, is that Descartes creates these problems for himself. Having correctly distinguished philosophical from nonphilosophical ways of talking about God, he fails to insist on that distinction. The Bible includes countless stories in which God changes his mind, expresses ignorance, or promises to reward or punish individuals, all of which, Bayle assures his readers, "are incompatible with supreme perfection."[95] Whatever else has happened when the Bible implicates God in deception, we can rest assured that God did nothing of the sort. Scripture, so the saying goes, speaks the language of man, and Bayle is less restrained than Descartes in summarizing this principle: "Vulgar minds being not able to raise themselves to the most perfect being, it was necessary that the prophets should bring God down to man, and make him stammer with us, as a nurse stammers with a child whom she suckles." When we discuss God as he is, we must discuss him in the proper metaphysical terms. In support of this position, Bayle borrows a programmatic statement from the late seventeenth-century thinker Pierre Sylvain Régis's *System of Philosophy*. "When I wish to speak about God with precision," Régis writes, "I must neither consult myself, nor use ordinary language. Rather, I must raise myself in spirit above every created thing in order to investigate the vast and immense idea of an infinitely perfect being." Perhaps in a moral treatise one might describe God in emotional terms, Régis concludes, "but this is in no way acceptable in a purely metaphysical treatise in which precise language is required."[96]

Régis states nothing that Descartes had not already asserted, and Bayle's effort to employ Descartes's own ideas against their author results in a rather uncharitable, even incorrect, interpretation of Descartes's account of divine deception. Descartes himself is in part to blame here with his imprecise references to "deception." Imprecision, however, like our vulgar way of talking about God, is a relative thing, and Bayle's dissatisfaction with Descartes's handling of scripture owes more to the latter's success in prying the language of metaphysics free from scripture than Bayle recognizes. Bayle, as well as Régis (who, it is worth noting, never worries about divine deception at any point in the metaphysical section of his *System*), simply take for granted what Descartes still needs to accomplish. This becomes evident when, after distinguishing between malicious and beneficial deceptions, Descartes raises what he considers to be a more "important point." Putting aside the Bible, he considers an apparent case of divine deception drawn from the natural world. "From time to time," Descartes writes, "it does appear that we really are deceived by the natural instinct that God gave us, as in the case of the thirst felt by those who suffer from dropsy. These patients have a positive impulse to drink which derives from the nature God has bestowed on the body in order to preserve it; yet this nature does deceive them because on this occasion the drink will have a harmful effect."[97] Descartes assures his readers that this example does nothing to impugn God's veracity and goodness, but it certainly might seem otherwise to the suffering individual.

Relative to the sufferer, it appears that God deceives him or, at the very least, constructed him to be deceived. Descartes contends that this is entirely the wrong way to approach the problem. To interpret the sufferer's thirst in this manner is to interpret it from a purely human or "vulgar" (as Bayle would have it) perspective and is no different from assuming scripture offers a literal account of God's emotional state when it describes him as angry or vindictive. Worse, it assumes God intends to deceive *this* person, in *this* way, at *this* moment. By contrast, if we consider the problem philosophically, that is, if we consider it from God's perspective, any hint of deception and malice vanishes. At first this may not seem to be a very promising approach. In the *Principles of Philosophy*, Descartes argues that nothing happens without God's willing it to happen. "We perceive in [God]," Descartes writes, "a power so immeasurable that we regard it as impious to suppose that we could ever do anything which was not already preordained by him."[98] And so it may well seem that the philosophical perspective reveals a God who predestines every evil in the world, every illness and ounce of human suffering. How could God be anything but malicious and our deceptions intended?

Descartes rejects this way of framing the problem and cautions his readers against inquiring into God's intentions. Finite beings like us can have no truck with the infinite, and we "should not be so arrogant as to suppose that we can share in God's plans," he writes in the *Principles*, adding, "We should instead consider him as the efficient cause of all things; and starting from the divine attributes which by God's will we have some knowledge of . . . see . . . what conclusions should be drawn concerning those effects which are apparent to our senses."[99] We must not, in other words, ask why God made the world. Rather, we must ask how he made it given the kind of being he is. What kind of being is God? Descartes believes, as did everyone who preceded him, that God is perfect and all-powerful. Perfection entails immutability because if change were possible it would imply an absence and future fulfillment of goodness not yet possessed. In God, all perfection is fully realized in the simple unity of his unchanging being. God's will, therefore, is also immutable, constant, even as it simultaneously predestines and sustains everything that occurs and exists. Deception is utterly incompatible with such a being because "in every case of deception some imperfection is to be found."[100]

Theologians from Augustine to Calvin had sought to explain how deception could be made consistent with God's nature. Descartes reframes the problem and asks, How can God will all things in such a way that he does not deceive and yet, from our perspective, it appears that he does? Descartes begins at the beginning, drawing out the creative implications of God's nature and essence. As efficient cause, God is the creator of the universe, the "general" source of all motion and energy within it. His constancy and immutability guarantee that he sustains this universe as it was created, preserving always "the same quantity of motion in matter."[101] God is infinitely wise and good, so we know his laws structure the universe in as benevolent a manner as possible. Put differently, the universe is a collection of matter in motion, organized through a minimal set of constant and unchanging laws designed to establish the best possible and most beneficial system in which beings like ourselves, souls embodied, can exist and thrive.[102] Given God's nature, we can rest assured that the established relation between body and soul, like the universe as whole, will also be most beneficially, intelligently, and wisely arranged. Our understanding is undeniably limited, but even here we have no right to complain that the role God assigns us "is not the principle one or the most perfect of all." God is no deceiver, and he has given us the ability to avoid error and secure certainty. While God could have made us impervious to deception, we must assume that he has his reasons for constructing us the way he did. "I cannot deny," Descartes writes, "that there may in some way be more perfection in the universe as a whole because some of its parts are not immune from error, while others are immune, than there would be if all the parts were exactly alike."[103]

Even in such a divinely orchestrated and law-governed world— take the case of dropsy—it may well seem that these laws intentionally deceives us. Again, Descartes warns, this is to consider God's work relative to human interests. We cannot pretend to understand God's intentions, nor can we pretend to understand our place in creation. We can, however, count on God's constancy and goodness. He is not malicious in his designs. In the case of dropsy, Descartes explains, the false sense of thirst is the unavoidable consequence of a human body created in the best possible fashion given the structures of this creation. "It is much better," Descartes writes, "that it should mislead on this occasion than it should always mislead when the body is in good health."[104] In his 1680 *Treaty on Nature and Grace*, the French Oratorian priest Nicholas Malebranche offers a decidedly Cartesian elaboration on the relation between general laws and individual suffering. "These laws, on account of their simplicity, necessarily have unhappy consequences for us," he explains, "but these consequences do not warrant that God change these laws into more composite ones. For his laws have a greater proportion of wisdom and fecundity to the work they produce than all others which he could establish for the same design." Perhaps God could avoid "unhappy consequences" through "an infinite number of specific volitions," Malebranche notes, "but his Wisdom which he loves more than his work, and the immutable and necessary order which is the rule of his volitions do not permit this."[105] God's immutability checks random alterations within the order of a creation whose "unhappy consequences" can be discovered, even rectified, through attention to his unchanging laws.

God loses the ability to deceive as soon as he loses the ability to speak, and he loses the ability to speak as soon as he prefers the system to its moments.[106] To imagine a God that speaks is to imagine God in human terms, a God who cares about individuals, who laughs, forgives, and punishes, who is invested and involved in the moment. The theological tradition could never escape this conception of God, because God had revealed himself through a historical narrative of exceptional and singular events—in the story of the Fall and our ever-lengthening exile from paradise, through the lying mouths of prophets, in the disguised incarnation of his only

son, and in Satan's endless stratagems. These revelations of purposefully deceptive divine interactions with men needed to be ra-
tionalized with God's goodness, even if only through forever vague
allusions to God's incomprehensible wisdom. For every satanic
sophistry, God responds as the perfect and nobly upright orator,
undoing cruel cunning with perfect prudence. Descartes's philosophical redescription of God can allow for this narrative only as
the dangerous exception to the rule. Divine revelation, Descartes
admits, guarantees that there will be "some changes" to the immutable order of things, certain events inconsistent with the universe's general laws and rules. Concerned he has granted too much,
he then immediately qualifies and limits these supernatural intru-
sions into a divinely instituted order, "but apart from these we
should not suppose that any other changes occur in God's works,
in case this suggests some inconstancy in God."[107]

Bayle takes all this for granted. As they did with everything
they touched, he argues, Scholastic theologians made a mess of
scripture, needlessly complicating its simple and self-evident clarity. Bayle hasn't the slightest doubt that every biblical story in
which God deceives includes the keys for its own translation into a
properly philosophical idiom through which God's individual interventions in the world disappear into the orderly system of creation itself. Never mind centuries of exegetical labor that found
it impossible to deny God's deceptions. Never mind all those
fourteenth-century theologians fascinated with God's absolute and
incomprehensible power, his ability to do all possible things. Bayle,
following Malebranche following Descartes, accepts a God "who
does not disturb the simplicity and uniformity of his ways in order
to avoid a particular disaster."[108] All of this Bayle asserts in the
name of a metaphysical conception of God, a God without human
attributes, without emotion. Never mind, finally, that this is an impossible dream and any human conception of God will conceive of
God in human terms. Bayle inherited Descartes's greatest success,
convincing God to give up rhetoric in exchange for the dreams of
the philosophers, and the philosophers, evidently, dreamt of a curiously compromised world. A world in which paradise would no

longer be found in the memories of Eden, a garden without trouble or illness, but in the ruin once thought to have been the result of the Devil's lie, the ruin of a fallen world now oozing with disease, requiring our endless toil. For the philosophers, the Devil, like God, never had to say anything, because God had always already listened to him and learned.

CHAPTER THREE

Human Beings

EVERY LIE IS A SIN

Over twelve hundred years of theological debate on deception ended in parody and vitriol. While the parody preceded, English readers encountered the vitriol first.

In the preface to his 1657 translation of Blaise Pascal's satirical dismantling of post-Reformation Catholic ethical thought, *The Provincial Letters*, Henry Hammond, a widely respected royalist and Anglican cleric, could find nothing but insidious and dangerous scheming in "the mystery of Jesuitisme." The Jesuits, Hammond contends, seek "to grasp all the world to themselves, and to usurp an universal empire over men's consciences." Rejecting God's precepts and rules, they endeavor to win people over with a laxity that transforms sin into virtue. Unlike the first Christians, who willingly suffered persecution and calamity, never acquiescing to the false demands of the world, the Jesuits dispense "with all the obligations of evangelical purity" and treat every ethical rule "like a wax nose capable of all forms" as they "level the precepts of the gospel to the passions of men [and] make our tendency to future Beatitude consistent with the pleasures and enjoyment of this world." In a final burst of outrage, Hammond writes, "Such societies of men are Academies of dissimulation and sycophancy, diabolically embarked in a design, of not only practicing, but maintaining and justifying whatever is most horrid and abominable in the sight of God and man."[1]

Hammond's preface and Pascal's work notwithstanding, every Catholic theologian, Jesuit or otherwise, believed lying was a sin.

To have claimed otherwise would have been to contradict centuries of accumulated argument and authority beginning with the towering figure of Augustine, whose rejection of lies could hardly have been clearer. Every lie is a sin, the great bishop had argued, and every sin must be avoided. No hoped-for benefit, no amount of good to be achieved or evil to be prevented, can justify our lies. Augustine was adamant about this and believed the Bible itself supported his confidence. Near the very beginning of *Against Lying*, a treatise composed in 420, Augustine approvingly quotes from Paul's letter to the Romans: "Thou hatest all the workers of iniquity; thou wilt destroy all that speak a lie." There is no room for misinterpretation here, Augustine contends, no suggestion that God looks favorably on certain lies, unfavorably on others. The apostle "has brought forth a universal proposition, saying, 'Thou wilt destroy all that speak a lie.'"[2] To think anything different is to run up against irrefutable authority, insurmountable ethical problems, irresolvable contradiction and paradox. No good can come from evil, and no virtue can come from vice.

Augustine wrote *Against Lies* in response to questions he had received from an ascetic named Consentius, who had taken an active role in combating a Spanish heretical group that had formed in the late fourth century around the teachings of Priscillian. Doctrinal errors aside, the Priscillianists had proven difficult to uproot because they found it perfectly acceptable to lie in order to protect and conceal their true beliefs. When questioned, Consentius explains, they happily shield themselves behind claims of an orthodox faith that they in no way accept. Consentius's solution to such mendacity was simple—for the good of the Catholic Church, we must lie to the liars, we must pretend to be the very heretics we are trying to root out, for "in no other way can we discover the hidden wolves dressed in sheep's clothing, secretly and seriously preying upon the flock of the Lord."[3] Augustine would have none of Consentius's tit-for-tat ethical reasoning, and *Against Lying* reads as a wholesale assault on dishonesty, dissimulation, and lies, not just in cases concerning the faith and the fight against heresy, but in every case, no matter what the circumstances, no matter what the repercussions.

Augustine understood how harsh his prohibition might seem to others. He understood the grief it might cause. Imagine unjust persecutors come pounding at your door seeking the location of an acquaintance, a friend you have hidden away under the floorboards, in a back room, or across town. Or perhaps you are a doctor tending a critically ill patient whose feeble system can no longer tolerate any tumult, neither trauma nor tragedy. "How is my son?" he asks, and you think about the news you just received concerning the boy's death from the same accident that has left his father in such fragile shape. These may well be the sort of over-baked cases that philosophers love, but they trouble Augustine, and he writes movingly about them. "Because we are men and live among men," he writes, "I confess that I am not yet in the number of those who are not troubled by compensatory sins. Often, in human affairs, human sympathy overcomes me and I am unable to resist" lying. Think what will happen if you choose to speak the truth in these cases. Your friend will suffer a horrible death at the hands of his enemies, or the patient will die from shock and sorrow even as people accuse you "of loving homicide as truth."[4] All this might be true, Augustine admits, but such considerations are irrelevant before God, who is the final arbiter of our virtue and of our salvation, and it is God himself who has declared every lie to be a sin and demanded that every sin must be avoided.

Not everyone agreed with Augustine, but their disagreements had little traction. Augustine's contemporary Jerome, famous for his Latin translation of scripture, believed the Bible did in fact authorize the use of dissimulation and deception to help secure the salvation of nonbelievers. Hadn't Paul supported such beneficial trickery when he wrote to the Corinthians, "To the Jews I became a Jew so as to win the Jews"?[5] And, in a nod to the enduring tradition of the Devil's mousetrap, Jerome notes that Jesus himself practiced dissimulation when he hid his divinity within human flesh. Despite his own fondness for the mousetrap, Augustine rejected Jerome's arguments in a series of forceful and uncompromising letters and, with few (and entirely inconsequential) exceptions, the subsequent theological tradition sided with Augustine, whose absolute prohibition against lies quickly became something of a commonplace.[6] The sixth-century Spanish bishop and encyclopedist Isidore of Seville concurred with him, as did Gregory the Great. In the twelfth century, Peter Lombard made Augustine's prohibition the centerpiece of his own analysis of lying, which itself was part of his more general analysis of the Ten Commandments in the third book of his *Sentences*.[7] After Peter, no aspiring theologian, from the Franciscan Alexander of Hales in the early thirteenth century to the Dominicans Gabriel Biel and Antoninus of Florence in the fifteenth century, not mention such influential sixteenth- and seventeenth-century writers as Domingo de Soto, Thomas Cajetan, Juan Azor, and Francisco Suarez, failed to rehearse and endorse Augustine's opinion that every lie is a sin. Given the near-universal assent that theologians gave to Augustine's prohibition, it is not at all surprising that when, in the early seventeenth century, the Englishman John Downame took up the cause in his aptly named essay, *A Treatise Against Lying*, he happily relied again and again on Augustine's enduring treatise *Against Lies*.[8]

Yet despite almost unanimous acceptance of Augustine's prohibition, the Catholic theological discussion about lies and deception outraged Henry Hammond and proved ripe for Pascal's satire. Perhaps Jesuit theologians condemned all lies as sinful, but they had accomplished this (so their critics would argue) through verbal tricks, tendentious redefinitions, and willful obfuscation. As evidence of their mendacity, Hammond cites the Jesuit support of such suspect techniques of subterfuge as "Equivocation, mental restrictions [and] shifting and direction of the Intention."[9] Pascal would consider all these techniques in the ninth of his *Provincial Letters*. Written under the guise of the country gentleman Louis de Montalte, Pascal's letters purport to record a series of discussions with an enthusiastic Jesuit all too convinced of the brilliance of his order's novel moral teachings. The ninth letter takes up the theme of alleged Jesuit laxity as Montalte's interlocutor runs through some of the "very easy, very sure and quite numerous" means the Jesuits employ to secure their salvation.[10] Having discoursed on a variety of topics, including how to eat well during fasts and the virtues of self-centered complacency, he turns to some of the "methods we have developed in order to avoid sin in worldly conversation and intrigues." How, for example, can a good Christian avoid lying in situations where telling the truth might be inconvenient? There is, of course, the tried-and-true method of equivocation, the use of ambiguous words that we know our listeners will understand one way, but which we understand differently. Useful as it is, this method has its limits because sometimes there are no equivocal words appropriate to the situation. In such cases, the Jesuits offer the strategy of mental reservation. Pascal's interlocutor explains, quoting from the writings of the late sixteenth-century Jesuit theologian Thomas Sanchez: "A man can swear that he did not do something, even if he really did it, understanding to himself that he did not do it on a certain day, or before he was born, or under similar conditions, without his actual words having any indication that this is what he means."[11]

Shocked, Montalte interjects that this practice sounds like little more than sheer lying and perjury. The Jesuit disagrees. It is intention, he explains, that determines the moral quality of our actions, and if we intend our spoken words to mean something different than our listeners will take them to mean, so much the worse for them. When we employ the technique of mental reservation, we intend that our spoken words (false when considered on their own) are part of a larger statement, a statement made true by the addition of those unheard words. Of course, this complex balancing act between public statement and careful qualifying thought can be difficult to achieve and, perhaps, may even be beyond the ability of most people. The Jesuit admits this and happily announces that his order has even found a way for less talented people to make use of the technique of mental reservation. The less able can confidently go ahead and assert that they have not done things they have done so long as they silently include "the general intention to give their words the sense that a capable man would have given them." Enthralled with his order's ingenuity, the Jesuit asks, "Be candid now and confess, if you have not often felt yourself embarrassed, in consequence of not knowing this?" Montalte can do little else but respond, "Sometimes."[12]

Vitriol is one thing, analysis another, and parody, however effective, is not the same as argument. While Pascal's *Letters* would forever tarnish the sixteenth- and seventeenth-century Catholic theological discourse concerning truth-telling and lies, they did so at the expense of ignoring the internal tensions that had fueled that discourse and the external forces that had shaped it. Augustine had declared every lie a sin, and the theologians followed suit, only to discover the suit did not fit as well they had hoped or needed. Caught between the demands of theology and the challenges of the world, theologians sought a middle ground, both wholly Catholic and wholly useful, recognizing both the absolute demands of faith and the vagaries of life in a fallen and maddeningly complex world. For Pascal, the very desire to accommodate marked the essence of our spiritual misery, a misery so deep that, in the end, even he could not entirely escape it.

EVERY SIN IS A LIE

In *Against Lying*, his letter to Consentius, Augustine repeatedly invokes consequentialist arguments in favor of his prohibition against lying. Consentius must not lie to uncover deceitful heretics, because lies never achieve the good ends we intend. If we lie to people who already lie to hide their faith, aren't we teaching them that lies are acceptable and, in the long run, making it that much harder to identify and convert them? If they believe our lies, won't we only confirm them in their heresy? If they discover we are lying, why should they ever trust anything we say? Our lies can only backfire on us.[13] No doubt Augustine took these arguments seriously, but the real basis for his prohibition against lies had little to with outcomes and everything to do with our relationship to God, to the Word, and to the Word made flesh in the incarnation of Christ.

Both stoic ideas and scripture shaped Augustine's philosophy and theology of the Word and of language. From the Stoics, Augustine drew on and then modified a distinction between words and meaning.[14] In one of his sermons on the Gospel of John, for example, Augustine asks his audience to look within themselves, to observe their own hearts, and to watch how language works. Augustine's reliance on visual metaphors is intentional. Before we speak, Augustine suggests, we have a thought, something we wish to express, an inner word or concept already present in our heart and "waiting to be uttered." This inner word is immaterial, preexists all languages, and is something we discover already within us when we look within ourselves using the eyes of our heart. Vision requires light, and just as the sun makes things in the world visible to us, so God illuminates these hidden contents of our mind, Augustine argues, which are "confined by no language" but make all language possible. The inner word is neither Latin nor Greek, but if we are Roman, we will express it in Latin and, if we are Greek, we will express it in Greek. Nor should we confuse this inner word with the silent thoughts or hymns that "run through our mind." When we quietly think things to ourselves, we use the same language that we use to express ourselves to others, a language that exists and changes over time. The inner word, by contrast, is the unchanging truth, the concept, the idea that we seek to express whenever we speak. Words, in effect, are "significant sounds" whose meaning derives from and depends on the truth of the inner word made known to us through divine illumination.[15]

For Augustine, the dependence of language on the inner word shapes the ethical demands of all discourse. If verbal signs signify mental concepts, then, Augustine reasons, they exist for the sake of correctly expressing our inner states and ideas to others. "There is no reason for us to signify something," Augustine writes in *On Christian Doctrine*, "that is, to give a sign, except to express and transmit to another's mind what is in the mind of the person who gives the sign."[16] While Augustine believed the subordination of language to inner word indicated that our spoken words be truthful, it was scripture that transformed this linguistic insight into a criterion of moral and spiritual rightness. In the Gospel of John, the evangelist describes the entire history of salvation as a series of speech acts. "In the beginning was the Word," the evangelist proclaims in the opening lines of his gospel, "and the Word was with God, and the Word was God." John the Baptist, "a man sent from God," testifies to the coming of "the true light" and, in good order, that true light appears when "the Word became flesh and lived among us . . . as of a father's only son, full of grace and truth."[17] Augustine asserts that the movement from God to Word and from Word to Word made flesh both clarified and was clarified by the structure of human language, which moves from illuminated inner word to language. "The Father," Augustine explains, "as though uttering Himself, begot the Word, equal in all things to Himself. For He would not have uttered Himself completely and perfectly, if there were anything less or more in His Word than Himself. . . . And therefore this Word is truly Truth, since whatever is in that knowledge from which it was born is also in the Word."[18] The Father's speech begets the Word, Augustine contends, and the Word's own speech produces the incarnation. "For just as our word in some way becomes bodily sound by assuming that in which it may be manifested to the senses of men," he writes, "so the Word of God was made flesh by assuming that in which he might also be manifested to the sight of men."[19]

On this reading of scripture, language provides an explanatory model for all action, divine and human. "The beginning of every work is the word," Augustine notes, and just as God made all things through "His only-begotten word, so there are no works of man which are not first spoken in the heart." Our gestures and actions, no less than our spoken words, signify the inner word and its eternal truth, and whether or not we choose to embody and obey that truth reveals our own relation to Christ, who is the Word embodied. "The Son alone," Augustine writes, "who is the word of God, was made flesh . . . in order that by our word following and imitating His example, we might live rightly, that is, that we might have no lie either in the contemplation or in the work of our word."[20] Every lie is a sin because, fundamentally, every sin is a lie, every sin takes the form of false signification. Every sin is a lie because sin is nothing but a turning from and rejection of the truth, a refusal to signify and express it, to speak it, in our lives. Like the snake whose motions depend on "the most minute movement of its scales," this rejection begins subtly and imperceptibly as we slowly slip away from the good "with the perverse desire of becoming like God." Augustine's allusion to the snake recalls Adam and Eve, whose transgression, he believed, made sense only if they had already inwardly turned from God's Word, preferring to follow their private passions and pleasures rather than obey God's command.[21]

It is this fear of the subtle and unperceived turn from God that gives force to Augustine's prohibition against all lies, against all false assertion. When we choose to sin, to lie, even if we sin and lie for the good, for the greatest good, we set ourselves up as arbiters of good and evil, we imagine ourselves to be like God, and the consequences of that error are all too obvious. "When a man lives according to truth," Augustine writes in *The City of God*, "then, he lives not according to self, but according to God; for it is God Who has said, 'I am the truth.' When he lives according to self, however,—that is, according to man, and not according to God—he then certainly lives according falsehood." In this turn from God, we imitate the Devil, who chose to live according to himself rather than abide in the truth. And, as Augustine is only too eager to remind his readers, "The devil is not only a liar, he is 'the father of lies': he was, indeed, the first to lie, and falsehood, like sin, began with him."[22]

Just as Augustine's prohibition against lies flows from his conception of God, so too does his definition of what it means to lie. In *On Lying*, a treatise he had written some twenty-five years before *Against Lying*, Augustine writes that the liar is a person "who has one thing in his mind but expresses something else with words or any other sort of indication." We lie when we embody falsity in words or in deeds and, in so doing, disrupt our likeness to God, who is Truth, and the Son, who is the full and total embodiment of that truth. According to this definition, the objective truth or falsity of what the liar says is irrelevant. We lie whenever we intend to assert what is false, whenever we keep one thing in our heart but say something else. We can even lie when we speak the truth, so long as we believe what we are saying is false. At times though, Augustine offers a slightly different definition of the lie. "The fault of the person who tells a lie," Augustine continues, "consists in his desire to deceive in expressing his thought."[23] In *Against Lying*, Augustine would frame this conception of the lie in the form that John Downame still repeated as definitive in the seventeenth century: "A lie is a false signification made with a will to deceive."[24] According to this second and admittedly more influential definition, the liar intends two things, both to state what is false and to deceive his listener.

Augustine is well aware that the will to assert what is false is not necessarily the same as the will to deceive, and he examines this difference in *On Lying*. Do we lie when we assert what we believe to be false without intending to deceive? Does the intention to deceive define all lies, or does it define a particular type of lie? To explore these problems, Augustine works through a variety of complex scenarios in which a person knowingly states a factual untruth or states the truth while thinking it is false, and in which a person states a falsehood precisely because he knows his listener will not believe him and, therefore, will end up believing what is true. At the end of these circuitous analyses whose subtleties are difficult to work through at best, Augustine concludes that it is safest to always speak the truth. "For there is no need to be afraid of any of those definitions," he writes, "when the mind has a good conscience as it utters what it either knows, or opines, or believes to be true, and has no wish to make anything believed but what it utters."[25] Perhaps the person who states what is false with the intention to deceive is the most obvious sort of liar, but we should always be wary of anything that involves us in falsehood and duplicity, of anything that threatens our always fragile likeness to God.[26]

Every lie may well be a sin, every sin may well distance us from God, but Augustine also recognizes that the intentions governing our lies matter. Some lies are worse than others, and he has little doubt that God will deal more harshly with liars whose sins are "committed in the spirit of harm" than with those "committed in the spirit of help."[27] Augustine contends there are three broad categories of lies—the malicious, the neutral, and the beneficial or officious. These three categories themselves can be subdivided into eight different species. There are, Augustine explains, three types of malicious lies, that is, three types of lies that are told to cause harm: there are lies spoken when teaching others about the faith (and this lie, Augustine warns, "is a deadly one which should be avoided and shunned from afar"), lies that harm someone and help no one, and lies that harm someone while helping someone else. The middle or neutral category of lies consists of two types, lies told simply for the love of lying (and this type, Augustine adds, "is a pure lie") and lies told to please others. Rounding out the list are three types of beneficial lies, which help others while causing no harm. There are lies that protect a person's temporal goods from unjust seizure, lies told to save the lives of the innocent ("with the exception of the case where a judge is questioning") and, finally, those lies we tell to save someone "from physical defilement."[28]

Augustine's division of lies into three categories and eight types, just like his prohibition, would become canonical, suggesting something like a hierarchy or ranking of lies from the most sinful to the least. While later writers would use Augustine's list to distinguish between those lies that are mortal sins and those that are merely venial and, perhaps, justifiable, Augustine himself never does this. On those few occasions when he considers whether some lies are worse than others, he does so only to shut down such speculation almost immediately.[29] We must never tempt God's mercy—we must never lie in the hope that the good we achieve will guarantee pardon for the sin we intentionally commit. In his mercy, Augustine explains, God may well pardon past sins for subsequent good works or forgive the person who, in a moment of crisis, performs "a deed of mercy and a deed of deception." These instances of God's mercy can in no way warrant choosing to sin for some hoped-for good. There are real differences between seeking atonement for sins already committed and choosing to "sin in order to do good," and they are differences we must never forget. "Whether we should ever tell a lie if it be for someone's welfare," he warns, "is a problem that has vexed even the most learned."[30] Vexatious or not, Augustine warns that it is a problem best avoided. In *Against Lies*, he asks Consentius to consider the story of Lot who, in an effort to prevent two male guests from being defiled, offers "the men of Sodom, both young and old," the pleasure of laying with his two daughters. Lot thought he should allow lesser sins to occur for the sake of avoiding greater ones, "since it is less evil for women to suffer violation than men." But Augustine fears Lot's is a losing gambit. "If we open this road to sins," he argues, "of committing lesser ones ourselves so that others do not commit greater ones, then, as though all barriers had been shattered and removed, every sin will enter and reign supreme." We will commit thefts to prevent greater thefts, incest to avoid murder, and every sort of lie will find a circumstance to sanction it.[31]

Perhaps God will concern himself with why we lie, will forgive some liars and punish others, but we should never presume to make such judgments ourselves. To do that is to follow the Devil's path, and that path leads nowhere but to our damnation.

BIBLICAL LIARS

Augustine's absolute prohibition against lies faced one great stumbling block. There are passages in the Bible in which it seems that lies are told and told well, that is, told without guilt and without sin. There are, for example, the Hebrew midwives who, when Pharaoh asked why they had not killed every male child as soon as it was born, replied, "Because the Hebrew women are not like the Egyptian women; for they are vigorous and give birth before the midwife comes for them." Jacob, following his mother's advice, pretends to be his brother Esau and obtains his blind father Isaac's benediction. In this case Jacob goes so far as to wear goatskin so that should his father touch him, he will feel like his hairy brother. Abraham at one point announces that his wife Sarah is his sister. There are even problematic moments in the Gospels. For example, following his resurrection, Jesus pretends to walk farther than he really intends.[32] Augustine worries repeatedly over the possible consequences of lowering his absolute standard and admitting the acceptability of certain sorts of lies. "He who says that there are some just lies," Augustine writes in *Against Lies*, "must be regarded as saying nothing else than that there are some just sins and, consequently, that some things which are unjust are just."[33] Not only does such a standard result in unacceptable logical and moral paradoxes, it also introduces a slew of practical problems. If some lies are acceptable, then how would we ever know when to believe a person's statements and when not to? More important, how could we be sure that any given passage from the Bible itself had been asserted as truth? On what basis could adjudication be made to determine whether on any particular occasion these words, this passage, were being offered sincerely or duplicitously, as models of holy behavior to emulate or sacrilege to condemn?[34]

Faced with these challenges, Augustine deploys his prohibition against lying as the basis for something like a nascent literary theory and hermeneutic for the Bible. Since God cannot lie and every lie is a sin, there can be no justifiable lies in the Bible. In all these cases of apparent Biblical deception, Augustine will therefore find it necessary to argue that either the alleged lie is no lie at all or that, if it clearly is a lie, the lie itself is not approved, not held up as a model of virtuous behavior. In the case of the midwives, for example, God rewarded them, not for lying, but for saving the lives of the Hebrew babies. Augustine suggests that even their ignorance, their acculturation into the ways of the Egyptians, not to mention the impossibility before the dispensation of Christ of their having clearly known the ethical imperative of truth-telling, all served as mitigating factors in God's eyes.[35]

By contrast with this clear case of Biblical lying, Augustine adopts a variety of different strategies to remove the taint of falsehood from other alleged cases of scriptural untruthfulness. Considering Abraham, Augustine distinguishes concealing the truth from lying. Abraham speaks the truth because he and Sarah share the same father (although not the same mother). He simply "conceals something of the truth." Extending this line of thought, Augustine writes, "It is not a lie when truth is passed over in silence, but when falsehood is brought forth in speech."[36]

Jacob's apparent lie presents a much tougher case, but one that Augustine resolves by stressing, again, the dangers of assuming there are acceptable lies in the Bible. The very possibility of reading parts of scripture allegorically, as mysteries or figures, depends upon this prohibition. "If we call it a lie," writes Augustine, "then all parables and figures for signifying anything which are not to be taken literally, but in which one thing must be understood for another, will be called lies."[37] In other words, the presence of an apparent false statement or deceptive act in the Bible, one that is neither condemned nor shown not to be a lie at all (as in Abraham's case), provides something like the justification, even the need, to engage in a figurative reinterpretation of the act that will render it truthful. As Augustine puts it in *On Lying*, the prophets of the Old Testament "did and said all that is related about them in a prophetic manner."[38] While it would certainly seem as if Jacob lied to his father when he announced, "I am Esau thy firstborn" and deceived him when he extended his goatskin-covered hand, Augustine will claim that Jacob had no intention of deceiving Isaac, much less of lying to him. Here it is a matter of relocating Jacob's words and deeds within a broader context, not as a response to his father's question, a question posed at a specific time and at a specific place, but rather in terms of what Jacob intended to signify, the transference of the elder brother's primacy and inheritance to the younger, of the future transference of God's covenant from the Jews to the Christians. Augustine attempts to reel in the potential for interpretive excess when he contends that what is presented as a mystery in one place in scripture must be presented clearly and openly in another—the Bible as a whole forms the proper context for interpreting such speech acts.[39] And yet, this strategy reveals a deeper problem that Augustine seems to recognize but ignores. How do such prophetic cases from the Bible relate to ordinary, nonbiblical, nonprophetic acts of communication in which, given the proximate causes and contexts, not to mention the reasonable expectations of the other participants, such statements and actions could hardly seem to be anything if not deceitful?

AUGUSTINE AMONG THE SCHOLASTICS

If Augustine's legacy loomed large for medieval theologians, it was an odd legacy when they concerned themselves with the problem of lying. In a sense, not a single medieval theologian agreed with the great North African bishop's analysis of mendacity. Certainly, they all endorsed Augustine's claim that every lie is a sin and quoted approvingly from his writings, but not one of them ever agreed with Augustine's reasons for believing that every lie is sin. They didn't agree with it because, it seems, they didn't know anything about it. Scholastic analyses of lying never draw from Augustine's treatise *On the Trinity*, where he elaborates his Christological analysis of lying and sin. Rather, they focus almost entirely on the two treatises he devoted exclusively to the topic of lying, *On Lying* and *Against Lying*, or on similar passages from his *Enchiridion*. Moreover, given that Scholastic theologians consistently made use of the same few sections from these treatises, it is likely they rarely, if ever, read the treatises themselves and certainly not in their entirety. What they seem to have known about Augustine's ideas they knew mostly from collections of excerpts, such as the ones Peter Lombard had included in his *Sentences*.[40] Scholastic writers, in other words, read these passages without their surrounding contexts in Augustine's own works, contexts in which he often qualified or amended their meaning. Scholastic writers did not so much follow Augustine as borrow some of his statements to serve as the basic building blocks for their own analyses of mendacity. As a result, they often sound Augustinian even as they diverge, often radically, from Augustine's own opinions. This is particularly evident in Scholastic discussions about the way in which the liar offends against the virtue of truth and in the importance they place on intention, on why the liar lies.

Writing in the 1260s, the Dominican theologian Thomas Aquinas has no doubt that every lie is a sin. "Words by their very nature," he writes, "being signs of thought, it is contrary to their nature and out of order for anyone to convey in words something other than what he thinks."[41] Though many subsequent theologians would take this assertion as self-explanatory, as if lying were a sin simply because the liar misuses language, Aquinas means something more, something else. The liar does in fact misuse language, but he misuses it because he offends against the virtue of truth. Significantly, Thomas links truth with justice, the virtue that defines how we should interact with and treat others. The virtue of truth, like justice, Thomas contends, obliges us to engage in honest, fair, and open dealings with others. It is an obligation rooted in our nature as social and intellectual animals, and it requires that our statements and actions reflect who we are and what we care about. Just as "justice sets up a certain equality between things," Thomas explains, "so does the virtue of truth, for it equals signs to the things which concern man himself."[42] The liar offends against justice because he fails to render to others the truth that he owes them. Thomas is very clear about this, and this is why, like Augustine, he locates the essence of the lie, not in the intention to deceive, but in the intention to say or to show what is false, to embody dishonesty. The desire to deceive, he explains, directs this initial inequality toward others, when we assert or show what is false in order to deceive someone. "Deception," Thomas explains, "belongs to the perfection of lying."[43]

And it is precisely the lie's perfection, according to Thomas, that determines its severity. Adopting Augustine's division of the sin of lying into three categories and eight types, Thomas contends that lies committed in the spirit of harm, lies against charity, are more grievous than those committed for the good. Lies told against charity are mortal sins, whereas officious lies, lies told for the benefit of our neighbors, are merely venial. Augustine himself had suggested that malicious lies were more serious than beneficial or compensatory lies, but he had refused to pursue the matter, and this refusal speaks to his contention that lying is at the basis of all sin. When we sin, we turn from God and from the Truth as we mimic the Devil in his fatal descent into unlikeness. Augustine's

two treatises on lying resonate with the emotional tension he suffers between the demand to love God and his occasional belief that
a minor sin might save the life of a loved one. His anguish arises
from the profound abyss that he believes every false assertion
carves out between sinner and God. While Thomas is no less vocif-
erous in his assertion that every lie is a sin, his decision to discuss
the nature and severity of different kinds of lies, to separate them
into mortal and venial sins, suggests a lessening of that tension
that so tortured Augustine. Much of this derives from Thomas's
decision to annex truth to justice. When we lie, we offend against
justice defined primarily in terms of our obligations to ourselves
and others, and those violations are less severe when they entangle
us in venial as opposed to mortal sins. Augustine had considered
the danger of lying entirely in terms of the liar's relation to God.
Thomas emphasizes the positive or negative consequences that our
lies will have on others.[44]

Despite this, Thomas, in good Augustinian fashion, condemns
all lies, even the most seemingly beneficial, as offenses against truth
and justice, arguing that good cannot come from evil and virtue
cannot come from vice. In the heat of the moment, when good
options seem few and a simple false assertion might save the life of
an innocent fugitive, the danger of a beneficial lie may well be invisible to us, but Thomas fears there is rot, perceived or not, at the
base of such calculations. Left to themselves, the will and intellect
have "no fixed limits," Thomas contends, and can proceed indefi-
nitely such that the individual who acts against justice one time,
can do so again, "and the more the will tends to undue ends, the
more difficult is it for it to return to its proper and due end."[45]
Once we find reasons to act against truth and justice, it will be
easier to find additional reasons, and soon irrationality will come
to characterize all our actions as we endeavor to create justice
from injustice. Commenting on Aristotle's *Ethics* in the early fourteenth century, the University of Paris arts master John Buridan
would express Thomas's deepest fears with great clarity. While we
might think it admirable to commit beneficial lies that achieve
great goods, Buridan promises this can never be the case. With

every lie, the liar destroys his own soul, undermining his ability to make and act on rational judgments, to be human, as he fools himself into imagining that he can achieve good ends through depraved means. The prohibition against lies becomes something like the limit beyond which we risk the loss of our very humanity and undo the possibility of human society.[46]

Precept is one thing, elaboration another. When Thomas turns to those classic cases of apparent biblical deception—the Hebrew midwives, Abraham and Sarah, Jacob and Isaac—he is compelled to stretch his concept of truthful discourse in surprising ways. In the case of Abraham, for example, Thomas notes the difference between "hiding the truth" and telling a lie, suggesting that Abraham did the former, not the latter. A little later in the same set of responses, however, Thomas pushes this line of thought a bit further when he notes that while "it is unlawful for anyone to lie in order to rescue another, no matter what the peril, one may, however, prudently mask the truth, as Augustine explains."[47] It is not at all clear that this is what Augustine explained, or at least had intended his readers to think he had explained. Perhaps Abraham's claim that Sarah was his sister required this sort of justification in order to render it truthful, but Augustine never holds up the patriarch's words as a model for his readers to follow. When difficult choices must be made, he much prefers the example of the bishop Firmus's resolute devotion to truth, maintained despite torture at the hands of Roman prosecutors, to Abraham's coy dissimulations. For Thomas, by contrast, Abraham's concealment is perfectly acceptable, not just for the Old Testament patriarchs, but for all of us.[48]

This alteration to Augustine's standards, however muted in Thomas's writings, becomes more evident in a line of thought that had already begun to develop among certain Franciscan writers. Pondering Jacob's claim to be his brother Esau, Alexander of Hales, in the 1230s, considers a problem that Augustine himself had noticed, only to more or less pass over, when he suggests that it might well be objected that Jacob really had intended to persuade his father that he was Esau. Alexander meets the objection, for all intents and purposes, by accepting it. "It ought to be said," he writes, "that given the circumstances, Jacob may have intended this, but principally he intended to claim for himself his due benediction; his statement was therefore simply true."[49] Alexander invokes something like a hierarchy of intentions. Jacob primarily intended his words and actions to signify at the allegorical or figurative level. In order to accomplish this allegorical signification, it was necessary, given the specific circumstances in which he found himself, for Jacob to speak and act in ways he knew would deceive his father. Whereas Augustine simply ignored the more practical implications of Jacob's performance, Alexander suggests that they cannot be ignored. Given the communicative context in which Jacob speaks, the meaning of his words, the expectations of his audience, Jacob's actions are deceptive. It is his primary intention to signify figurative truth, an intention known only to Jacob, that renders that intended deception something less than sheer lying.

Alexander's willingness to complicate Jacob's speech act, to recognize the multiple interpretive contexts it inhabits and intentions it contains, combined with his very Augustinian stance against lying, no doubt plays a part in his distinction between words and deeds. Repeating and affirming Augustine's definition that a lie is a false statement made with the intention of deceiving someone, Alexander adds, in a decidedly non-Augustinian move, that this definition does not strictly apply to deeds. Unlike words, actions are not instituted for the sole purpose of communication, for revealing to others what is in our minds, and as a result there is some leeway in how we can use them to communicate.[50] Alexander contends that there are three categories of praiseworthy simulations, that is, types of actions in which a person, without incurring guilt, without lying, can pretend to be someone he is not or pretend to do something he does not intend to do. Citing the usual array of biblical examples, he defines these as prudent, instructive, and figurative deceptions. Jehu, for example, engaged in prudent deception when he pretended to be a member of the cult of Baal so that he could kill their priests.[51] Jesus, by contrast, engaged in instructive deception when he pretended to continue walking when he and his disciples had reached the village that was their destination. He was, Alexander explains, teaching them about the importance of deeds of mercy and hospitality. Finally, when he donned goatskin and stated, "I am Esau your firstborn," Jacob did not lie so much as engage in a figurative deception. In each case, the action is laudable because of the overarching intention and goal, to instruct or to signify a spiritual truth.[52] Regardless, the immediate action with its potentially deceptive aspects remains.

Another Franciscan, Duns Scotus, writing in the early 1300s, would extend the importance of intention in his own *Sentence* commentary. Accepting the Augustinian standard that all lies are sinful, Scotus asks why. Following his fellow Franciscan Bonaventure, Scotus argues that the sinfulness of lies cannot rest in the alleged fact that every lie turns us from God. Lies, Scotus contends, are not "immediately opposed to the first truth, but to the truth of some particular thing one is talking about." Scotus next considers and rejects what he understands (incorrectly) to be Thomas's argument that lies are necessarily sinful because they misuse language. Appealing to the divine omnipotence, Scotus argues that if God so chose, he could revoke the commandment "Thou shalt not kill," in which case we could blamelessly kill others. Scotus considers the example of Abraham and Isaac. God ordered Abraham to kill Isaac, and had Abraham followed through on this command (as he intended), his action would have been meritorious. If God can render murder virtuous, Scotus reasons, then he can certainly allow licit lies, "for the precept of not deceiving is not more binding than the precept of not killing—indeed one's neighbor loses less if occasionally given a false view . . . than he would if deprived of bodily life, in fact, there is no comparison here."[53]

If the sinfulness of lies does not rest in a misuse of language, Scotus argues, it must rest entirely in the liar's intention to deceive. To prove his point, he analyzes the lie into its component parts. The word "lie," he explains, refers to the conjunction between a certain act and its "malice" or "deformity." He clarifies this claim through comparisons with adultery and theft. Adultery does not simply name the act of "natural copulation," which on its own can be sinless, "but also the impropriety that it is not done with one's own spouse." Likewise, there are circumstances in which it is perfectly legitimate to take another's property. "Theft" names the act of taking property illegally and against the owner's will.[54] By extension, we lie when we make a false assertion with the intent of deceiving someone. It is the evil intention that deforms the false assertion and transforms it into sin.

The consequences of Scotus's subtle interpretive shift, his exclusive emphasis on bad will and evil intention, show up in his handling of those now well-trod biblical examples. Considering the case of the Hebrew midwives, Scotus first offers as "probable" an interpretation that extends at least as far back as Augustine's *Against Lying* and that had been more or less repeated verbatim ever since. The midwives did in fact lie, and because that sin precluded an eternal reward, God granted them a temporal one for their charity. Significantly, Scotus then proceeds to what he believes to be an even more probable interpretation. "One could say," he writes, "that theirs was a polite lie, because it was useful in saving the Jewish children and harmed no one. Therefore, God would have rewarded their motives and good will and would still not have denied them eternal life, since their sin was only venial."[55] In other words, Scotus's emphasis on will and intention enables him to enter even more fully than Thomas into the very sort of moral calculating that Augustine had been so keen to avoid.

With the case of the midwives in mind, Scotus immediately asks whether "because of a powerful motive of charity" one should commit a venial sin, tell a venial lie. For Scotus, it is no longer simply a question of the gravity of our charitable lies but rather our duty, should the circumstances warrant it, to sin to avoid sin. Although he chooses to postpone a full examination of the problem, Scotus's own position is clear: "Since such an evil is of itself not eternal but temporal," he concludes, "it does not seem one ought to omit something which of itself is the cause in some way of an eternal good."[56] Perhaps every lie is a sin—indeed, Scotus is clear about this, as clear as Thomas, Alexander, and Augustine were before him—but that does not prevent him from sometimes recognizing the need and even the reward for telling them.

Augustine would have sympathized with Scotus's dilemma, even if he would have condemned Scotus's final position. Augustine, no less than the Scholastics, understood that we live in a world full of entanglements, dilemmas, and confusions, a world in which a simple lie might often seem like the only means to achieve the good. His two treatises against lying repeatedly stress how harsh, unfair, and cruel his exceptionless ban against lying might at times appear. For all that, Augustine feared nothing was more cruel to ourselves and to others than violating our duty to God. When we lie, for whatever reason, we embody falsity in our refusal to honor our image and likeness to God, who is truth, and to Christ, who suffered death as the incarnation of God's true Word. No temporal reward, no worldly good or beneficial outcome can make good the sinner's rejection of God's infinite love and truth. The divide between truth and falsity, likeness and unlikeness, is absolute, and not even the best of intentions can do anything to bridge it. By contrast, even as they clung to his absolute prohibition against lies, Augustine's Scholastic readers repeatedly considered the forms our lies can take. Why we lie matters even though we must never lie.

The consequences of this moral predicament show up quite clearly in the thirteenth-century Dominican theologian Albert the Great's influential commentary on Aristotle's *Ethics*. At one point, Albert asks whether one could lie to prevent a great harm from befalling the state.[57] Albert opts to investigate the problem from two different perspectives, the political and civil, on the one hand, the spiritual and theological, on the other. This division foreshadows Thomas's decision to annex truth to justice and to analyze lies in terms of what we owe others. From the perspective of civil virtue, Albert writes, which is ordered toward the temporal and finite good of the state, opposed courses of action can be compared, their respective outcomes and benefits weighed. At least in certain cases, intention and outcome will determine an action's moral status. If a person lies to protect the state from some great harm, considered politically, the lie is not evil at all and might even be virtuous. According to the perfection of political virtue, Albert concludes, a person can occasionally stoop to mendacity and can sometimes "lie in words or in deed, namely, he can present himself as something other than he is, other than as things really are." From the perspective of theological virtue, which is ordered toward an infinite good, an entirely different rule applies. Considered theologically, Albert argues, one ought never lie because no temporal advantage can ever outweigh or even be commensurable with the infinite goodness of salvation.[58]

Theological concerns ultimately trump the political, and Albert, following tradition, asserts that every lie is a sin and must be avoided, but the drift from Augustine's Christological rejection of lies cannot be denied. For Albert and Thomas, for Bonaventure and Scotus, for the entire subsequent theological tradition, lies were no longer understood as always and necessarily opposed to God. Rather, they were merely one of the many evils that plague this fallen world, worse than some, better than others. Bonaventure gives voice to this Scholastic development in his commentary on Peter Lombard's *Sentences* when he attempts to explain why every lie is a sin and begins with a contrast between lies that oppose created truth (lies about the things and people that populate this world) and those that oppose the uncreated truth (lies about God and the faith). The distinction between these two types of lies, Bonaventure contends, might seem to hold open the prospect that in some possible world lies against created truths could be virtuous. In language that would later influence Scotus, Bonaventure argues, "If God, therefore, can dispense with his commandments [as he did in the case of Abraham and Isaac] so that someone can destroy a created good ... it would seem he could act similarly with regard to created truth." Bonaventure allows this reasoning to stand, only later to locate the intrinsic and essential sinfulness of lying in the "intention to deceive."[59]

The thirteenth-century distinction between lies against God and lies against creation reflects a much broader transformation in Scholastic thought, a transformation at least partly dependent on the unique institutional and religious setting in which thirteenth-century intellectuals found themselves. If, to borrow Albert's terminology, Augustine had believed there was only one frame within which to evaluate our actions, Scholastic writers discovered an alternative frame: the civil, the political, the secular—the world itself. Nowhere is the conceptual novelty of this development made clearer than early in Thomas's *Summa of Theology*, when, as part of his investigation into the nature of truth, he asks whether "there is only one truth according to which all things are true?" As Thomas himself notes, the Benedictine monk Anselm of Bec had asked the very same question nearly two hundred years earlier, determining that "there is only one truth by which all things are true." While Thomas does not entirely disagree with Anselm, he believes that Anselm does not consider the question from all sides.[60]

Anselm addresses the problem in *On Truth*, a work he composed in the 1080s in the form of a dialogue between a younger monk and his teacher. Anselm argues that there is only one truth by which all things are true and that truth is determined entirely through each thing's relationship with God. Much like Augustine before him, Anselm begins with language and then extends his analysis to encompass the truth of all natural things, of all human action. Just as statements are true when they assert that what is is, that is, when they do what they ought to do, natural things signify truly when they do what they ought to do. Fire, Anselm offers by way of example, does what it ought to do, signifies truly, when it heats other objects. Rational beings differ from nonrational beings because rational beings choose to act as they do, that is, they can choose to do or not do what they ought to do.[61] Anselm then rephrases his initial question to bring out the moral, ethical, and ultimately the theological dimensions of true signification and action. Since truth is nothing but doing what ought to be done, it is the same as rendering what is owed, what ought to be repaid.[62] Truth, accordingly, falls under the category of rightness and rectitude, of acting correctly. Asking "[w]hether there is only one or many truths in all things which we say are true" is the same as asking if there is one or many rightnesses by which all action is judged to be correct. For Anselm the answer to that question is unambiguous—there is only one such rightness, and it is God. Rectitude names a single and universal demand that all natures act as they ought to act, that they be true, and the truth and rightness of all created natures is nothing but their indebtedness to the Supreme Truth, God, who is the single truth of all beings and is himself indebted to nothing. Failure to maintain one's right relation to God, to exist in the truth, to exist with rectitude, is a moral failure that incurs immediate guilt against the infinite.[63]

Thomas never denies that in a primary sense all things are true only insofar as they are conformed to the divine truth—"And this is the truth of which Anselm speaks," Thomas writes in his *Disputed Questions on Truth*—but, he adds, in a secondary sense, truth can also be predicated of the human intellect, insofar as it is able to know created things.[64] By this, Thomas does not mean that there can be truths about the world, philosophical truths, that contradict the truths of faith. In fact, he argued strenuously against arts masters Siger of Brabant and Boethius of Dacia, who held such positions. Rather, he means that something can also be called true if it is knowable to the human intellect, if "it is such as to cause a true estimate of itself." In this sense, Thomas explains, there are "many truths about many true things and even many truths in many minds about one true thing."[65] It might seem as if there is no disagreement here between the two writers. Anselm certainly recognizes a sense in which there are many truths. Spoken affirmations, he notes, are said to be true when we assert them correctly (when, for example, we say, "It is day" during the daytime).[66] Anselm, however, quickly adds that "truth is improperly said to be 'of this thing' or 'of that thing.' For truth does not have its being *in* or *from* or *through* the things in which it is said to be." There is only one truth, one rightness, the Supreme Truth, and created things are called true when they accord with that one absolute and unchanging standard.[67] By contrast, Thomas contends there is a legitimate and proper, if secondary, sense in which things in this world can be called true, are true—when, for example, we know them for what they are. It is precisely this difference between truths and Truth, Thomas argues, that distinguishes philosophy from theology. The philosopher considers the characteristics that belong to things according to their nature—the upward tendency of fire, for example. The theologian considers things only in terms of their relation to God.[68]

Later Thomists, such as the early sixteenth-century Italian cardinal Thomas Cajetan, would radicalize the split between truths and Truth, introducing the notion of "pure nature" into Thomas's thought. Natural things, even human beings, have natural ends wholly distinct from their supernatural ends in God. In the state of pure nature, they argued, human beings can only desire natural ends, and it is philosophy that reveals these independent and self-sufficient natural ends.[69] While these distinctions are foreign to Thomas, they are latent in his division between truths and Truth, and that division (or variations on it) supports the Scholastic contention that not every lie is a lie against the first and uncreated truth. Some lies are about things in this world, created things—the good of the state, the whereabouts of an innocent fugitive—and these lies can be weighed and evaluated, judged to be mortal or merely venial. No longer immediately defined as an offense against the infinite God and the infinite good of salvation, the culpability of these lies depends on context and the liar's intention to help or to harm. Scotus would push this line of thought far enough to speculate on the possible theological merit of our lies, but even he never denied, in the end, that every lie is a sin. Albert is no different, undercutting the implications of his division between the theological and the civil and concluding that no temporal benefit can outweigh the harm the soul suffers when we lie. Thomas's discussion of truth mirrors these various analyses of deception. Having located a place for the philosophical examination of the world, he limits it. The desire for knowledge becomes mere curiosity and blameworthy unless it is ultimately referred to God, divine truth, divine mandate, and our final ends.[70]

INSTITUTIONAL TRANSFORMATIONS

Thomas may have argued that the theologian considers things only as they relate to God, but the practical demands of his position required he consider quite a few other things as well. These considerations did much to shape the Scholastic discourse concerning deception. This becomes clear if we return to Anselm, whose work everywhere reflects its origins in the daily life of the monastery, in which every activity and every duty was always already understood (at least ideally) as an act of devotion to God, and this applied no less to studying, teaching, or working in the kitchen than it did to reciting the Psalter or attending mass. Anselm describes one of his works, *The Monologion*, as a meditation. For a monk, "to meditate" did not mean simply to reflect on and analyze an idea. It also had practical and moral connotations that encompassed more than just study. Meditation was a physical and spiritual activity involving the intelligence, the heart, and the tongue. The word *meditation* also named the first moment of contemplative prayer, the moment when the monk strove to conform himself to the text, to embody the prayer.[71] Anselm explicitly joins together all these senses of meditation at the conclusion of the *Proslogion*, when he writes, "Meanwhile let my mind meditate upon it; let my tongue speak of it. Let my heart love it; let my mouth talk of it. Let my soul hunger for it; let my flesh thirst for it; let my whole being desire it, until I enter into your joy, Lord, who are ever the three and the one God, blessed forever and ever. Amen." The *Proslogion* is both a speculative treatise and a prayer. Indeed, its speculative or philosophical aspects must not be disentangled from its overall setting as a prayer. It is a prayer even when it is speculative, and the act of speculation is the performance of a duty to pray, an act of piety and devotion, the repayment of a debt to God.[72]

The monastic setting not only lends form to Anselm's writings (the dialogue, the prayer, the meditation) but even shapes their content. Since speculation is prayer, it always assumes the perspective of the monk's immediate relation to God. No other perspec-

tive ought to matter to the monk, whose life signifies truly and
rightly only when it signifies its love of God. But this singleness of
perspective is exactly what Thomas finds mistaken in Anselm's theory of truth. Anselm, to hear Thomas tell it, lacks that perspective
which contemplates the truth of created things independently of
God and the first truth. If the institutional setting of the monastery
itself organizes and shapes Anselm's conception of truth, the university plays no less a role in shaping Scholastic conceptions of
truth. Even though early governing statutes for the university at
Paris borrowed from monastic ideals concerning the relation between virtue and study, the university would never have been mistaken for a monastery.[73] Much of this had to do with the sheer size
of the university and its charge to educate not only theologians but
also future bureaucrats, arts masters, doctors, and lawyers. To accomplish this most effectively, standards needed to be set, pedagogy unified, and the various fields of study organized. This applied to the teaching of grammar and dialectic as much as it did to
theology which, in the twelfth century, began to be treated as an
academic discipline for the first time. Under these pressures, theology became a field of study, a body of knowledge to be mastered,
and great effort was undertaken to create texts in systematic theology capable of "meeting the needs of professional theological
education."[74]

Thomas explicitly refers to these new educational demands in
the prologue to the *Summa*, where he explains that his goal is to
organize coherently and concisely all of theological science for the
beginning student. In the context of the university, theology, indeed all fields of study, became bodies of knowledge to be learned
and debated, mastered, refined, and extended. There is even linguistic evidence for this new conception of study. Over the course
of the twelfth century, the term "speculation" (*speculatio*), which
for monks like Anselm had implied a devotional exercise related to
contemplation (*contemplatio*), came to refer to a teachable activity
of the mind independent of religious emotion.[75] It is at precisely
this point that the institutional structure of the university appears
to guide the content of Thomas's thought. Once speculation is freed

from devotion and conceived as an activity detachable from prayer, it becomes possible to study things in themselves and not solely as they stand in relation to God, and so it becomes possible to consider the truths and lies of this world as they relate to the things of this world. Even the division of the university into different faculties, each with its own area of expertise and texts, set the stage for this reconceptualization of truth and deception. As early as the 1220s, masters in the faculty of arts claimed a certain autonomy from the theological faculty, the right to a philosophical and natural as opposed to theological and supernatural perspective. By institutionalizing the split between theology and the other faculties, the university institutionalized a system of studies practically demanding that, in some sense, things be considered outside their immediate relation to God.

While the institutional and pedagogical imperatives of the medieval university might provide some explanations for the conceptual distinctions at work in Scholastic discussions of truth and lies, they don't explain why theologians almost inevitably used these distinctions as excuses to expand the limits of acceptable speech. No doubt one factor at play is the extremity of Augustine's prohibition, an extremity that attracts and troubles even modern ethicists, not to mention Augustine himself.[76] Another factor, more immediately relevant to the thirteenth century, was the moral and pastoral expectations that the mendicant religious orders placed on their members to live a life of witness in both word and deed. It was an obligation that brought problems concerning truth and falsity, appearance and reality, simulation and deception, to the foreground.[77] University theologians not only experienced these anxieties in their role as preachers, but studied and wrote about them in numerous handbooks designed to assist their brothers. In his thirteenth-century guide *On the Formation of Novices*, for example, the Franciscan David of Augsburg gives voice to these concerns when he suggests that there will be times when even the best of novices must present a false front. "If you should lack interior devotion," he writes, "at least humbly maintain discipline and a grave exterior demeanor out of reverence for God and as an example to others."[78] No Scholastic theologian would have objected to this advice, would have judged such behavior to be deceitful, but it is worth noting that Scholastic discussions of lying almost inevitably conclude with discussions of hypocrisy, discussions themselves that almost inevitably focus on those who present themselves as holy while lascivious or at least lukewarm emotions stir within them. What exactly is the difference between laudable deception and vile hypocrisy?[79]

These are concerns that move us to the very heart of mendicant life—to the public preacher with his duty, not merely to edify and instruct his audience, but also to move and excite them with the desire to confess. In this respect, the thirteenth-century Dominican Humbert of Romans's *On the Formation of Preachers* is unique only because of its sustained examination of the preacher's need to cultivate his public persona. Humbert makes it clear that the preacher must adapt his words and appearance to an ever-changing set of circumstances and audiences, while simultaneously maintaining a careful watch on his intentions. The preacher must make sure that the dramatic and rhetorical effects he deploys are never intended for self-glorification but only for the good of his listeners.[80] Dominican and Franciscan training manuals and exempla indicate how difficult maintaining this balance could be. Writing in the fifteenth century, the Dominican Johannes Nider confronts the problem directly in his discussion of hypocrisy when he asks if a person sins who simulates sanctity to edify his neighbors. Clearly, Nider answers, a person who simulates holiness to win fame and renown sins, but consider a different case. Imagine a member of the church, a priest or mendicant who, when he preaches to the laity, pretends to be holier than he would ever dare pretend when with his fellow brothers. If he does this for the sake of more effectively edifying his audience, Nider reasons, not only does he not sin, but his actions are meritorious. Nider looks to the story of the bishop Diego, a friend of Dominic, the founder of Nider's order, to support this bit of justified fakery. Disgusted at the pomp and pageantry of the abbots he met in 1206 in the south of France, Diego declared they would do a much better job of converting the Albigensians if they presented themselves on foot and in blessed poverty, rather than on horseback and in fine clothes.[81] While Diego meant this as both a bit of sound advice and a rebuke of ecclesiastics whose faith had gone tepid, there is no hint of critique or correction in Nider, merely permission to pretend to a sanctity one doesn't possess, a simulation rendered virtuous through intent and calculated outcome.

EQUIVOCATION, MENTAL RESERVATION, AND AMPHIBOLOGY

Thirteenth-century theologians bequeathed their successors a set of questions to be repeatedly pondered and answered. When is simulation and pretending acceptable, and when is it nothing but base duplicity? What distinguishes concealing the truth from fabricating its false likeness? Long-standing and unquestionable interpretations of scripture helped to generate these questions and to provide clues to their solution. Theologians knew that Jacob was not guilty of duplicity when he pretended to be his brother Esau and that Christ did not offend against truth when he pretended to walk past the village of Emmaus. They knew this, just as they also knew that Abraham did not lie when, asked if Sarah was his wife, he responded, "She is my sister." Thanks to Augustine's prohibition against lies, these interpretations of biblical narrative had achieved the status of exemplary facts in need of an explanation, and the entire Catholic theological discourse on lies and deception can be read as a vast exercise in abductive reasoning, a search for the most reasonable set of premises to support them.[82]

External pressures also shaped this search. As human beings, theologians experienced the challenges and dilemmas that the world posed to the religious and laity alike. As preachers, they experienced the complicated dialectic between performer and audience, between appearance and reality, between simulation and dissimulation. As institutionally sanctioned authorities, they were expected to reflect on all these topics, to offer advice and guidance. Even the sacraments could generate dilemmas about truth and falsity. In sixteenth-century Spain this became strikingly obvious when the confessor's duty to maintain the secrecy of sins heard in confession, an injunction already made clear in 1215 in the canons of Lateran IV, came into conflict with the Inquisition's desire to root out and extinguish heresy. To what extent should priests protect secrets learned in confession? When pressed, could a confessor deny having heard what he in fact had heard in the private forum of confession? And there would be additional pressures, especially in the wake of the Reformation as Catholics and Protestants, persecuted and threatened with torture or death, wondered if they could, in deed and in act, pretend to beliefs they in no way accepted, publicly reject beliefs they privately held.[83]

The popular and influential fifteenth-century Florentine bishop Antoninus set the stage for much of what was to follow in his *Summa of Sacred Theology*. Reflecting on those ever-popular biblical examples, Antoninus offers a simple principle for distinguishing between sinful and sinless simulation. Our simulations and pretenses are sinful only when they signify nothing and are made up out of whole cloth. When they refer to something, an idea, a lesson, a sacred mystery, they are not lies but "figures of the truth." Jacob's claim to be his brother refers to the future favor that Christians will see in God's eyes, and when Jesus pretends to walk past the village of Emmaus, he is figuring his future ascent into heaven.[84] Nider, who was one of Antoninus's contemporaries, would explain this distinction between simulations that refer to something and those that refer to nothing in terms of the difference between concealing and deceiving. Referencing Thomas Aquinas, Nider explains, "A person verbally lies when he signifies what is not, not when he is silent about what is, which is sometimes allowed." By extension, Nider suggests that simulation is sinful when, through deeds, we signify something that is not, not if someone neglects to signify what is. "This is why," Nider concludes, "a person can hide his sin without sin."[85] The existence of this hidden meaning, higher lesson, or invisible reference renders true what would otherwise be a lie.

With this principle in mind, fifteenth-century theologians began to explore the connections among words, contexts, and both the speaker's and listener's intentions, between what others might take our words to mean and what we intend them to mean. Antoninus addresses these connections when he takes up the question of concealment. "It is sometimes licit to hide the truth when necessary," he writes, "and this pertains to prudence." Although he does not cite Thomas, his Dominican predecessor's discussion of concealment during moments of peril clearly frames Antoninus's explanation. Antoninus turns to the tried-and-true story of Abraham's assertion that Sarah is his sister. Like previous theologians, Antoninus agrees that this is not a lie, because Sarah was both Abraham's wife and half sister, but Antoninus takes the analysis a step further, deriving from it a rule for determining when our concealments are licit. "When there are many reasons for something, an agent, free from the vice of lying, can assign one of the lesser reasons, remaining silent about the others." To explain this, Antoninus looks to the story of Samuel, whom the Lord sent to Bethlehem to announce that Isai's youngest son David was to replace Saul as king of the Jews. When Samuel expresses concern that Saul would rather kill him than allow this news to be spread, the Lord advises Samuel to bring along a calf for Isai to sacrifice. Arriving at the gates of Bethlehem, calf in tow, and asked if he comes to the town peaceably, Samuel responds, "Peaceably, I am come to sacrifice to the Lord, sanctify yourselves and come with me to the sacrifice." As Antoninus notes, Samuel does not lie. He simply conceals his principal reason for coming to town while offering up another true, but secondary, reason.[86]

Antoninus then adds that it is perfectly acceptable to employ sophistical words and equivocal expressions for the sake of countering evil. Specifically, Antoninus notes that we can take advantage of words with multiple meanings, using them so that our listeners will understand them one way while we understand them in another. If asked by persecutors whether a man they intend to kill passed this way, it is acceptable to respond, "He did not pass here," by which we mean he did not pass over the very spot on which we stand. While this example clearly plays on the equivocal meaning of the word "here" in conjunction with an added mental qualification specifying which meaning the speaker intends, Antoninus's next example seems to do something more. A priest approaches the entrance to a city, and the gatekeeper asks whether he has money to pay the entrance fee. Although the priest has the money, he responds no. Antoninus contends that this is not a lie so long as the priest intends his response to mean, "I do not have the money in the sense that the religious are not obligated to pay such fees." Although the priest intends this hidden meaning, Antoninus adds, he intends the gatekeeper to believe that he has no money whatsoever. To support this practice, Antoninus invokes the story of Tobit's meeting with the angel Raphael, who had taken form of a beautiful young man. When Tobit asks who he is, Raphael responds that he is one of the children of Israel, Azarias son of Ananias. Much like Jacob before Isaac, Antoninus claims that Raphael's words, literally false though they may be, are made true through the angel's intention to speak figuratively, to give them a special meaning indicating his true identity as a glorious creature worthy of seeing and helping God.[87]

In cases like these, the line between licit simulation and sheer duplicity, between concealment and lying, becomes vanishingly fine, perhaps nonexistent. All of Antoninus's methods of concealment depend on forms of mental reservation, the speaker's silent specification of meaning, his intent that his words mean something other than what an ordinary listener would take them to mean. As Antoninus makes clear in his discussion of the priest at the city gates, the priest wants the gatekeeper to believe he has no money at all. This bit of misdirection is possible because of the difference between thought and speech, but that very difference implicates Antoninus's technique in the very duplicity that defines the liar. Antoninus knows this well, as he makes clear early on in his discussion of lies, when he writes, "Where there is a doubleness of heart such that one says one thing and intends something else, there is a lie." While it is possible that equivocal words (like "here") might avoid the charge of speaking against one's mind, it is much more difficult to make that argument in the case of the priest at the city gates. It becomes more difficult still when, following both

Bonaventure and Thomas, Antoninus locates the perfection of lying in the "intention of generating a false opinion in the listener" and several lines later defines duplicitous and sinful simulation as rooted in the intention to deceive.[88] In these cases, there is every intention to deceive.

Although Antoninus seems oblivious to this potential inconsistency, he certainly recognizes the potential for these techniques to be abused, and he sets limits on their legitimate employment. We can equivocate to forestall evil, but we should never silently qualify our words (à la the priest at the gate) when such reservations will cause scandal if discovered or when a just judge questions us.[89] Subsequent theologians would take a similar tack to avoid abuse. Sylvester Prierias, a Dominican writing late in the fifteenth century, following Antoninus, divides the various types of licit concealment into four distinct categories, the last, like Antoninus's priest at the city gates, involving mental reservation. Imagine we are asked about something that we are not free to discuss. In such cases, we can respond that we do not know, while to ourselves adding the appropriate clause to render our statement true. Sylvester looks to the Gospels for support. When Mark asks Christ when the day of judgment will occur, the Lord responds that he doesn't know, no doubt adding to himself, or so Sylvester believes, "such that I should reveal it to you." Significantly, Sylvester begins this entire discussion with a crucial caveat. We are free to employ these techniques only in those cases in which we are not bound to respond according to our questioner's intentions and, at the very end of his discussion, warns that we must avoid all these methods of concealment when they might give rise to scandal, when we are before a just judge, or when they concern something that we are bound to confess. Exceeding these limits, our words will become dishonest, and we will become liars.[90]

While everyone who had written on the subject agreed that context and intention shape the severity our lies, whether they are malicious or beneficial, whether they are mortal or venial, they also agreed that the difference between telling the truth and telling a lie was an entirely private and internal matter, depending solely on the speaker's intention to make a false assertion. While it might well have public consequences, the essence of the lie itself had nothing to do with the liar's audience and everything to do with the liar's decision to let his words misrepresent his thoughts. It doesn't matter what Isaac understands when Jacob claims to be Esau, just as it doesn't matter what the Egyptians understand when Abraham tells them that Sarah is his sister. It doesn't matter if they are deceived (which they are—Alexander of Hales had already admitted as much, as if what is obvious requires admitting), all that matters is what the speaker says and what the speaker intends, and if the speaker intends a true statement, then he has not lied. Having over the centuries worked through what, in retrospect, can only seem like the necessary implications of Augustine's interpretation of scripture, though certainly not his Christology, these fifteenth-century writers suddenly uncovered a nearly limitless range of seemingly licit, deceptive, yet nonmendacious, communication.

This entirely internal and self-referential conception of lying helps to explain why the various limits that Antoninus and Sylvester place on the use of mental reservation seem so ad hoc and irrelevant to the question of our honesty and dishonesty. Since the difference between thought and speech no longer determines whether we lie, Antoninus and Sylvester have little alternative but to look to context as a moral check on the words we use. In response to the exact same question, we can offer the exact same response, and yet, they contend, depending on the situation and the person with whom we are speaking, our words and intentions remaining entirely unchanged, we may be telling the truth or speaking a lie. The internal incoherence of this effort stems from the disconnect between intention and context in traditional conceptions of mendacity. Whether or not our words cause scandal or stave off evil, whether we are responding to a just or unjust judge, or are speaking with someone to whom we are or are not obligated to respond, are entirely different questions from whether our responses are true or false. The entire point of these techniques, or so claimed their supporters, is that they keep us from lying, and this means they do not depend on the speaker making a false assertion. If the use of mental reservation, selective response, and equivocation in and of themselves do not entangle us in lies, then it should hardly matter why we use them so long as we don't use them for sinful purposes, and even if we do use them for sinful purposes, they are still not lies. Our intentions might be evil and our sins many, but our words remain true.

It was Martin Azpilcueta, more famously known in his day as Dr. Navarrus, who resolved this incoherence. An Augustinian canon and professor of canon law at the university of Salamanca before moving to Rome, where he died in 1586, Navarrus argued that the very nature of language rendered silent qualifications to our spoken words perfectly truthful.[91] Navarrus made this case most fully in his *Commentary on the Chapter "Human Ears,"* a philosophically tinged reflection on a famous passage from Gregory the Great's *Moralia on Job*. "The ear's of men judge our words as they sound outwardly," Gregory writes, "but the Divine judge hears those things we profess within ourselves. Men know each other's will and intention through various words; but we shouldn't consider words, but the will and the intention, for the intention ought not depend upon the words, but the words on the intention." To test the implications of the idea that God hears both our spoken and our silent words, Navarrus considers a case of decidedly devious behavior. Imagine that a man, with no intention of making good on his vow, privately tells a woman, "I take you for my wife." Later, when a judge asks him, "Did you speak those words," the man responds that he did not, adding silently to himself, "with any intention of actually doing so." Navarrus then asks three questions: Did the man lie before God? Even if he didn't lie before God, did he perjure himself before God? And, finally, even if he neither lied nor committed perjury, did he commit some other sin?[92]

While the idea that God hears, sees, and understands all our communicative acts is hardly a controversial idea, Navarrus draws a rather unexpected consequence from it. If it is true that God understands both our spoken and silent words, then he can understand sentences and ideas composed out of both as single statements. "Through which it is obvious," Navarrus concludes, "that the man did not lie before God because in his divine majesty he knows and sees the truly intended sense," and this is case even though the judge or anyone else who heard what the man said would judge the statement to be false. Navarrus finds additional support for his theory of "mixed speech" or "amphibology" in the writings of the dialecticians who teach that there are many different kinds of language, "purely mental, purely vocal, purely written and a mixture of these." When we judge the truth or falsity of our own or someone else's statements, we need to take all these parts into account. Imagine the following mixed statement, Navarrus offers by way of example, "God is an angel," of which the first two words are spoken aloud, the last two mentally. Although the spoken part is perfectly orthodox, the statement as a whole must be considered heretical. Navarrus, picking up on an argument from Prierias, even suggests that scripture and Church practice supports this conception of mixed language. "Our lord Jesus Christ, who was and is the way, the truth and the life," Navarrus argues, employed amphibology when he claimed not to know the date of the final judgment. Considered as purely vocal speech, Christ's claim is surely false because he knows all things most truly, but when taken in conjunction with its mental qualification, "such that I should reveal it to you," the statement is true. The privacy of confession likewise demonstrates the reality of mixed speech. When asked if a confessant committed some sin, the Church considers it perfectly acceptable and honest for the confessor to respond, "No he did not," even if he did, so long as the confessor has added the appropriate mental statement to render the completed statement true.[93]

Although Navarrus agrees that every lie is a sin, that the essence of the lie rests in false assertion, its perfection in the desire to deceive, the theory of mixed language is utterly foreign to the spirit of Augustine's thought.[94] Augustine had rooted his objection against lies in Christ's incarnation as the Word made flesh and his willingness to witness Truth publicly and openly on the cross. It was the incarnation that demanded the identity between inner thought and spoken word, guaranteeing that false assertion was necessarily sinful. By contrast, Navarrus's theory of mixed statements creates the possibility that no matter what we say, we will never have to speak against our mind. Antoninus and Sylvester had attempted something similar but failed to offer an internally consistent account of why mental reservations were at times truthful, at other times mendacious. They were, therefore, compelled to look to external factors to discriminate honesty from dishonesty, even as their definition of what it meant to lie remained entirely internal to the liar. Navarrus sidesteps this entire problem, offering a theory of language that guarantees the honesty of mental reservations. Given the amphibological nature of language, properly conceived mixed statements are never lies. His test case makes this abundantly clear. The man who privately tells a woman "I take you for my wife" neither lies nor perjures himself when he tells the judge that he never vowed marriage to her, adding silently to himself "with the intent of actually marrying her." If his statement is not a lie, then, considered on its own, neither is it a sin. It is, in a sense, morally neutral. With the question of dishonesty bracketed, context, circumstance, and intention will entirely determine whether the man's actions are sinful or not. In fact, having undone the link between dishonesty and deception, Navarrus creates the possibility of honest deceptions, deceptions in no way tainted by sin. Our simulations are good, "useful" as Jerome put it, when we use them "prudently and ordinately with just cause, and without evil intent and foxlike craftiness [*astutia vulpinus*], and apart from any lying words or deeds." By contrast, they are bad when we simulate "evilly and inordinately without just cause, or not caring whether or not they lie."[95] In this case, the man acted with evil deceit [*dolo malo*] if he deceived the woman in order to have sex with her outside wedlock. On the other hand, if he deceived her in order to keep himself unmarried and, therefore, able to enter holy orders, he acted with good deceit [*dolo bono*].[96]

The theory of mixed speech represents something like the culminating moment of an ethical trajectory begun some four hundred years earlier in Peter Lombard's *Sentences*. If the entire tendency of Scholastic thinking about lies had been to frame their moral status in terms of the world, in terms of good achieved or evil avoided, in terms of intention and circumstance, Navarrus completes this process. Language, now liberated from theology, becomes entirely part of the world and, as part of the world, becomes good or bad, rewarded or punished, depending on its relations to the world. Not only are we perfectly right to use mixed statements when unjust judges or evil questioners interrogate us, we can also employ them to avoid all sorts of "negligent" sins committed in the course of daily life. If a friend asks us for money or for a book, we are free to respond "I don't have it" even if we do, so long as we silently add, "such that I would give it to you." Mixed speech also has great political value, Navarrus adds, and even kings have been known to use it, telling pleasant falsehoods rendered true through silent adumbration to members of their court.[97]

There were dangers here, and Navarrus's critics noted them. Theologians had long argued that the fabric of society would collapse if lies were sometimes thought to be acceptable, and that collapse seemed all the more imminent in a world of mixed speech. Citing Angelus of Clavasi and Prierias, along with Navarrus, as the main proponents of mixed speech, the sixteenth-century Jesuit theologian Juan Azor feared that if such subterfuge were freely allowed, "every sort of lie could be excused," and "all human intercourse and charity destroyed."[98] By lumping Navarrus together with Angelus and Prierias, it is not at all clear if Azor appreciates the crucial differences between their theories. Certainly Navarrus would have denied that his theory sanctioned any type of lie. Subtleties aside, Azor admitted the licit use of mental reservations, while simultaneously placing the same sorts of limits on them as had Angelus and Prierias. Navarrus had done the same, arguing that mixed statements are licit when employed for just causes, when they do not offend against charity, when we are not bound to respond in the sense our interrogators or questioners understand. When we violate these limits, our words become sinful but not mendacious. By contrast, Azor and most of the other Jesuits who came after Navarrus, who would reject the theory of mixed

language while accepting more traditional versions of mental reservation, argued that when we exceed the limits of just cause our
words become lies.[99]

These specific differences must not obscure how all these later
writers had reversed the role of context in the discourse of lies.
Scholastic theologians, interested in pushing the range of licit
speech, looked to intention and circumstance to reduce the culpability of certain sorts of lies, to render them merely venial and almost negligible. With the theory of mixed statements and the practice of mental reservation, theologians looked to context and the
notion of just cause to restrain a theory of language that threatened to make it impossible ever to know how to understand the
meaning of a speaker's words. Let loose into the world, it seemed
as if only the world could help hold back our deceit.

FROM PASCAL TO AUGUSTINE AND BEYOND

Like Juan Azor before him, Pascal most likely did not perceive the
difference between Navarrus's theory of mixed speech and the Jesuit doctrines of equivocation and mental reservation that he pillo-
ried in his *Provincial Letters*. It wouldn't have mattered if he had.
Pascal's disdain for such techniques was not rooted in the niceties
of detail but in the rejection of an entire theological conception of
ourselves and our place in the world that Henry Hammond would
describe as the "mystery of Jesuitisme." As it turned out, it was not
exactly a Jesuit mystery, even if Jesuit theologians were the ones
who had refined and promoted it, written about it, defended it
and, in time, popularized it. Its immediate roots could be traced
back to the writings of fifteenth-century theologians like the Dominican friar Antoninus of Florence and the Augustinian canon
Martin Azpilcueta, and its conceptual possibility extended even
further back, to the medieval university, to John Duns Scotus,
Thomas Aquinas. and to Peter Lombard's *Sentences*. Pascal's critique begins at precisely that point where Scholastic writers first
diverged from Augustine, when they took seriously the idea that
they could evaluate the moral gravity of our lies, deploying ideas

about intention and context, the civil, the political, means and ends, to determine which are mortal and which are venial.[100]

Pascal makes this case most clearly in the seventh of his *Provincial Letters* when he accuses the Jesuits of being more concerned with policy than with religion. Learning Jesuit views concerning the right to kill another in defense of one's honor or in retaliation for slander or "a saucy gesture," Montalte (Pascal's stand-in) reminds the Jesuit father with whom he is speaking that God prohibits killing. The Jesuits agree with God's prohibition, the father responds, but they have their own reasons for accepting it. Quoting a fellow Jesuit, he clarifies: "Although the opinion that we may kill a man for calumny is not without its probability in theory, the contrary one ought to be followed in practice; for in our mode of defending ourselves, we should always avoid doing injury to the commonwealth."[101] At the heart of this approach to morals, Pascal contends, is a turn from God to the world, a turn rooted in the sin of pride and a self-love capable of justifying any desire, forever transforming falsehoods into apparent truths, as we unknowingly drift further from any hope of salvation.[102] And so it is, Pascal contends, that the Jesuits find it perfectly reasonable to modify any tenet of faith as they see fit. Even the most fundamental beliefs about Jesus Christ are ripe for reinterpretation. "Where the doctrine of a crucified God is accounted foolishness," the Jesuit father blithely announces to a horrified Montalte, "they suppress the offense of the cross and preach only a glorious and not a suffering Jesus Christ."[103] What is left, Pascal argues, is nothing but a "criminal neutrality" in which the Jesuits remain utterly indifferent to what is true and what is false, to the Gospel and their own ideas, as they forge a horrible alliance between Jesus Christ and the Devil.[104]

Parody allows Pascal to make mental reservation and equivocation look like the shape-shifting practices of egotistical hotheads and avaricious cowards, but he roots his parody in Augustinian ideas of grace and original sin. Pascal is simply not interested in entering into Scholastic debates about the fine lines that separate licit from illicit speech, concealment from mendacity. Lying for him is less a linguistic or ethical problem than it is a profound spiritual and ontological disorder whose source extends back to Adam and Eve and the Fall. "Man is, therefore, only disguise, falsehood and hypocrisy," he writes in his *Pensées*, "both in himself and in regards to others. He does not want to be told the truth. He avoids telling it to others. And all these dispositions, so far removed from justice and reason, have a natural root in his heart."[105] Perhaps the world abounds in moral conundrums, but the real problem rests in our fallen faculties, our imperceptible desires and constant distractions, in a pride and self-love that blinds us to ourselves even as we set ourselves up as gods, judging good and evil. These are the sad consequences of original sin, a punishment we all suffer because of one man's transgression, a punishment so contrary to human conceptions of justice that it appears irrational and, appearing irrational, remains forever inaccessible to human reason.[106]

Original sin leaves us no choice but to cleave to God and to his self-revelation in scripture as the only fixed point to which we can secure ourselves and our judgments, and at the heart of scripture there is Jesus Christ, prophesied in the Old Testament, memorialized in the New Testament.[107] In opposition to what he refers to as "Jesuit neutrality" toward the world in which reason fits religious doctrine to worldly need, Pascal looks to the first centuries of the Christian faith, when there was an "essential distinction between the world and the church ... as between two irreconcilable enemies, such that the one persecuted the other without end." The Romans savaged the Church so relentlessly that men "conceived a dreadful difference between them."[108] To enter the Church required a commitment to reject the world, to leave it behind and to abandon all its ideas and values. There was little choice. The Church countered Roman pride with Christ's incarnation and the humility of his crucifixion.[109] There can be no middle ground, Pascal contends, no room for compromise nor human invention, for "Jesus Christ is a God whom we approach without pride and before whom we humble ourselves without despair."[110] But all these distinctions, he laments, are now obscured because the Church has made peace with the world, and at the very moment we are born into the world, so also are we born into the Church, the absolute difference between the two lost. Even as we partake in the sacraments, Pascal laments, we "enjoy the pleasures of this world."[111]

With the model of the early Church's refusal to accommodate to the ways of a sinful world, Pascal recuperates something like the purity and simplicity of Augustine's original prohibition against lies—the unwavering example of the Bishop Firmus, the total rejection of Consentius's deceptive tactics to root out hidden Priscillianist heretics. But no recuperation is total, if only because the passage of time wearies and shifts that original vision once lost and now inevitably regained from a different vantage point. Pascal, admittedly, says little or nothing about Augustine's actual prohibition. He condemns Jesuit moral theology as sinful because he believes it condones lies and sets reason up as its own god determining good and evil. Less polemically, Pascal believes the Jesuits credit reason with too much power, too much discernment, that they credit human beings with the ability to determine their own salvation. If our very essence as fallen beings is one of self-deception, if lies and deceit constitute our very nature, then it cannot be enough to ask how reason ought to operate in a deceptive world, nor can it be enough to analyze the fine gradations of culpability among different sorts of lies, between licit and illicit speech. For Pascal, these approaches are fundamentally insufficient because they fail to take account of our inherent sinfulness, the fact that we lie to ourselves even as we confront a world full of liars. Reason is not simply weak, it is treacherous.

Pascal treats the lie entirely as a problem in spiritual anthropology that leaves us incomprehensible and paradoxical to ourselves. This is the starting point of his famous wager, which places us in the midst of uncertainty and confusion while simultaneously appealing to our own self-interest. Should we bet on God's nonexistence for a possible share of the world's paltry and finite pleasures, or bet on God's existence and the possibility of eternal happiness and salvation? If we accept the wager, we will have to enact that crucial, if now lost, distinction between Christian and Roman, Church and world. We will have to act differently than we had before. We will have to submit reason to the will of Christ and give up the "poisonous pleasures" of human glory and luxury, even as we now attend mass and accept the sacraments. We will act as if we believe, even if we don't, in the hope that someday we will. There are no assurances, and Pascal clearly distinguishes belief from faith. Habit can form belief and prepare us for grace, but grace cannot be earned and comes from God alone. If this seems to verge on the very sort of self-centered hypocrisy he deplores in his *Provincial Letters*, Pascal doubles down, stressing that whether or not habit leads to belief and belief to faith, the bettor will still profit as his peers take him to be "faithful, honest, humble, grateful, generous, a sincere friend."[112]

In this life, the simulation of Christian virtue offers its own rewards, has its own benefits, entirely independent of our salvation. Perhaps the spiritual for Pascal will always trump the worldly, but the worldy benefits remain, calculable, potentially separable.

PART TWO

Courtiers and Women
Ask the Question

CHAPTER FOUR

Courtiers

FLATTERERS, WHEEDLERS, AND GOSSIPMONGERS

"The flatterer is the enemy of all virtue," John of Salisbury warns in the *Policraticus*, a work he composed in 1159, "and forms as it were a cataract over the eye of him whom he engages in conversation." With seemingly kind and encouraging words, pledges of love and fidelity, fine manners and concerned gestures, the flatterer blinds his victim, fills his ears with lies, and stokes his vanity. "Men of this type," John continues, "always speak to give pleasure, never to tell the truth. The words in their mouths are wicked guile which, even when friends are in error, bellows Bravo! Bravo! to their undoing."[1] And there are others lurking around the court, no less pernicious, no less evil. To the ranks of the flatterer, John adds the timeserver, the wheedler, and the gift giver, the actor and the mimic, the pervert, the procurer, and the gossipmonger. The only thing that surpasses their variety, John fears, is their number, "for the foul inundation of their cancerous disease seeps into all so that there is rarely anyone left uncontaminated."[2]

Perhaps John exaggerates. The history of social commentary all too often seems like little more than the history of fears and proclamations that the current generation has gone to seed, that corruption runs rampant and morals have decayed beyond hope of redemption. In the 1520s, some 350 years after John despaired of his contemporaries, Baldassare Castiglione, the Mantuan-born envoy for the court of Gonzaga, would blame the elderly for this

153

tendency to believe that "all things imaginable are always moving from bad to worse." Why? "For myself," Castiglione writes in *The Book of the Courtier*, "I think that the reason for this faulty judgment in the old is that the passing years rob them of the favorable conditions of life."[3] As our bodies and minds wither, the world around us seems to wither as well. Whether John was aged or not (he was in his late thirties with more than half his life still ahead of him when he composed *The Policraticus*), his observations should be taken seriously, since he was as well placed as anyone during his life to observe the "frivolities" or "non-sense" of the courtiers. An emissary for kings and popes, not to mention a fervent letter writer who ended his days as bishop of Chartres, there can be little doubt that John was intimately acquainted with the nature of medieval court life, its forms and foibles, its pleasures and poisons and, especially, its temptations.[4] "The most dangerous situation . . . that men of eminence have to face," John writes at the very beginning of the first chapter of the first book of the *Policraticus*, "lies in the fact that the enticements of fawning fortune blind their eyes to truth. The world heaps upon them its wealth and its pleasures and thereby kindles and fosters their craving for self-indulgence. The soul, deceived by allurements of many kinds, proving false to its own inner light, by a sort of self-betrayal goes astray as the result of its desires amid the deceptions of the outer world."[5]

John was not alone in his depiction of the court as a place of lies and deception. During the first decades of the fifteenth century, Alain Chartier who, among other things, served as private secretary to Charles VII, received a request for assistance from his brother Jean, who hoped to obtain a position at court. Alain was less than thrilled with his brother's plans and did his best to dissuade him in a letter known as the *Curial*. Although Alain alludes to the official burdens of his position, to the "miseries" he suffers each day due to his public services, he has little else to say about his onerous civic and political duties.[6] On the other hand, he has a tremendous amount to say about life in the court, and nothing he has to say about it is good. The courts of high princes overflow with an assortment of deceivers and bullies, of envious men, flatterers, and false accusers, all endeavoring to hinder and somehow undo "the good will of honest men." Sadly, human nature is weak and, just like John's man of eminence, Alain fears that no matter how good a person is when he enters the court, he will all too quickly "follow the habits of others and begin to do as they do."[7] If a man has been studious, rising early each morning, soon he will be out late at night carousing, wasting his time on idle thoughts as he begins to lose "mastery" over himself.[8] The court constantly replicates itself, breeding new flatterers and liars as it cons men into exchanging proper morals for prideful dreams. "For the court," he adds, "nourishes people who by fraud and simulation endeavor to draw from each other such words by which they may persecute them . . . taking more pleasure in false reports than in true words."[9] His language growing more florid by the line, Alain laments that "to those who understand it well, the court is a gathering of people who, under the pretense of the common good, assemble in order to deceive one another."[10]

Alain contrasts the perils of court life with the Edenic plea-sures of the country, where a man is free to be himself. "Oh fortu-nate men, who live in peace," Alain writes in praise of bucolic tran-quillity, "blessed family, where honest poverty is content with reason, without eating the fruits of other men's labor. O blessed house in which virtue reigns without fraud and strife and which is honestly governed in the dread of God and the good moderation of life. There enter no sins and there is a true and rightful life."[11] Of course, the simple pleasures of the countryside were not enough to keep Alain himself from falling for the lure of the court, nor, as it turned out, would they keep his brother Jean's attention for long. None of this is surprising. How could the merely Eden-like pleasures of the country satisfy, if the real pleasures of Eden itself were not enough to keep Adam and Eve from transgressing God's command in favor of the serpent's illusory promises of power, prestige, and divinity? When John of Salisbury and Alain Chartier describe the dangers of the court and the transformations it works on its victims, they are doing little more than offering an updated version of the oldest story in the world.

Scripture reports that almost as soon as Adam took and ate the fruit that his wife had already tasted, their "eyes were opened and they knew that they were naked; and they sewed fig leaves together and made loincloths for themselves."[12] According to the sixth-century Spanish bishop Isidore of Seville, whose account of this event was included and popularized in the *Glossa Ordinaria*, a combination of shame, cunning pride, and salacious desire motivated the first couple to conceal themselves with leaves and lies. Now fallen, having violated God's command, Adam and Eve no longer see themselves and the world as they had before. Their nakedness, once the sign of their innocence, suddenly appears shameful to their corrupted eyes. The experience of shame itself is significant, revealing their loss of innocence as "they make girdles, hiding their genitals, that is, hiding their innocence, about which a cunning pride now embarrasses them." The fig-leaf clothing behind which they conceal themselves signifies the salacious yearnings their souls now "suffer as a result of carnal desire and the pleasure of lying. This is why," Isidore concludes, "people who love to joke are called liars, because in jokes, deception is key."[13]

If deception was the key to humor, it was also the key to courtly life. Already in the eleventh century, the reforming monk and future cardinal Peter Damian discerned the structural element of court society that so efficiently transformed men into liars and the world into a veil of false fronts. Railing against clergy who serve in the imperial courts in the hope of eventually receiving bishoprics of their own, Damian argues that no one can enter the secular courts without falling into sin. Advancement requires that clerics "must both be lavish with their money and not forget to ingratiate themselves with their patrons by fondling them with fawning compliments." Whenever possible, "he will smother his lord with affable words" and "delight him with fawning flattery." Having handed himself over in vassalage to the whims of his new lord, the cleric is no longer his own man. No matter what his lord does or says, the cleric must make his approval known, shivering should the king appear cold, growing weary should the king want to sleep, belching should the king have eaten too much. Flattery transforms the cleric into a liar because his only goal in speaking is to please his lord. "For sinners," Damian warns, "use deceptive words when with flattery they suggest that something wicked be done, or praise you when you have done it."[14] Just as John would warn of the courtier's self-betrayal, Damian demonstrates how the very dynamics of court society compel its members to take on deceptive coverings, to lie and become someone other than themselves. In keeping with his own reformist inclinations, Damian sees nothing for it but to avoid the court completely.

About one hundred years later, one of John of Salisbury's students, Peter of Blois, would castigate himself for having ignored Damian's advice. Reflecting on his own experiences, Peter would bitterly observe that "the life of the curial is the death of the soul, and it is damnable to be a cleric who has immersed himself in courtly and worldly business." Damnable or not, Peter cannot forget how that business seduced him, how ambition had intoxicated him, how the prince's sweet promises had undermined him, so that he willingly and knowingly conspired against his own life.[15] For medieval writers, the structure of courtly life revealed more clearly than anywhere else the conditions of life after Eden, as it staged unending reenactments of our fall and, fallen, leaving us with no recourse but to lie in our own self-defense like Adam before a questioning God. "Some offering an excuse for their sin and preferring the coverings of the old Adam," Peter notes, "when asked why they follow after the court, rather than God and salvation, argue that these two ends are not opposed and they introduce examples from antiquity to color and support their ambition. Wasn't Moses sent to correct and instruct Pharaoh, Jeremiah to Sedechiam, Helias to Ahab, Joiadas to Josaih?"[16] But Peter knows this recourse to precedents from antiquity is nothing more than the Devil's work, contorting scripture to serve one's own ends. God did not send Peter to court, nor did he send any of Peter's peers. Just as temptation got the better of Peter, so had Adam and Eve already exchanged the simple pleasures of paradise for the serpent's sham promises. And the consequences for all of them, for Adam and Eve and for all their descendants, would be the same—a world of pride and envy and lust, of concealment and disguise, deception and lies.

East of Eden, Adam and Eve find the court.

EARLY MODERN UNCERTAINTY AND DECEPTION

How should a person, John's "man of eminence" or Alain's "honest man," respond to a situation of rampant illusion, ever-present deception, and constant uncertainty? This is an important question for at least two different, if related, reasons. To begin with, it is an important question because it is a question that matters to John, to Alain, to any number of medieval writers. Peter Damian and Alain Chartier may have advised one and all to avoid the court, but Damian went on to become a cardinal, the head of his own court, and Alain maintained his position long after he had unsuccessfully warned his brother away from following in his footsteps. Even Peter of Blois recognized the need for courtly and secular involvements in a fallen world. Before his own disappointments and frustrations had gotten the better of him, he had defended the role of clerics at court, and he would do so again as offended clerics demanded an apology for the slanders they had found strewn across the pages of his epistolary diatribe against their profession. "I do not condemn the life of clerics," he would write in a subsequent letter, "who remain engaged in prayer and contemplation, are concerned with the utility of the commonweal and frequently carry out the work of salvation."[17] The court was a necessary evil of a fallen world that required institutions, laws, and armies to maintain peace and order. Avoiding the court was not an option, not a real option anyway, so knowing how to adapt to it in order to shape it toward the good was too important a duty simply to abandon.

But it is an important question for another reason as well, a reason having to do with how historians think about the development of European society. For many historians, the response to illusion, deception, and uncertainty functions as a central explanatory device in popular and enduring accounts of Europe's transition from a medieval or premodern society to an early modern one. According to these varied interpretations of the sixteenth and seventeenth centuries, the origins of European modernity depend in large part on how people reacted to the specter of uncertainty and skepticism, the result of a widespread crisis of confidence in which long-held religious, cultural, and scientific institutions and beliefs had become unstable, even untenable.[18] Members of the early modern court were hardly immune to these pressures, and scholars have long wondered about the rather cheerful tone of Castiglione's great work, even as his characters discuss the ominous consequences of life in the newly emerging absolutist states. It is in the court that the epistemological and ethical crises in early modern Europe came together most dramatically.[19]

One particularly useful way into this enormous historiographic debate focuses on two distinct types of response to uncertainty: those that privilege the theoretical intellect and those that privilege the practical intellect.[20] Descartes offers an example of the first approach when he famously addresses the problem of uncertainty in his *Discourse on Method*. Describing his time spent at one of Europe's most esteemed colleges, Descartes informs us that the upshot of his education was the disheartening discovery that there is practically nothing upon which everyone agrees. Every authority has its detractors and every theory its objectors.[21] In the *Meditations on First Philosophy*, Descartes would radicalize this uncertainty through a series of thought experiments culminating in his invention of a "malicious demon of utmost power and cunning" whose sole purpose is to deceive us about all things, all the time. Descartes responds to the threat of global uncertainty with a drastic limitation or restriction concerning what qualifies as knowledge. He will accept as true only those opinions that are indubitable, necessarily true, and incapable of being false. Certainty, Descartes argues, is the only feasible response to uncertainty.[22]

While this approach may well have proved useful for the natural philosopher, it was hardly practical for anyone else, even that same natural philosopher in daily life, where certainty can rarely, if ever, be had. The second response to early modern uncertainty, an approach that privileged the practical intellect and the faculty of prudence, addressed precisely these more immediately pressing concerns. Accepting uncertainty as an unavoidable feature of our lives, any number of early modern writers and thinkers turned to rhetoric and dialectic as a means of making sense of themselves and their actions in the world.[23] In a series of lectures from the 1570s on Aristotle's *Rhetoric*, the Oxford scholar John Rainolds argues that we must reject the Aristotelian notion of scientific demonstration based on first principles because we possess few, if any, real first principles. Proponents of Aristotle, Rainolds writes, "wish a demonstrative proof to be understood with reference to nature, not to us." The problem, Rainolds contends, is one of perspective. By demanding that knowledge must begin with necessary first principles, Aristotelians fail to consider the real limitations that frame and condition our attempts to know the world. "Being men with wits enslaved to error," Rainolds argues, "we scarcely know what might be 'first principles,' 'unmediated terms,' and 'necessary propositions' for ourselves, much less for nature." The evidence of our confusion is everywhere, he adds: just look at the disagreements among the Skeptics, the Epicureans, and the Pythagoreans.[24] For Rainolds, dialectics replaces demonstration precisely because the rules and tools of rhetoric provide the individual with a means for evaluating and selecting among the competing choices that confront us in our lives. "Rhetoric," Rainolds reminds his readers, "does not create probabilities, but instead perceives them."[25]

Rhetoric may have provided the analytic and interpretive tools, but it was prudence, the practical intellect, that put those tools to use. Rainolds argues that prudence can apply dialectical techniques to practically any question, and even the most summary review of sixteenth- and seventeenth-century literature reveals that he was not alone in this belief. The French skeptic Pierre Charron argues that prudence "is a general guide and conduct of the other virtues, and of our whole life . . . in a word, the art of our life, as physic the art of our health."[26] A good thing this is, too, as our uncertainty about things extends far beyond the confines of natural philosophy. "[O]bserve how all mankind are made up of falsehood and deceit, of tricks and lies," Charron writes in his most famous work, *Of Wisdom*, "how unfaithful and dangerous, how full of disguise and design all conversation is at present become, but especially, how much more it abounds near [the prince], and how manifestly hypocrisy and dissimulation are the reigning qualities of princes' courts." Given "the great uncertainty and inconstancy of human affairs," the fickleness of human nature, and "the inexpressible variety of accidents, circumstances, appurtenances, dependencies and consequences, the difference of times and places and persons" that constantly surround and confront us, there can be few hard-and-fast rules to guide our conduct, few principles on which we can always rely.[27] In such circumstances, demonstration gives way to dialectic, and it is left to prudence, Charron contends, to determine when we ought to follow "established laws and customs in common use" and when we will be "obliged to go off the beaten road, and have recourse to difficult stratagems and unusual methods."[28]

In *The Book of the Courtier*, Castiglione would offer similar advice for similar reasons. Modeling his own dialogue on Cicero's skeptically tinged treatise *The Orator*, Castiglione leads his characters through a series of conversations that, in true rhetorical fashion, consider every question from both sides, generating doubt and a general distrust of first principles and dogmatic positions. Before embarking on his depiction of the ideal courtier, one of those characters, Count Ludovico, warns that "to recognize true perfection in anything is so difficult as to be scarcely possible; and this is because the way of opinions vary."[29] When it comes to questions of aesthetics, morals and ethics, not only do different people prefer different things, but even each change of circumstance requires its own unique response. During the second evening of discussion among the guests at the Court of Urbino another character, Federico, advises that "in everything he does or says" the perfect courtier should follow "certain general rules." Before speaking or acting, the courtier should match his words and deeds to the ever-changing demands of the moment. If he hopes to succeed, "he should consider well what he does or says, the place where he does it, in whose presence, its timing, why he is doing it, his own age, his profession, the end he is aiming at, and the means that are suitable."[30] Only through these careful dialectical and prudential calculations will the courtier be able to act in the most pleasing, the most useful, and most beneficial manner.

Beneficial for whom? The importance of early modern Europe's alleged rhetorical turn, historians contend, depends on how sixteenth- and seventeenth-century writers answered this question. Machiavelli's response is, no doubt, the most infamous, but he is really only the very representative tip of the proverbial iceberg. Machiavelli's valorization of a prudential politics is but one example of an alleged separation of prudence from not only its traditional religious but even its ethical moorings.[31] Confronted with the vagaries of fortune and a dangerous populace ("Men," Machiavelli famously notes, "are ungrateful, fickle simulators and deceivers, avoiders of dangers, greedy for gain"[32]), the prince must act in his own self-interest, and this might require dissimulation, hypocrisy, and lies. Life in the court was no different, and behind the urbane conversations of Castiglione's noble men and women is a constant awareness that the court is a dangerous place, full of intrigue, deception, and self-serving sycophants ceaselessly seeking their own success at another's expense. In this atmosphere, prudence becomes a tool of self-defense and self-interest, demarcating ever more clearly the courtier from his surroundings, his inner thoughts and intentions from his outward performance. Dissimulating one's thoughts, parrying dangerous and intrusive questions with ambiguous or witty responses, is the stock-in-trade of the successful courtier. In *The Book of the Courtier*, Gaspare Pallavicino fears that Federico reduces the courtier to a liar. Federico does little to dispel these concerns, adding that "even if it is deception it is not to be censured."[33]

From uncertainty to probability and from prudence to deception, historians trace a path that severs early modern Europe from its medieval past, leading us forward into a modernity that privileges the interior over the exterior, the individual over the community, utility over truth. Unfortunately, neither the path nor the destination were entirely new. Medieval writers knew all too well the perils of the court and how to respond to them. What changed between the twelfth and seventeenth centuries, between John of Salisbury and Castiglione, between Pierre Charron and Bernard Mandeville, was not the recognition that sometimes we must lie but rather the role that lies play in human society.

UNCERTAINTY AND SKEPTICISM IN THE MEDIEVAL COURT

In *The Treasure of the City of Ladies*, an early fourteenth-century handbook for women at court, Christine de Pizan considers the daily dangers that face the princess or noblewoman. Christine asks her readers to imagine the noble lady glorying in her position and possessions as she awakes in the morning wrapped in her luxurious bedding, in her well-appointed room, surrounded by her ladies-in-waiting. Temptation, always ready to seduce, whispers in her ear, "By Almighty God, is there in this world a greater lady than you or one with more authority?" Her vanity and pride begin to swell and soon, forgetful of who she is and how she should behave, she comes to believe there is nothing she does not require, no pleasure she should not satisfy. Temptation encourages her with more baseless compliments: "It's no more than your deserve."[34]

Christine undoubtedly understood the seductions of court life. Having grown up in and around the court of Charles V of France, first as the daughter of the king's physician, later as the wife of one of his courtiers, she would have witnessed, perhaps even experienced, them. In Christine's writings the court teems with danger, and the unwary noblewoman, filled with false and illusory promises of power, riches, and comfort, can all too easily plunge headlong into her own undoing. John of Salisbury had warned of precisely the same dangers in the *Policraticus* when he invoked his decidedly Platonic analogy to describe the courtier's relationship to the court. Just as the soul can all too easily lose itself to bodily sensations and "by a sort of self-betrayal go astray as the result of its desires amid the deceptions of the outer world," so too can the unwary courtier lose himself amidst the false delights of the court. Forgetful of his own interests and nature, he chases hungrily after tantalizing diversions and base pleasures, degrading himself so that man, who was made in the image of the Creator, "is transformed into a beast by a sort of similarity of character."[35]

Christine may well have read John's treatise, either in the original Latin or in the French translation that Charles V had requested from Denis Foulechat in the 1370s.[36] In any event, they speak with one voice when it comes to diagnosing and responding to the nature of court life. Both Christine and John describe the court as a place of deception in which the illusion of truth stands in for the truth itself, and at the heart of these illusions are the flatterers in all their treacherous variety. Whereas Plato stressed the dangers of sensation and warned his followers against those insidious pleasures and pains "that rivet the soul to the body and . . . weld them together,"[37] John stresses the dangers of language, of false words and feigned gestures. "One who is called flatterer in the strict sense of the word," John explains, "is he who whitewashes another's fault, and, that the latter may not see himself, spreads before the eyes of his victim a cloud, as it were, of vanity and fills his ears with encomiums."[38] Christine, likewise, warns her readers against accepting anyone at face value. "There is not the least doubt," she writes, "that according to the way of the world and the movements of fortune, there is no prince so grand in this world, however just he may be, nor was there ever a lord or lady or any other man or woman who was loved by everyone."[39] Even Jesus had so-called friends plotting his arrest and crucifixion, and the noble woman must never forget that behind even the kindest words and most innocuous asides there can lurk dishonesty and treachery, false counsel and pointed gossip.

Confronted with the ever-present threat of deception, both John and Christine counsel their readers to approach the court with a carefully cultivated caution and suspicion. While Christine simply assumes this approach throughout the *Treasure*, John elaborates its philosophical underpinning and justification when, in the prologue to the *Policraticus*, he proclaims his allegiance to the ancient Academic skeptics.[40] In a slightly earlier treatise, the *Metalogicon*, John aligns himself with a form of ancient Academic skepticism whose followers "do not precipitate an opinion concerning those questions that are doubtful to a wise man."[41] John associates this type of skepticism with Socrates's pupil Antisthenes, who distinguished between self-evident things and things known through experience. While we can know the former, our knowledge of the latter is never so secure. What we know through experience, what usually happens, John cautions, need not always happen. About these sorts of things, things that are credible if not certain, Antisthenes advised moderation in judgment and speech. We should restrain and qualify our words, adding phrases like "I believe" or "I think."[42] In the *Policraticus*, John refers to this sort of knowledge in terms of probability. "In philosophy," he writes, "accepting as I do the Academic system, I have admitted that which seems to the best of my judgment likely or probable." John claims that both Cicero and Augustine had ascribed to this cautious approach to human knowledge, recognizing that while there are some questions we cannot doubt, "no one speaks with greater safety who is circumspect in language just to guard himself from falling into error."[43]

Skepticism reveals apparent certainties to be mere probabilities. Probability, John explains in the *Metalogicon*, is one of the three branches of logic, "the science of argumentative reasoning."[44] Unlike demonstrative logic, which focuses on principles and "rejoices in necessity," and sophistry, whose "only objective is to lose its adversary in a fog of delusions," probable logic concerns itself with "propositions which, to all or to many men, or at least to the wise, seem to be valid."[45] Probable logic itself consists of two parts, dialectic and rhetoric. The difference between dialectic and rhetoric is one of focus and, perhaps, purpose.[46] Dialectic investigates and seeks answers to questions of a general nature. John offers an example drawn from the field of moral philosophy: "Is it better to obey one's parents or the laws when they disagree?" Unlike logical demonstrations, which begin with necessary first principles, the dialectical proof will begin with propositions or "theses" that themselves "are well known to all, or to the leaders in each field."[47] A dialectical proposition is probable if it "holds true in several cases," if it can counter most, even if not all, objections. By contrast, rhetoric analyzes particular cases. The orator will construct a persuasive speech based on hypotheses that derive from the circumstances. "Such circumstances," John adds, citing Boethius's *Topics*, "are: 'Who, what, where, by what means, why, how and when.'"[48]

We need the methods of dialectical and rhetorical analysis, John argues, because our knowledge of the world is limited, imperfect, sometimes confused, and too often wrong. Late in the *Metalogicon*, John serves up a list of impediments to human understanding that includes our invincible ignorance concerning the truths of faith, the frailty of the human condition, and the brevity of our lives. As serious as these obstacles are, none is more pernicious than sin, which "separates us from God, and bars us from the fountain of truth."[49] John's emphasis on the connection between sin and human ignorance places his entire discussion of skepticism in a decidedly theological framework. By the same token, it also allows John to conceive of sin, in its root causes at least, almost entirely in epistemological terms. We sin when we pursue idle and useless knowledge and claim to know with certainty things that lie beyond our understanding. Curiosity is a sin, John warns, and those pagan philosophers who occupied themselves with investigating the "hidden causes" of things became vain through their own fault. John repeats these warnings in the *Policraticus*, again citing the example of the pagan philosophers who "reared on high the structure . . . of their own genius in a war against heaven" only to find themselves unknowingly barred from truth.[50] Curiosity itself, however, is really more symptom than cause of our broken human condition. The pagan philosophers pursued their investigations beyond proper bounds because they forgot who and what they were. Having become mysteries to themselves, they thought they were wise when in fact they were fools. "When the mind is over-occupied with numerous questions that do not greatly concern it," John writes, "it wanders far afield from itself, and often becomes oblivious of itself and no error can be more pernicious than this."[51]

And so it is that John's skepticism returns him to the court with its flatterers and tempters, with its amnesiac courtiers and noblewomen forgetful of themselves, their stations, and their duties as they chase after false goods and fleeting pleasures. "Returns" may even be the wrong term. John's discussion of skepticism, demonstration, and dialectic never left the court. While John's stated purpose in the *Metalogicon* is to defend the traditional educational program of the liberal arts from a new breed of critic, he is quick to remind his readers that these critics are none other than his peers and opponents. "Utterly at a loss to evade the snapping teeth of my fellow members of the court," John contends that he had no choice but to respond to them in writing.[52] But John is defending more than a pedagogy and style of learning. He is defending his position at court. In the hothouse of the court, pedagogical attacks become personal attacks, and the personal is always already political. "Being respectful of all and injuring no one," John laments, "used, of yore, to assure one of popularity." Clearly the old ways have been forgotten, and with his status at court in question, John has no choice but to strike back against his enemies' daily carping.

John's desire to prevail in his own particular courtly squabbles is not sufficient, however, to motivate the *Metalogicon*'s composition. He is equally clear that his overarching philosophical ideas must be immediately relevant to life in the court. "Any pretext of philosophy," he explains, "that does not bear fruit in the cultivation of virtue and the guidance of one's conduct is futile and false."[53] John's skepticism, in other words, is more than a set of philosophical theorems. It is, as well, an antidote to the poisonous and deceptive atmosphere of the court, a technique of calculated suspicion and doubt, of wariness and care, that trains the individual to take nothing at face value. John's fourteenth-century translator, Denis Foulechat, took this to be the *Policraticus*'s main goal. Describing John's book as a guide to virtuous living, Foulechat contends that virtue requires wisdom, and true wisdom of the sort required by kings, princes, courtiers, and judges consists of two rules. "In the first book of the *Sophistical Refutations*," writes Foulechat, "the Philosopher notes that there are two works of wisdom: to speak the truth without lying about things that one knows and to be able to reveal the liar and his lies."[54] To hear Foulechat tell it, the good prince, like a lamb among wolves, is surrounded by innumerable "subtle liars" hiding under the facade of goodness and waiting for their moment to pounce. Unschooled in the ways of the world, the prince imagines that everyone acts only in terms of what is good and true. As a result, he is easily taken in, and "thinking that he preserves justice, destroys it and, when he wishes to please God, sins dearly."[55] Everything hinges on the good prince's ability to identify liars. He must be trained in the ways of the deceitful, must understand their plots, their secrets, their treasons, so that they will not lead him to his own self-destruction.[56]

It is the faculty of prudence, John contends, that bridges the divide between theory and practice and transforms philosophical skepticism into a strategy for courtly survival. Prudence takes up the tools of the "science of argumentative reasoning" and uses them to discern the truth or, failing that, to determine what is useful and probable when certainty is not possible. As a result, John connects prudence with wisdom, "whose fruit consists in the love of what is good and the practice of virtue."[57] Successfully distinguishing true goods from transitory pleasures has real consequences. The person who mistakes the transitory for the true, the apparent for the real, will find himself oppressed under the "yoke of vice." Enslaved to morbid desires like Cornificius, John's loudest critic, he will forget the teachings of philosophy in his mad pursuit of money, deeming "nothing sordid and inane, save the straits of poverty." He will, in short, become a flatterer. But having said this much, John cuts short his account of flatterers in the *Metalogicon*. "I will not discuss their ways here," he explains, "for my *Policraticus* delves into the latter at length, although it cannot hope to ferret out all their tricks, which would be beyond the powers of any mere human."[58]

ENTANGLED IN LEVIATHAN'S LOINS

The move from the *Metalogicon* to the opening books of the *Policraticus* certainly involves a shift in topics, from a defense of philosophy to a critique of the court, but it is something else as well. It also marks a shift in the deployment of prudence. In the *Metalogicon*, John defends the importance of dialectic with the tools of dialectical reasoning. He constructs arguments using probable theses, that is, theses approved and accepted by the wise. In the *Policraticus*, he does something different. He constantly moves from dialectic to rhetoric, from thesis to hypothesis, from general questions to specific instances. John himself signals this difference in the *Metalogicon*, with his brief allusion to the *Policraticus*. No one can spell out, account for, or predict all the deceptions, plots, and schemes of the courtiers. Their vanity and avarice know no limits, and the wise man, the man of eminence struggling against the illusory attractions of the court, must always be ready to adapt to each new challenge. Dialectics, with its reliance on generally approved principles, has its uses, but in the daily life of the court, the questions that confront us are always already "hedged in by a multitude of circumstances."[59] Rhetorical practice provides the tools the man of eminence needs to determine the best course of action, not in the abstract, not in most cases, but in this case, at this moment, against these opponents.

John is heavily indebted to Cicero for this conception of rhetoric. In *On Duties*, Cicero depicts the wise and honorable man as the perfect orator. Just as the orator must always match his words and gestures to the demands of the moment if he hopes to sway his audience's opinion, so must the honorable man always match his words and actions to the demands of the moment if he hopes to do the right thing. We do the right thing, Cicero argues, when we honorably and appropriately fulfill our duties. This requires a particular sort of knowledge. We cannot know what duty demands of us, what we should do or say in any given situation, unless we know who we are, and who we are, Cicero believes, requires an awareness of the two different roles with which Nature "dresses" us. The first role, Cicero writes, "is common, arising from the fact that we all have a share in reason and in the superiority by which we surpass brutes." In everything we do, we must always endeavor to act as rational creatures, tied with bonds of love and fellowship to our family and fellow citizens. The second role "is that assigned specifically to individuals." Each of us has different strengths and weaknesses, peculiarities of character. Some people are smarter, others stronger, still others are more or less humorous, forthright, or conniving.[60] We must consider these roles, what demands they place on us, what duties they require from us, so that we can meld our actions together in the most virtuous, seemly, and decorous manner possible. "All action," he adds, "should be free from rashness and carelessness; nor should anyone do anything for which he cannot give a persuasive justification: that is practically the definition of duty."[61] We must, as Cicero puts it, become "good calculators of our duties."[62]

Quite early on in the *Policraticus*, John adopts a version of Cicero's distinction between common and specific duties. "The principles of nature are binding upon all alike," John informs us, "considerations of duty, upon particular individuals."[63] Appropriate action for John, as for Cicero, depends on self-knowledge. The man of eminence must understand his boundaries, his limits and frailties. He must know "what is within him, what without, what below, what above, what opposite, what before, and what after."[64] Tellingly, John also suggests that he must understand and adapt to the specific contexts in which he seeks this knowledge. Immediately before embarking on his critique of flatterers, John distinguishes between two kinds of self-knowledge, the knowledge we acquire through faith and the knowledge we acquire through learning. While faith trumps learning in the long run, learning cannot be ignored. "Let the rule of faith be deferred," John writes, "as it will be discussed in its own time and place. Learning then involves knowledge of self, which cannot be attained if it fails to measure its own strength or if it is ignorant of the strength of others."[65]

John's skepticism compels him, as it would John Rainolds in the sixteenth century, to adopt a fundamentally rhetorical orientation toward the world. "Those things are of doubtful validity," John writes, "which are supported by authority of neither faith, sense or apparent reasons and which in their main points lean towards either side." While at first this might sound as if it holds open the possibility for quite a bit of certainty about things, John's subsequent list of doubtful subjects rather quickly quashes any such hope. We can have no certainty, he tells us, concerning providence, "the substance, quantity, power, efficacy and the origin of the soul," nor about fate and free will. Nor do we possesses any certainty about an increasingly vast array of moral and ethical matters such as "the use, beginning and end of all virtues and vice, whether everyone who possesses one virtue possesses all, or whether all sins are equal and to be punished equally." Human ingenuity is also at a loss when it comes to determining the status of "duties and the various kinds of situations which arise in reference to agreements and quasi agreements; to misdemeanors and quasi misdemeanors or to other matters."[66] Lacking universally binding first and certain principles to serve as regulative ideals in guiding our behavior, we are forced to make do with merely probable theses, whose applicability to any given situation is always open to modification depending on the ever-changing situation at hand.

The significance of John's adoption of a rhetorical approach to the world and ethics in the *Policraticus*'s opening books appears in a variety of guises. More often than not, it shows up when John suggests that generally accepted ethical principles be modified or ignored in certain situations. John, for example, goes on at length about the indignity of hunting, referencing such authorities as Horace, Valerius Maximus, scripture, and the Church fathers. Hunting, he informs us, debases noble natures, rendering hunters worse than peasants and barely on par with the animals themselves. Toward the end of this diatribe which, for all intents and purposes, forms something like a dialectical argument from probable principles against hunting, John adopts a rhetorical mode of analysis. Is hunting necessarily bad? Not at all. While it is all too often abused, considered on its own it is a morally indifferent activity. "Therefore," John concludes, "it is quite possible, depending upon the circumstances, time, manner, individual, and purpose, for hunting to be a useful and honorable occupation."[67] John performs precisely the same move from dialectical to rhetorical analysis when he considers gambling, an activity to be abhorred, "in which one becomes more depraved in proportion as his skill in it increases."[68] This probable moral thesis notwithstanding, John then argues that there is nothing wrong with gambling given the proper circumstances. John writes, "The circumstances that regulate all freedom from restraint are dependent upon a preceding consideration of place, time, individual, and cause. It is this consideration which makes all transactions appear beautiful or condemns them as morally ugly. In each individual case many roles are to be considered since nature, situation, and fortune each invests a man with its own garb and from these he must choose that which in his own case is becoming."[69] Circumstances, when properly concatenated, can override even the most probable of probable theses.

While few would object to the occasional hunt or roll of the dice, John applies his rhetorical ethics to other, more morally dubious endeavors. Having raged against the flatterers throughout most of the *Policraticus*'s third book, John asks, in the final chapter, if there is anyone the man of eminence is allowed to flatter. John answers, famously, yes. "It is lawful to flatter him whom it is lawful to slay," he writes, "and it is not merely lawful to slay a tyrant but even just and right."[70] And so, there are special circumstances in which flattery itself becomes morally appropriate. While the flattery and assassination of tyrants is the most extreme case John considers, the power of circumstances to free us from normal moral restraints against flattery and lying shows up in numerous places throughout the early sections of the *Policraticus*. Midway through his discussion of flatterers, John abruptly and without warning offers some surprisingly underhanded tips. "The art of flattery," he writes, "is very effective when you appear to be negligent of your own interests and attend to those of others; speaking of your own profit never or rarely, but always, or at least often, of his whose favor you are currying."[71] Several pages later, he adds, "If you are ambitious to outstrip those who are lavish with promises and gifts, in the esteem of him with whom you are currying favor, you should associate yourself with his financial secrets. . . . You must worm your way into his secrets at any cost."[72] No doubt these are exceptions to standard moral principles, but they are legitimate exceptions made acceptable by the circumstances.

John is in no way suggesting anything like a moral free-for-all in which the man of eminence can justify any action whatsoever through recourse to difficult circumstance. Each of us has our duties, our role to fulfill, the moral "garb" that fits us best, and those duties, to ourselves, our fellows, our state, and to God, must determine how we act at any given moment.[73] In normal circumstances, perhaps these decisions are easy and recourse to standard and generally accepted moral principles can successfully guide us. Unfortunately, the court, perhaps this entire fallen world, is no normal place. Self-serving duplicitous courtiers ("those whose intercourse is not in the heavens," as John describes them at one point) surround and attempt to deceive us. To people like these, John contends, we can afford neither "affection nor friendship."[74] John often describes the world as a comedy or tragedy, a stage play in which people have taken on false roles. Just as often, he invokes metaphors of combat and warfare. If negotiating one's way through the world of the court is akin to combat, then the rules of combat apply, and John wholly approves the use of *strategemmata*, cunningly wrought military deceptions, in overcoming our enemies.[75]

Medieval canon lawyers and theologians had a word for the epistemological condition associated with these sorts of impossibly confused types of ethical conundrums: they called it "perplexity." Court writers from at least as early as the twelfth century and continuing without interruption for the next six or seven hundred years consistently depict the world as a place in which the individual is in a near-constant state of moral perplexity, in which uncertainty proliferates with every chance encounter, leaving the individual with no morally pure alternatives. Sometimes we must sin to avoid greater sins, to achieve some great good, or prevent some great harm, and sometimes we must sin simply to avoid incurring displeasure, anger, or social embarrassment. In his *Decretum*, the great legal treatise from the mid-twelfth century, the Bolognese canon lawyer Gratian, drawing on ideas from Gregory the Great and others, suggested that we do indeed face such moments of perplexity when, say, we are caught between lying or breaking an oath. In such cases, Gratian contends, when "an inescapable danger compels us to perpetrate one of two evils, we must choose the one that makes us less guilty." The glossators whose commentary accompanies Gratian's work, as well as Thomas Aquinas, argue that such moments of moral perplexity are entirely subjective, "arising only in the mind and from foolish opinion."[76] The glossators assume that any and all moral perplexities can be resolved through analysis of the situation and the options it presents, even if the sinless choice with which we are left is a difficult one.

Gratian, by contrast, seems to assume that the world itself is morally ambiguous, offering us few good options, fewer certainties, and all too many situations that require us to sin, if only to avoid worse sins. This is what it means to live east of Eden, in the Devil's world. Gratian quotes Gregory to describe our predicament. "The sinews of the Leviathan's loins are entangled because the purpose of his suggestions is entangled with tangled devices," he writes. "Thus, many commit sins because hoping to avoid one, they cannot escape the snare of another."[77] In response to Gratian's depiction of a morally perplexed world, the glossators assert the existence of a world whose moral contours are much more clearly delineated. "It must be stated," they write, "that no one can really be in doubt between two evils in this way. For it would then follow that necessity can make one do something evil. But the canons say that God will never punish anyone unless he has done wrong voluntarily."[78] But this is Gratian's point entirely: the world itself generates profound moral dilemmas, leaving us with no choice but to sin. "When there are walls on all sides," he writes in a memorable metaphor, "and the way of escape is closed to prevent flight, the one fleeing throws himself off where the wall is lowest."[79]

While the entire courtly tradition would share Gratian's vision of a morally perplexed world, it would reject his belief that when necessity compels us to choose the lesser evil, we are still guilty of sin.[80] For John, the uncertainties the man of eminence faces justify deceptive ruses and tricks. Lies beget lies, and in the *Policraticus*'s prologue, John simply notes the wisdom of the psalmist's observations that "every man is a liar."[81] Occasionally, John will deplore lies and mendacity. More often than not, he ignores Augustine's well-known prohibitions and theses against lying, never mentioning them once, while admitting that he himself has had recourse to lies when it has suited his purposes.[82] In the *Entheticus*, his poetic account of twelfth-century pedagogy and life in the court, John argues that "that deception is good which effects benefits, and by which joys, life and salvation are looked after." The man of eminence must be all things to all people, feigning many things, to draw the sinful from their sins. Often, there is simply no other way. "The work of infiltration," John notes, again invoking the language of combat and espionage, "recalls from vices those whom simple reason cannot recall."[83]

CHRISTINE DE PIZAN AND JUST HYPOCRISY

Christine de Pizan's *Treasure of the City of Ladies* is a decidedly more practical and streamlined work than anything John ever wrote. A handbook to teach noblewomen how to negotiate the complicated personal, social, and political challenges of early fifteenth-century France, Christine simply assumes John's entire philosophical and rhetorical framework as she plunges her readers into the maelstrom of the medieval court. Christine is quite up-front and unabashed about her work's this-worldly orientation, and much of it is given over to the lessons of "Worldly Prudence," whose "teachings and admonitions are not separate from those of God, but come from them and are based on them." With her valorization of worldly prudence, Christine rejects those who would utterly condemn the active life in favor of a life of religious seclusion and prayer. There are two paths to God, Christine writes, the contemplative and the active, and while the contemplative life is the better life, the life most agreeable to God, the active life "has more use in the world."[84] Utility, as it turns out, has its value both here and in heaven. "It does not displease God," Christine writes, "for a person to live in this world morally, and if she lives morally she will love the blessing of a good reputation, which is honor." Even Augustine, Christine adds, had warned that to live well a person needs both a good conscience and a "good reputation."[85] Christine not only links morality to the possession of a good reputation, she also emphasizes their interconnection. While living morally results in a good reputation, successfully maintaining one's good reputation is a sign of moral worth.

Honor and good reputation, Christine notes, have little if anything to do with worldly riches and everything to do with "good manners and behavior."[86] In order to live an honorable life, Worldly Prudence suggests the noblewoman obey two overarching principles. She must carefully organize her daily activities in order to increase her standing in the court, and she must maintain a constant vigilance over her behavior.[87] Nothing should be taken for granted, and her every activity must be calculated to achieve its maximum effect. Each day, she should rise early, say her prayers, and attend morning mass. Religious devotion, important though it is for our spiritual well-being, must be made to serve practical ends as well. "This lady will have such a good, orderly system," Christine elaborates, "that as she leaves her chapel there will be some poor people at the door to whom she herself with humility and devotion will give alms from her own hands." She will deal with her daily duties carefully and thoughtfully, surrounding herself with wise counselors, and later, when she has free time, she will share in useful activities with other women and girls, laughing and engaging with them so that "they will love her with all their hearts."[88] When it comes to her behavior, she will obey the counsel of sobriety, which governs how much she should sleep, drink, and eat. It will help her dress properly, and it will "correct, chastise and control the mouth and the speech of the wise lady." Most important, sobriety will teach the princess to "hate with all her heart the vice of lying. She will love truth, which will be so habitually in her mouth that people will believe what she says and have confidence in her as one has in a lady whom one has never heard lie."[89]

Christine's condemnation of lying, much like John of Salisbury's condemnation some 250 years earlier, is decidedly flexible. Prudent behavior cannot consist in blind obedience to general principles, if only because principles in this perplexing world can all too easily come into conflict with other principles. This becomes clear when Christine turns from Prudence's two overarching principles to seven additional "teachings which, according to Prudence, are necessary to those who wish to live wisely and wish to have honor." The first of these is that every lady must "love her husband and live in peace with him, or otherwise she will have already discovered the torments of Hell."[90] Easy advice to follow when her husband is devoted to her, but not all husbands are kind, nor faithful. Christine acknowledges these possibilities only to stress that what matters is the woman's honor and good reputation, and these require that she always maintain a facade of devotion to her husband. Imagine he has strayed into an affair with another woman. If there is nothing the princess can do to end it, Christine writes, "she must put up with all this and dissimulate wisely, pretending that she does not notice it and that she truly does not know anything about it."[91] While Christine says little in this case about how far such dissimulation should go, whether the woman should quietly feign ignorance or go so far as to deny verbally any knowledge of the affair when others ask about it, the justification for such less than forthright behavior is never in doubt—to act otherwise is to risk angering her husband. "He will perhaps leave you," she writes, "and people will mock you all the more and believe shame and dishonor, and it may be still worse for you."[92]

What at first remains implicit soon becomes explicit. In the fourth lesson, Worldly Prudence warns that the envious are everywhere, and the better and more virtuous a person is, the more her enemies gather round to bring her down with their plots and schemes, their murmurings and gossip. Christine, echoing her advice concerning adulterous husbands, recommends that the good lady pretend not to notice these people and to continue to treat them as friends. Christine's advice then becomes much more specific. The princess must appear to defer to them and to seek their advice "in confidential meetings (as she will pretend them to be), where she will tell them ordinary things with a great show of secrecy and confidence and keep her real thoughts to herself."[93] If a friend should warn her that these people are out to seek her ruin, she will rebuke the informer and assert that far from being enemies, they are her closest friends. All this must be done with great show and calculation. She will make every effort to appear simple and ignorant of their schemes. "But in spite of all of these things and her great dissimulations," Christine writes, "she will watch them as carefully as she can and stay on her guard."[94]

Throughout *The Book of the Three Virtues*, Christine recommends the deployment of deception, dissimulation, and lies as weapons for warding off the attacks of the envious while simultaneously allowing the princess to maintain the demeanor of a good and honorable lady. It is tempting to read all this with something of a cynical slant and to imagine that Christine is more concerned with the mere appearance of honor and virtue than with their reality. As a result, it might seem that she effectively collapses the distinction between moral worth and a good reputation in such a way that, for all intents and purposes, moral worth is nothing but the possession of a good name, no matter how she achieves and sustains it. The practical nature of *The Book of Three Virtues* adds to this impression. If the princess wishes to win over her husband's friends and family so that they will protect her from her enemies and come to her aid in difficult times, she must honor and praise them. The evidence of this sort of behavior, Christine writes, "will give still greater proof of the love and loyalty that she has for her husband."[95] To make these actions even more effective, Christine writes at another point, the lady "will want her behavior to be apparent and known to everyone and not at all kept secret."[96] It is only through such words and actions that people develop their opinions about us. "One cannot judge the intention of good people," Christine notes, "except by their deeds, which if they are good testify to a good person, and vice versa."[97] Whether or not you love your husband, respect his family, or feel any goodwill toward the poor and those around you in court, pretend that you do, and your place will be secure.

Good deeds serve as witness to a person's character, but deeds can be faked, intentions hidden. Christine admits as much and advises women to exploit such possibilities when necessary in order to protect themselves and their good name. She even recognizes how difficult this work of self-suppression and concealment can be because it requires the lady "to master and correct [her] own heart and will," and that "is a thing beyond nature." She must act against her natural inclinations to be honest. Still, it is worth the trouble because "it is a sign of very great strength and steadfastness of heart, which is one of the most excellent cardinal virtues."[98] Again and again, Christine emphasizes, not simply the practical necessity of this behavior, but also its moral and religious importance. Survival matters, but it is not an end in itself, and Christine tries to restrict the range of acceptable duplicitous behavior through the ties that link the active life with God's "teachings and admonitions." The woman who serves God through the active life leads a life of charity, and for the princess this means she must strive to "be the means of peace and concord."[99] Unlike men, who by nature are more courageous and hotheaded, women are more timid and of a sweeter disposition, Christine explains, "and for this reason, if they are wise and if they wish to, they can be the best means of pacifying men."[100]

Christine introduces the role of the princess as peacekeeper when discussing how the honorable princess should work to defuse those tensions that can lead to war, but it is clear that it is a more general principle that frames her entire conception of the woman's social function. The noblewoman, for example, must act as an intermediary between the poor and her husband, winning their trust and, in so doing, curtailing potential riots and civil unrest. Her behavior toward her husband and the envious can likewise be translated into this higher register of creating peace and concord. Both her genuine concern for her husband and, if the situation should arise, feigned ignorance of his sexual dalliances work to establish domestic peace and a setting in which she can continue to act as a moderating element in his governance of the state. Pretending friendship with the envious does something similar. By refusing to acknowledge their ill will, the princess avoids potential quarrels and arguments, keeps her friends from becoming involved in injurious affairs, and forestalls the possibility that her husband, learning of her enemies, might side with them.[101] If people are judged by their external signs, it seems all the clearer that the truest proof of the princess's honor and good reputation will be in her effect on the state, the fruit of her works of charity, and in her promotion of peace and harmony.[102]

While the larger goal of civic charity both justifies and sets limits on the noblewoman's actions, Christine admits her advice poses problems, possibly serious problems. Nowhere is this more clear than when she presents the fifth teaching of Worldly Prudence. The noblewoman must cultivate the goodwill not only of the barons and aristocracy but also of the middle classes and the common people. The friendship and admiration of these people will profit her in a variety of ways. They will include her in their prayers, praise her in their sermons and, if the need arise, "their voices and words can be a shield and defense against the rumors and reports of her slanderous enemies and can negate them."[103] To gain their favor, the lady should socialize and meet amiably with intelligent and influential members of the clergy. Whenever possible, she should make sure that her acts of charity and almsgiving are made public and recorded "in perpetual memory on tablets in their churches so that the people will pray to God for her."[104]

A thin, perhaps vanishing line separates these recommendations from sheer hypocrisy. A hypocrite, according to long-accepted definition, is a person who makes excessive show "through genuflections and prayers" of virtues they lack. The hypocrite is more concerned with how others perceive her, with the public acclaim and belief in her virtue, than with actually being virtuous.[105] Christine acknowledges how perilously close her advice comes to advocating hypocrisy and that she may, in fact, actually be endorsing it. "It may seem," Christine writes, "that she has a small streak of hypocrisy or that she is getting a name for it, yet it may be called a 'just hypocrisy,' for it strives towards the good and the avoidance of evil."[106] There is danger here because the very actions needed to secure her reputation and good name are the same sorts of actions that can undo all she has achieved. It doesn't take much for "just hypocrisy" to look like hypocrisy plain and simple. "We repeat," Christine concludes, "that this kind of 'just hypocrisy' is almost necessary, especially to princes and princesses who must rule over others and to whom more reverence is due than to other people."[107]

Lies will always be lies, but for Christine, as for John, in this fallen world context and circumstance can render them virtuous, praiseworthy, and pleasing to God.

FROM LIES TO CIVILITY

With their advocacy of the well-timed lie, the pious fraud, and just hypocrisy, both John of Salisbury and Christine de Pizan completed the intellectual journey from uncertainty to probability to deception that so many early modern thinkers would make. What they discovered is remarkably similar. John and Christine, not to mention Peter Damian, Peter of Blois, and Alain Chartier, all stress the epistemological dangers of the court, how it overflows with liars and deceivers, spewing verbal illusions that make it all too easy for the courtier to lower his guard as he eases into a life of indolence and for the noblewoman to expect the fulfillment of her every passing whim. In both cases, they mistake the false for the true, the illusion for reality. These mistakes matter. Identifying themselves with what appears, they dress themselves in the garb of truth's simulacrum and become someone else, someone they are not, debased, degraded, endangered. If courtly life is a struggle waged on the battlefield of our fallen world, as John of Salisbury would have it, then it is a struggle in which the possibility of deception must always already be assumed, and this assumption profoundly shapes how we must think about ourselves and others. Constantly on guard against his peers' countless plots and schemes, the courtier cannot help but be aware that menacing and unknown secrets may well lie veiled behind smiling faces. By the same token, how can he not be aware of his own secrets, the difference between his unspoken intentions and his outward appearance, as he assumes misleading and false gestures to mask his goals from those around him? Deception becomes the only remedy against deception. John explicitly signals this distinction between surface and depth, appearance and reality, not to mention the need to exploit it in one's own self-defense, in the Platonic analogy with which he begins and frames the *Policraticus*. Just as the soul must be separated from the body, so must the man of eminence keep his distance from the world and its seductive temptations.

To many amused early modern observers, courtiers were more than happy to erase the line between appearance and reality in their eager rush toward self-interested sycophancy and flattery. In his 1547 satire of court life, *The Philosopher of the Court*, Philibert de Vienne gleefully contrasts the philosophers of old with the newest crop of courtiers. Unlike philosophers who, in the manner of the Stoics, believe that they must search out secrets hidden deep in the nature of things and invisible to the eye, courtiers attend only to surfaces, "to little civilities and good facades."[108] While ancient philosophers stressed that if we follow nature and the dictates of natural reason we can avoid doing evil, the courtier seeks only to do what is seemly and decorous.[109] Indeed, Philibert claims that to be prudent simply means to be seemly, to be able to do what needs to be done, like playing the lute, the guitar, the harp or the harpsichord, the violin or the lyre, or knowing any of a dozen styles of dance.[110] Should we master the expectations and etiquette of courtly life, all our actions will be "honest and virtuous and we will be judged to be wise, prudent and full of knowledge." For virtue, Philibert announces, is nothing other than "to live after the manner of court." What is the practical consequence of the courtier's philosophy? In language that could have been lifted directly from the pages of Peter Damian and Alain Chartier, Philibert writes, "The gentleman courtier is not subject to himself; if it is necessary to laugh, he laughs, if it is necessary to grieve, he cries, if it is necessary to eat, he eats and if it is necessary to fast, he fasts."

He will, in short, do whatever is necessary to please his company, even if it goes against his own desires. Without the teachings of this philosophy, Philibert assures his readers, a person will not be able to fool and deceive even the simplest of minds.[111]

Philibert's satire hit close enough to home that at least some of his readers, including his English translator, mistook it for a serious guide to courtly life and success.[112] Their mistake is easy enough to forgive, since the real things were ever quick to stress the importance of conforming oneself to others. In *The Refin'd Courtier*, his self-described English "paraphrase" of Giovanni della Casa's immensely popular 1558 treatise *Galateo: Or, the Rules of Polite Behavior*, Nathaniel Walker emphasizes that a man must know how to manage his life so that "in his *familiar* intercourse with others, he may gain a reputation of a *neat*, and an *amiable*, and a *well-manner'd* person; which truly is either really a virtue, or else for its resemblance very near of kin to it."[113] To these ends, Walker advises his readers that it is "meet whatsoever you are, to frame and compose your self and actions, not according to your *own private* Will and Fancy, but according to the prescriptions and Garbs of *those* among whom it is your lot to live." Perceiving the satirical excesses to which such counsel might lead, he cautions, "Not that you are *entirely* to resign your Freedom to the imperious dictates of other men, but that, by no means affecting Singularity, you should yield a ready Compliance in all things which are *indifferent*, still retaining a due respect to your own native right and Liberty." It is a matter of learning how to "demean ourselves acceptably" before our superiors, without appearing willing "to lick the very spittle from under their feet."[114]

Maintaining one's self-respect and identity in an environment designed to reduce its inhabitants to the level of groveling yes-men was undoubtedly a challenge for the early modern courtier, and it was far from the only one. Walker returns to an age-old theme later in his treatise when he addresses the dangers of flattery, "a disease that *reigns* in the *Courts* of *Kings*." Walker warns that "*Flattery* fills us with *wind* and *corruption* till we *burst*, and a strong gust of *underserved applause* quite overturns and ruins us, if we are not well-balast'd." Suddenly switching metaphors to give full scope to the true horrors of this dread practice, he compares it to a "*subtil poison* [that] steales *insensibly* into the very bones, and drinks up the marrow and yet never breaks the skin, but pleases it with a soft gentle touch."[115] Stefano Guazzo, who served as a diplomat for the ruling Gonzaga family of Mantua, agreed with Walker and in very similar terms. In his 1574 fictional dialogue *Civil Conversation*, Guazzo has his brother William, who has grown cynical about courtly society, warn his interlocutor, the doctor Anniball Magnocavalli, of flatterers whose words are like an infected breath that "poisons the very souls of those who hearken to them."[116] If Walker's advice was to avoid these liars at all costs, Anniball realizes this is much easier said than done. "It is very difficult, not to say impossible," to distinguish a friend from a flatterer, he replies to William, because "an artful Flatterer puts the garment so artificially on the back of him whom he would disguise with it, that the seams shall not be discerned; and works up his false material so curiously that you can scarce know them from what are real and genuine."[117] Perhaps we can identify some of the flatterers but certainly not all, and even the ones we identify may have fooled everyone else, secretly assaulting us while successfully maintaining a good reputation.

Left with few good options, many individuals sought to hide in plain sight. At the very beginning of the first chapter of his treatise *On Honest Dissimulation*, for example, Torquato Accetto, a seventeenth-century secretary to the rulers of Andria in Southern Italy, recalls Adam and Eve's predicament during that fatal moment in the Garden. "From the instant the first man opened his eyes and realized he was naked," Accetto writes, "he was concerned to hide himself from the view of his Creator, thus the effort to conceal was born with the world itself and the appearance of the first fault." Adam's concerns are still our own, Accetto adds, and there are many people who now try to hide themselves "by means of dissimulation."[118] Accetto, about whom almost nothing is known, who published his book in Naples in 1641 to no critical notice whatsoever, counts himself among the dissimulators. The secretary, who for all intents and purposes remained invisible until his work was rediscovered in the early twentieth century, could not have intended a more fitting historical and literary legacy. The dissimulator, aware of the dangers and lies that surround him, endeavors to slip from view, to vanish even as he interacts with those around him. Dissimulation, Accetto notes at one point in his brief treatise, is a "trade that consists in not revealing things as they are." To accomplish this a person must set up "a veil made of honest shadows and violent courtesies" to deflect unwanted attention and to conceal himself from prying and intrusive inquiries until the time is right to respond to them. Nature behaves no differently, Accetto adds, obscuring things at night that it illuminates during the day.[119]

Accetto steps back from openly claiming to endorse dishonesty, arguing that it is "never licit to abandon the truth." Drawing on a standard distinction, he contrasts dissimulation with its evil doppelganger, simulation. "One simulates what is not," Accetto explains, and "one dissimulates what is."[120] This was as much a truism as any other in the early modern period, and even before. Thomas Aquinas had invoked it in the thirteenth century to explain how concealing what is true differs from pretending something false, and biblical exegetes had long found it useful as a way to distinguish the Devil's simulating serpentine disguise in the Garden from Christ's dissimulating decision to conceal his divinity within a human body.[121] Just like these earlier usages, Accetto's own examples suggest that dissimulation always maintains an uneasy relationship with the morally questionable activity of simulation, of pretending to be something you are not, of deceiving, lying. He asks his readers to consider a scene from the first book of Virgil's *Aeneid*. A savage storm has destroyed all but seven Trojan ships, which now limp into a natural harbor on the Libyan coast. Aeneas speaks to his men, hoping to rally their sagging spirits. Virgil writes, "His face feigned hope, but his heart hid a profound sadness." Aeneas conceals and dissimulates his misery with a show of hope, but the show inevitably requires pretending to be something one is not. "This verse," Accetto explains, "contains the simulation of hope and the dissimulation of sadness." It is impossible, it would seem, to dissimulate something without simulating something else in its place, to conceal one thing without pretending another. These two practices become yet more intertwined in Accetto's second example, this time taken from late in Homer's *Odyssey*, when Ulysses, disguised beneath rags and pretending to be the great grandson of King Midas, speaks with his unsuspecting wife Penelope, reducing her to tears with an elaborate and fictitious story about her long-lost husband. Accetto quotes Homer: "Ulysses contemplated his wife's misery; but without a flutter of his lids, his eyes seemed like horn or iron; for his ruse to work, it was necessary that he hide his own tears."[122] Accetto marvels over the prudence with which Ulysses places a check on his own tears at the very moment they need to be hid, but Accetto pretends to be something he is not as well.

Accetto simulates throughout his treatise. He confesses as much in the prefatory letter when he writes, "A year ago this treatise was three times as large as the one you see today, and many people know this; but if I had wanted to delay still more before handing it over to the printer, it would have been in a way reduced to nothing due to the many wounds which destroyed, rather than enriched it." Those who remember the original text, he adds, will all to easily recognize the "scars" that mark the places where he has amputated parts of his treatise.[123] Of course, it was the nurse Eurycleia who recognized Ulysses under his disguise of rags when she noticed his childhood scar, and Accetto's recounting of Ulysses's meeting with Penelope bears its own scars, excising the very line that describes Homer's assessment of the kind of words that make up Ulysses's tear-inducing story: "He made all these lies sound so convincing."[124] Ulysses's prudence puts over the lie, and without the lie the prudent restraint of tears would have been for nothing. The slippage from dissimulation to simulation appears again in Accetto's treatise when he contrasts the two practices. He would have happily examined the art of simulation, explaining fully the art of pretending in those cases where it seems to be necessary, but he opts not to, not because it is sinful and tantamount to lying, but merely because "it has a reputation so horrible, that I judged it best to abstain from such a discussion, although there are any number of people who say, 'That person does not know how to live, who does not know how to pretend.'"[125]

If Accetto preferred to conceal the potentially mendacious nature of the practices he found necessary to live a safe and happy life, Guazzo's characters freely admit them, offering advice that has much in common with Christine's advice to her female readers. Surrounded by flatterers and liars, identified or not, Anniball argues that we must conceal our knowledge and suspicions for fear that acting otherwise will make things worse for us. Even if it "goes against your conscience to keep them company," he states, do not call them out if their reputation at court is good. The court judges people on their appearances, and to condemn an apparently reputable person will appear rude, utterly uncalled for, and deserving of "public censure."[126] Returning to this predicament a few pages later, he observes that "without doubt that man is mistaken, who thinks he may lawfully despise or ridicule any, besides those that are notedly scandalous and who therefore deserve it."[127] Given the constraints of courtly life, Anniball counsels a practice of strategic feigning in which we "salute those, who, we imagine are our Enemies." Invoking a variety of military metaphors to justify these deceptions, as had John of Salisbury before him, he compares this tactical dissembling to fencers who pretend to aim at the head in order to wound the leg or to the "Generals of armies who deceive the enemy, when, by making a feint of attacking one way, they fall upon them another." There is nothing wrong with this sort of mendacity, he argues, and then rather suddenly adds, and "not only among enemies, but among friends and acquaintances, colourable dealings are tolerable, when they are not prejudicial in their consequences." This is why, for example, it is perfectly acceptable to lie to a friend in order to avoid his invitation to attend a play in which you have little interest.[128] Although Anniball condemns liars as "impudent and shameless," as so many had and would continue to do, he carefully qualifies his disdain. "I readily own, that on some particular occasions, a lie may be necessary, and even commendable, if it be for some honest purpose."[129] As his own examples demonstrate, honest purposes need hardly be important ones.

If Walker's condemnation of lies and liars at first seems more robust than that of Guazzo's characters by the time he finishes with his own qualifications, there is little difference between the two authors. The truth, Walker asserts, is the "beginning of Heroical virtue," whereas lies are as unreasonable and ugly "as the shadows of the night." They are squalid and deformed, not to mention "a violation of that tacit universal contract of Mankind implied in all their commerce and intercourses."[130] Without missing a beat, he then admits in true courtly fashion that lies have their time and place. "But I would not be thought over rigid," he continues, "doubtless we may speak untruths in some cases." We can lie to children for their benefit, as can doctors to their patients. We can commit "pious frauds" on the impious to draw them to the true faith, and we can lie to save lives. Walker justifies these exceptions as consistent with religious virtue. "Charity is better than Truth," he explains, "and every man is willing to be cozen'd into his own advantage."[131] Christine de Pizan would not have disagreed, and suddenly the exclusive requirement for truth in human affairs, in our commerce and intercourses, appears much less certain. Truth might be a heroic virtue, but too much truth can be a dangerous thing, and ignoring the demands of charity might be even worse. In a fallen world, in the world of the court, deception, duplicity, and dishonesty are natural and naturally useful qualities, perfectly fitted to our benefit and the benefit of others.

Walker invokes charity to justify his lies, and Guazzo insistently reiterates the need for the courtier to be a good Christian. Still, something other than, something in addition to, religion seems to be at work in their conception of proper courtly behavior, be it honest or dishonest. Walker refers to it as "refinement," the thing that delights the "greatest part of mankind" and that requires knowing "what is fit to be done, and also what to be avoided, to render our conversation sweet and gracefull."[132] For his part, Guazzo, true to the title of his treatise, calls it "civil conversation," that is, "an honest, virtuous, and sociable kind of living in the world."[133] French writers in the seventeenth century would convert this notion of courteous behavior into the ideal of the *honnête homme*. However termed, all these writers believe that the courtier's actions and words must be "comely and amiable," and even if they do not "gratify the senses," at the very least they must not "trouble any of them."[134] Not only must the courtier always imagine himself on display, he must adapt that display, his words and actions, to the expectations of his courtly audience, for only their approval will guarantee that he is refined, civil, and virtuous. Nearly a century later, François duc de La Rochefoucauld would capture this notion of the refined courtier perfectly when he succinctly noted, "To be willing to live continuously under the eyes of gentlemen is to be a gentleman indeed."[135]

While medieval courtiers were no less interested in their appearance and in how people responded to them, the early modern emphasis on refinement reflects a repositioning of the role that deceit plays in society. Both Christine and John contend that exceptional circumstances require exceptional measures, and sometimes for our own good and the good of our family and the state we must lie. To hear Christine tell it, princesses and noblewomen might spend much of their lives in such dire straits, carefully orchestrating a litany of daily hypocrisies to keep their enemies at bay. Be that as it may, princesses and noblewomen are, by any estimation, exceptional figures, so it should not be all that surprising that they spend their lives doing exceptional things. In this respect, early modern writers were no different, fully recognizing the just use of lies to stave off threats to oneself, one's family, even one's state. But they recognized something else as well—without lies, society could not exist. La Rochefoucauld captured this insight in his collection of maxims: "Social life would not last long if men were not taken in by each other."[136] While lies might occasionally threaten civil society, they also make it possible.

Walker, with at least a pretense of reluctance, highlights society's dependence on lies, large and small, in the opening pages of *The Refin'd Courtier*. Having ranked the demand for charity above the demand for truth, and thus justifying the occasional lie, he adds, "But this is to be understood warily and practiced with a great deal of sober caution, according to the comedian's rule, only when truth produces an insufferable mischief; and in that case it is pardonable, not laudable and noble."[137] Of course, the entire point of his handbook is to demonstrate that crass and "unrefined" behavior is the very essence of insufferable mischief. The only way to avoid being insufferable is to adopt the appearance civil society demands, whether honestly or deceptively. For his part, Guazzo suggests the social necessity for deception when William recommends the courtier employ flattery to make his mark in the world. "The world is full of and subsists by flattery, which is more in fashion than peeked beards and large ruffs," he explains to Anniball. "You see how all persons for the sake of peace, and to avoid contention, and that they may appear agreeable in company, comport themselves in the best manner they can to other men's talk and behavior."[138] And, as one example among others, he describes how parents "flatter their children to encourage them in virtue." While Anniball refuses to let anything good be said about flattery, he accomplishes this through an arbitrary redefinition of terms that does nothing to undermine its social importance. When good intentions accompany our flattery, we do not flatter so much as feign. When we overly praise our children "for some trifling action that is not worth notice," we cannot be said to flatter because our praise "is a commendable kind of deceit which has a good end in view and that brings advantage to the party deceived."[139] But the good ends achieved can be our own as well, and so it is, Anniball continues, that we can feign friendship with our enemies and respect for our inferiors. Perhaps feigning can really be distinguished from flattery, but it is deceptive nonetheless, occasionally mendacious and, it would seem, absolutely necessary for the success of human society.

BERNARD MANDEVILLE AND THE WORLD LIES BUILT

Published first to little notice in 1714, the 1723 revised and expanded edition of Bernard Mandeville's *Fable of the Bees: or Pri-*

vate Vices, Publick Benefits met with outraged howls of disgust (and sold copies by the thousands). In a letter that appeared in the *London Journal* on July 27, 1723, addressed to Lord John Carteret, First Earl of Granville, one Theophilus Philo-Brittanus, roiling with impatience and pugilistic brio, writes, "The Jest of it is, my Lord, that these *Scribblers* would still be thought *good moral men*. But, when Men make it their Business to *mislead* and *deceive* their Neighbours, and that in Matters of *Moment*, by *distorting* and *disguising* Truth, by *Misrepresentations* and *false* Insinuations; if such Men are not guilty of *Usurpation*, while they take upon them the Character of *good Moral Men*, then 'tis not Immoral, in any Man to be *false* and *deceitful*." While it is bad enough that Mandeville has filled his book with lies, what particularly offends Philo-Brittanus's sensibilities is that Mandeville lies about lying— lies when he claims that society depends for its very existence on all manner of vice, deception, and flattery. What more need be said, Philo-Brittanus contends, for Mandeville convicts himself of such seditious ideas and, as evidence, he quotes directly from *The Fable's* conclusion: "What we call *Evil* in this World, *Moral* as well as *Natural*, is the *Grand Principle* that makes us sociable Creatures, the *solid Basis*, the *Life* and *Support* of all Trades and Employments without Exception . . . and that *the Moment Evil ceases, the Society must be spoli'd, if not totally dissolv'd*."[140]

As always, the Devil is in the details, and if Mandeville's readers too quickly honed in on words like "evil," passing over such qualifiers as "what we call," Mandeville himself could not deny the privileged place he had granted to all manner of lies in the formation and maintenance of human society. Fallen man, he explains, is a pride-filled creature, so supremely arrogant and vain that it is impossible "he should act with any other view but to please himself while he has the use of his organs, and the greatest extravagance of love or despair can have no other center." Our desires and caprices are limitless, welling up within us continuously and uncontrollably with such force that "all civil commerce would be lost, if by art and prudent dissimulation we had not learned to hide and stifle them." If we weren't such able hypocrites, veiling our true intentions behind sociable facades and amicable words, we would be "insufferable to each other." Of course, self-centered egotists that we are, we wouldn't worry about being insufferable unless our bad manners and overweening self-regard somehow prevented us from satisfying our desires. Fortunately, Mandeville argues, because such blatant bad behavior so often does backfire on us, we learn to regulate our conduct and disguise our base intentions. This is why the undertaker, even as he gleefully thinks about his fee, maintains a grave expression, and why the dance instructor mimics enthusiasm as he stumbles through lesson after lesson with students, each less talented than the one before.[141] Even our most seemingly charitable actions are nothing but shams. "Where is the man," Mandeville asks, "that has at no time covered his failings, and screened himself with false appearances, or never pretended to act from principles of social virtue and his regards to others, when he knew in his heart that his greatest care had been to oblige himself?"[142]

As Mandeville famously put it near the beginning of *The Fable of the Bees*, "The nearer we search into human nature, the more we shall be convinced, that the moral virtues are the political offspring which flattery begot upon pride."[143] From earliest childhood we are trained to respond to flattery and soon after to use it on others. In order to teach toddlers manners, Mandeville writes, we praise their simplest fumbling acts of courtesy in terms so extravagant they would be considered "abominable lies" by anyone "above the capacity of an infant." When, a little older, those same children become annoyed that the praise they once so happily sopped up is now poured willy-nilly on their younger siblings' malformed efforts, we pull them aside. "It is only to please baby," we explain, assuring them that since they are now adults, we can let them in on the secret. Their vanity sated, the cycle begins again as the older children now join their parents, leading the lying hordes and "rejoicing in the superiority of [their] understanding" over their younger brothers and sisters. We lie to others to get what we want, but when others falsely praise us, we assume their words are true estimates of our noble nature in order to feed our voracious hunger for approbation and love. We should know better, Mandeville contends, but we don't. "There is no man of what capacity or penetration soever that is wholly proof against the witchcraft of flattery, if artfully performed, and suited to his abilities."[144] The entire world depends on these endless charades and deceptions. "Thus every Part was full of vice," Mandeville writes in "The Grumbling Hive, or Knaves turn'd Honest," the poem that prefaced his controversial work, "Yet the whole Mass a Paradise."[145] In Mandeville's story of civilization, when the whole mass turned honest, paradise was undone.

Shocking though his ideas may have been, no one would have denied the ubiquity of flattery and lies in a fallen world. In his mid-seventeenth-century collection of worldly-wise aphorisms, *The Pocket Oracle and Art of Prudence*, the Spanish Jesuit Baltasar Gracián may have lamented his age's fall from truth and openness into a world of malice, from an Age of Gold into the Age of Iron in which "good men . . . seem to be the relics of better times," but John of Salisbury had already groaned that lament more than five centuries earlier.[146] The entire tradition of court writing had declared, as if with one voice, that the world was full of liars and flatterers, illusions and facades, and that in such a world we might sometimes need to lie to the liars, flatter the flatterers. Mandeville's promotion of flattery and lies to the status of unadulterated goods draws deeply from this tradition but also, especially, from the early modern emphasis on courtesy, refinement, and civil conversation. Even if writers like Guazzo and Walker stressed the need to be good Christians, they also understood that it was well nigh impossible to distinguish the truly virtuous from those who merely play the part for ulterior motives. It was precisely this fascination with acting appropriately that gave particular weight to the age-old metaphor of world as stage. "I am convinced that in many situations," writes Antoine Gombaud, the self-appointed Chevalier de Méré, "that it is not without benefit that one looks at what one is doing as theatre, and imagines oneself as a character in a play."[147] Madeleine de Souvré, the Marquise de Sablé, whose mid-seventeenth-century Parisian salon would prove an incubator for the style of maxim for which La Rochefoucauld would become famous, remarked on this phenomenon with a tinge of regret. "If we had as much care to be what we should be as we have to deceive others by disguising what we are," she writes, "we would be able to show ourselves just as we are, without having the trouble of disguising ourselves."[148] Gracián would make a similar observation when he noted, "Things don't pass for what they are, but for how they appear. Few look within and many are content with appearances."[149]

While many writers mourned this alleged loss of interest in real virtue, a few couldn't help but note that it hardly mattered to society itself. Whatever the reasons that motivated people to behave courteously, the effect was the same. The Jansenist theologian Pierre Nicole latched onto this curious phenomenon in his essay from the 1670s, *Of Charity, and Self-Love.* "Although there is nothing so opposite to charity," he writes, "which relates all to God, as self-love, which relates all to self, yet there is nothing so resembling the effects of charity, as those of self-love." Self-love, the consequence of original sin, makes men incapable of caring for anyone but themselves, rendering them tyrannical, "violent, unjust, cruel, ambitious, flatterers, envious, insolent and querulous."[150] However much we love these passions in ourselves, we despise them in others, and if it were possible we would make everyone submit to our most passing egotistical whims. But this is simply not possible, and as much as we love dominating others, Nicole contends, so much the more do we love ourselves and want others to love and respect us, to flatter and admire us.[151] So begins the slow process of adapting our prideful selves to other prideful selves as we conceal our rapacity and will to dominate behind acceptable and useful actions. We perform acts of kindness and courage, are courteous and solicitous to others, not because we care about them, but simply because such actions will bring us praise, adulation, and honors. "There is hardly any action," Nicole explains, "whereto we are carried by charity that would please God, whereunto self-love cannot engage us to please men."[152] And this, Nicole contends, is the sum total of human civility.[153]

Not only is it impossible for others to discern the true motivation of our actions, our motivations are often, perhaps always, invisible even to ourselves. La Rochefoucauld stressed this problem throughout his volume of maxims, observing that "we are so used to disguising ourselves from others that we end up disguising ourselves from ourselves."[154] Nicole suggests something similar, arguing that we often act out of sheer habit, without really attending to our motivations at all.[155] Significantly, Nicole suggests that God himself makes it impossible even for the virtuous to know whether their actions are just. Human nature is so corrupt that such knowledge would overwhelm us. If we knew we were virtuous or, at the very least, that some of our actions were virtuous, we would all too easily become self-satisfied, vain, and proud, with what little virtue we did possess soon destroyed. "This obscurity does not take away virtues from him," Nicole explains, "but hinders him from losing them, by keeping him always in humility and fear, and making him mistrust all his works, and to rely on God's mercy."[156] If our lack of self-knowledge keeps us humble, it also renders charity completely irrelevant, at least here and now, in this world, in this society. From John of Salisbury to Nathaniel Walker, it was charity that had justified our lies, deceptions, and hypocritical civilities. In this tradition, intentions mattered in the difficult prudential calculations that each and every one of us needed to make to navigate our way through a world full of lies. The early modern conception of refinement, courtesy, and civil conversation, with its emphasis on decorum and amiability, may have trivialized the significance of these judgments, but these writers still framed their discussions in terms of charity and virtue. Even Gracián, whose *Pocket Oracle* ranks among the most cynical accounts of how to survive in "civil society," concluded with a lengthy aphorism, "*In a word, a saint*," in which he stressed that "virtue links all perfections and is the center of all happiness."[157]

Certainly Nicole cared about the difference between true charity and self-love. It was for him the difference between those whose futures rested with God and those whose futures promised to be much less pleasant. Important in principle, as Nicole works through what he takes to be the implications of his ideas, it is a distinction that proves meaningless in our lives. Self-love's deceptions are so subtle, so perfectly suited to resemble virtue, that love of self can even drive us to imitate the devoutly religious, saints and holy men, and it can motivate us to live lives of brutal asceticism, penance, and more. "In fine," he writes, "self-love is also capable to make us suffer even death with joy and to the end there may be no certain way to distinguish it from charity by martyrdoms, the saints do teach us after St Paul, that there are martyrs of vanity as well as of charity." Even if such religious exertion were not almost always undone through pride, Nicole recognizes that few are capable or even motivated "to embrace this kind of life so contrary to nature."[158]

With human happiness through religious austerity ruled out, Nicole sees nothing for it but to foster the mysterious machinations of self-love so as to foster at least an imitation of a charitable society. "Thus one may say truly," Nicole concludes, "that absolutely to reform the world, that's to say, to banish all the vices and the gross disorders therein, and to make mankind happy even in this life, there needs only instead of charity, to give everyone a harmless self-love which may be able to discern its true interests, and to incline thereto by the ways of which true reason shall discover to it." Laws promoting socially useful behaviors, shaming and punishing deleterious behaviors, can create an enlightened self-love motivated toward the facade of goodness, even in the utter absence of charity. Such a society would be no less corrupt before God, but Nicole seems willing to accept a society built on lying and deceptive self-interest, yet so constrained through appropriate laws that "we should see everywhere nothing but the form and characters of charity."[159]

It was precisely this false form of charity that Mandeville sought to uncover, and especially the lies that people told about their so-called charity. Mandeville, like Nicole, had no doubt that self-interest was the hidden hand that led to a healthy society, but he had no patience with the hypocrites who considered their self-serving behavior to be truly good. "Virtue is a very fashionable word, and some of the most luxurious are extremely fond of the amiable sound," Mandeville explains in the preface to *The Fable of the Bees*'s second volume. "All court philosophers are agreed, nothing can be lovely or desirable, that is mortifying or uneasy," and all the world requires of the so-called virtuous man is "a civil behavior among the fair in public, and a deportment inoffensive both in words and actions is all the chastity the polite world requires in men." But, of course, this isn't virtue in any real sense. Not only does society's emphasis on courtesy provide men the needed cover to revel in every form of vice in private and when out of sight, it flatters their vanity, shielding them from the self-interested hypocrisy that motivates their every public deed.[160]

"If we would know the world," Mandeville writes, "we must look into it," and when Mandeville looks into it, he sees a world shot through with self-interested flattery and hypocrisy, with lies and deception.[161] No one would have disagreed. But what we don't see can be as important as what we do see and, like Nicole, Mandeville does not see charity or anything that could reasonably be thought to be the effects of charity at work in our actions. Nicole still believed in charity but had found himself lost in a world where it had become invisible, untraceable, effectively if not truly irrelevant. Mandeville, by contrast, simply ignores it. The world is the world as he finds it, a world devoid of charity, and this is why Mandeville can give so different an answer to the question that had so long troubled writers in the courtly tradition, the question that so desperately worried John of Salisbury: How should we respond to this morally perplexing world so riven with illusions? Mandeville's answer is simple: Don't respond to it, just accept it. We are all both deceivers and easily deceived, full of self-love and thank goodness for that. The mysterious operations of self-interested pride accidentally result in a better social order than any intentional human planning blinded by false notions of charity could ever have hoped to achieve.[162]

This was hardly the answer Mandeville's critics wanted to hear. In *Remarks on the Fable of the Bees*, published in 1724, William Law contended that Mandeville incoherently, not to mention heretically, blurred the difference between truth and lies, good and evil. "Now, the Religion of our Country tells us that God is *Truth*, and the Devil the Author of *Lies*. And if I should ask you why one should be worshipp'd rather than the other, I should puzzle your profound philosophy, as much as if I ask'd you which was the finest Flower; for you cannot tell that one of the Beings is really good, and the other really evil, and yet maintain, that there is no real Goodness in Truth, nor any real Evil in Lies and Falsehood."[163] But it was precisely the dream of such straightforward distinctions that Mandeville found lacking in a world in which flattery and deception so often seemed to pave the way to a thriving society. And not just Mandeville. The entire tradition of court writing had recognized the value of lies, whether virtuous, pious, necessary, or expedient. This is what it meant to live east of Eden, in the court, in a fallen world in which moral perplexity and confusion abound.

Lies had always had their place, only now they no longer needed the fig leaf of charity.

CHAPTER FIVE

Women

LESSONS ABOUT LIES

There are liars and there are women, and every woman is a liar.

A difficult lesson learned and unwanted, but impossible to avoid, even behind closed doors in the solitude of one's own room. This is where Christine de Pizan learns it, after a long day of exhausting study. Tired of working her way through oversize treatises full of subtle and difficult arguments, she scans the shelves that surround her for some light poetry. She reaches up for a book she doesn't recognize and, discovering it is by Matheolus, smiles. Although she has never read it, she has "often heard that like other books it discusses respect for women." Before she can begin reading, her mother calls her to supper, and so it is only the next morning, having returned to her study, that she discovers the volume is not at all what she had heard it to be. Full of lies and vicious slanders about women, poorly written and unpleasant, she quickly puts it down in favor of something "more elevated and useful [for] study."[1]

Unfortunately, she cannot forget what she has read. Her thoughts keep returning to Matheolus, and not only to him but to all the other men, often learned and respected philosophers, orators, poets—all of whom as if with one voice have filled their books and treatises with "many wicked insults about women and their behavior." She thinks of herself and her friends, of the princesses, noblewomen, and members of the lower classes with whom she has spoken over the years. Nothing about their lives, neither

199

their actions nor their conversation, supports the vile assertions that these men have written about women, and yet their writings exist. Nearly every moral treatise she has ever read contains at least one, if not several, chapters denigrating women. Under the weight of such revered and accumulated authority, Christine finds herself reduced to tears and despair, doubting herself and accepting what she has read. "And I finally decided," she writes, "that God formed a vile creature when He made woman, and I wondered how such a worthy artisan could have deigned to make such an abominable work . . . the vessel as well as the refuge and abode of every evil and vice." Wishing she could have been born a man, she suddenly detests not only herself but all women, condemning one and all as little else than "monstrosities in nature."[2]

Jehan le Fèvre would not have disagreed with Christine's conclusion, nor would Matthew of Boulogne. Together they were responsible for the poem that precipitates Christine's plummet into the depths of self-doubt, Matthew as its originator, Jehan as its very creative translator. Matthew composed *The Lamentations of Matheolus* sometime quite late in the thirteenth century as a warning to his acquaintances "lest they submerge themselves in the burdensome war of wedlock."[3] Claiming the poem to be a sort of autobiography, Matthew describes himself as a once-successful cleric and attorney involved in the ecclesiastical bureaucracies in and around Orléans, successful, that is, until he met, then married, a lovely widow named Perrette. For violating canon law, Matthew lost everything, his status and his wealth, all for the love of a woman whose beauty quickly vanished, leaving behind nothing but an increasingly horrid character with which to torture him the remaining days of his life. Though not widely read, Matthew's poem fascinated Jehan le Fèvre, "a legal representative, at the royal parliament in Paris."[4] In the 1370s, Jehan translated Matthew's poem into French, while doubling its length with additional venom, vitriol, and over-the-top misogyny.

As Jehan would have it, and it is his version that Christine most likely read, Matheolus all too soon realizes that Perrette has deceived him. Had he met Medusa, who transforms men into

stone, it would not have been as bad as meeting this "most horrible monster."[5] Later, embellishing his theme, he adds that Nature
herself, "having embarked on creation, was shocked when she
contemplated her mistake and blushed" before the monstrous
hermaphrodite that is woman.[6] And what makes women most
horrendous and insufferable, what makes them most evil and
despicable, is that they speak—constantly, self-servingly, seduc-
tively, and always dishonestly. Jehan again and again returns to
their shrill incessant babble, their mindless chatter, and the lying
sophistry with which they connive to make men their perpetually
unrewarded servants. Caught in bed beneath her heaving lover, a
woman will convince her cuckolded husband that nothing is hap-
pening, that he is deluded, dreaming, suffering from melancholy
and must publicly apologize for the outlandish charges he has
brought against her, his devoted, now suffering, wife.[7] Women nag
and whine and scheme, they break promises, they contradict and
disobey. "Whoever gave them the gift of speech was out of their
mind," Jehan exclaims at one point. "If one dare accuse God, He
would not be able to defend Himself against the charge of giving
perverse women deadly weapons when He gave them many
tongues."[8]

Jehan's was hardly a solitary voice bemoaning man's entrap-
ment to deceptive woman. The late fourteenth-century anonymous
poem *The Fifteen Joys of Marriage* presents a world in which
women are in league against men, in which wives, maids, mothers,
and their friends form secret societies plotting and scheming
against their exasperated and never less than befuddled spouses,
telling lies to avoid their conjugal duties as they eagerly await late-
night or midday rendezvous with their younger and always more
virile lovers. When caught, women lie shamelessly, blaming their
lovers, their husbands, calling in their mothers and acquaintances,
gossips one and all, to help them escape the predicaments of their
uncontrollable passions, filling the air with a cacophony of words
and more words and every one false but effective, leaving men
helpless in their endless echo.[9] The author of the anonymous early
fourteenth-century French poem *The Vices of Women* would not

have disagreed. "Outwardly she's well-behaved/but by her nature, she's depraved," he writes. "Her words are sugar-clad/To lure a man and drive him mad."[10] Most popular of all was Jean de Meun's *Romance of the Rose*, written in the 1270s, in which he announces, "There is so much vice in woman that no one can recount her perverse ways in rhyme or in verse" before immediately going on to do just that, describing how wives seduce secrets from their husbands using sweet words, fallacious arguments, tears, and exposed breasts.[11] Should any woman complain that these depictions of her sex are false, as Christine de Pizan later would when confronted with Jehan le Fèvre's rhymed misogyny, Jean replies that authority is on his side. "I shall never lie," he contends, "in anything as long as the worthy men who wrote the old books did not lie. And in my judgment they all agreed when they told about feminine ways."[12] Christine's despair begins precisely where Jean's confidence takes root.

Women lie, but doesn't everyone? In the book of Psalms, David famously proclaimed that every man is a liar, and who could disagree with that judgment? Certainly not John of Salisbury, who invoked David's authority in the opening pages of his *Policraticus*. The court, John writes, teems with liars, flatterers, and slanderers leaving us with no choice but to lie in our own self-defense, to beguile the beguilers. The man of eminence resorts to lying and simulation out of necessity, as a last expedient in a world in which no other strategy will succeed in bringing about the good. Christine agreed. In *The Treasure of the City of Ladies*, she counsels princesses and noblewomen to practice simulation and holy pretense in order to protect themselves from the envious backbiters who everywhere surround them.

Every man is a liar, and every woman too, but that hardly renders them or their lies equal, hardly renders identical their place in the world and the challenges they must overcome. To hear John tell it, the courtier's need to lie is less a reflection of who he is than of the impossibly confused and confounding world in which he finds himself. He lies, but he is not a liar. Not so for the princess or noblewoman, at least not simply so and certainly not so simply.

Even if necessity and charity motivate her deceptions, trustworthy authority affirms that when women lie they lie because they are women, as if the effects of the Fall had somehow bypassed men, only to be redoubled in feminine nature itself. Why are women so talkative, so prone to falsehood, idle gossip, and argument? Jehan found one answer in the book of *Genesis*: "Because they are made of bone, while our bodies are fashioned of clay: bone makes more noise than clay. . . . It is their nature that makes them foolish and proud."[13]

When a woman lies, she lies because she is a woman, and every woman is a liar. This is the lesson Christine learns in her study the morning she skims through Jehan le Fèvre's poetic slanders and reflects on well over twelve hundred years of endlessly repeated authority transmitted in the form of religious doctrine, natural philosophy, and stories, poems and plays, jokes and anecdotes. After all, Jehan and Jean de Meun were hardly saying anything new. Augustine's spiritual mentor, the bishop Ambrose of Milan, had already set the stage for their literary productions when, in midst of his commentary on *Genesis*, he pointed out that it was hardly surprising which sex sinned first.[14] Prior to Ambrose, Tertullian, the Carthaginian convert to Christianity who died in A.D. 225, had already raised the proclaimed dangers of women to hyperbolic extremes when he infamously condemned all women. "Do you not believe that you are (each) an Eve?" he exclaims. "The sentence of God on this sex of yours lives on even in our times and so it is necessary that the guilt should live on, also. You are the one who opened the door to the Devil, you are the one who first plucked the fruit of the forbidden tree, you are the one who first deserted the divine law; you are the one who persuaded him whom the Devil was not strong enough to attack. All too easily you destroyed the image of God, man. Because of your desert, that is, death, even the son of God had to die."[15]

Variations on Tertullian's and Ambrose's laments would reverberate through the centuries, through the Middle Ages in the writings of Jehan le Fèvre, Jean de Meun, and so many others, and long after them, in mushrooming crops of plays and pastoralia, witchcraft manuals, and philosophical treatises. Heinrich Kramer and James Sprenger gave voice to such condemnation in their notorious late fifteenth-century work *The Hammer of Witches* when they stressed that women are naturally more susceptible to demonic influence and evil because of their incredible credulity, their slippery tongues, weak intellect, and uncontrollable carnality.[16] Easily deceived, women find it even easier to deceive. Or so it might seem. But situations like this require caution.

When potential deception lurks everywhere, both within us and without, we have no choice but to proceed with care, to question, to reflect, and to doubt. This is John of Salisbury's advice to the man of eminence: be skeptical and never mistake mere appearances for reality, flattery for truth. Virtuous action requires self-knowledge, and lacking that we can only lose ourselves to vice, and the lies we fall for will be the lies that undo us. A lesson Christine takes to heart: she uses the opening pages of *The City of Ladies* to dramatize the mechanisms—the religious, the scientific, and philosophical arguments, even the civic institutions and traditions—that men use to demean and oppress women, to convince women of their alleged inferiority and inescapably deceitful nature. Christine understood that the question *Is it ever acceptable to lie?* would always be a more difficult question when asked about women, when asked by women, because the weight of tradition had worked to blind women to their own true nature. In order to answer the question *Is it ever acceptable for women to lie?* Christine realized that she would first have to learn who she was and that this knowledge could be acquired only through methodical excavation and critique of the misogynist tradition itself, a tradition that would have to be understood before it could be refuted, debunked before it could be replaced. To borrow Christine's own metaphor, she would first have to clear away the accumulated dirt of male slander before she could lay out the true foundation of female virtue.[17]

And there was a lot of dirt to excavate. The misogynist discourse that not only supported the claim that every woman is a liar but made it sound reasonable depended on ideas that, at times, might seem at best tangentially related to the problem of lies and lying. This was its power, this was how it convinced. Its claims cohered so fully with a much larger and diverse set of authoritative scientific and religious ideas that the inherently mendacious nature of all women seemed to flow from them like logical corollaries. Christine first, and then those she inspired, would search out these hidden assumptions in order to clarify the disparate elements that sustained the belief that all women are liars. Since the misogynists depended so profoundly on a certain understanding of what transpired in the Garden of Eden, it became necessary to return to the first pages of Genesis to determine precisely what they believed it taught about women. Similarly, since the misogynists also believed that natural philosophy, the disciplines of medicine and biology, confirmed and extended the conclusions of their biblical exegesis, it became necessary to understand why they believed the biological differences between men and women rendered women inconstant and deceptive. Only by revealing and critiquing these traditions and ideas could Christine and her heirs begin to reframe and redirect them, replacing a theory of feminine deceit with an account of human nature.

ALL ABOUT EVE, ALL ABOUT WOMEN

If Rupert of Deutz is sure of anything, he is sure that the evils of women reach back to Genesis, to the Garden of Eden, and to the very first recorded words a woman ever spoke.

In his commentary on the Bible's opening book, Rupert, a twelfth-century Benedictine monk and theologian, lingers over each and every word of the Woman's response to the serpent's question, words that prove the corruption, weakness, and fickleness of her mind. The serpent, incorrectly phrasing God's prohibition against eating from the Tree of the Knowledge of Good and Evil, asks, "Why has God forbidden you from eating from every tree in the Garden?" The Woman, unwilling to ignore the serpent, proves equally unwilling to restate God's prohibition verbatim. She changes it, simultaneously strengthening one part, weakening another, while altering yet a third. She strengthens it when she falsely claims, not only that God has forbidden them from eating from the Tree of the Knowledge of Good and Evil, but also that he has prohibited the first couple from even touching it. She immediately goes on to undermine God's prohibition when she introduces a hint of doubt about the consequences of violating God's law—"lest perchance we will die," she informs the serpent. Finally, Rupert, almost alone among commentators, observes that the Woman actually misidentifies the forbidden tree. "We may eat of the trees in the garden," she states, "but God said, 'You shall not eat of the tree that is in the middle of garden.'" But this is simply false, Rupert notes. God placed the Tree of Life at the center of the garden, and he certainly did not prohibit them from eating from it.[18]

The Woman says too much, and what she says is knowingly false and blasphemous. Rupert contends that her words reveal how quickly she has become impatient with God's commands, complaining about them, criticizing them, as if God had reserved the real treasure at the center of paradise for himself, while granting to Adam and herself the dubious honor of eating from the more worthless trees that surround it. Rupert invokes the book of Revelation and its author, John, who warns of the punishments that await anyone who tampers with God's Word. Should a person add words to God's book, "He will add to that person the plagues described in this book," Rupert writes, quoting scripture: "if anyone takes away from the words of the book of this prophecy, God will take away that person's share in the tree of life and in the holy city."[19] All of which makes clear, Rupert concludes, that though the Devil first spoke through a visible serpent, a body, now he speaks "inside the ear of her heart." Rupert draws from this a lesson and a warning. Every work of diabolical lust and adultery begins with those subtle and hidden movements that delight the soul and move us from God's Word.

A general lesson maybe, but a lesson that inevitably explains more about the Woman than Adam, more about women than men. Rupert argues at length that Eve does not merely see the tree, eat from it, and hand the fruit to Adam. She sees that it is good for food and a delight to the eyes. She gazes at it, contemplates it. She knows God's threat and the serpent's promise, and she must judge between them. Unfortunately, the serpent's words already have infected her with pride and desire, have confused her so that she no longer understands the import of God's prohibition. Rupert invokes a distinction between our interior and exterior eyes. Her interior eyes now darkened with concupiscence, she no longer fears transgressing God's mandate but only delights in the tree's apparent beauty. Looking at it, she concludes that God has lied and the serpent speaks the truth. How could this tree cause death when its fruit looks so good to eat, when it is so delightful to the eyes? Appearances and surfaces, the superficial and the transitory, sway her, and then she sways Adam. The Apostle Paul assures us that only the Woman was deceived, not the man, and so Rupert concludes, "By compelling rather than deceiving, by enjoining more than pretending, she accomplishes this, so that the man obeys her voice rather than God's." However she accomplished it, she accomplished it with lying words, and those words welled up from a pride-filled and lustful soul, words that concealed a horrible truth behind their falsely promised pleasures.[20]

Nothing Rupert describes is particularly original, but that is the value of his commentary. With its occasional rhetorical flourish for added froth, Rupert's commentary flows along the very mainstream of the tradition, caught up in its most basic assumptions about Eve and women. Already in the sixth century, Alcimus Avitus, bishop of Gaul, would describe Eve as prone to pride, "open to seduction . . . too ready to believe . . . [and] perversely gullible."[21] And everyone agreed that Eve was the lesser of the two first humans, formed second, from Adam's rib. Augustine would take this as evidence that she lacked reason, certainly lacked Adam's reason. In the thirteenth-century treatise *The Golden Legend*, Jacobus Voragine would cite Eve's inferiority as the reason the serpent approached her and not her husband: "she was not so prudent and more prone to slide and bow."[22] Vincent of Beauvais would give this interpretation his encyclopedic stamp of approval later in the same century when he linked Eve's natural inferiority to her creation after Adam. "For the woman is the glory of the man, not the image of God . . . and more, the woman is under the man, and since she is not the origin of everything, as he is, and she was not made by God immediately, but formed from the man's side, and because she did not have reason from the start, as did the man, whence she was seduced by the Devil, not the man."[23] Seduced by words and appearances, she seduces with words and appearances.

Greek and Roman literature, scripture, even Aristotelian and Galenic ideas about the body and medicine made it easy for the Church fathers to equate all women with Eve and to allow Eve's actions to reveal the true nature of all women. Individual women, whether virtuous or vicious, vanished into the abstract notion of "woman," a universalized essence impervious to anything so transitory as a writer's actual experience with real women. Those same lines from Paul's letter to Timothy declaring that only the Woman, not Adam, was deceived also made it clear that Eve's subjection to Adam named every woman's permanent state in a fallen world. Women were to dress simply, without unnecessary adornment, with their heads covered and, most important, they were not to speak. "Let a woman learn in silence," Paul writes, "with full submission. I permit no woman to teach or to have authority over a man; she is to keep silent."[24] The *Glossa Ordinaria*, quoting extensively from Augustine's exegesis of Genesis at this point in Paul's letter, makes clear that it was the Woman's frailty, her failure to obey, her attempt to speak and teach, that rest at the heart of women's current subjection to man.[25] Silence: the imposed penalty for having rephrased God's prohibition to the serpent and for turning the serpent's wiles on Adam.

But women didn't need to speak to lie. In his third-century treatise *On Female Apparel*, Tertullian, having bluntly asserted that every woman is an Eve, quickly adds that there is more than one way to tarnish God's Word. When a woman paints her face with rouge or powder, her mouth with lipstick, when she decorates herself with silver or gold or jewels, dresses in elaborate and richly colored clothing, she effectively criticizes God, suggesting with every daub of makeup another way he could have improved on his work. Invoking language reminiscent of John the Revelator's warning against altering even the slightest word of scripture, Tertullian contends that women censure God "when they amend, when they add to, his work; taking these additions, of course, from the adversary artificer. That adversary artificer the devil. For who would show the way to change the body, but he who by wickedness transfigured man's spirit?" Women recapitulate the Fall when they adorn themselves and, at the root of the Fall, at the root of all sin, is the lie. "How unworthy of the name Christian that you bear!" Tertullian rages, "To have a painted face, you on whom simplicity in every form is enjoined! To lie in your appearance, you to whom lying with the tongue is not allowed.... To commit adultery in your appearance, you who should eagerly strive after modesty! ... How can you keep the commandments of God if you do not keep in your own persons the features which He has bestowed on you?"[26] For Tertullian, when Adam and Eve cover themselves with leaves and hide among the trees of the Garden, they do not merely symbolize the lying words they will soon use to conceal and excuse their transgression against God. They are discovering new methods of deceit and simulation.

Although Tertullian warns men against adorning themselves, his real concern is with women because women are essentially connected to adornment, to amendment, and excess. "Female toilet," Tertullian writes, "has two possible purposes—dress and make-up," and dress and makeup serve only two purposes: to satisfy female ambition and to prostitute the body.[27] But just as women do not need to speak to lie, they do not even need to go to the trouble of caring for their appearance to attract the male gaze. A woman's mere presence can ignite carnal yearnings better left unlit in men, leaving them helpless before the temptation that is the female sex. While a woman's natural "comeliness is not to be censured," Tertullian explains, "as being a bodily happiness, as being an additional gift of the divine Sculptor, and as a kind of fair vestment of the soul, it must be feared because of the affront and violence on the part of those who pursue it."[28] Simply put, a woman's body is little different from cosmetics and fine clothes. Just as the latter adorn the body, the former adorns the soul. Women are naturally adorned, naturally fictitious and deceitful. They are natural liars, and this means that it is never enough for women to reject "the display of false and studied beauty." They must use "concealment and negligence" to obliterate even their "natural grace." Being a woman is synonymous with seduction and deception. It doesn't matter that a woman has no intention of arousing the man whose leer lands on her. It does not even matter that she is utterly unaware of the effect she has on him. It does not matter, because she is a temptress nonetheless and despite herself, by her very nature. She deceives simply in virtue of being a woman in the presence of a man who (unknown to her) desires her, who mentally performs the deed that a lust-filled gaze inspires. Perhaps she is not guilty, but odium and infamy attach to her nonetheless as the unwitting sword of man's perdition.[29]

A woman is her body, and it is her body that defines her. If her body is a "garment of her soul," then, like any garment, it is a covering, something extra, an alteration and correction always bordering on the precipice of sin. Tertullian's identification of women with the body and deception fell in line with, would draw from and in turn nourish, a long tradition that identified men with the soul and with reason, women with the body and the senses. The first-century Jewish exegete Philo of Alexandria exploits this tradition in his commentary on Genesis when he resignedly notes that the joy and perfection of paradise could never have lasted long. Nothing is stable in this world, and eventually something had to give. Scripture quickly proves his pessimism true when the Woman arrives on the scene and, with her, the start "of a blameworthy life."[30] Philo reads the entire Temptation scene as an allegory for the soul itself. Adam symbolizes reason, the Woman symbolizes the body's senses, and the serpent symbolizes all those many pleasures that seep in through the senses and deceive the soul.[31] Although subsequent commentators, such as Origin and Ambrose, would pick up on Philo's allegory, it merely made explicit what even the most literal of expositors would find in the story of the Fall. The serpent tempts the Woman with promises of power and pleasure, it plays on her senses, her ears and her eyes, her sense of touch and taste. The Woman is fickle, persuadable, inconstant, easily confused, lacking in self-control—and without self-control, Philo observes, "the soul softens and tends towards death."[32]

These feminine stereotypes appear everywhere in patristic literature. They appear in Jerome's writings when he stresses woman's "fickle-mindedness" and the "softness of her soul" and in the works of John Chrysostom, who fears that a salacious feminine nature could all too easily replicate itself in even the most religious of men should they incautiously let down their guard. Warning against the dangers of "spiritual marriage" between male and female ascetics, Chrysostom warns that regular contact with women makes men "softer, more hot-headed, shameful, mindless, irascible, insolent, importunate, ignoble, crude, servile, niggardly, reckless, nonsensical, and, to sum it up, women take all their corrupting feminine customs and stamp them into the souls of men."[33] These ideas underwrite Rupert of Deutz's commentary on Genesis and the twelfth-century writings of both Hugh and Andrew of St. Victor, who see all women as more fleshy and less rational than men and certainly more prone to sin.[34] Along a multitude of such currents and eddies, these ideas flowed practically unchanged into the books of men like Jehan le Fèvre and Jean de Meun, books that leave Christine awash in an ocean of self-loathing.

THE BIOLOGY OF FEMININE DECEIT

Natural philosophy, biology, and medicine, no less than religious tradition, abetted this reduction of women to evil woman, rooting the differences between men and women in their respective bodily makeup, their different temperatures and, eventually, in the medical theory of complexion. Aristotle's writings stand at the origin of this tradition with their confident pronouncements concerning the male's superiority over the female, a superiority rooted in man's greater heat. According to Aristotle, heat purifies and invigorates the man's semen, transforming it into an active, creative, and ensouling principle. Women produce semen as well, evident in the moisture and liquid they produce when aroused, but their bodies being cooler, their semen is less refined, passive rather than active, the mere material on which the male principle operates. Greater heat at conception results in a male, whose perfect form, greater strength, and powers of intellect all manifest his superiority. Women, by contrast, are cooler, their bodies and intellectual abilities less developed. Women, as Aristotle famously puts it, are nothing but "mutilated males" and "imperfect men."[35]

The second-century physician Galen would refine these ideas so common to the Hellenistic culture of the Roman Empire. "Just as mankind is the most perfect of all animals," he writes in *On the Usefulness of the Bodies Parts*, "so within mankind the man is more perfect than the woman, and the reason for this perfection is his excess of heat, for heat is Nature's primary instrument."[36] With these assumptions in place, Galen developed a general theory of complexion, and from Galen's writings it passed on through various routes to medieval and early modern thinkers. Galen reasoned that since all living creatures consist in different combinations of the four basic elements (earth, air, fire, and water), they must also possess different and defining combinations of the four basic elemental qualities (hot, cold, dry, wet). While health required that a being have the right complexion, that is, the proper balance of these qualities, everyone agreed that different animals possessed different complexions. Fish were moister than lions, birds warmer than worms. In addition, environmental conditions, dietary regimes, and astrological forces could shape a creature's complexion.[37] As a result, even individuals of the same species possessed, within the limits defined by the species' formal principles, different ratios of the four elemental qualities. Among human beings, for example, these external factors not only played a part in determining a race's characteristic appearance, its typical skin and hair color, its average size and strength, but even its general disposition and psychological makeup, whether members of the race were, say, more or less courageous, intelligent. or humorous than members of other races. John Buridan, the fourteenth-century University of Paris arts master, would argue that there are two kinds of complexion, one derived from a creature's birth, another through its experiences. Summarizing these ideas, while emphasizing the import of celestial influences, the late thirteenth-century Dominican theologian John of Paris adds, "Complexions vary with varied causes. This proposition is self-evident, since under this and that constellation we have this and that complexion and mores and figure and color and disposition." This is why, he concludes, "all Saxons are of the same sort, and Frisians and Poles and Thuringians, because they are nourished in the same place and by the same constellation."[38]

Significantly, not only did the standard complexion of human beings differ from those of other animals, and even between different groups of people, the complexion of men and women differed. Writing in his thirteenth-century encyclopedia *On the Property of Things*, Bartholomew the Englishmen explains, "The male passes the female in perfect complexion, for in working, in wit, in discretion, in might and in lordship. In perfect compleation, for in comparison the male is hotter and dryer, and the female the contrary."[39] While some men were more warmly complected than others, some more coolly, and even some women warmer than men, in general men were warmer than women, and this difference mattered, supporting assumptions about fundamental differences between the sexes. As a result of greater warmth, male virtues are "formal and shaping and working," whereas female virtues are "material, suffering and passive." Not only does the male in every species tend to be stronger and larger than the female, it is also cleverer and wiser, more capable of avoiding dangers and peril. "Therefore," Bartholomew adds, claiming Augustine as his source, "a man passes a woman in reason and sharpness of wit and understanding." From medical theory to Augustine, Bartholomew then slides easily to scripture, when he adds that "by the authority of the apostle he sets a man before a woman in dignity and worthiness of the Image and likeness of God." And so it is that Bartholomew brings his discussion of the differences between male and female complexion back to the dangers of female speech, quoting from Paul's letter to the Corinthians: "I suffer not a woman to teach in Church or congregation: For it is written: Under man's power thou shalt be, and he shall be thy Lord."[40]

Complexion theory provided biological support to long-standing misogynist attitudes, particularly the notion that every woman is a liar. Sometimes these attitudes would be presented in a matter-of-fact tone, a neutrality of language underlining the objectivity of analysis. In his *Questions on the Eight Books of Aristotle's Politics*, John Buridan cites female complexion as the central reason why women cannot be judges, why their counsel cannot be trusted. Judges and counselors, he explains, must be wise, prudent, and in control of their passions. But these are traits rarely found in women, because of a general complexion that puts female reason at the mercy of their out-of-control passions, that renders their judgments fluid and inconstant and certainly not subject to right reason.[41] Significantly, Buridan later adds that women cannot even properly be said to possess prudence, the virtue that allows us to identify what is truly good and to select the most appropriate means to achieve it. Women only seem to possess prudence and right reason. In reality, they possess mere cunning (*astutia*), which allows them to seek their own private good or, by mere luck, the common good.[42] Several decades later, Nicole Oresme, an eminent theologian and member of Charles V's court, would echo these ideas in his translation and gloss of Aristotle's *Politics*, arguing that prudence is so rarely found in women because their deliberation lacks maturity, and "the softness of their nature" means their advice can never be firm.[43]

Cunning was hardly a neutral term. Aquinas had defined it as the vice opposed to prudence and rejected its use outright. In the *Summa of Theology*, for example, organizing his discussion of cunning or craftiness around the authority of Paul's second letter to the Corinthians, he writes, "The Apostle says, 'We renounce the hidden things of dishonesty, not walking in craftiness, nor adulterating the word of God.' Therefore, cunningness is a sin."[44] The contrast between prudence and cunning would surface in other, equally telling, places. Both Aquinas and Bonaventure employed the distinction to elaborate the absolute differences between Christ's incarnation and the Devil's stratagems. It is Christ's prudence that counters the Devil's cunning, thus rendering the incarnation, life, and crucifixion of Christ the perfect antidote and response to the Devil's evil machinations and lying schemes.[45]

But it was Aquinas's famous mentor, Albert the Great, who brought out the real difference between male prudence and female cunning. Late in his treatise *Questions on Animals*, Albert asks whether men are more easily trained in morals than women. Perhaps not, he begins, offering in dubious defense of female educability the fact that women are more like children and children are more easily trained than their elders. Authority might support this position as well, for hadn't Aristotle contended that women possessed more prudence than men? But Albert will have none of this. He counters both the alleged values of female childishness and Aristotle's authority with what he assumes everyone takes to be unimpeachable common, proverbial, and popular wisdom. "Women are great liars," he writes, "weak, diffident, shameless, deceptively eloquent, and in a nutshell, woman is nothing other than a devil disguised in human form." Popular opinion finds its intellectual support in complexion theory. Women, Albert explains, are more humid than men, and while this makes it easier for women to receive information, it also makes it difficult for women to retain that information.[46]

The consequences of a moist female complexion, Albert warns his readers, are awe-inspiring in their horror. Excessive humidity renders women fickle and inconstant, prone to passion, and always embroiled in sin. Invoking language that could be mistaken for something out of the *Lamentations of Matheolus*, Albert notes their temperament leaves women perpetually unsatisfied and forever in search of new pleasures. When a woman is beneath one man, he writes, she cannot help but wish she were already under another. Countering Aristotle's claim that women possess more prudence than men, Albert contends, as Buridan would later, that properly speaking women only seem to possess prudence, when in fact they possess mere cunning. Invoking the age-old association of women with the body and the senses, men with the soul and reason, Albert observes that "the senses move woman towards every evil, just as the intellect moves man towards every good." Albert roots female dependence on the senses in a deficiency "in the intellectual operations, which consist in the apprehension of the good, the deliberation of truth and the avoidance of evil." As a result of these deficiencies, woman is "directed by sensory appetites which incline her towards evil." In short, Albert writes, woman is a defective man, and whatever she cannot acquire through honest means, she endeavors to acquire "through lies and diabolical deceptions," and this is why every woman ought to be shunned "like a venomous snake and horned devil."[47]

Albert's comments return us to the very sorts of writings Christine had in mind as she pondered woman's wretched ways. So far as Christine knew, Albert most likely had written one of them. In the opening pages of *The City of Ladies*, Christine mentions *Women's Secrets*, a book popularly ascribed to Albert, although most likely written and then glossed by a student and followers. *Women's Secrets*, a key source for the most influential of all witch-hunting treatises, *The Hammer of Witches*, describes itself as a handbook designed to "bring to light certain hidden, secret things about the nature of women" so that confessors will know how to interrogate them and what sorts of penances to assign for their sins. Unsurprisingly, the treatise depicts women as overflowing with sin and deceit in large part because they "are so full of venom in the time of their menstruation that they poison animals by their glance; they infect children in the cradle; they spot the cleanest mirror and whenever men have sexual intercourse with them they are made leprous and sometimes cancerous."[48] Feminine deceitfulness arises from a woman's very body, from her very essence. Kramer and Sprenger, those close readers of *Women's Secrets*, glossing an entire religious and scientific tradition, would put it this way in *The Hammer of Witches*: "For she is lying in speech just as she is lying in nature."[49]

CHRISTINE DE PIZAN, MISOGYNY, AND SELF-KNOWLEDGE

Alone in her room, books proudly proclaiming the biological inferiority and inescapable sinfulness of women surrounding her, Christine carefully dramatizes the plight of women who have heard nothing but misogynist slander their entire lives. "Alas God," she writes, "why did You not let me be born in the world as a man, so that all my inclinations would be to serve you better, and so that I would not stray in anything and would be as perfect as a man is said to be?"[50] But Christine does not mean this, and she knows that it is men who lie to women, who lie about women. Christine takes it upon herself to reveal and prove those lies for what they are.

Unlike John of Salisbury in the *Policraticus*, unlike her own book, *The Treasure of the City of Ladies*, in *The Book of the City of Ladies*, Christine does not ask if it is acceptable to lie. Instead, she wants women to see themselves for what they really are and the world for what it really is. In this sense, *The Book of the City of Ladies* is, at one and the same time, critique, diagnosis, and therapy. The actions women can take to confront an aggressively deceptive world depend entirely on the possibilities they find within themselves, on the self-knowledge that generates those possibilities. The practical importance of this kind of knowledge appears in *The Treasure of the City of Ladies*, the handbook for women that Christine presents as the companion piece to *The Book of the City of Ladies*. In the former, Christine advises that the noblewoman must know who she is and whether she is best suited to the contemplative or the active life. While the contemplative life is dearer to God, the "active life has more use in this world." If a woman opts for the active life, she must be completely clear about her standing at court. She must be able to distinguish what is truly good from what only appears to be good, and having made these discriminations, she must know how to respond.[51] She must, in other words, possess and exercise the faculty of prudence, the faculty that, as Thomas Aquinas notes, allows us to match proper means to proper ends. But this is precisely the faculty that the misogynists, drawing on both biblical exegesis and natural philosophy, so strenuously asserted that women lacked. Without it, women can only be cunningly disguised deceivers, incapable of either virtue or honesty, little different from the Devil in the Garden of Eden.

In *The Book of the City of Ladies* Christine, along with three allegorical figures—Ladies Reason, Rectitude, and Justice, who ap-

pear suddenly and without warning in her locked study—sets herself the task of undercutting and refuting misogynist claims that
women lack prudence.[52] She adopts a variety of strategies to accomplish this. Among other things, she questions the misogynists'
motives. Why do men say such hateful things about women? Some
men slander women in a misguided effort to help other men, de-
meaning the object of their lust to help free them from the sinful
chains of desire. Other men are simply cruel and vicious, taking
pleasure in slander and vice. Some, having led dissolute lives in
their youth, wantonly deceiving and seducing women, are now old
and decrepit, impotent, angry, and unrepentant as they vainly recall past pleasures forevermore out of reach.[53] This was certainly
the case with Matheolus, Lady Reason tells Christine, "who himself confesses that he was an impotent old man filled with desire."
Whatever the cause, she assures Christine that such blanket con-
demnations can arise only from a wickedness of heart that blinds a
man to "the good deeds which women have done for him" and,
without doubt, such assertions are contrary to nature, "for there is
no naked beast anywhere, nor bird, which does not naturally love
its female counterpart."[54]

Highlighting the motivations behind male misogyny, Christine
highlights something else as well. The misogynist always moves
from the particular to the universal, generalizing from one bad experience with some specific woman (whether imagined or real) to
universalizing claims about all women. Just as Tertullian and Jerome had indulged in this tactic so many centuries before, so do
Christine's contemporaries. In *The Letter to the God of Love*, a
poem Christine composed in 1399, several years before beginning
work on *The Book of the City of Ladies*, she had already pointed
out this dubious practice, bemoaning its presence in the sorts of
poems and verses that fill the workbooks assigned to young boys
in school. The clerics who write these books, Christine complains,
fill them with doggerel like "Adam, David, Samson, and many
other men were deceived by women both early and late: what living man will escape? Others say that women are very deceitful,
crafty, false, and worthless. Still others say that they are highly

untruthful, changeable, inconstant, and flighty."[55] More galling is the double standard that allows men to make these generalizations about women, never about themselves. Late in *The Book of the City of Ladies*, Lady Rectitude points out that men seem to expect and demand more from women than they do from themselves and other men. When men waver, when men sin, they brush it off as nothing of consequence, as being simply the result of human nature. By contrast, when "a few women lapse (and when these men themselves, through their own strivings and their own power are the cause), then, as far as these men are concerned, it is completely a matter of [feminine] fragility and inconstancy."[56] As Tertullian had it, every woman is an Eve.

Christine's response to this homogenizing account of women is telling. Taking her lead from scripture as opposed to biology, she stresses God's power and perfection. God would never make something evil or imperfect, and those men who suggest that God created women as flawed versions of the human species demean him and his goodness.[57] Christine's argument is more nuanced than the one the misogynists put forth. On the one hand, her emphasis on God's power, goodness, and perfection undercuts the misogynists' belief that biology necessarily makes women evil. God created both men and women perfectly and in accord with his wishes. On the other hand, she does not counter their stereotyped depiction of all women as essentially evil with another stereotype of her own portraying all women as essentially good. It is not our sex that makes us saints or sinners, she writes, it is what we do, what we make of ourselves. "The man or woman in whom resides greater virtue is the higher," Lady Reason tells Christine, "neither the loftiness nor the lowliness of a person lies in the body according to sex, but in the perfection of conduct and virtues."[58]

As both a writer and thinker, Christine's inclination is to avoid generalizations and to dwell with the particular, to move away from the demands of universal law and toward the demands of the moment. At one point, for example, Lady Reason explains that "God has ordained man and woman to serve him in different offices" and that this is why it "would not be at all appropriate for [women] to go and appear so brazenly in court like men, for there are enough men who do so." But, Lady Reason immediately adds, what is generally the case need not always be the case. "If anyone maintained that women do not possess enough understanding to learn the laws," she continues, "the opposite is obvious from the proof afforded by experience, which is manifest and has been manifest in many women."[59] Natural and divine hierarchies matter, but they are not absolute, and in extraordinary circumstances women must act in extraordinary ways. Lady Reason assures Christine that "a woman with a mind is fit for all tasks," and the bulk of *The Book of the City of Ladies* bears this claim out as the three allegorical ladies provide example after example of women who performed remarkable and virtuous actions when circumstances demanded it. Christine relates stories of empresses and queens who, suddenly finding themselves widowed, threatened on all sides, take control of their countries, rule them wisely, develop laws, defend them from attacking enemies, and conquer neighboring countries.

But if these stories are meant to demonstrate what women can do, they also, crucially, demonstrate what women are. However diverse their motives or flawed their logic, the lies men tell about women are grounded in stories that reveal famous women to be nothing but liars and temptresses. History seems to support misogyny and, as Jean de Meun wrote in defense of his accounts of deceitful woman, his stories are true so long as the "worthy men who wrote the old books did not lie." If the misogynist argues from example to rule, Christine's final move is to undercut their examples, to demonstrate that the very stories men tell to demonstrate that all women are liars are themselves lies, mistruths, and implausible exaggerations. History itself becomes the battleground to disprove the misogynist reification of women into deceitful woman. Until now, Christine claims, no one has contested the slanderous histories men write, so their unchallenged lies thereby become authorities, and such authority is the guarantor of truth. "Just as you yourself once said regarding this question," Lady Rectitude says, reminding Christine of her earlier poem *The Letter of the God of Love*, "whoever goes to court without an opponent pleads very much at his ease." In that earlier poem, Christine had no doubt that "[i]f women had written all those books, I know the works would read quite differently, for well do women know this blame is wrong."[60]

It is, at first glance, a curious strategy. To counter traditional claims that women are liars, claims rooted in long-accepted histories, stories, and exempla, Christine will rewrite those stories, rewrite accepted history to exonerate women. On the surface, it seems she is doing little else than confirming worst suspicions, countering authority with falsification, creating fictions to counter truths, lying to prove women aren't liars. Christine, unsurprisingly, deflects these claims, sometimes implicitly, sometimes explicitly. On a number of occasions she looks to her own experience as a woman, her knowledge of herself and of other women, to justify her alterations to commonly told stories. Lady Justice reminds her, for example, that all she needs to do is think about herself and her own body to know that *Women's Secrets* is nothing but a pastiche of absurd and puerile fantasies, just as all she needs to do is reflect on the lives of friends and acquaintances to know that more often than not women, far from ruling their husbands like the serfs of imperious queens, suffer more from their husbands' cruelties and beatings "than if they were slaves among the Saracens."[61] Often reflection on the lives of her contemporaries serves as the basis for making sense of the lives of women long since dead, a reflection rooted in the commonly held belief that human nature remains constant over time.[62]

Nowhere is Christine's dependence on her own experience to rewrite history more evident than in the story of the young and beautiful Tertia Aemilia, who learns that her aged husband, the legendary Roman general Scipio, has taken up with a mere servant girl. Giovanni Boccaccio had included this story in *Famous Women*, a sort of encyclopedic collection of brief stories of well-known women that he composed between 1361 and 1362. Boccaccio praises Tertia's loyalty to her husband. She lets no one know about the affair, concealing her own emotional pain in order to protect the reputation of her much-respected husband. Having lauded her discretion, Boccaccio cannot help but move from Tertia's story to general reflections about women. Tertia, Boccaccio suggests, like all women, was a weak and suspicious creature suffering from low self-esteem, and this makes her actions all the more marvelous precisely because they are so unexpected from a woman. Had she been like most women, she would have called in her family and friends, filling "their ears with slander and complaints" while harassing her "husband in public with tearful protests," ruining the reputation of a person "who in all other respects was a man of spotless honor."[63] For her part, Christine, who composed *The Book of the City of Ladies* with a copy of Boccaccio's work at hand, praises Tertia, who "never ceased to serve her husband loyally, to love him, and to honor him." Unlike Boccaccio, rather than assess Tertia's behavior in light of some abstracted conception of feminine nature, Christine simply notes that her behavior is hardly uncommon. "I have seen similar women," she tells Lady Rectitude, including most recently a young and beautiful countess in Brittany who "thanks to great constancy and goodness did the same."[64]

Christine emphasizes examples of constancy to counter claims that all women are fickle and inconstant. These claims found their biological support in a theory of complexion that held women to be moister than men and, therefore, less rational, less able to retain moral lessons, and all too easily led astray by the senses and physical pleasures. As Albert the Great, John Buridan, and a host of others had surmised, the female body itself renders women merely cunning, never prudent, naturally prone toward evil and every sort of deception. Christine attacks these ideas at the very beginning of her biographies, when she praises Eve's body. The first woman was created in paradise itself, not from vile mud, but from "the noblest substance which had ever been created . . . the body of man."[65] Nor did she deceive Adam, Christine argues in *The Letter to the God of Love*. She believed what the serpent said, repeated it to Adam in good faith, with neither fraud nor guile, and things said with no hidden spite "must not be labeled deceptiveness."[66]

Perhaps Eve was not deceitful, but this account of her actions certainly opens her to charges of dull-wittedness and inconstancy. No doubt with this concern in mind, Christine quickly turns to the story of Semiramis. Following the death of her husband, King Ninus of Nineveh, Semiramis took control of his empire, expanded and secured its borders, built fortresses, and founded cities. A notoriously infamous figure, Boccaccio had already included her story in *Famous Women*, suggesting that Semiramis initially took control of Ninus's army through deceit, pretending to be her young beardless son. While this example of feminine wile does not seem particularly to perturb Boccaccio, Semiramis's private life is another matter. "Like others of her sex," he writes, "this unhappy female constantly burned with carnal desire and it is believed she gave herself to many men," including her own son, whom she eventually married. Appalled, Boccaccio asserts that Semiramis's lust deranged her judgment. She became "heedless of time or circumstances" as base pleasure dragged her ever closer to the abyss. In a cunning attempt to cover her crimes, she passed laws allowing every sort of sexual impropriety, hoping her own sick pleasures might pale in comparison with those of her subjects. No good could come from any of this and, in the end, her own son slaughtered her, whether through fear others would interfere with his incestuous nights or because he had grown disgusted with himself Boccaccio refuses to say.[67] Overflowing with deceit, lust, and depravity, Boccaccio's telling of Semiramis's life seems perfectly modeled on Scholastic accounts of woman, all women. They lack prudence and have no concern with the common good. They desire nothing but their own satisfaction, never hesitating to employ corrupt means for even worse ends.

To Christine, this entire reading of Semiramis's life is flawed. Christine simply ignores Semiramis's cross-dressing, even as she admits that the widow did marry her son. Questionable though this behavior might seem to us, Christine adds that the widowed queen had good reasons for acting as she did. Had her son married another woman, Semiramis may well have lost some of her power and, the implication goes, the state some of its security. More im-

portant, Christine notes, in those early days "people lived according to the law of nature, where all people were allowed to do
whatever came into their hearts without sinning."[68] The appeal to
ancient custom, to the differences between life before and after
the introduction of law, is hardly original with Christine. In the
late thirteenth century, Vincent of Beauvais had employed it in his
Speculum Doctrinale to explain away both Abraham's adultery
("In Paradise God praised marriage, he did not condemn adultery") and Lot's incestuous relations with his two daughters ("Lot
and his holy daughters acted for the sake of posterity, otherwise
the human race would have died out, thus their public service
excuses their private guilt").[69] While Vincent is mostly interested
in clearing the names of the long and revered dead, Christine is
doing something much more interesting. Christine argues that
not only were Semiramis's actions moral given their time and
place, she acted with foresight and a concern about the common
good, about what she could and must do to maintain the security
of her empire. Far from being "heedless of circumstance," as Boccaccio claimed, she knew exactly what was allowed and what
was needed. She acted with reason and prudence, not with lust
and cunning, properly weighing means and ends for the good of
her state.

Christine takes up the topic of prudence again a bit later in the
text. After listening to Lady Justice recount the lives of several
women of great learning who could "conceive, know and retain all
perceptible things," Christine asks "whether women can reflect on
what is best to do and what is better to be avoided, and whether
they remember past events and become learned from the example
they have seen, and, as a result, are wise in managing current
affairs, and whether they have foresight into the future."[70] Lady
Justice responds that Nature bestows prudence on both men and
women, some receiving more, some less, and then supports her
contention with accounts of the lives of particularly prudent
women such as Gaia Cirilla (the wife Tarquin, king of Rome),
Dido of Carthage, and Ops, the queen of Crete. She concludes with
the life of Aeneas's wife, Lavinia. Suddenly widowed and pregnant

with Aeneas's son, Lavinia fled to the woods fearful that "Aeneas' son by another woman would have the child put to death in his desire to rule." Despite these hardships and her long widowhood, Lavinia never remarried, treasured the memory of her dead husband, and treated her stepson so well he eventually "harbored no evil against her or his half brother." She founded cities and governed wisely until her son was of age and assumed power.[71] Perhaps not all women can be this prudent, this virtuous, but neither can all men. One should not expect anything more, nor anything less.

The recovery of prudence as both a male and female virtue is at the absolute center of Christine's ideological critique of the misogynist tradition and her rediscovery of who she is and what she can do. It is also at the absolute center of her contention that women are not natural liars. Christine offers no shortage of examples to disprove misogynist claims that all women are seductive and deceitful temptresses, and such stories go a long way to demonstrate that women are perfectly capable of considering context and circumstance, of matching means to end, to achieve the good. Prudence frees women, just as it frees men, from slavishly following after the senses and the sordid satisfaction of every base desire. It allows the virtuous woman to reflect on and respond to whatever situation confronts her. Unfortunately and all too often, she will confront a world filled with lies and deception, with treachery and violence. In such circumstances, the noblewoman is no different from John of Salisbury's man of eminence, no different from the heroes and heroines of vernacular romance. Lady Rectitude includes any number of stories of women who lie virtuously and out of necessity. Hypsipyle places herself in grave danger when she lies to protect the life of her father, as does Lady Curia to save her husband, and Tertia Aemilia, embodying the very wisdom Christine recommends in *The Treasure of the City of Ladies*, lies to conceal her husband's extramarital affair.[72] If possession of the faculty of prudence frees women from the charge of being natural liars, it also sets them free to lie when circumstance requires and virtue demands it.

ALL MEN ARE LIARS

Revealing long-revered authority to be false, purposefully distorted to demean and slander women, reveals that authority to be nothing but base deception. Whether or not women are natural liars, men also lie and, all too often, those lies are anything but virtuous.

Pietro de'Zorzi, the eldest son of Moderata Fonte, who died giving birth to her fourth child in Venice in 1592, certainly understood this. Pietro appended two sonnets to the front of his mother's posthumously published treatise, *The Worth of Women*, praising her efforts to call out the deceivers for what they really were. "Up to now," he writes, "men could conceal all their misdeeds, but now their flaws, as well as women's true qualities, will be known from one end of the world to the other."[73] Fonte's book appeared in 1600, eight years after her death—all things considered, a relatively bad year for the reputation of men, at least in Venice. That same year another Venetian woman, Lucrezia Marinella, published her own table-turning work, *The Nobility and Excellence of Women and the Vices and Defects of Men*, a spirited response to Giuseppe Passi's 1599 diatribe *On the Defects of Women*, an all too typical, if particularly rabid, attack on the female sex. Marinella makes her intentions abundantly clear from the very outset: "My desire is to make this truth shine forth to everybody, that the female sex is nobler and more excellent than the male."[74] Nobler, according to Marinella, not simply because women possess all the virtues—prudence, intelligence, kindness, courage, and constancy— that men so often claim they lack, but nobler too because it is men themselves who lack those very virtues. Fonte would not have disagreed, and despite the stylistic differences between their two works, both Marinella and Fonte share an unshakable belief in the almost innate dishonesty of all men, a belief that every man is liar and that this belief must guide a woman's every word and every deed.

Marinella and Fonte stand at something of a crossroads in the literary history of the defense of women. Among the most famous Venetian women writers of the late sixteenth century, they would build on the arguments of Christine de Pizan and more immediate predecessors, while resituating and reframing them. The social and cultural world of turn-of-the-century Venice may well have encouraged women to deeper reflection and reassessment of their place in the world. The forced enclosure of so many Venetian noblewomen, both before and after marriage, contrasted not only with the freedom that foreign female visitors experienced but also with Venice's famous and quite visible courtesans, not to mention actresses, who had only recently begun to appear onstage. The variety of roles women played in Venetian society almost begged for analysis.[75] Not content, as Christine had been, to unmask the lies men pass off as truths about women, Marinella and Fonte return slander for slander, or better, argue that when men lie about women, they reveal the truth about themselves and in so doing reveal a truth about all men and all women. Their critique is subtle. If a tradition dating back as least as far as Tertullian had argued that women are natural liars because they are essentially artificial, covered, and adorned, Fonte and Marinella argue that to be human, male or female, is to be adorned. The difference between men and women does not rest in adornment but in the vile adornments men adopt to suppress and oppress women.[76]

Whereas Christine de Pizan worked her way through the slanders of the misogynists behind closed doors in dialogue with three allegorical figures, Fonte stages her attack as a conversation among seven women who, "despite their great differences in age and marital status," are good friends. They often set aside time to gather together for "quiet conversation; and on these occasions, safe from any fear of being spied on by men or constrained by their presence," they can speak freely on any topic they desire. On this day, Fonte tells us, the women have convened for the afternoon at Lenora's house, a beautiful residence along one of the Venetian canals with a lovely and secluded courtyard garden filled with flowers and fruiting trees. The oldest member of the group, Adriana, a widow "of great discernment," describes the garden as a paradise. Corinna, a young single woman, quickly adds that among the garden's most charming aspect is "that there are no men here."[77] Men might be physically absent, but from the beginning they are the topic of conversation, spurred on, no doubt in part, by the arrival of Helena, just returned from her honeymoon and still in the first thralls of love with her new husband.

When Adriana's unmarried daughter Virginia asks if Helena is happy, Leonora sarcastically chimes in, "How can you ask such a thing, when everyone already knows the answer? For popular opinion dictates that no new bride can be anything but happy." Helena's response, however, is decidedly lukewarm. Although she enjoys her husband's company, already he seems to be too controlling, prohibiting her from leaving the house to attend weddings and banquets. The others do little to comfort her, noting that newlyweds almost always suffer illusions of happiness that blind them to the reality of their new status in life. "What you mean," Leonora clarifies, "is that everything seems lovely when it has the charms of novelty."[78] Married mere weeks, Helena has no response to Leonora's somber pronouncement. Already, experience is putting the lie to popular opinion and received authority, revealing promises of marital happiness to be mere illusions that all too quickly give way to a cruel reality threatening ever new dangers and novel forms of suffering.

Fonte makes the dangers of popular illusions and false appearances explicit when the ladies ask Leonora to explain the symbolism of six statues, exquisitely sculpted figures of beautiful women each holding emblems and scrolls, that surround a fountain situated at the very center of her courtyard garden. Before describing them Leonora reminds everyone that her aunt, from whom she inherited the house and who had vowed from the time she was a little girl never to marry, procured the fountain and its statues "as a statement of the way in which she intended to live her life and of the views she held against the male sex." The first three, Leonora explains, offer the keys to female independence, illustrating the need for chastity, solitude, and liberty. The next three emphasize the threats that men pose to such independence. The fourth figure is Naïveté, which signifies those women who "put too much faith in the false endearments and empty praises of men," believing their husbands will always be kind and charming and, so deceived, "allow themselves to be caught in their snares and fall into the fire that burns and devours them." Next comes the emblem of False-hood, which "tells of the deceit and falsity of men" and the glaring divide between their sweet words and their vile hearts. Finally, there is Cruelty, which speaks to the violence men commit against the women "who become involved with them" and the feigned compassion men pretend for their victims.[79]

Now sitting around the fountain, the women decide to engage in a friendly debate, making official what has already become the central topic of conversation, the worth of men. They nominate Adriana to be queen and judge, and she, in turn, nominates Le-onora (assisted by two others) to "the task of speaking as much evil" about men as she can and Helena, who is still "so captivated by the charms of her husband, along with two others, to speak in defense of men."[80] From this moment forward, the entire conversa-tion will replay the same concerns about uncertainty, illusion, flat-tery, and lies that characterize court handbooks, but now explicitly transposed onto the register of gender and sexual difference. From the perspective of these women, it is men who lie constantly and uncontrollably. The discussion of husbands, invariably cruel and violent, prone to anger, fond of prostitutes and gambling, finally gives way "to talk about the worst type of man there is: the false and deceitful lover."[81] Adriana warns that this is a topic so vast, she "can't imagine you'll be able to cover the tiniest part of what there is to say on the subject." Virginia, speaking on behalf men, argues that lovers, true lovers at least, cannot possibly be as flawed "as you have shown other conditions of men to be." She refuses to believe that "a well-mannered young man, behaving respectfully, sensibly and politely," neither begging for favors nor complaining of unsatisfied desires, a young man "showing with his burning sighs and other subtle signs" that he loves me, could be a deceiver. "On the contrary," Virginia contends, "it would seem to me as though I could see his heart lying open before me and I should be overcome by his displays of love and humility and would not help loving him in return."[82]

Cornelia warns Virginia against too easily mistaking appearance for reality. "You have just painted the outward semblance of a lover," she counters, "as though his inner self must necessarily correspond to this appearance." Fearing that Virginia has no real experience with men, Cornelia embarks on a scathing portrayal of lovers, young and old, who stop at nothing as they lie and scheme their way to a woman's dishonor and ignoble rejection. Young men are too impetuous and hotheaded, quick to demand favors and even quicker to brag about them to anyone that will listen. Their only advantage is that youth and lack of experience makes it easier to strip away their lies, revealing that all their kind manners and bashful stutters are merely a "false coat," like "bronze with a layer of gilding." Middle-aged men are even worse: experience adds to their false charms as they lay "down traps for every woman they see, trying out each one in turn, deceiving them all, saying the same words to all and laying down the same nets." Middle-aged men, Cornelia concludes, have one dubious advantage over younger men. Concerned with their reputation, at least they keep quiet about their self-serving seductions. If anything, old men are the worst of the lot. Having long lost their looks and their charms, deficient in so many ways, they would be better off finding happiness at the bottom of a bottle than in chasing pretty girls.[83]

While there is nothing original about depicting lovers, liars, and flatterers in terms of false facades, Cornelia's reference to Virginia's having "painted the outward semblance of a lover" links this discussion of male deceit with another discussion, one that takes place on the next day, when the women have reconvened in Leonora's courtyard garden. Having begun a wide-ranging conversation about men, women, and natural philosophy, the women eventually turn to a discussion of the seemingly miraculous power of paintings to preserve the fame of heroes in noble poses, at their moment of greatest triumph or saddest defeat. Lucretia dreams of her own military victory, fighting for freedom from male tyranny like the Amazons of old, bearing the emblem of the phoenix "to boast of her chaste resolve to live forever without a mate."[84] Explaining the power of such symbols, Adriana notes that "[a]ll these various emblems and colors are like a language that doesn't use words, that allow people to reveal the innermost reaches of their heart in a delightful manner." Having apparently forgotten the previous day's critique of false lovers, Leonora counters that she prefers the language of sighs to the language of emblems. For sighs constitute the most truthful and eloquent form of speech. For her part, Cornelia opts for the language of the eyes, those "eloquent orators" that "can in all truth be said to speak and to reveal in their outward gaze the innermost secrets of the heart." Coming to the defense of sighs, Corinna replies that "eyes very often deceive . . . showing one emotion in place of another," but the language of sighs never lies, "for it has to be admitted that although one can pretend to sigh without meaning it, it's very easy to detect the lie."[85]

As if suddenly coming to her senses, Leonora cuts short this digression on different forms of speech and immediately quashes any hope of an inherently truthful and transparent language enabling us to see the reality beneath the surface, the soul hidden within the body. "In men, everything is feigned: looks, sighs, colors, words, deeds. You can never discover the truth of their souls or tell whether they are acting sincerely—except when they are perpetrating some particularly grave offence against women."[86] Men are not just liars, they are inveterate liars. They are natural liars in precisely the same way that men claim women are liars.

Throughout *The Worth of Women*, Fonte undoes the traditional coupling that associates women with the body and men with the soul. Men are nothing but painted surfaces and superficial languages. At the very beginning of their conversation about the arts, Corinna contends that poetry is to painting as the soul is to the body. "Painting," she argues, "is like a body the soul has left, while verse is like a soul without a body; and so just as the soul is far nobler than the body, so composition in words is far nobler than one in colors."[87] Of course, it is Corinna who, throughout this second day of conversation, has quoted various lines of poetry, some of which the women suspect to be her own. By contrast, the women consistently associate men with the body, with makeup and adornment. Men will spend "a thousand years combing and setting the few paltry hairs they have on their head," and when they are not wearing ludicrously long ties, more like napkins than clothing, tied so tightly around their necks they look like puppets, they will surrender hours each day to selecting from among any number of tight breeches with long doublets that make them look like frogs.[88]

Unlike Tertullian, who condemned adornment outright as altering the holy word of God's creation, a trespass and lie against God's truth, the ladies in Leonora's garden place a positive valence on style and fashion. Style, Corinna says, should not simply be tolerated, "but accepted and praised, just as much as any other feminine adornment. Because this is nothing more than a fashion, a custom, and a pastime of ours."[89] But adornment can be more than mere fashion as well. Surfaces can, sometimes, reveal hidden truth, and the "refinement and neatness of our appearance is a sign of nobility of soul." In her treatise *On the Nobility and Excellence of Women and the Vices and Defects of Men*, Lucrezia Marinella extends this conception of adornment beyond fashion. All the great handbooks on courtly life, she argues, such as the works of della Casa and Castiglione, advise the courtier to be "elegant and polished," and if this applies to men why shouldn't it apply to women, "since beauty shines brighter among the rich and elegantly dressed than among the poor and rude"?[90] Beauty is like a gift from God that must be cherished, protected, enhanced. Men are no different. If a man is naturally strong, a gladiator or solider, for example, doesn't he do everything he can to maintain his strength? Don't courageous men learn the arts of war in order to take advantage of their fearlessness? If men adorn and improve their natural gifts and talents, why shouldn't women? Invoking Augustine's authority, however dubiously rendered, Marinella even contends that the Church fathers recognized the importance of feminine adornment.[91]

No one can deny that men always and in every way adorn themselves, Marinella asserts. How many men dress themselves in fine clothes to distract attention from their unattractive faces, dye their beards "when the dread arrival of old age causes them to turn white?" Men spend hours before mirrors primping their hair, powdering their face, scenting their body, while wearing shoes many sizes too small in order to make their feet seem more petite. Hortensius, "the famous orator," spent whole days gazing at himself in the mirror, adjusting the folds of his clothing. Demosthenes, "the glory of Greek eloquence," was no better, and Marinella's list rolls onward with a litany of famous men who painted their faces, bleached their skin, and spent all their wealth on clothes and jewelry, extravagances that left them and their families destitute. If these sorts of examples seem to link adornment to feminine vanity, critiquing men when they become more like women, Marinella stresses that manliness itself is nothing but a kind of adornment. Try to find a man, she asks her readers, "who does not swagger and play the daredevil. If there is such a one people call him effeminate." Men dress themselves up in uniforms and swords, with medals and boots, making sure everyone knows they are armed and dangerous. "What are these things," Marinella concludes, "but artifice and tinsel? Under these trappings of courage and valor hide the cowardly souls of rabbits or hunted hares, and it is the same with all their other artifices."[92]

As Fonte puts it, there are many types of languages: spoken languages and the language of sighs and of the eyes, the language of emblems, and the language of fashion. Men speak of their courage when they dress like soldiers and pace through the streets with a determined pounding gait no less than women speak of the beauty, refinement, and nobility of their souls when they color their hair or dress in clothes dyed in rich purples and gold. Of course, both Marinella and Fonte agree that each sex uses these languages differently. The languages that men use are almost always false and illusory facades to strike fear in other men and to seduce their next would-be and unsuspecting female conquest, whereas the language of women strives for truth, revealing their simple honest natures, even as they attempt to calm their husbands' unruly tempers. However men and women put these languages to use, they are all forms of adornment, no longer understood as pertaining essentially to women but to both men and women, equally and essentially. If a popular Renaissance proverb asserted that "women are words, men are deeds," then both Marinella and Fonte suggest that deeds are simply visible words and that men, no less than women, depend on them.

A threatening reduction for men, no doubt, and no men experienced that threat to their alleged superiority over women more intensely than rhetoricians and orators, that is, men who made their living plying that most feminine of things, language. In 1458, Pico della Mirandola famously contrasted the philosopher with the rhetorician, demanding that philosophy remain free from the feminine poison of rhetorical adornments. "Who will not condemn synthetic beauty, or rouge, in a reputable maiden? Who would not curse it in a Vestal?" he asks. "For what else is the task of the rhetor than to lie, to entrap, to circumvent, to practice sleight of hand."[93] Rhetoricians, like women, it would seem, are garrulous and decorative, wordy and deceitful. Faced with this dilemma, rhetoricians attempted to distinguish within rhetoric itself between a masculine and feminine style. The first-century Roman rhetorical theorist Quintilian had already contributed to this project when he contrasted a virile, "natural and unaffected" style of speech, like the body of a healthy man "enjoying a good circulation and strengthened by exercise," with an emasculated style, more akin to "the man who attempts to enhance these physical graces by the effeminate use of depilatories and cosmetics." Renaissance writers would pick up on these distinctions, contrasting a virile style of speech with a soft feminine style.[94] Borrowing from Cicero, for example, the English rhetorician Henry Peacham invoked military metaphors to guarantee the masculinity of at least some forms of eloquence. Figures of speech, he explains, "are as martial instruments both of defense and invasion; and being so, what may be either more necessary, or more profitable for us, than to hold those weapons always ready in our hands."[95]

Countering style with style as a means of demarcating the allegedly absolute differences between male and female seems a losing proposition even before begun, as if certain kinds of style are not styles at all. Peacham merely gives added credence to Marinella's sarcastic description of all those men, carefully decked out in soldier's uniforms, attempting to fool the world into thinking they are as brave as they pretend to be. Male rhetoricians may have tried to cordon off an effeminate style, but their efforts simply revealed that rhetoric was style all the way down or, in their language, inescapably feminine.[96] If this troubled men who were worried about their masculinity, it troubled women too, though for a different reason. This final problem is less clear in Marinella's treatise than in Fonte's dialogue.[97] So confident is she in her argumentation, Marinella offers no room for doubt, uncertainty, or second thoughts in her encomium for women, her deprecation of men. Women are prudent, intelligent, temperate, and strong. Men overflow with anger and envy. They are obstinate and ungrateful liars and deceivers. Certainly the women in Leonora's garden would agree with all this, but where Marinella's evisceration of male pretension operates entirely at the level of argument and assertion, confident in its proofs and exempla, seemingly freed from the tyranny of male deception, Fonte's characters are not nearly as secluded in Leonora's courtyard garden as they would like to be. Like the snake that slipped its way into Eden, the outside world constantly makes itself felt, intruding into the conversation often unrecognized, leaving the women confused, uncertain, and always already ensnared in a world of masculine lies.

Fonte signals this condition from the very start of her treatise when Helena voices concern about her husband's sudden and unforeseen insistence that she remain at home, and then with the need for the other women to remind her repeatedly of this potentially dread development.[98] But it appears in other places as well. During the second day in the garden, a discussion about lawyers and judges suddenly transforms into praise of Venice's leaders who, "like loving fathers, work unceasingly, unstintingly, and unwaveringly for the benefit of all, without any thoughts of the cost to themselves, in money and energy, of their labors for the common good."[99] Only after quite a while does Leonora free her friends from this propaganda that they have long accepted at face value. "Good Lord!" she exclaims, "I can't believe what I am hearing. . . . Are not all these official functions exercised by men, against our interests?" But even Leonora finds herself deluded, if only momentarily, when, recalling a popular *canzone*, she accepts its platitudes about the truth of lovers' sighs. Everything in society, it would seem, conspires to fool women, to make them act against their own interests, to accept second-class status and culturally sanctioned domestic violence. Perhaps this is most obvious in the lies men tell to seduce women, but these lies are everywhere, in institutions that limit a woman's choices in life and in the love and devotion they are made to feel for their state, in well-known songs and poems, in sayings, maxims, and learned treatises. "For if we are their inferior in status," Leonora explains, "but not in worth, this is an abuse that has been introduced into the world and that men have then, over time, gradually translated into law and custom; and it has become so entrenched that they claim (and even actually believe) that the status they have gained through their bullying is theirs by right."[100] And the power and ubiquity of these institutionally sanctioned lies are enough to fool women explicitly engaged in conversation to critique, unmask, and condemn them.

Nowhere does male duplicity create greater uncertainty and fear than in marriage. Near the end of conversation on the second day, Virginia, now convinced of the dangers men pose to women, claims she no longer wishes to marry. Her mother, Adriana, responds that her uncles claim she must in order to keep the family fortunes safe.[101] But what if her husband proves violent, boorish, prone to anger or jealousy? If this is the case, Adriana responds, her daughter will have to work to change his nature with compassion, constancy, and humility. Leonora repeatedly counters that none of these strategies work—men don't change but if they do, they only change from bad to worse. In that case, the women agree that Virginia will have to choose carefully and make sure she finds one of the few decent men that exist. Sadly, masculine nature undercuts even the value of this seemingly sound advice. Male duplicity runs deep and long, unperceived for years, carefully and purposefully hidden until it is too late for the deceived woman to escape. Men who have no good qualities, certainly none of the qualities a woman would want in a lover and husband, Cornelia explains, "often succeed very well (much to our harm and peril), in concealing their falsity and ill intentions beneath an appearance of decency. So even if a man does seem, over a long period, to display that loyalty and true love that we have talked about, I should advise any woman who is sensible, well-respected, and virtuous to proceed cautiously, if she values her virtue and reputation."[102]

Perhaps not every man is a liar, but sadly, Leonora and her friends have no choice but to assume otherwise.

MADELEINE DE SCUDÉRY, THE SALON, AND THE PLEASANT LIE

There are any number of ways to ruin a conversation. Discussing how to ruin them, it turns out, is not one of them.

Madeleine de Scudéry, the most popular author of the seventeenth century and sponsor of the Saturday Society, an influential Parisian salon, stages her conversation about bad conservations as a gathering of amiable and eminently polite men and women, placing it at beginning of her 1680 collection of interlinked set pieces, *Conversations on Various Subjects*. Of course, the point of this conversation is not to dwell on the incompetent, not to ridicule and insult the boorish and dull—that would hardly be polite and amiable. Rather, as Cilenie, one of the women, puts it, "Before we can determine what most contributes to the charm and beauty of conversation, everyone here must recall those annoying conversations that have most bothered them."[103] Focusing on the bad will help to illuminate the good, and the value of good conversation is inestimable according Cilenie, who describes it as the most essential bond of human of society. Good conversation is "the greatest pleasure of well-bred people, the most ordinary way to introduce, not only politeness to the world, but also the purest morals and the love of glory and virtue."[104] When conversation goes wrong, more than boredom is at stake.

Unlike Christine de Pizan, unlike Moderata Fonte and Lucrezia Marinella, in her *Conversations* Scudéry neither attacks men
nor defends women. Instead, she teaches them how to behave and
how to converse, hardly a surprising role for an aristocratic woman
in seventeenth-century France. Although often connected with the
Enlightenment Republic of Letters, the salon, from its inception in
the waning years of the sixteenth century and well into the nine-
teenth century, was ultimately a retreat for the rich and aristocratic. Offshoots of the royal and noble courts, places where
women had long played a central role in maintaining harmony
among potential adversaries through enforcement of the codes of
chivalry and gallantry, the salons, too, were places where the rules
of courtliness and courtly sociability held sway. And in the salon,
just as in the court, it was women who played the role of peace-
keepers and civilizers.[105] Men must know how to talk and so must
women, because friendship and society depend on it. Which, as
Scudéry's conversation about conversations develops, is little different from asserting that friendship and society depend on lies.

Given the seemingly trivial examples of bad conversations the
group discusses, it is at first difficult to discern why Cilenie places
so much importance on it. Several of the women bemoan the hours
lost, as if doing penance, having listened to women who do nothing but complain about their servants, their daily chores, or one
who rapturously described "syllable by syllable the first stutterings
of her three year old son." Some women speak incessantly about
their clothes, lying about how much they paid for them or the
trouble they had procuring them. Others gossip cruelly and insip-
idly about other women, their loves and losses and lack of looks.[106]
And the list continues with men coming off little better as they
prattle on endlessly about the minutiae of their business affairs,
estates, and sunken boats. While one or two of the women present
suggest that when men converse they tend to be more rational, albeit more serious, than women, whose discussions too often de-
volve into nothing but inane triviality, this doesn't prevent some
men from disagreeably talking only of great historical events or
others from focusing on nothing but the nonevents of daily life.[107]

In a later conversational set piece, "On Speaking Too Much or Too Little," Amilcar pays a visit to Plotina, who makes him promise not to be so boorish as the two men she had met with earlier in the day, the one who spoke so much she was reduced to silence and the other who spoke no more than four words during his entire stay.[108]

Asked toward the end of dialogue what can be learned from these various examples of conversation gone wrong, Valerie suggests that most any topic is fit for proper conversation, but only if introduced at the right time and only if discussed for the right amount of time. "I believe that there is no topic that cannot be entered into; but it must be free and varied according to the time, the place and the people one is with; and the key is that one always speaks nobly of base things, simply of noble things and gallantly of gallant things, without undo haste or affection."[109] While successful conversation requires both the wit and judgment necessary to be able to fit our words to the moment and to the audience, truly refined conversation must appear effortless. Valerie adds that the sort of person she has in mind, the sort, no doubt, that Scudéry depicts herself and her friends to be, must speak so easily and gracefully that "they don't seem to reject any of their thoughts, as if saying whatever comes to mind, without any affected design of saying one thing rather than another."[110] Conversation must flow smoothly among all participants, moving seamlessly from one person to the next, back and forth and always forward.

Scudéry had already emphasized the importance of effortless conversation nearly forty years earlier in the introduction to her 1642 work, *Illustrious Women or Heroic Harangues*, in which she imagined twenty great speeches delivered by famous women of the past, such as Cleopatra, Agrippina, and Sappho. Although Scudéry was widely known to be the work's creator, her brother Georges appears in it, as he so often does, as the alleged author. The introductory letter, written in his voice, takes up an objection that some men might make to her depictions of these women. Some men, Scudéry writes, might find it strange "that I have chosen women to express my thoughts because they imagine that the art of oratory" is unknown to them. If the ancients really did praise women for possessing great oratorical skills, then why doesn't Scudéry assiduously follow the rules of rhetoric as taught in the schools, organizing her speeches with such key rhetorical elements as exordiums, narrations, exaggerations, metaphors, digressions, antitheses, "and all the other beautiful figures that typically enrich works of this sort?" These figures of speech are present, Scudéry responds, but hidden, for "the most delicate art consists in pretending there is none at all," just as a woman might carefully set the curls and ringlets of her hair with a negligence so subtle and a nonchalance so agreeable that "anyone would suspect it was the wind, rather than her hands" that had arranged it so beautifully.[111]

Artifice concealed behind an effortless facade defines Scudéry's conception of conversation, and she explicitly contrasts it with the rhetoric of the schools, with the language of lawyers at court, merchants at their trading houses, generals before their armies, and kings before their counselors. Amilcar announces the basis for this distinction at the very beginning of "On Conversation," when he asserts that "all of these people speak expertly of their concerns and affairs, but they lack the agreeable talent of conversation which is the sweetest charm of life and is, perhaps, more rare than is commonly believed."[112] Of course, the distinction between these two types of rhetoric mirrors a social distinction between places where women were allowed to speak and places where they were institutionally and legally barred from speaking. Women were not allowed to participate in such public arenas as the Sorbonne, courts of law, and the military. In opposition to these sites of public speech, Scudéry proposes the salon as a place with its own superior form of rhetorical practice, where both men and women can participate as equals.[113] Just as important, Scudéry delimits the field of private rhetoric through a series of exclusions. It is not like public speech. It is not like all those examples of conversation gone wrong. As Amilcar's comment suggests, self-interest governs these other types of speech. The lawyer wants to win his case, the merchant seeks to maximize his profits, and bad conversationalists insist on imposing their personal obsessions on anyone and everyone who will listen.

Polite conversation bonds together noble society because in the privacy of the salon, removed from the competitive hustle and bustle of the outside world, the participants put personal interest aside in favor of entertaining conversation that has no end beyond itself.

If conversation is the bond of all civil society, then complaisance is the most basic bond of conversation.[114] Complaisance names that all-important skill that allows individuals to conceal their own interests and yield to the wishes of others. In "On Complaisance," Clearque notes that "complaisance yields without weakness, praises without flattery . . . without affectation and baseness, renders society agreeable, and life easier and more diverting." Sometimes, for the sake of others, we will pretend happily to discuss topics we don't much care about, participate eagerly in activities we would rather forgo. Complaisance names the ability to ignore the foibles and eccentricities of others, to cede our own personal pleasures to the pleasures of those we are with, and so with "a thousand other little things, which without offending reason, and going against justice, manage effectively to make mankind better."[115] More than merely ceding to the wishes and desires of others, for complaisance to do its work, we must appear sincere. We must conceal our own wishes and desires behind an effortless facade of agreement so that those we are with can truly believe we mean what we say, otherwise our alleged agreement will reveal a not so hidden self-interest. "There is nothing more insupportable," announces Clearque, "than those people who adopt a false complaisance and who are willing to do whatever you want to do, so that you will be willing to do what they want."[116] Finally, we mustn't be overly complaisant, agreeing with everything proposed so that conversation dwindles into the boring silence of automatic agreement. There must be enough disagreement and wit among the participants to lend conversation its needed traction, to allow it to progress and for everyone to come together in a shared act of entertainment, but not so much that it grinds to a halt in strongly held positions, silence, boredom, or anger.[117]

Scudéry's conception of conversation as a model of social cohesion depends on the concealment of self-interest beneath a carefully contrived appearance of nonchalance and naturalness. The most clever bit of carefully planned banter must appear as if it springs immediately and naturally to mind. Even a moment's hesitation between saying one thing or another betrays the possible hidden presence of a self-interest calculating between its most beneficial options. Conversation succeeds, society forms and bonds, when nothing disturbs these smooth exterior appearances, when nothing gives us cause to worry about what those appearances might hide. In a different conversation, "On the Knowledge of Ourselves and Others," for example, Cephise claims that in order "to pass one's life sweetly, it is necessary to remain on the surface of things, for should you penetrate any deeper, a person may find that those same pleasures are bitter."[118] In our dealings with others, we should be satisfied with facades and appearances. Hoping to discover and know something more, something deeper, something real, will only lead us into "a thousand sorrows."[119] When another person complains that Cephise would have us lead our lives potentially deceived about our dearest friends, Cephise simply acknowledges that to "look deeper is to risk those surfaces being proven false." We can think we have known someone for years only to discover, suddenly and unexpectedly, the most dismaying imperfections in their character. The best we can do is make conjectures about others, knowing full well that more often than not we will be proved wrong.[120]

Invoking the sort of world-weary truism found in critiques of court life from as early as the eleventh century, Telesile supports Cephise's favorable assessment of superficial human relations when he adds that it is simply impossible to know when and if people are disguising themselves. Who can tell if anyone is the person he presents himself to be: the courtier before his lord, the lover before his lady, even a friend before his friend? "One cannot know the heart," he concludes, "through words or actions."[121] Significantly, Scudéry complicates this vision of global uncertainty and latent duplicity with a dose of Jansenist self-loathing. Not only can we never be sure if others are being truthful, worse, we cannot even be sure about ourselves. We continually mask our own passions and envies, disguising them without realizing it, so charmed by our defects that we believe ourselves noble and caring when we are actually base and cruel. "People love themselves more than all the rest of the world," Cephise notes, "and though they do not know themselves, they esteem themselves, they praise themselves without knowing why and even as they attempt to deceive others, they deceive themselves as well."[122] Although the bulk of the dialogue consists of a friendly debate between Cephise and Telesile about whether, with work, it is easier to know something of ourselves or others, the final word belongs to a third participant, Timocrates. "I believe that the two of you will agree," he concludes, "that the greatest difficulty in knowing others well, and even ourselves, derives from the same cause that makes us see distant objects confusedly and makes us unable to discern those things that are too near to us. Similarly, we can say that others are too far from us and we are too close to ourselves in order to know either the one or the other perfectly."[123] Too close to ourselves and too far from others, everything becomes blurred, uncertain, unknown.

Whether truthful or false, society coheres so long as it skirts smoothly along a polished surface of diverting pleasures that conceal the possibility of ulterior motives and self-interest, of jealousy and envy. Universal civility, Cephise will claim, is a way of living, a tool we can use to make our way through the world as we see fit. Others can interpret our civility however they wish, and many may interpret our actions "as the beginning of friendship. This being so, wouldn't it be brutal to disabuse them of their error?"[124] Predictably, it is precisely this gap between what appears and what exists, between superficial complaisance and hidden interests, that renders the utility and convenience of civility problematic. Essential for social harmony, complaisance is, at the same time, dangerous, capable of abetting vice as much as virtue. On the one hand, as Clearque states in "On Complaisance," "It is necessary to the society of all mankind, it promotes all pleasures; maintains friendship and without it we should be ever in a state of war and irritated." On the other hand, he adds, "As sincerity is of all virtues that which is most peculiar to persons of honor, complaisance is of all virtues that which the sordid, the self-interested, the treacherous and flatterers most commonly abuse."[125] Behind a mask of complaisance, we can flatter and goad and harm others for our own benefit.

Amilcar, a little later in "On Complaisance," attempts to limit its domain and potential for abuse. "In proper speech," he asserts, "we can say that complaisance is the queen of trifles, and it is appropriate when the question is whether to stroll in one direction or the other, to dance or not to dance, to sing or not sing."[126] But it is clear that complaisance's kingdom extends much further than the realm of mere social niceties, that it extends into every aspect of our dealings with others. Clearque will point out that there are "self-interested complaisances, habitual complaisances, complaisances of love, esteem and friendship, ambition, sordid and counterfeit complaisances, complaisances of the court and the city, serious complaisances, jocund and eloquent complaisances, true and false ones and thousands of other sorts."[127] Ideally, complaisance has no "particular interest," aiming instead at "the world's convenience" even as it strives to avoid dissimulation, lying, and flattery. But these are less rules than mere suggestions, for complaisance has no rules, and its proper performance requires judgment and virtue.[128] Sadly, our inability to know either ourselves or others renders these moral decisions suspect, a situation made all the more problematic because flattery is simply complaisance misused. "The civility and gallantry of the world," Scudéry writes, "at first conceals flattery, then custom admits it, and we are so used to it we are no longer capable of recognizing it."[129] Behind every act of complaisance lurks the possibility of flattery, deceit, and deception.

There was nothing Scudéry could have done about this, nothing anyone could have done to erase the always threatening difference between what we say and what we mean. With those hidden depths of self-interest forever imperceptible, Scudéry opts for what we can perceive, reducing civil society to a seamless flow of words always leading to more words, each sentence expressly designed to delight even as it conceals the intentions that motivate the speaker. Complaisance is the price she pays to purchase a place free from the contest and troubles and misogyny of the public world of male-dominated competitive discourse. Ultimately, the challenge Scudéry confronts is no different from the problem Moderata Fonte confronted in *The Worth of Women*. But whereas Fonte saw nothing for it but to dream of a utopian world of women freed from the impenetrable and ensnaring lies of men, Scudéry converts that world of women into the idyllic dream of a civil society rooted in nothing but false pleasantries, uniting both men and women in the private refuge of the salon.

The problem of lying and hypocrisy, present yet veiled in every preceding chapter of *Conversations on Diverse Subjects*, finally surfaces in first volume's last dialogue, "On Dissimulation and Sincerity." The speakers wonder if it is possible to distinguish complaisance from flattery, sincerity from hypocrisy, truth from lies. "But as for sincerity," Lucinda announces, "all the world boasts of it and wants to have it; and those who are the greatest dissimulators cover themselves no less in sincerity, for without it their dissimulation would be ineffectual."[130] Mathilda wishfully suggests that sincerity and hypocrisy can be distinguished, for "sincerity must of necessity carry along with it all the beauty of truth, all the charms of freedom, all the sweetness of confidence." Sincerity reveals itself not in words but in an open heart, in guileless eyes and agreeable expressions. "In a word," she concludes, "it is like beauty without paint, which fears neither to be seen in the truest light nor closely examined."[131] But everyone else present at the conversation realizes, as had the women in Moderata Fonte's *Worth of Women* and, indeed, as Bernard Mandeville would assert some forty years later, that this is little more than a dream. The success of civil society depends on concealing intentions and interests behind white lies, false pleasantries, and insincere gestures. Women cannot help but perceive each other as rivals, and men are too competitive to ever really open themselves to one another.[132] "When I examine myself," Padilla states, "I am all too aware that sincerity often quits me. I have said a hundred times to women of my acquaintance that I thought them beautiful and well dressed, well made, that they danced admirably, yet I believed nothing of all this. We conceal love, hatred, ambition, and we only show what we believe may please or be useful. The world has ever took this course and ever will."[133]

And saying this, the conversation continues. Indeed it must continue. Deftly diverted to less pessimistic topics, the artful banter of the salon will proceed through another volume of conversations, skimming along on a beautiful pleasant surface, where lies no longer matter so long as they add to the conversation.

The Lie Becomes Modern

In the *Discourse on the Origins of Inequality*, Jean-Jacques Rousseau offers his own account of the origin of lies and deception. Invoking no sacred garden, neither God nor serpent, Rousseau tells the story of wild men and women, once solitary but contented wanderers, now coming together to form the first families and, soon, the first societies. Settled in gatherings of primitive huts, they slowly develop language and tools, the first farms, and the art of metallurgy. With agriculture, they discover the need to divide land, to assign each lot to the man who tills it and, over time, from years of repeated use, these lots become that man's personal property. Property, in its turn, requires a system of justice, for "as men began to look to the future and as they all saw themselves with some goods to lose, there was not one of them who did not have to fear reprisals against himself for wrongs he might do to another."[1]

Had all men been naturally equal, Rousseau suggests, equally strong and clever, industrious, and thrifty, none of these changes would have been so problematic. Unfortunately, men are far from equal and, as a result, they began to perceive themselves and each other in new and troublesome ways. Differences in wealth, prestige, and status, in mind, beauty, strength, and skill, stirred the envy of the less well-off, while it goaded the pride of the successful. "And these qualities being the only ones which could attract consideration," Rousseau ominously notes, "it was soon necessary to have them or affect them; for one's own advantage, it was necessary to appear to be other than what one in fact was. To be and to seem to be became two altogether different things; and from this distinction came conspicuous ostentation, deceptive cunning, and all the vices that follow from them."[2]

Rousseau narrates a secular fall from the state of nature in which men present themselves to one another just as they are, hiding nothing because they have nothing to hide, to the state of civil society in which "suspicion, offenses, fears, coldness, reserve, hate, and betrayal constantly hide under that uniform and false veil of politeness, under that much vaunted urbanity we owe to the enlightenment of our century."[3] Extending a line of thought already present in Augustine's meditations on Adam and Eve's disobedience, and revived in both Jacobus Acontius's *Satans Strategems* and John Milton's *Paradise Lost*, Rousseau asks what it was about the first couple, about any of us, that makes it possible for us to sin. "You say we are sinners because of our first father's sin," Rousseau writes to the bishop Beaumont of Paris in 1763, "but why was our first father himself a sinner? Why wouldn't the same reason by which you explain his sin apply to his descendants without original sin?"[4] This question troubled Augustine, who saw nothing for it but to suspect a hidden and always present and percolating pride in the first couple, already tilting them toward evil even before the serpent arrived on the scene. Every subsequent medieval and Reformation theologian rejected Augustine's solution because it suggested that God had created mankind with an innate propensity toward evil. Whatever hidden steps led to that initial disobedience, Augustine and the theologians all agreed that the consequence of that fateful action was the hereditary stain of original sin, the continuing source of human perversity.

For his part, Rousseau simply rejects the entire notion of original sin because it explains nothing. As he argues in his letter to Beaumont, to invoke original sin as the reason for our evil actions is to do little more than to argue that mankind is corrupt because it is corrupt. Rousseau, by contrast, claims to have an account of how mankind, born naturally good, becomes corrupt.[5] As men and women formed the first families and groups, they became aware of one another, learned to speak and began the long, slow, everconstricting and enslaving process of human socialization. "Each one began to look at the others and wanted to be looked at himself, and public esteem had value," Rousseau explains in the *Discourse on Inequality*, "and that was the first step towards inequality and, at the same time, towards vice. From these first preferences were born on the one hand vanity and contempt, on the other shame and envy; and the fermentation caused by these new leavens produced compounds fatal to happiness and innocence."[6]

We lie, Rousseau argues, because we are social, have become social, valuing more what people think about us than what we really are, and as society develops, as the arts and sciences develop, our lies become ever more refined and inescapable. "Before Art had molded our manners," Rousseau writes, "and taught our passions to speak an affected language, our morals were rustic but natural." But now we worry so much about public opinion that no one "dares to appear as he is," and "a base and deceptive uniformity prevails in our morals" as we restrain our impulses and carefully compose our every word and deed, rendering us unknown to everyone else and everyone else unknown to us. "Even to know our friends," Rousseau writes, "we must await some critical and pressing occasion; that is, until it is too late; for it is on those very occasions that such knowledge is of use to us."[7] Many writers from the prior century—Marquise de Sablé, François La Rochefoucauld, and Madeleine de Scudéry among them—had made precisely these sorts of observations, noticing that in the courts and salons of Europe, the facade of virtue had replaced any concern with real virtue. We compliment others whom we have no desire to compliment and exchange courtesies with people we despise because that will make things easier for us. Social cohesion and the public good require that we tell such lies, and what is good for society is good for us. Rousseau suggests something very different. Society divides us against ourselves: it opposes our natural inclinations and sentiments with its own standards. Confused, we become lost to ourselves, inauthentic and insincere. As Rousseau writes in *Emile*, "Always in contradiction with himself, always floating between his inclinations and his duties, he will never be either man or citizen. He will be good neither to himself or others."[8] No inherent perversity of will, no original sin, just human beings grown prideful and deceptive through historical circumstance, alienated from themselves, tricked into believing that hypocrisy provides the surest route to happiness.

All of which means the problem of lying, of whether it is ever acceptable to lie, takes quite a different shape in Rousseau's writings. He explicitly discusses lying in the fourth of his *Reveries of the Solitary Walker*. Long pained by the memory of a youthful lie, Rousseau believes he has ever since assiduously cultivated a life devoted to truth, going so far as to claim for his personal motto a variation on a line from the Roman writer Juvenal's *Satires*, "To consecrate one's life to truth."[9] A mere moment's reflection, however, brings to mind all the occasions he has lied and prevaricated without any remorse, neither at the time nor later when reflecting on his actions. He begins with a definition of lying, one he claims to have read "in a Philosophy Book that to lie is to conceal a truth we ought to make manifest."[10] This definition frames the question of lying in the language of debt. When do we owe someone else the truth? When do we owe ourselves the truth? What are the sorts of things we can owe to others and to ourselves? These are complicated questions that grow only more complex as the essay continues, but it is a complexity Rousseau refuses to evade. Repeatedly stressing that what matters most is what can be put into practice, he simply rejects all those many austere moralists who steer clear of these problems by arguing we must never lie, no matter what the consequence. Such men, Rousseau dismissively notes, offer little more than "idle chatter impossible to put into practice."[11]

Not only does he reject the austere advice of moralists, he rejects truth as an absolute good in and of itself. While general and abstract truths are precious, allowing us to reason and conduct ourselves toward our due ends, particular truths can be beneficial, harmful, or simply irrelevant. He clarifies the distinctions between useful, harmful, and indifferent truths through a comparison. Imagine a man, the sort whom most of the world calls truthful, a man who faithfully ensures the accuracy of every trivial little fact he states but who, when it comes to himself and his own interests, adopts colorful language and, even if he doesn't lie, is more than happy to mislead others for his own benefit. Now imagine a different sort of man, a man, no doubt, of the sort Rousseau imagines himself to be, a man so perfectly indifferent to all those trivial details that "he will scarcely have scruples about amusing a group of people with contrived facts from which no unjust judgment results." But, when it comes to truths that matter, when it comes to things pertaining to his own interest or the interests of others, "he is solidly truthful, even against his self-interest." For Rousseau this is the man who exemplifies what it means to be truthful because he renders what is owed, and only things that matter, things that have value, are things that can be owed. "The truth that is owed is that which interests justice," Rousseau writes, "and this sacred name of truth is debased if applied to vain things whose existence is indifferent to all and knowledge of which is useless for anything."[12] Scrupulous adherence to justice can even justify certain lies, and Rousseau recalls two episodes from his youth in which he lied to protect friends from what he perceived would have been unjust punishment and then adds, "and a hundred others of the same nature have happened to me in my life."[13]

Between Augustine and Rousseau everything seems to have changed. Perhaps this is not surprising, and it may even be obvious, but it is worth pointing out. Augustine had argued, and argued repeatedly, that the very essence of sin and, therefore, the very essence of lying as the prototype of all sin consisted in the belief that we can discriminate between good and evil when we decide that this act, this lie, is no sin at all. "When a man lives according to truth, then he lives not according to self, but according to God; for it is God Who has said, 'I am the truth,'" Augustine writes in *The City of God*. "When he lives according to self—that is, according to man, and not according to God—he then certainly lives according to falsehood."[14] In sharp contrast, though within limits, Rousseau seems to make himself the arbiter of what is moral and immoral, true and false. As he puts it near the very end of the "Fourth Walk," "From all these reflections, it follows that the commitment I made to truthfulness is founded more on feelings of uprightness and equity than on the reality of things, and that in practice I have more readily followed the moral dictates of my conscience than abstract notions of the true and the false."[15] We act with justice when we act in accord with our inner sentiments, when we replace the insincerity that society demands of us with the sincerity that we can, with effort, demand from ourselves.

Rousseau accepts this justification for the occasional lie even as he admits that it displeases him and does not clear him of all guilt. "In weighing so carefully what I owed others," he asks, "have I sufficiently examined what I owed myself?"[16] The truthful man, Rousseau will argue, must above all else be "jealous of his self-esteem, this is the good that he can least get along without, and he would feel a real loss in acquiring the esteem of others at its expense."[17] But does he pay himself his just due when he spices up sterile conversation with innocent lies, or does he instead sell himself cheaply to a society that asks him to play the liar and hypocrite so that others perceive him as he wishes to be perceived? These lapses are so much the worse given his motto that publicly proclaims his absolute commitment to truth. Rousseau's response is not to side with the austere moralists but to lower his sights. When he has lied, it has been out of weakness, not a desire to be false. "With a weak soul we can at the most preserve ourselves from vice; but to dare to profess great virtues is to be arrogant and rash." When we learn who and what we really are, we sometimes learn that we must "presume less" of ourselves, expect less from ourselves.[18] Rousseau counters the socially sanctioned and instituted hypocrisy that alienates us from ourselves, that renders us insincere, with the ideal of personal integrity and unity, with personal sincerity as a good in and of itself, as an end in itself. We are sincere when we act and speak according to our inner sentiments and nature, even if those inner sentiments cannot live up to the ideals we think we hold.[19]

∞ ∞

If there is a before and an after in the history of lying, then Rousseau's *Discourses* may well mark the moment when the one becomes the other. Although he was far from the only eighteenth-century thinker to question the notion of original sin, Rousseau's critique is without doubt the most intense, the most developed, the most devastating.[20] With Rousseau, deception and lying become natural problems, problems with natural causes and, hopefully, natural solutions. While this development was never inevitable, the history of lying certainly suggests how it became possible, in what Rousseau both retains and rejects from that history. On the one hand, he is inescapably beholden to the long-held belief that we have fallen from a state of perfection into a state of corruption. His narrative of that fall may differ markedly from the one that so many had accepted for so long, but the beginning and end of the stories, however told, remained the same. On the other hand, his sense of disgust with our current state seems more profound than it was for many of his immediate predecessors and contemporaries.

Even before the eighteenth century, writers had gradually been coming to terms with what they understood to be our inherent penchant for deception and lying. Jacobus Acontius had recognized that our inability to interpret God's Word with total clarity, with total accuracy, while unfortunate, simultaneously provided a basis for harmonious coexistence among the many varied Protestant sects. While the theologians never gave up their contention that every lie is a sin, they ceaselessly worked to mitigate the culpability of beneficial lies and to expand the range of deceptive and misleading (though never mendacious) behavior. In the tradition of courtly writing, the value and function of lies had steadily expanded, from a means of countering the deceits and evil intentions of others to providing the very foundation of social harmony and, to hear Mandeville tell it, prosperity as well. Something similar occurs with female writers responding to charges of their inherent deceitfulness. From Christine de Pizan to Madeleine de Scudéry, women writers made a concerted effort to demonstrate why women can engage in prudential deceptions and lies, while rehabilitating the role of coverings, appearances, and deceptive pretenses. A cynical reading of Scudéry's *Conversations on Diverse Subjects* suggests that the seventeenth century's most popular author believed the only society in which men and women could coexist in peace would be a society of mere appearances, innocent fabrications, and carefully structured lies.

Everywhere, it seems, lying and deception had already become normalized, not so much secularized and stripped of their roots in Genesis, as unquestionably fitted into the successful and harmonious operation of a fallen world. If this book's central question, *Is it ever acceptable to lie?* was always really a question about how we should live in a corrupted world, whether we should accommodate ourselves to it or reject it, a number of writers leading up to and during the eighteenth century had increasing difficulty imagining a world in which we did not lie, a world that did not need our lies. Unable to return to paradise, this world, the world in which the fallen Adam and Eve found themselves, in which all their descendants had and would continue to find themselves, had always been corrupt and full of liars. In a very real sense, the history of the human race was the history of an always already-corrupted species and, as a result, the only options were to accept or reject the ways of this world. Rousseau discovers a third option: recovery. For him, the fall from honesty and innocence into mendacity and corruption is a historical event, an event that occurred and continues to occur in this world, in the complicated interplay between individual and society. The recovery of what has been lost, Rousseau admits, will never be total. We live in the aftermath of society, forever in its wake, and whatever innocence we regain will be rooted less in honesty than in a state of personal integrity and sincerity, in remaining true to our deepest and most personal sentiments—and sentiments can conflict with principles. We might lie and feel justified in our hearts, even as we recognize that it goes against our ideals, and this is fine.

While the late eighteenth-century German philosopher Immanuel Kant would hardly take so tolerant an attitude concerning lies, his work reveals how fully the problem of lying after Rousseau had become a new problem, our problem. Kant conducts his entire investigation in entirely human terms, examines it as a strictly human phenomenon. "The greatest violation of a human being's duty to himself regarded merely as a moral being (the humanity of his own person)," Kant writes in the second part of *The Metaphysics of Morals*, first published in 1798, "is the contrary of truthfulness, *lying*." When we lie, whether for charitable or evil reasons, we violate the purpose of human communication, which consists in the honest revelation of our thoughts to another. As a result, when the liar lies, he renounces his personality and becomes "a mere deceptive appearance of a human being, not a human being himself."[21] Kant prohibits lies because falsehood contradicts and debases our very essence as rational beings. "To be truthful (honest) in all declarations," Kant writes in *On a Supposed Right to Lie from Philanthropy*, a brief essay he published in 1797, "is therefore a sacred command of reason prescribing unconditionally, one not to be restricted by conveniences."[22]

Although Kant alludes to scripture, noting that the Bible dates the first crime not to Cain's murder of his brother Abel but to the first lie, and that "it calls the author of all evil a liar from the beginning and the father of lies," he does this solely to make a philosophical point. The ground and possibility of the human propensity toward hypocrisy is inaccessible to reason, impossible to deduce from any actual lie itself.[23] But for Kant, biblical revelation no longer picks up where human reason fails, offering answers to questions unanswerable to us on our own. In *Conjectures on the Beginning of Human History*, Kant turns to Genesis to think, not so much about the origin of human mendacity, but about the origin of human freedom. Before proceeding with this biblically inspired thought experiment, Kant carefully qualifies its usefulness. Such speculations, he notes, "should not present themselves as a serious activity but merely as an exercise in which the imagination, supported by reason, may be allowed to indulge as a healthy mental recreation." Removed from its earlier role as a historical account of the source and origin of all human misery, the tragedy in the Garden now offers the exhausted philosopher a vacation from the hard work of rational inquiry, a "pleasure trip," as Kant refers to it at one point.[24]

The ground shifts, and the question of lying finds itself irrevocably separated from God and the Devil. Even as we continue to ask *Is it ever acceptable to lie?* and even as the answers we come up with appear unaltered (yes, no, sometimes, never), the framework is new. Beneath a settled and seemingly unchanged facade, everything has changed, as if, having lived too long in exile, we one day realized paradise had never existed in the first place.

Notes

INTRODUCTION: IS IT EVER ACCEPTABLE TO LIE?

1. Dante Alighieri, *Dante's Inferno: The Indiana Critical Edition*, trans. Mark Musa (Bloomington: Indiana University Press, 1995), canto 18, in order, ln. 114, 35, 133–36. Virgil's more general description of Malebolge occurs earlier, canto 11, ln. 52–69: "Fraud, that gnaws the conscience of its servants,/can be used on one who puts his trust in you/or else on one who has no trust invested.//This latter sort seems only to destroy/the bond of love that Nature gives to man;/so in the second circle there are nests//of hypocrites, flatterers, dabblers in sorcery,/falsifiers, thieves and simonists,/panders, seducers, grafters and like filth.//The former kind of fraud both disregards/the love Nature enjoys and that extra bond/between men which creates a special trust;//thus, it is in the smallest of the circles,/at the earth's center, around the throne of Dis,/that traitors suffer their eternal pain."
2. *Dante's Inferno*, canto 32, ln. 36.
3. *Dante's Inferno*, canto 11, ln. 25–27.
4. Matthew 26:25. Unless otherwise noted, all biblical passages come from the *New Standard Revised Version, with Apocrypha* (Oxford: Oxford University Press, 1995). On sin and placement in the *Inferno*, see Marc Cogan, *The Design in the Wax: The Structure of the* Divine Comedy *and Its Meaning* (Notre Dame: University of Notre Dame Press, 1999), 36–75.
5. *Dante's Inferno*, canto 23, ln. 142–45.
6. *Dante's Inferno*, canto 33, ln. 91–150.
7. On plants, insects, and spiders, see Natalie Angier, "The Art of Deception: Sometimes Survival Means Lying, Stealing or Vanishing in Place," *National Geographic*, August 2009, 70–87. On primate deception, Euclid O. Smith, "Deception and Evolutionary Biology," *Cultural Anthropology* 2 (1987): 50–64.
8. Robert Feldman, *The Liar in Your Life: The Way to a Truthful Relationship* (New York: Twelve, 2009), 14–15. On evolutionary aspects of human deception, David Livingstone Smith, *Why We Lie: The Evolutionary Roots of Deception and the Unconscious Mind* (New York: St. Martin's Press, 2004), 11–12, writes, "Nature selected those mental capacities that helped spread our genes, and those that proved unhelpful were ineluctably snuffed out. As any seducer knows, honesty and reproductive success are not necessarily

good bedfellows. Because deception and self-deception helped our species to succeed in the never-ending struggle for survival, natural selection made them part of our nature."

9.   The contemporary literature on lying is immense. An accepted and accessible starting point for most philosophical discussions is Sissela Bok, *Lying: Moral Choice in Public and Private Life* (New York: Vintage Books, 1999, 2nd ed.), also, David Nyberg, *The Varnished Truth: Truth Telling and Deceiving in Ordinary Life* (Chicago: University of Chicago Press, 1993). For lying in politics, see Martin Jay, *The Virtues of Mendacity: On Lying in Politics* (Charlottesville: University of Virginia Press, 2010), and for a sociological perspective, J. A. Barnes, *A Pack of Lies: Towards a Sociology of Lying* (Cambridge: Cambridge University Press, 1994).

10.   Bernard of Clairvaux, *On Humility and Pride*, trans. G. R. Evans, in *Bernard of Clairvaux: Selected Works* (New York: Paulist Press, 1987), 114. The scriptural passages come from Psalms 118:75 and 115:11 respectively.

11.   Perez Zagorin, *Ways of Lying: Dissimulation, Persecution, and Conformity in Early Modern Europe* (Cambridge: Harvard University Press, 1990), 330. Also, Albert R. Jonsen and Stephen Toulmin, *The Abuse of Casuistry: A History of Moral Reasoning* (Berkeley: University of California Press, 1988), which organizes itself around the era of "high casuistry," roughly the sixteenth and seventeenth centuries. There are, of course, histories of medieval attitudes about lying, including a series of essays by Arthur Landgraf, beginning with "Definition und Sündhaftigkeit der Lüge nach der Lehre der Frühscholastik," *Zeitschrift für Katholische Theologie* 63 (1939): 50–85, as well as innumerable essays and books focusing on specific medieval writers.

12.   Zagorin, *Ways of Lying*, is the authoritative work on this topic. Also, John Sommerville, "The New Art of Lying: Equivocation, Mental Reservation, and Casuistry," in *Conscience and Casuistry in Early Modern Europe*, ed. Edmund Leites (Cambridge: Cambridge University Press, 1988), 159–84.

13.   Niccolò Machiavelli, "Letter #179, To Franceso Guicciardini, 17 May 1521," in *The Letters of Machiavelli: A Selection of His Letters*, trans. and ed. Allan Gilbert (New York: Capricorn Books, 1961), 200. Recent valuable monographs on deception and the Renaissance court include Jean-Pierre Cavaillé, *Dis/simulations. Jules-César Vanini, François La Mothe Le Vayer, Gabriel Naudé, Louis Machon et Torquato Accetto. Religion, morale et politique au XVIIe siècle* (Paris: Honoré Champion, 2002), and Jon Snyder, *Dissimulation and the Culture of Secrecy in Early Modern Europe* (Berkeley: University of California Press, 2009).

14.   Snyder, *Dissimulation*, 184, ft. 23, discusses some of the background to this maxim.

15.   Sylvester Prierias, *Sylvestrinae Summae*, pars secunda, "De Mendacio & Mendace" (Lyon: Mauricius Roy & Ludovicus Pesnot, 1555), 225.

16.   Dante, *Inferno*, canto 27. Fittingly, Guido fell victim to false counsel himself, believing he could commit and repent of a sin at the same time, ln. 98–102: "He asked me to advise him. I was silent,/for his words were drunken. Then

he spoke again:/'Fear not, I tell you: the sin you will commit,/it is forgiven.
Now you will teach me how/I can level Palestrina to the ground.'"

17. Niccolò Machiavelli, *The Prince*, trans. Peter Bonadanella (Oxford: Oxford
University Press, 1979), ch. 18, 58–59. Lionel Trilling, *Sincerity and Authenticity* (Cambridge: Harvard University Press, 1972), 13–14, takes this contrast between Dante and Machiavelli as definitive of the differences between
medieval and early modern attitudes about truth-telling.

18. Medievalists themselves may have inadvertently abetted this process. Most
work on lying in the Middle Ages focuses exclusively on the Augustinian-
inflected theological and pastoral traditions, and on what were known as the
"sins of the tongue." See, for example, two very good books, Carla Casagrande and Silvana Vecchio, *Les péchés de la langue: Discipline et éthique de
la parole dans la culture médiévale*, trans. Philippe Baillet (Paris: Les Éditions
du Cerf, 1991), and Edwin D. Craun, *Lies, Slander, and Obscenity in Medieval English Literature* (Cambridge: Cambridge University Press, 1997).

19. The best recent book to make these sorts of claims is John Jeffries Martin's
otherwise excellent *Myths of Renaissance Individualism* (New York: Palgrave MacMillan, 2004), 7, which attempts "to approach the history of the
Renaissance self from a new angle, neither Burckhardt's nor Greenblatt's,"
arguing instead that "there were multiple models of identity in the Renaissance," almost always concerned "with what we might call, provisionally
at least, the relation of the internal to the external self." The great virtue of
Martin's methodology, one I have used in this book, is his refusal to reify
a Renaissance conception of self, offering instead case studies of different
ways different sorts of people adapted to the world. Still, when it comes
time to define what is novel about these Renaissance developments, Martin
invokes contrasts between medieval theologians and monks and all variety of
Renaissance people. See, for example, his discussion of prudence, 48–53, and
concordia and sincerity, 109–17.

20. While theologians agreed that any lie was always sinful, there was debate
about whether the lies of holy men were worse than the lies of the ordinary
religious. See, for example, Bonaventure, *Sententiarum*, III, in *Opera Omnia*,
4 vols. (Quaracchi: Collegii S. Bonaventura, 1882–89), dist. XXXVIII,
quaest. 847–49, where he asks, "Utrum omne mendacium sit mortale viris
perfectis?"

21. For two rather different defenses of the use of "perennial questions" as a
mode of historical inquiry, see Mark Bevir, "Are There Perennial Problems
in Political Theory?" *Political Studies* 42 (1994): 662–75, and John Patrick
Diggins, "The Oyster and the Pearl: The Problem of Contextualism in Intellectual History," *History and Theory* 23:2 (May 1984): 151–69.

22. I use the term "tradition" here in somewhat the same sense as Mark Bevir,
The Logic of the History of Ideas (Cambridge: Cambridge University Press,
1999), 200–220, uses it in his defense of the history of ideas against its con-
textualist critics. At 203, for example, he writes, "Because traditions persist
only through teachers initiating pupils into shared understandings, we must
avoid hypostatising them. We must not ascribe traditions an occult or Platon-

ic existence independent of the beliefs of specific individuals. Traditions are not fixed entities people produce by their own activities. The exponents of a tradition bring it into being and determine its progress by developing webs of belief in the ways they do."

23. Augustine, *Against Lying*, trans. Harold B. Jaffee, in Augustine, *Treatises on Various Subjects*, ed. Roy J. Deferrari (Washington, D.C.: Catholic University of America Press, 1952), ch. 10 (23), 152.

CHAPTER ONE. THE DEVIL

1. Which is not to say later Jewish interpreters were uninterested in the first couple. See James L. Kugel, *The Bible as It Was* (Cambridge: Harvard University Press, 1997), 67–82.
2. Luke 3:23–38.
3. Romans 5:14.
4. Romans 5:12–14.
5. Romans 5:19. Jaroslav Pelikan, *The Emergence of the Catholic Tradition (100–600)* (Chicago: University of Chicago Press, 1971), 141–55, notes that it was not until the second century that Irenaeus, developing ideas already present in liturgical practice, provided a theological underpinning for the correspondence between Adam and Christ. For the deeper background, Henry Angsar Kelly, *Satan: A Biography* (Cambridge: Cambridge University Press, 2006), 175–82.
6. The best overall review of the history of interpretations of the early chapters of Genesis remains J. M. Evans, *'Paradise Lost' and the Genesis Tradition* (Oxford: Clarendon Press, 1968). On developing conceptions of Satan, see Neil Forsyth, *The Old Enemy: Satan and the Combat Myth* (Princeton: Princeton University Press, 1987). For studies of medieval interpretations, see Eric Jager, *The Tempter's Voice: Language and the Fall in Medieval Literature* (Ithaca: Cornell University Press, 1993). Useful works on Renaissance and Reformation interpretations include Arnold Williams, *The Common Expositor: An Account of the Commentaries on Genesis, 1527–1633* (Chapel Hill: University of North Carolina Press, 1948), Lise Wajeman, *La parole d'Adam, le corps d'Eve: le péché originel au XVI siècle* (Geneva: Droz, 2007), and Kathleen M. Crowther, *Adam and Eve in the Protestant Reformation* (Cambridge: Cambridge University Press, 2010). On the seventeenth century, see Philip C. Almond, *Adam & Eve in Seventeenth-Century Thought* (Cambridge: Cambridge University Press, 1999).
7. Augustine, *The City of God*, trans. and ed. R. W. Dyson (Cambridge: Cambridge University Press, 1998), bk. 14, ch. 12, 607.
8. Alcimus Ecdicius Avitus, *The Poems of Alcimus Ecdicius Avitus*, trans. George W. Shea (Tempe: Medieval & Renaissance Texts & Studies, 1997), 72.
9. Martin Luther, *Lectures on Genesis, Chapters 1–5*, in *Luther's Works*, vol. 1, ed. Jaroslav Pelikan and trans. George V. Schick (St. Louis: Concordia Publishing House, 1958), 141.

10. Augustine, *The Literal Meaning of Genesis*, trans. John Hammond Taylor (New York: Newman Press, 1982), bk. 11, ch. 6, 139.

11. Jacobus Acontius, *Satans Strategems or the Devils Cabinet-Council Discovered* (London: John Macock, 1648).

12. 2 Corinthians 1:3.

13. John 8:20–44.

14. Luther, *Lectures*, ch. 3, 146.

15. Bonaventure, *Commentarius in Evangelium S. Ioannis*, in *Opera Omnia*, vol. 6 (Quaracchi: Collegii S. Bonaventurae, 1893), 366.

16. John Chrysostom, *Homilies on Genesis: 1–17*, trans. Robert C. Hill (Washington, D.C.: Catholic University of America Press, 1985), 209.

17. Nicholas of Lyra, *Postilla*, in *Bibliorum Sacrorum cum Glossa Ordinaria . . . et Postilla Nicolai Lyrani* (Venice, 1603), col. 1167. The twelfth-century Benedictine abbot and theologian Rupert of Deutz, *In Genesim*, lib. III, cap. IV, in *Opera* (Paris: Caroli Chastellain, 1638), 38–39, recognizing that questions are not commonly thought to be true or false, argues that the serpent's question is a lie because he uses it to conceal his knowledge of God's prohibition and to lead the woman into disobedience.

18. John Calvin, *Commentaries on the First Book of Moses Called Genesis*, vol. 1, trans. John King (Edinburgh: Calvin Translation Society, 1847), 146.

19. Psalms 116:11.

20. Romans 3:4.

21. Ambrose, *Paradise*, in *Hexameron, Paradise, and Cain and Abel*, trans. John J. Savage (New York: Fathers of the Church, 1961), ch. 12 (68), 339. Michael P. McHugh, "Satan and Saint Ambrose," *Classical Folia* 26:1 (1972): 94–106, surveys Satan's presence in Ambrose's work.

22. Astruc was building on the work and insights of earlier exegetes such as Jean le Clerc and Baruch Spinoza. See Pierre Gibert, "De l'intuition à l'évidence: la multiplicité documentaire dans la Genèse chez H. B. Witter et Jean Astruc," in *Sacred Conjectures: The Context and Legacy of Robert Lowth and Jean Astruc*, ed. John Jarick (New York: T&T Clark, 2007), 174–89.

23. For a brief overview of theories concerning these divisions of the text, including contemporary evangelical Christian assertions of a unitary, Mosaically authored text, see Victor P. Hamilton, *The Book of Genesis: Chapters 1–17* (Grand Rapids: William B. Eerdmans Publishing Company, 1990), 2–38. Also useful, Joseph Blenkinsopp, *The Pentateuch: An Introduction to the First Five Books of the Bible* (New York: Doubleday, 1992), 54–97.

24. Augustine, *Literal Meaning of Genesis*, vol. 1, bk. 4, 103–45.

25. Calvin, *Commentaries on Genesis*, ch. 1, 78.

26. Calvin, *Commentaries on Genesis*, ch. 2, 109.

27. Philo of Alexandria, *On the Creation of the Cosmos according to Moses*, trans. David T. Runia (Leiden: E. J. Brill, 2001), chaps. 22 and 23, 88–90.

28. Augustine, *Literal Meaning of Genesis*, bk. 8, ch. 2, 33. Elizabeth A. Clark, "Heresy, Asceticism, Adam and Eve: Interpretations of Genesis 1–3 in the Later Latin Fathers," in *Genesis 1–3 in the History of Exegesis: Intrigue in the Garden*, ed. Gregory Allen Robbins (Lewiston: Edwin Mellen Press,

1988), 99–133, notes that Augustine himself was simultaneously drawn toward and suspicious of allegorical interpretations of the first three chapters of Genesis. For a brief overview of Augustine's exegetical practice, Thomas Williams, "Biblical Interpretation," in *The Cambridge Companion to Augustine*, ed. Elenore Stump and Norman Kretzman (Cambridge: Cambridge University Press, 2001), 59–70.

29. Origen, *Contra Celsum*, trans. Henry Chadwick (Cambridge: Cambridge University Press, 1965), bk. 4:39, 214.

30. Augustine, *Literal Meaning of Genesis*, bk. 8, ch. 1, 34.

31. Luther, *Lectures on Genesis*, ch. 1, 4.

32. Luther, *Lectures on Genesis*, ch. 3:1, 144.

33. Guillaume de Saluste Sieur du Bartas, *The Divine Weeks and Works of Guillaume de Saluste Sieur du Bartas*, vol.1, ed. Susan Snyder and trans. Joshua Sylvester (Oxford: Clarendon Press, 1979), 316.

34. John Milton, *Paradise Lost*, ed. Merritt Y. Hughes (New York: Odyssey Press, 1935), bk. 9, ln. 220–25.

35. Genesis 3:1.

36. Kugel, *The Bible as It Was*, 72–75.

37. John Chrysostom, *Homilies on Genesis*, homily 16 (4), 209. On the Jewish origins of this identification and Chrysostom's innovation, see Evans, *Paradise Lost*, 32–35 and 88–89.

38. Augustine, *Literal Meaning of Genesis*, bk. 11:4, 135–36.

39. Calvin, *Commentaries on Genesis*, ch. 3, 141.

40. On Nicholas's life and his approach to biblical commentary, see Deeana Copeland Klepper, *The Insight of Unbelievers: Nicholas of Lyra and Christian Readings of Jewish Text in the Later Middle Ages* (Philadelphia: University of Pennsylvania Press, 2007), 1–60.

41. Luther, *Lectures on Genesis*, ch. 3:14, 184.

42. Nicholas of Lyra, *Postilla*, cap. 3, cols. 87–90. Another tradition, with roots in *The Book of Watchers* and Philo of Alexandria and culminating in seventeenth-century writings of the German mystic Jacob Boehme, suggests that the serpent seduced a lust-filled Eve. See Almond, *Adam & Eve*, 173–77, and Vita Daphna Arbel, *Forming Femininity in Antiquity: Eve, Gender and Ideologies in the Greek "Life of Adam and Eve"* (Oxford: Oxford University Press, 2012), 17–37.

43. Nicholas of Lyra, *Postilla*, cap. 3, col. 88.

44. Peter Lombard, *The Sentences: Book 2, On Creation*, trans. Giulio Silano (Toronto: Pontifical Institute of Mediaeval Studies, 2008), dist. 21, ch. 6, 95. For Hugh of St. Victor's formulation see *On the Sacraments of the Christian Faith (De Sacramentis)*, trans. Roy J. Deferrari (Cambridge: Mediaeval Academy of America, 1951), bk. 1, pt. 7, 9, 124.

45. John Chrysostom, *Homilies on Genesis*, homily 16 (3) and (4), 208–9.

46. John Chrysostom, *Homilies on Genesis*, homily 16 (5), 210.

47. John Chrysostom, *Homilies on Genesis*, homily 16 (5), 210.

48. John Chrysostom, *Homilies on Genesis*, homily 16 (4), 209.

49. John Chrysostom, *Homilies on Genesis*, homily 16 (6), 210.

50. John Chrysostom, *Homilies on Genesis*, homily 16 (9), 212.
51. Augustine, *On Free Choice of the Will*, trans. Anna S. Benjamin and L. H. Hackstaff (Indianapolis: Bobbs-Merrill Company, 1964), bk. 3, ch. 25, 146.
52. Hugh of St. Victor, *On the Sacraments*, bk. 1, pt. 7, 4, 122.
53. Hugh of St. Victor, *On the Sacraments*, bk. 1, pt. 7, 4, 122.
54. Nicholas of Lyra, *Postilla*, Genesis, cap. 3, col. 90.
55. Augustine, *Literal Meaning of Genesis*, bk. 11, ch. 30 (38), 161–62.
56. Augustine, *City of God*, bk. 15, ch. 13, 608.
57. Augustine, *Literal Meaning of Genesis*, bk. 11, ch. 30 (39), 162. William S. Babcock, "The Human and Angelic Fall: Will and Moral Agency in Augustine's *City of God*," in *Augustine: From Rhetor to Theologian*, ed. Timothy D. Barnes (Waterloo: Wilfrid Laurier University Press, 1992), 133–49, discusses the theological and philosophical significance of this problem for Augustine. It is worth noting that there was considerable discussion among the early Church fathers concerning the relation between envy and pride, not only in Adam and Eve, but in the character of Satan himself. See Sophie Lunn-Rockliffe, "The Diabolical Problem of Satan's First Sin: Self-Moved Pride or a Response to the Goads of Envy," *Studia Patristica* 63:11 (2013): 121–40.
58. Ambrose, *Paradise*, ch. 12 (54), 333. J. Patout Burns, "Creation and Fall According to Ambrose of Milan," in *Augustine: Biblical Exegete*, eds. Frederick Van Fleteren and Joseph C. Schnaubelt (New York: Peter Lang, 2001), 71–97, discusses the overall structure of Ambrose's exegesis of Genesis.
59. Bonaventure, *Sententiarum*, II, dist. 21, art. 1, quaest. 3, sed contra 3, 496.
60. Ambrose, *Paradise*, ch. 12 (54), 333.
61. Ambrose, *Paradise*, ch. 12 (58), 338. Neil Forsyth, *The Satanic Epic* (Princeton: Princeton University Press, 2003), 45–49, provides historical context for the identification of Satan with heretical readings of scripture in the early church.
62. Ambrose, *Paradise*, ch. 12 (55), 335.
63. Revelation 22:18–19.
64. Ambrose, *Paradise*, ch. 12 (55), 334. On the Devil as sophist, see Eric Jager, *The Tempter's Voice*, 115–23.
65. Ambrose, *Paradise*, ch. 13 (61), 342.
66. Ambrose, *Paradise*, ch. 13 (62), 342–43.
67. Augustine, *Literal Meaning of Genesis*, ch. 31 (39), 162. On Augustine's warnings against reading the literal as figurative or the figurative as literal, see Jager, *The Tempter's Voice*, 75–82.
68. Ambrose, *Paradise*, ch. 6 (32), 310.
69. Augustine, *Literal Meaning of Genesis*, bk. 6 (12), 42.
70. Ambrose, *Paradise*, ch. 6 (34), 312.
71. Augustine, *Literal Meaning of Genesis*, bk. 11, ch. 30 (39), 162.
72. 1 Timothy 2:13–14.
73. Nicholas of Lyra, *Postilla*, Genesis, ch. 3, col. 94.
74. Hugh of St. Victor, *On the Sacraments*, bk. 1, pt. 7, ch. 10, 125.
75. Bonaventure, *Sententiarum*, II, dist. 22, art. 1, quest. 2, resp. 519.
76. Ambrose, *Paradise*, ch. 13 (65), 344. On the significance of clothing in Gen-

esis, Edgar Haulotte, *Symbolique du vêtement selon la Bible* (Paris: Aubier, 1966), 186–90.

77. Luther, *Lectures on Genesis*, ch. 4, 237.
78. For a general contrast between medieval and reformed readings of Genesis, Crowther, *Adam & Eve*, 9–51. Reformation emphasis on *sola scriptura*, and the literal sense of scripture tends to be overstated. See, for example, David C. Steinmetz, "Divided by a Common Past: The Reshaping of the Christian Exegetical Tradition in the Sixteenth Century," *Journal of Medieval and Early Modern Studies* 27:2 (Spring 1997): 245–64.
79. Luther, *Lectures on Genesis*, ch. 3:1, 146.
80. Luther, *Lectures on Genesis*, ch. 3:1, 146–47.
81. Nicholas of Lyra, *Postilla*, Genesis, ch. 3, col. 90.
82. Thomas Aquinas, *Summa of Theology*, trans. Fathers of the English Dominican Province (New York: Benziger Brothers, 1947), II-II, quest. 163, art. 1, reply 4, 1463.
83. Nicholas of Lyra, *Postilla*, Genesis, ch. 3, col. 93.
84. Hugh of St. Victor, *On the Sacraments*, bk. 1, pt. 7, ch. 8, 123–24. The first part of this translation is mine, rendered freely and a bit more clearly. See *De sacramentis Christianae fidei*, in *Patrologiae Latinae*, vol. 176, 289: "Primum enim promissam excellentiam per superbiam appetiit; deinde promissam abundantiam (et qualis talem excellentiam decebat) per avaritiam concupivit." Peter Lombard, *The Sentences*, bk. 2, dist. 21, ch. 5, 6, 95, attributes this analysis incorrectly to Augustine. For a prominent later version of this analysis, see Vincent of Beauvais, *Speculum Morale* (Venice: Dominic Nicolini, 1591), lib. III, pars II, dist. XI, 168v–169r.
85. Bonaventure, *Sententiarum*, II, dist. 21, art. 2, quest. 1, 3, 499.
86. Luther, *Lectures on Genesis*, ch. 3:1, 148.
87. Luther, *Lectures on Genesis*, ch. 2:9, 94.
88. Luther, *Lectures on Genesis*, ch. 3:1, 146.
89. Luther, *Lectures on Genesis*, ch. 3:1, 152.
90. Calvin, *Commentaries on Genesis*, ch. 3, 148.
91. Luther, *Lectures on Genesis*, ch. 3:6, 162.
92. Calvin, *Commentaries on Genesis*, ch. 3, 161.
93. Luther, *Lectures on Genesis*, ch. 3:12, 177.
94. Luther, *Lectures on Genesis*, ch. 3:10, 175.
95. Susan Schreiner, *Are You Alone Wise? The Search for Certainty in the Early Modern Era* (Oxford: Oxford University Press, 2012), 79–129.
96. George Gyfford, *A Discourse on the subtill Practices of Devilles by Witches and Sorcerers* (London: Toby Cooke, 1587), E2. Jeffrey Burton Russell, *The Prince of Darkness: Radical Evil and the Power of Good in History* (Ithaca: Cornell University Press, 1988), 167, suggests that the Devil "reached the height of his power just at the time when the intellectual structure supporting him began to crumble," that is, during the sixteenth century. Heiko Oberman, *Luther: Man between God and the Devil*, trans. Eileen Walliser-Schwarzbart (New Haven: Yale University Press, 1989), 102–6, briefly summarizes Luther's relationship with the Devil. On the general concern over

the Devil and diabolical illusions during the sixteenth and seventeenth centuries, see Stuart Clark, *Vanities of the Eye: Vision in Early Modern European Culture* (Oxford: Oxford University Press, 2007), 123–60, and Russell, *The Prince of Darkness*, 167–85.

97. Luther, *Selected Psalms III*, in *Luther's Works*, vol. 14, ed. Jaroslav Pelikan and trans. Edward Sittler (Philadelphia: Fortress Press, 1958), 288. Luther is quoting 2 Corinthians 11:14.

98. Luther, *Catholic Epistles*, in *Luther's Works*, vol. 30, ed. Jaroslav Pelikan and trans. Walter A. Hansen (Saint Louis: Concordia Publishing House, 1967), 240.

99. Luther, *The Sermon on the Mount*, in *Luther's Works* vol. 21, ed. and trans. Jaroslav Pelikan (Saint Louis: Concordia Publishing House, 1956), 212 and 251.

100. John Farrell, *Paranoia and Modernity: Cervantes to Rousseau* (Ithaca: Cornell University Press, 2007), 200.

101. James Simpson, *Burning to Read: English Fundamentalism and Its Reformation Opponents* (Cambridge: Belknap Press of Harvard University Press, 2007), 118–22.

102. Acontius, *Satans Strategems*, unpaginated prefatory material. Spelling and punctuation have been silently updated.

103. Acontius, *Satans Strategems*, 3. Random capitalizations and italicization found in the original.

104. On Acontius's life see W. K. Jordan, *The Development of Religious Toleration in England: From the Beginning of the English Reformation to the Death of Queen Elizabeth* (Cambridge: Harvard University Press, 1932), 303–17, Gary Remer, *Humanism and the Rhetoric of Toleration* (University Park: Pennsylvania State University Press, 1996), 112–15, and Aart de Groot, "Acontius's Plea for Tolerance," in *From Strangers to Citizens: The Integration of Immigrant Communities in Britain, Ireland and Colonial America, 1550–1750*, ed. Randolph Vigne and Charles Littleton (Brighton: Sussex Academic Press, 2001), 48–54.

105. Acontius, *Satans Strategems*, 8.

106. Acontius, *Satans Strategems*, 15.

107. Acontius, *Satans Strategems*, 16.

108. Acontius, *Satans Strategems*, 83–84. The literature on this debate is immense. For an introduction, see Jaroslav Pelikan, *The Reformation of Church and Dogma (1300–1700)* (Chicago: University of Chicago Press, 1984), 189–203.

109. Acontius, *Satans Strategems*, 85. Put differently, Acontius believes that most religious controversies arise over adiaphora (inessential interpretive details). In this he has something in common with other Northern Humanists interested in healing divisions within Christendom. See Gary Remer, "Hobbes, the Rhetorical Tradition, and Toleration," *Review of Politics* 54:1 (Winter 1992): 5–33, here, 25.

110. Acontius, *Satans Strategems*, 60.

111. Cited in Remer, *Humanism and the Rhetoric of Toleration*, 122 and, more generally, 118–22, for a good discussion of these topics in Acontius. See Jor-

dan, *Development of Religious Toleration*, 351–56, on the value of inquiry and skepticism in Acontius.

112. I suspect this facet of Acontius's writings accounts for the debate concerning whether or not he even accepts the Devil's existence. For opposed positions in this admittedly very minor controversy, see De Groot, "Acontius' Plea for Tolerance," 50, who takes issue with Jeffrey Burton Russell's *Mephistopheles: The Devil in the Modern World* (Ithaca: Cornell University Press, 1986).

113. Milton, *Paradise Lost*, bk. VIII, ln. 560–70. The classic discussion of this thesis is Millicent Bell, "The Fallacy of the Fall in Paradise Lost," *PMLA* 68:4 (September 1953): 863–83, and her contributions to Wayne Shumaker and Millicent Bell, "The Fallacy of the Fall in Paradise Lost," *PMLA* 70:5 (December 1955): 1185–203, especially 1187–95. Compare with Forsyth, *Satanic Epic*, 265–68, who connects Eve's misreading of scripture directly with her conversation with the serpent.

114. Milton, *Paradise Lost*, bk., IX, ln. 253.

115. Milton, *Paradise Lost*, bk. IX, ln. 364–65.

116. Milton, *Paradise Lost*, bk. IV, ln. 635–38.

117. Milton, *Paradise Lost*, bk. IX, ln. 322–36.

118. Milton, *Paradise Lost*, bk. IX, ln. 372.

119. Augustine, *City of God*, bk. XIV, ch. 13, 610.

CHAPTER TWO. GOD

1. Augustine, *De symbolo ad catechumenos*, ed. R. Vander Plaetse, in *Corpus Christianorum Series Latina* 46 (Turnholt: Brepols, 1969), 185–86.

2. René Descartes, *Meditations on First Philosophy*, "First Meditation," in *The Philosophical Writings of Descartes*, 2 vols., vol. 2, trans. John Cottingham, Robert Stoothoff, and Dugald Murdoch (Cambridge: Cambridge University Press, 1985), 14.

3. Descartes, *Meditations*, "Third Meditation," 35.

4. Augustine, *De symbolo*, 186. Descartes, *Principles of Philosophy*, in *Philosophical Writings*, vol. 1, 1.40, 206.

5. Nicholas of Lyra, *Postilla*, Genesis 3, 87.

6. Augustine, *Literal Meaning of Genesis*, vol. 2, bk. 11, ch. 13, 145. Neil Forsyth, *The Old Enemy*, 421–34, discusses Augustine's Genesis commentaries in connection with his struggles against Manichaeism. On Augustine's actual experience with and rejection of Manichaeism, see Jason David BeDuhn, *Augustine's Manichaean Dilemma, I: Conversion and Apostasy, 373–388 C.E.* (Philadelphia: University of Pennsylvania Press, 2009).

7. Augustine, *Literal Meaning of Genesis*, vol. 2, bk. 11, ch. 11, 143–44.

8. Lombard, *Sentences*, lib. I, dist. XLVI, cap. 3.11, 316.

9. Calvin, *Commentary on Genesis*, 94.

10. Calvin, *Institutes of the Christian Religion*, vol. 1, trans. Ford Lewis Battles (Philadelphia: Westminster Press, 1960), bk. 1, ch. 18, 228–35.

11. *The Aberdeen Bestiary*, Aberdeen University Library MS 24, 7r–7v. The

entire bestiary is reproduced with transcription, translation, and commentary at http://www.abdn.ac.uk/bestiary/intro.hti.

12. Isidore of Seville, *The Etymologies of Isidore of Seville*, trans. Stephen A. Barney, W. J. Lewis, J. A. Beach, and Oliver Berghof (Cambridge: Cambridge University Press, 2006), bk. XII, ch. ii.5, 251.

13. *Physiologus*, Robert Curley, trans. (Austin: University of Texas Press, 1979), 3–4.

14. *The Aberdeen Bestiary*, 7v. On later medieval bestiaries, see Debra Higgs Strickland, *Medieval Bestiaries: Text, Image, Ideology* (Cambridge: Cambridge University Press, 1995).

15. Augustine, *On the Trinity*, ed. Gareth B. Matthews and trans. Stephen McKenna (Cambridge: Cambridge University Press, 2002), bk. 13, ch. 14 (18), 124–25. For a now standard account of the Devil throughout history, see the three volumes by Jeffrey Burton Russell, *The Devil: Perceptions of Evil from Antiquity to Primitive Christianity* (Ithaca: Cornell University Press, 1987), *Lucifer: The Devil in the Middle Ages* (Ithaca: Cornell University Press, 1984), and *Mephistopheles: The Devil in the Modern World*.

16. Augustine, "Sermon 263," in *The Fathers of the Church: Saint Augustine, Sermons on the Liturgical Seasons*, trans. Mary Sarah Muldowney (Washington, D.C.: Catholic University of America Press, 1959), 392.

17. Augustine, "Sermon 261," in *The Later Christian Fathers: A Selection from the Writings of the Fathers from St. Cyril of Jerusalem to St. Leo the Great*, ed. and trans. Henry Bettenson (London: Oxford University Press, 1970), 222. The metaphor of the mousetrap has a double history. While Augustine used it to describe the cross as a trap for the Devil, a slightly earlier tradition uses it to describe how the Devil traps mankind through various, often sexual, temptations. On this prior tradition, see Paul G. Remly, "*Muscipula Diaboli* and Medieval English Antifeminism," in *English Studies* (1989): 1–14.

18. Gregory of Nyssa, in *The Later Christian Fathers*, 141. Nicholas P. Constas, "The Last Temptation of Satan: Divine Deception in Greek Patristic Interpretations of the Passion Narrative," *Harvard Theological Review* 97:2 (April 2004): 139–63, here, 139–49, situates Gregory's theory within the context of Arian and Stoic thought and traces the imagery of the fishhook to several biblical passages.

19. Gregory of Nyssa, in *The Later Christian Fathers*, 142. On Gregory's theory of redemption via deception, see David Satran, "Deceiving the Deceiver: Variations on an Early Christian Theme," in *Things Revealed: Studies in Early Jewish and Christian Literature in Honor of Michael E. Stone*, ed. E. G. Chazon, D. Satran, and R. A. Clements (Leiden: E. J. Brill, 2004), 357–64.

20. Eugene Teselle, "The Cross as Ransom," *Journal of Early Christian Studies* 4:2 (1996): 147–70, analyzes the differences and similarities among the various "ransom" theories of redemption in the early Church.

21. C. W. Marx, *The Devil's Rights and Redemption in the Literature of Medieval England* (Cambridge: D. S. Brewer, 1995), 7–15, offers a lucid explanation for God's just dealing with the Devil in early Christian writings.

22. Cyril of Alexandria, *A Commentary on the Gospel According to S. Luke*, trans. R. Payne Smith (Oxford: Oxford University Press, 1859), homily 12, 54.

23. Ambrose, *Expositio evangelii secundum Lucam*, in *Corpus Christianorum Series Latina*, vol. XIV, ed. M. Adriaen (Turnholt: Brepols, 1957), 113.

24. See, for example, Tyrannius Rufinus, *Expositio symboli*, in *Corpus Christianorum Series Latina*, vol. XX, ed. M. Simonetti (Turnholt: Brepols, 1961) 20, 14, 151–52, which dates to the first decade of the fourth century, and Leo the Great, *Letters and Sermons of Leo the Great*, in *Nicene and Post-Nicene Fathers*, 2nd series, vol. 12 (New York: Christian Literature Co., 1895), 130– 21.

25. Douglas Gray, *Themes and Images in the Medieval English Lyric* (London/ Boston: Routledge and Keegan Paul, 1972), 123, for example, quotes a sermon tag, a rubric around which a priest could compose an entire sermon, that reads, "Crux est/A barge to beren fro depe groundes/A targe to weren fro detly woundes/A falle to taken in the fend/And an halle to glathen in a frend." Thanks to Mary Agnes Edsall for this reference. On Anselm's theory of atonement, see Eileen C. Sweeney, *Anselm of Canterbury and the Desire for the Word* (Washington, D.C.: Catholic University of America Press, 2012), 277–302.

26. On Corpus Christi plays, see Alan H. Nelson, "The Temptation of Christ; or, The Temptation of Satan," in *Medieval English Drama: Essays Critical and Contextual*, ed. Jerome Taylor and Alan H. Nelson (Chicago: University of Chicago Press, 1972), 218–29.

27. Aquinas, *Summa of Theology* III, quest. 41, art. 2, resp. 2241–42.

28. Aquinas, *Summa of Theology* I, quest. 64, art. 1, resp. 4, 321.

29. Aquinas, *Summa of Theology* III, quest. 29, art. 1, reply 3, 2177. See George Duriez, *La théologie dans le drame religieux en Allemagne au moyen âge* (Lille: René Girard, 1914), 72–81, for a survey of theological opinion concerning this deception and how it filtered into German religious plays.

30. Jean Gerson, *Considérations sur Saint Joseph*, in *Oeuvres Complètes, VII: L'oeuvre Française*, ed. Palemon Glorieux (Paris: Desclée & Cii, 1966), 76. During his discussion of the Annunciation, Jacobus de Voragine, *The Golden Legend*, vol. 1, trans. William Granger Ryan (Princeton: Princeton University Press, 1993), 197, cites Bernard of Clairvaux as he relates the story of Joseph's deceptive role.

31. Meyer Schapiro, "Muscipula Diaboli: The Symbolism of the Mérode Altarpiece," *Art Bulletin* 27:3 (1945): 182–87.

32. Bonaventure, *Sententiarum* III, dist. 20, art. 1, quaest. 5, conclusio, 427–28.

33. Bonaventure, *Collations on the Six Days*, in *The Works of Bonaventure*, vol. 5, trans. José de Vinck (Patterson: St. Anthony Guild Press, 1970), 6th collation, 12, 13, 16. For a more detailed discussion, see Christopher M. Cullen, *Bonaventure* (Oxford: Oxford University Press, 2006), 96–104.

34. Bonaventure, *Sententiarum* II, dist. 7, pars 2, art. 1, quaest. 3.

35. Aquinas, *Summa of Theology* II-II, quest. 55, art. 3, resp. and reply 2, 1423.

36. William Langland, *Piers Plowman: A New Annotated Edition of the C–Text*,

ed. Derek Pearsall (Exeter: University of Exeter Press, 2008), Passus XX, ln. 163–65, 329.

37. Alan of Lille, *Liber poenitentialis* I.12, ed. Jean Longère, vol. 2 (Louvain: Editions Nauwelaerts, 1965), 29. For a brief survey of the circumstances and sin, see Dallas G. Denery II, *Seeing and Being Seen in the Later Middle Ages: Optics, Theology and Religious Life* (Cambridge: Cambridge University Press, 2005), 57–63.

38. Thomas Chobham, *Summa Confessorum*, ed. F. Broomfield, art. 3, dist. 2, quest. 2a (Louvain: Editions Nauwelaerts, 1968), 56–57.

39. Guido de Monte Rocherii, *Manipulus curatorum*, pars 2, trac. 2, cap. 9 (Strassburg, 1490).

40. Jacobus de Voraigne, *The Golden Legend*, vol. 1, 210.

41. Bonaventure, *Tractatus de praeparatione ad missam*, in *Opera Omnia* VIII, cap. I:1:3 (Rome: Quaracchi, 1898), 100.

42. Miri Rubin, *Corpus Christi: The Eucharist in Late Medieval Culture* (Cambridge: Cambridge University Press, 1991), 12–82, discusses the design and development of the mass.

43. William of Auxerre, *Summa Aurea* IV, ed. J. Ribaillier (Rome: Collegii S. Bonaventurae ad Claras Aquas, 1980) d. VII, cap. vii, quaest. 4, 173. William invokes this idea while arguing that priests should never deceive their parishioners about whether or not the host is consecrated. More typical is Bonaventure, *Sententiarum* IV, in *Opera Omnia* IV, dist. X, pars. II, art. II, quaest. II, ad. iii, 137, who considers the problem entirely within the context of sensory discrepancy, "Ad illud obicitur de deceptione, dicendum, quod in hoc Sacramento nullus sensus decipitur nec aliquid, quia est Sacramentum veritatis."

44. Cited in Ian Christopher Levy, *John Wyclif: Scriptural Logic, Real Presence and the Parameters of Orthodoxy* (Milwaukee: Marquette University Press, 2003), 127–28.

45. The literature concerning the development of Eucharistic theory is vast. For an excellent recent overview, see Levy, *John Wyclif*, 127–215.

46. Aquinas, *Summa of Theology* III, quest. 75, art. 1, resp., 2446.

47. John Pecham, *Quodlibet* IV, quaest. 41, in *Quodlibeta Quatuor*, ed. F. Delorme and G. J. Etzkorn (Grottaferrata: Quaracchi, 1989), 263.

48. For examples of these and other Eucharistic wonder stories, see Caesarius of Heisterbach, *The Dialogue on Miracles*, vol. 2, trans. H. Von E. Scott and C. Swinton Bland (London: George Routledge & Sons,, 1929), 105–69. On the value of miracle as a means of confronting the faithful with the incredible facts alleged about the Eucharist, see Steven Justice, "Eucharistic Miracle and Eucharistic Doubt," *Journal of Medieval and Early Modern Studies* 42:2 (2012): 307–32.

49. William Ockham, *De corpore christi in eucharistia*, in *Opera Theologica* , vol. 10, ed. Carolus A. Grassi (St. Bonaventure: Franciscan Institute, 1986), cap. 8, 107. For a defense of the sincerity of Ockham's Eucharistic orthodoxy, see Gabriel N. Buescher, *The Eucharistic Teaching of William Ockham* (Washington, D.C.: Catholic University of America Press, 1950), 1–14.

50. On Peter Aureol, see Katherine Tachau, *Vision and Certitude in the Age of Ockham* (Leiden: E. J. Brill, 1988), 84–122, and Denery, *Seeing and Being Seen*, 117–36.

51. William Ockham, *Quodlibeta* VI, quaest. 6, in *Opera philosophica et theologica*, vol. IX, ed. Gedeon Gál et al. (St. Bonaventure: Franciscan Institute, 1967–), 605. For brevity, I have greatly simplified Ockham's analysis. Philotheus Boehner, "The Notitia Intuitiva of Non-Existents According to William Ockham," in *Collected Articles on Ockham*, ed. Eligius Buytaert (St. Bonaventure: Franciscan Institute, 1958), 274–87, offers the clearest account of how Ockham situates this scenario within his broader epistemological and cognitive theories. Compare with Katherine Tachau, *Vision and Certitude in the Age of Ockham* (Leiden: E. J. Brill, 1988), 115–29, for a somewhat different interpretation.

52. Robert Holkot presents these objections to the doctrine of bodily presence at *Super sententias* (Lugduni, 1518, rprt. Frankfurt: Minerva, 1967) IV, quaest. III, primi principi, secundo. He responds with his own opinions at *Super sententias* IV, quaest. III, responsio, ad secundum.

53. Holkot, *Super sententias* IV, quaest. III, responsio, ad experientiam. At *Super sententias* IV, quaest. III, ad. secundo, he adds, "Dicendum est quod deus potest plus facere quam intellectus intelligere, et ideo non est inconveniens concedere quod deus posset totam machinam mundi convertere et facere existere sub speciebus unius musce." Gary Macy, *The Banquet's Wisdom: A Short History of the Lord's Supper* (Mahway: Paulist Press, 1992), 120, makes a similar point.

54. Holkot, *Super sententias* IV, quaest. III, responsio, ad secundo.

55. *Fasciculus Morum*, ed. Siegfried Wenzel (University Park: Pennsylvania State University Press, 1989) V.ii, 409.

56. Levy, *John Wyclif*, 125.

57. Robert Holkot, *Sententiarum* II, quest. 2, in *Seeing the Future Clearly: Questions on Future Contingents*, ed. Paul A. Streveler and Katherine H. Tachau (Toronto: Pontifical Institute of Mediaeval Studies, 1995), 156. Here I follow the lead of both Katherine Tachau, in two separate articles, "Robert Holcot on Contingency and Divine Deception," in *Filosofia e teologia nel Trecento: Studi in ricordo di Eugenio Randi*, ed. L. Bianchi (Louvain-la Neuve: Fédération internationale des instituts d'études médiévales, 1994), 178–78, and "Logic's God and the Natural Order in Late Medieval Oxford," *Annals of Science* 53 (1996): 235–67, here, 250–55, and especially, Hester Gelber, *It Could Have Been Otherwise* (Leiden: E. J. Brill, NV, 2004), 191–222. Neither of them address these problems in relation to Eucharistic theory.

58. Holkot, *Sententiarum* III, quaest. 1, BBB, "Probatur quod deus potest fallere, sexto."

59. Holkot, *Sententiarum* III, quaest. 1, CCC, responsio.

60. Holkot, *Sententiarum* III, quaest. 1, primo through tertio, A. The edition is unpaginated. These questions are raised in the very first column of the question.

61. Holkot, *Sententiarum* III, quaest. 1, art. 5, MM.

62. Heiko A. Oberman, "*Facientibus quod in se est deus non denegat gratiam*: Robert Holcot, O.P. and the Beginnings of Luther's Theology," in *The Dawn of the Reformation* (Edinburgh: T&T Clark, 1986), 84–103.

63. John Wyclif, *De eucharistia*, ed. Iohann Loserth (London: Wyclif Society, 1892), cap. 3, 57.

64. Stephen E. Lahey, *John Wyclif* (Oxford: Oxford University Press, 2009), 102–34, and Gordon Leff, *Heresy in the Later Middle Ages: The Relation of Heterodoxy to Dissent, 1250–1450* (Manchester: Manchester University Press, 1967), 499 and 550. On scripture and church councils, see Maurice Keen, "Wyclif, the Bible and Transubstantiation," in *Wyclif in His Times*, ed. Anthony Kenny (Oxford: Clarendon Press, 1986), 11–3, and Ian Christopher Levy, "*Christus qui mentiri non potest*: John Wyclif's Rejection of Transubstantiation," *Recherches de Théologie et Philosophie* 66:2 (1999): 316–34.

65. On medieval Eucharistic practices and devotion see, E. Dumoutet, *Le Désir de voir l'hoste et les origins de la dévotion au saint-sacrament* (Paris: Beauchesne, 1926). On Wyclif's reactions to these practices, see J. I. Catto, "John Wyclif and the Cult of the Eucharist," in *The Bible in the Medieval World: Essays in Memory of Beryl Smalley*, ed. Katherine Walsh and Diana Wood (Oxford: Blackwell, 1985), 269–86, here, 279–82, and Heather Phillips, "John Wyclif and the Religion of the People," in *A Distinct Voice: Medieval Studies in Honor of Leonard E. Boyle, O.P.*, ed. Jacqueline Brown and William P. Stoneman (Notre Dame: University of Notre Dame Press, 1997), 561–90, here, 572–75.

66. The Parisian theologian Gregory of Rimini attempted to refute the possibility of a deceptive God using similar arguments. See Dominik Perler, "Does God Deceive Us? Skeptical Hypotheses in Late Medieval Epistemology," in *Rethinking the History of Skepticism: The Missing Medieval Background*, ed. Henrik Lagerlund (Leiden: E. J. Brill, 2010), 171–92, here, 181–84.

67. Wyclif, *De eucharistia*, cap. III, 73.

68. Wyclif, *Sermones*, ed. Iohann Loserth (London: Wyclif Society, 1889), vol. III, XVIII, 139.

69. Wyclif, *De benedicta incarnacione*, ed. Edward Harris (London: Wyclif Society, 1886), ch. 5, 76–77. Lahey, *John Wyclif*, 32–64, describes "the Oxford context of Wyclif's thoughts."

70. Wyclif, *De eucharistia*, cap. IV, 109.

71. Luther, *Lectures on Genesis*, vol. 5, 151. Gustaf Aulén, *Christus Victor: An Historical: Study of the Three Main Types of the Idea of Atonement*, trans. A. G. Herbert (New York: Macmillan, 1954), 103–11, discusses the connections between Luther's and the Church fathers' conception of Christ's work.

72. Luther, *Lectures on Genesis*, vol. 5, 150–51.

73. Luther, *Lectures on Genesis*, vol. 4, 93–97.

74. Alister E. McGrath, *Luther's Theology of the Cross: Martin Luther's Theological Breakthrough* (Oxford: Basil Blackwell, 1985), 158–60.

75. Luther, *Selected Psalms*, in *Luther's Works*, vol. 14, 31.

76. Luther, *The Bondage of the Will*, in *Luther's Works*, vol. 33, ed. and trans. Philip S. Watson (Philadelphia: Fortress Press, 1972), 140.

77. John Calvin, *Commentaries on the Prophet Ezekiel*, lecture XXXVIII, 58.

78. Calvin, *Commentaries on Ezekiel*, lecture XXXVIII, 57–58.

79. Calvin, *Commentary on Corinthians*, vol. 2, trans. John Pringle (Edinburgh: Calvin Translation Society, 1849), 2 Corinthians 4:1–6.

80. Calvin, *Commentaries on Ezekiel*, lecture XXXVIII, 58–59.

81. Calvin, *Commentaries on Ezekiel*, lecture XXXVIII, 59–60. On Calvin and biblical style, see William Bouwsma, *John Calvin* (New York: Oxford University Press, 1988),104–6.

82. Calvin, *Commentaries on Ezekiel*, lecture XXXVIII, 59–60.

83. Calvin, *Institutes*, bk. 1, ch. 18:4, 237.

84. Pierre Bayle, *Dictionaire [sic] Historique et Critique*, 4th ed., "Gregoire (de Rimini)" (Amsterdam: P. Brunel et al., 1730), 57. On reading seventeenth-century natural philosophers as "secular theologians," see Amos Funkenstein, *Theology and the Scientific Imagination from the Middle Ages to the Seventeenth Century* (Princeton: Princeton University Press, 1986), 3–9.

85. Descartes, *Meditations*, "Second Set of Objections," 89–90.

86. Gregory of Rimini, *Lectura super primum et secundum Sententiarum*, vol. 3, ed. A. Damasus Trapp and Venicio Marcolino (Berlin: Walter de Gruyter, 1979), lib. 1, dist. 42–44, quaest. 2, 391.

87. Bayle, *Dictionaire*, 57.

88. Descartes, *Meditations*, "Second Set of Replies," 101–2.

89. Descartes, *Meditations*, "Second Set of Replies," 102.

90. Descartes, *Meditations*, "Sixth Set of Replies," 289. For a brief account of Descartes's studies and education, see Geneviève Rodis-Lewis, *Descartes: His Life and Thought*, trans. Jane Marie Todd (Ithaca: Cornell University Press, 1999), 8–23.

91. Descartes, *Meditations*, "Dedicatory Letter to the Sorbonne," 3–4.

92. Descartes undertakes this analysis most explicitly at *Meditations*, "Second Meditation," beginning at 17, when he asks, "What then did I formerly think I was? A man. But what is a man?"

93. Descartes, *Meditations*, "Second Set of Replies," 102.

94. Bayle, *Dictionaire*, 57.

95. Bayle, *Dictionaire*, 57.

96. Pierre Sylvain Regis, *Système de Philosophie Contenant La Logique. La Métaphysique. La Physique et La Morale*, vol. 1 (Paris: Denys Thierry, 1690), 89.

97. Descartes, *Meditations*, "Second Set of Replies," 102–3.

98. Descartes, *Principles of Philosophy*, in *The Philosophical Writings of Descartes*, vol. I, 1.40, 206.

99. Descartes, *Principles*, 1.28, 202. Stephen Menn, *Augustine and Descartes* (Cambridge: Cambridge University Press, 1998), 237, elaborates on this idea.

100. Descartes, *Principles*, 1.40, 206. For a succinct list of what Descartes "learns" about God, see David Cunning, *Argument and Persuasion in Descartes'*

Meditations (Oxford: Oxford University Press, 2010), 208–9. On the relation between God's infinity and his perfection, see Jean-Marie Beyssade, "The
Idea of God and the Proofs of His Existence," in *The Cambridge Companion
to Descartes*, ed. John Cottingham (Cambridge: Cambridge University Press,
1992), 174–99, especially 193–96. Jean-Luc Marion, "Outline of a History
of Definitions of God in the Cartesian Epoch," in *On the Ego and God:
Further Cartesian Questions*, trans. Christina M. Geshwandtner (New York:
Fordham University Press, 2007), 161–92, here, 170–75, stresses the incoherence of Descartes's conception of God.

101. Descartes, *Principles*, 2.36, 240.
102. This is an extraordinarily condensed summary of the metaphysical super-
structure that supports Descartes's physics. For more, see Daniel Garber,
"Descartes' Physics," in *The Cambridge Companion to Descartes*, 286–334.
For an excellent account of Descartes's "metaphysical turn," see John
Henry, "Metaphysics and the Origins of Modern Science: Descartes and the
Importance of Laws of Nature," *Early Science and Medicine* 9:2 (2004):
73–114.
103. Descartes, *Meditations*, "Fourth Meditation," 42–43. For a nuanced account of Descartes's acceptable deployment of teleological explanations, as
captured in terms like "beneficial," see Alison J. Simmons, "Sensible Ends:
Latent Teleology in Descartes' Account of Sensation," *Journal of History of
Philosophy* 39:1 (January 2001): 49–75.
104. Descartes, *Meditations*, "Sixth Meditation," 61.
105. Cited in David Cunning, "Descartes on the Immutability of the Divine Will,"
Religious Studies 39 (2003): 79–92, here 87, and more generally 86–88 for
a very good and succinct account of the relations between philosophy and
theology in Descartes's thought. This paragraph relies heavily on his analysis.
On Malebranche, see Andrew Pessin, "Malebranche's Distinction between
General and Particular Volitions," *Journal of the History of Philosophy* 39:1
(January 2001): 77–99.
106. Gerald L. Bruns, *Inventions: Writing, Textuality, and Understanding in Literary History* (New Haven: Yale University Press, 1982), 94: "[I]n Descartes'
construction God, in creating the world, is not obliged to speak, He does not
say, 'Let there be light.' Even if he did say it, no light would therefore shine.
Systems are alogorithmic rather than logocentric, as Leibniz knew, which is a
way of explaining the Cartesian or rationalist thesis that God does not create
the world, he introduces procedures, in whose actual operation and results
he need not maintain any loving or mythological interest—or, as John Stuart
Mill thought, could not maintain an interest even if he wanted to. Hence
the old schoolroom joke that Descartes proved the existence of God only to
show how little God matters in the scheme of things."
107. Descartes, *Principles*, 2.36, 240.
108. Cited and translated in Robert C. Bartlett, "On the Politics of Faith and Reason: The Project of Enlightenment in Pierre Bayle and Montesquieu," *Journal
of Politics* 63:1 (February 2001): 1–28, here p. 12, ft. 13, and, generally, 9–
12. The line in its original context can be found in Pierre Bayle, *Ce que c'est*

que la France toute Catholique sous le règne de Louis le Grand, ed. Elisabeth Labrousse (Paris: J. Vrin, 1973), 46.

CHAPTER THREE. HUMAN BEINGS

1. Blaise Pascal, *Les Provinciales, or, The Mystery of Jesuitisme,* 2nd ed., trans. Henry Hammond (London: Richard Royston, 1658), (mostly) unpaginated prefatory material written by Hammond.
2. Augustine, *Against Lying,* ch. 1 (1), 126.
3. Augustine, *Against Lying,* ch. 6 (11), 137. Viriginia Burrus, *The Making of a Heretic: Gender, Authority and the Priscillianist Controversy* (Berkeley: University of California Press, 1995), 115–22, surveys Consentius's efforts.
4. Augustine, *Against Lying,* ch. 18 (36), 171–72.
5. 1 Corinthians 9:20.
6. Augustine, letters 28 and 40, in *Saint Augustine: Letters,* vol. 1 (1–82), trans. Wilifrid Parsons (Washington, D.C.: Catholic University of America Press, 1951), 93–98 and 172–179. For an outline of this debate, see Boniface Ramsey, "Two Traditions on Lying and Deception in the Ancient Church," *Thomist* 49 (1985): 504–33.
7. Lombard, *The Sentences,* bk. III, dist. 38, chs. 1–5, 157–61.
8. John Downame, *A Treatise Against Lying* (London, 1636), 15, sets the tone for the rest of the work when he begins his second chapter, "Wherein it is shewed what a Lye is," with one of Augustine's definitions of a lie: "Saint *Augustine* briefly defineth it thus; A Lye is a false signification with a will to deceive."
9. Pascal, *The Mystery of Jesuitisme,* unpaginated prefatory material by Henry Hammond. Random capitalizations found in the original.
10. Blaise Pascal, *The Provincial Letters,* trans. Thomas M'Crie (Boston: Houghton, Osgood and Company, 1880), "Letter IX," 270.
11. Pascal, *Provincial Letters,* "Letter IX," 277–78. I have slightly altered the translation. For the original see *Les Provinciales,* in *Pascal: Edition définitive des Oeuvres Complètes,* vol. II, ed. Fortunat Strowski (Paris: Libraire Ollendorff, 1926), 94.
12. Pascal, *Les Provinciales,* "Letter IX," 278.
13. Augustine, *Against Lying,* ch. 3 (4)–(6), 129–33.
14. For Augustine's philosophical influences, see Gerard Watson, "St. Augustine and the Inner Word: The Philosophical Background," *Irish Theological Quarterly* 54 (1988): 81–92, and Marcia Colish, "The Stoic Theory of Verbal Signification," in *Archéologie de signe,* ed. Lucie Brind'Amour and Eugene Vance (Toronto: Pontifical Institute of Mediaeval Studies Press, 1982), 17–43.
15. Augustine, *On the Trinity,* bk. 15, chs. 10 and 11 (18–20), 185–88. Christopher Kirwan, "Augustine's Philosophy of Language," in *The Cambridge Companion to Augustine,* 195–201. See also Paul Vincent Spade, "The Semantics of Terms," in *The Cambridge History of Later Medieval Philosophy,* ed. Norman Kretzman et al. (Cambridge: Cambridge University Press, 1982),

186–204, here, 188–90. Margaret Miles, "Vision: The Eye of the Body and the Eye of the Mind in Saint Augustine's *De trinitate*," *Journal of Religion* 63:2 (April 1983): 125–42, discusses the function of vision and visual metaphors in Augustine's theology.

16. Augustine, *De doctrina christiana*, 2.2.3, ed. and trans. R.P.H. Green (Oxford: Oxford University Press, 1995), 56–59. See also R. A. Markus, "St. Augustine on Signs," *Phronesis* 2:1 (1957): 60–83, here, 70–76.

17. John 1:1–16.

18. Augustine, *On the Trinity*, bk. 15 (23), 194–95.

19. Augustine, *On the Trinity*, bk. 15 (20), 187. On the Christological underpinnings of Augustine's theory of language, truth, and lies, see Mark D. Jordan, "Words and Word: Incarnation and Signification in Augustine's *De Doctrina Christiana*," *Augustinian Studies* 11 (1980): 177–96, and Thomas Feehan, "The Morality of Lying in St. Augustine," *Augustinian Studies* 21 (1990): 67–81.

20. Augustine, *On the Trinity*, bk. 15 (20), 189. Eileen Sweeney, "Hugh of St. Victor: The Augustinian Tradition of Sacred and Secular Reading Revised," in *Reading and Wisdom: The De Doctrina Christiana of Augustine in the Middle Ages*, ed. Edward D. English (Notre Dame: University of Notre Dame Press, 1995), 61–83, notes that Augustine makes similar arguments in the *De doctrina christiana*.

21. Augustine, *On the Trinity*, bk. 12 (16), p. 94. See Paul J. Griffiths's excellent discussion, *Lying: An Augustinian Theology of Duplicity* (Grand Rapids: Brazos, 2004), 85–100, from which I have learned quite a bit.

22. Augustine, *City of God*, bk. 14, ch. 3, 586.

23. Augustine, *On Lying*, in *Treatises on Various Subjects*, ch. 3 (3), 55–56. See also Thomas Feehan, "Augustine on Lying and Deception," *Augustinian Studies* 19 (1988):131–39.

24. Augustine, *Against Lying*, ch. 12 (26), 160.

25. Augustine, *On Lying*, ch. 4 (4), 59 (with minor alterations to the translation). He reaches the same conclusion after a similar analysis of scenarios at ch. 13 (22), 81–82, and in *Soliloquies*, trans. Thomas F. Gilligan (New York: CIMA Publishing, Co., 1948), bk. 2, ch. 9 (16), 399, where he distinguishes the falsity of storytellers from that of deceivers.

26. I follow Griffiths, *Lying*, 29, who writes, "Duplicity is, to say it again, the evil proper to lying, and I read Augustine as claiming that this is both necessary and sufficient for the lie. That the lie is usually also accompanied by an intention to deceive is true and of interest, but it does not pick out what is most deeply characteristic of the lie, and is not relevant to the exceptionless ban on the lie that Augustine advocates."

27. Augustine, *Against Lying*, ch. 15 (32), 166.

28. Augustine, *On Lying*, 14 (25), 86–88.

29. Augustine, *On Lying*, ch. 21 (42 and 43), 109.

30. Augustine, *Against Lying*, ch. 15 (32), 165–66.

31. Augustine, *Against Lying*, ch. 9 (20), 147. The story of Lot, his guests, and his daughters can be found at Genesis 19:1–11.

32. The story about the midwives appears at Exodus 1:19, Jacob's claim to be Esau at Genesis 27:1–40, Abraham's assertion that Sarah is his sister at Genesis 20:2, and Jesus's long walk at Luke 24:28.

33. Augustine, *Against Lying*, ch. 15 (31), 164.

34. Augustine, *On Lying*, ch. 8 (11), 70–71.

35. Augustine, *Against Lying*, ch. 15 (32–33), 165–67.

36. Augustine, *Against Lying*, ch. 10 (23), 151–52.

37. Augustine, *Against Lying*, ch. 10 (24), 152–53.

38. Augustine, *On Lying*, ch. 5 (7), 62.

39. Augustine, *Against Lying*, ch. 10 (24), 152–55.

40. Lombard, *The Sentences* III, dist. XXXVIII, chs. 1–6, 156–61. Marcia Colish kindly confirmed this suspicion when I asked her about it via e-mail.

41. Aquinas, *Summa of Theology* II-II, quest. 110, art. 3, resp., in 1666.

42. Aquinas, *Summa of Theology* II-II, quest. 109, art. 3, resp. and replies 1 and 3, 1662–63.

43. Aquinas, *Summa of Theology* II-II, quest. 110, art. 1, resp., 1664. This reading of Thomas is much indebted to John Finnis, *Aquinas: Moral, Political, and Legal Theory* (Oxford: Oxford University Press, 1998), 154–63.

44. I follow Griffiths, *Lying*, 173–75, who makes this observation about Thomas.

45. Aquinas, *Summa Contra Gentiles* III, trans. Vernon J. Bourke (Notre Dame: University of Notre Dame Press, 1975), cap. 12, n. 7, 65, cited and interpreted (though not quoted) in Finnis, *Aquinas*, 161, ft. 138.

46. John Buridan, *Super decem libros ethicorum* (Paris, 1513, rprt. Frankfurt: Minerva G.M.B.H., 1968), LXXXVIIIr. Dante offers a markedly similar account of the dehumanizing effects of lying in the *Inferno*. See Joan Ferrante, "The Relation of Speech to Sin in the Inferno," *Dante Studies* 87 (1969): 33–46.

47. Aquinas, *Summa of Theology* II-II, quest. 110, art. 3, reply 4, 1667. Zagorin, *Ways of Lying*, 28–31, notes the future importance of Thomas's creative reinterpretation of Augustine's exegesis. He ignores the significance of Thomas's alignment of truth and justice.

48. For the story of Bishop Firmus, see Augustine, *On Lying*, ch. 13 (23), 84–85. Emily Corran, "Hiding the Truth: Exegetical Discussions of Abraham's Lies from Hugh of Saint Victor to Stephen Langton," *Historical Research* (forthcoming), demonstrates that twelfth-century theologians were already debating how to make sense of Augustine's discussion of Abraham's claim that Sarah was his sister.

49. Alexander of Hales, *Summa theologica*, vol. 4 (Quaracchi: Rome, 1979), pars II, inq. III, tractatus II, sect. I, quaest. II, titulus VIII, cap. VI, 582A/B. The jury is still out on the complete authenticity of this treatise and the extent to which it contains redactions and interpolations from Alexander's students, especially Jean de la Rochelle. On the treatise's authorship and its continuing importance as a marker of mid-thirteenth-century Franciscan theology, see Casagrande and Vecchio, *Les péchés de la langue*, 143–44. For convenience, I will refer only to Alexander as the author.

50. Alexander of Hales, *Summa theologica*, inq. III, tractatus III, sect. II, quaest. II, cap. I, vol. 3, 402, and pars II, inq. III, vol. 4, 581b.

51. This interpretation would prove controversial, and both Thomas Aquinas and John Duns Scotus would reject it. The story can be found at 2 Kings 10.

52. Summarizing this lengthy section, Alexander of Hales, *Summa theologica*, pars II, inq. III, tractatus II, sect. I, quaest. I, vol. 4, 581a/b, writes: "Dicendum ergo generaliter quod mendacium de se dicit vituperabile et contrarium veritati, et ideo non potest recte fieri, sive sit in voluntate, sicut primo modo, sive in facto, sicut secundo modo, sive in dicto, sicet tertio modo. Solvendum ergo per interemptionem, cum dicit quod mendacium potest esse licitum in operibus simulatis. Non est enim mendacium simulatio cautelae vel doctrinae vel figurae in facto, sed illa quae est duplicitatis et fallaciae."

53. John Duns Scotus, *In librum tertium sententiarum*, dist. 38, quaest. 1, art. 1. For a facing-page translation of the entire question, see John Duns Scotus, *Duns Scotus on the Will and Morality*, trans. Allan B. Wolter (Washington, D.C.: Catholic University of America Press, 1986), 484–85. Richard Cross, "Duns Scotus on Goodness, Justice, and What God Can Do," *Journal of Theological Studies* 48 (1997): 67, n. 61, corrects several defects in Wolter's Latin text. For a concise summary of Scotus's conception of the relation between voluntarism and ethics, see Richard Cross, *Duns Scotus* (Oxford: Oxford University Press, 1999), 89–95. Scotus, Cross suggests, 192, n. 79, probably holds that while lying is not intrinsically evil, it can never be in accord with the intrinsic nature of things. "After all," Cross writes, "God can dispense from the obligation not to lie; and we presumably would want to claim that under such circumstances lying is not morally bad." For an overview of thirteenth-century ethical debates about voluntarism, see Bonnie Kent, *Virtues of the Will: The Transformation of Ethics in the Late Thirteenth Century* (Washington, D.C.: Catholic University of America Press, 1995).

54. Scotus, *In librum tertium sententiarum*, dist. 38, quaest. 1, art. 1, opinio 3, 486–87.

55. Scotus, *In librum tertium sententiarum*, dist. 38, quaest. 1, art. 2, ad. 4, in *Duns Scotus*, 496–97.

56. Scotus, *In librum tertium sententiarum*, dist. 38, quaest. 1, art. 2, ad. 4, in *Duns Scotus*, trans. Wolter, 496–97. Compare this reading of Scotus's position with Silvana Vechio, "Mensonge, Simulation, Dissimulation," in *Vestigia, Imagines, Verba: Semiotics and Logic in Medieval Theological Texts (XIIth–XIVth century)*, ed. Constantine Marmo (Turnhout: Brepols, 1997), 126, who stresses Scotus's "condamnation absolue du mensonge verbal."

57. For a brief overview of the commentary tradition on Aristotle's *Ethics*, see George Weiland, "The Reception and Interpretation of Aristotle's *Ethics*," in *The Cambridge History of Later Medieval Philosophy*, 657–72.

58. Albert the Great, *Super Ethica* IV, in *Opera Omnia*, vol. 14a, ed. W. Kübel (Münster: Aschendorff, 1968), lectio 14, 288. For a fuller account of Albert's position, see M. S. Kempshall, *The Common Good in Late Medieval Political Thought* (Oxford: Oxford University Press, 1999), 67–73. Anthony J. Celano, "The End of Practical Wisdom: Ethics as Science in the Thirteenth Century," *Journal of the History of Philosophy* 33:2 (April 1995): 225–43,

discusses the significance and lasting influence of Albert's distinction between the civil and the theological and its relation to prudence. "In Albert's science of ethics," he writes, 238–39, "prudence, supreme *in genere politicorum*, is merely a means to a superior good, when considered in relation to contemplative happiness."

59. Bonaventure, *Sententiarum*, III, dist. XXXVIII, quaest. 2, conclusio, ratio1 and confirmatio, 843. See John F. Quinn, "Bonaventure on Our Natural Obligation to Confess Truth," *Franciscan Studies* 35 (1975): 194–211. Contrast with Mireille Vincent-Cassy, "Recherches sur le mensonge au Moyen Âge," in *Études sur la sensibilité au Moyen Age*, Congrès national des sociétés savantes, France (1977), 165–73.

60. Thomas Aquinas, *Summa of Theology*, I, quaest. 16, art. 6, ad. 2.

61. Anselm, *De veritate*, in *Anselm of Canterbury*, 4 vols., vol. 2, ed. and trans. Jasper Hopkins and Herbert Richardson (Toronto: Edwin Mellen Press, 1974–76), ch. 5, 82–84.

62. Anselm, *De veritate*, ch. 8, 87–89.

63. Anselm, *De veritate*, ch. 13, 99–102. For a similar reading of Anselm's *De veritate*, see Eileen Sweeney, *Anselm of Canterbury*, 181–96. Compare with Sandra Visser and Thomas Williams, *Anselm* (Oxford: Oxford University Press, 2009), 41–56.

64. Aquinas, *Quaestiones disputatae de veritate*, quaest. 1, art. 4, reponsio, in *Opera Omnia XXII*, vol. I (Rome, 1975), 14.

65. Aquinas, *Quaestiones disputatae de veritate*, quaest. 1, art. 4, solutio, 14. On Thomas's arguments against Siger of Brabant and Boethius of Dacia, see John F. Wippel, *Medieval Reactions to the Encounter between Faith and Reason* (Milwaukee: Marquette University Press, 1995).

66. Anselm, *De veritate*, ch. 2, 78–81.

67. Anselm, *De veritate*, ch. 13, 102.

68. Aquinas, *Summa Contra Gentiles* II, cap. 4, 34–36. On Thomas's distinction between Truth and truths, see William Wood's very useful essay, "Thomas Aquinas on the Claim That God Is Truth," *Journal of the History of Philosophy* 51:1 (2013): 21–47, especially 42–44.

69. Henri de Lubac, *Augustinianism and Modern Theology*, trans. Lancelot Sheppard (New York: Herder and Herder, 1969), 126–27 and 207–16.

70. Aquinas, *Summa of Theology* II-II, quest. 167, art. 1.

71. Anselm, *Monologion*, in *Anselm of Canterbury*, vol. 1, pref., 3. On monastic education and devotion, see Jean Leclercq, *The Love of Learning and the Desire for God*, trans. Catherine Mishari (New York: Fordham University Press, 1961), 15–19, and Paul F. Gehl, "Competens Silentium: Varieties of Monastic Silence in the Medieval West," *Viator* 18 (1987): 126–60.

72. Anselm, *Proslogion*, in *Anselm of Canterbury*, vol. 1, ch. 26, 112. Paul Gehl, "Mystical Language Models in Monastic Educational Psychology," *Journal of Medieval and Renaissance Studies* 14:2 (1984): 219–43, and Edward Synan, "Prayer, Proof and Anselm's *Proslogion*," in *Standing before God: Studies on Prayer in Scriptures and in Tradition with Essays in Honor of John M. Oesterreicher*, ed. Asher Finkel and Lawrence Frizzell (New York:

KTAV Publishing House, 1981), 267–88. More recently, Ian P. Wei, *Intellectual Culture in Medieval Paris: Theologians and the University, c. 1100–1333* (Cambridge, Cambridge University Press, 2012), 52–71, who discusses the influence of context on monastic thought.

73. Wei, *Intellectual Culture*, 87–124, here, 122. Contrast with Marie Dominique Chenu, *Toward Understanding Saint Thomas*, trans. and corrected by A. M. Landry and D. Hughes (Chicago: Regnery Publishing, 1964), 299, and Jacques LeGoff, *Intellectuals in the Middle Ages*, trans. Teresa Lavendar Fagan (Oxford: Blackwell, 1992), 79–82.

74. Marcia Colish, "Systematic Theology and Theological Renewal in the Twelfth Century," *Journal of Medieval and Renaissance Studies* 18:2 (1988): 135–56, here 155.

75. G. R. Evans, *Old Arts and New Theology: The Beginning of Theology as an Academic Discipline* (Oxford: Clarendon Press, 1980), 93–95. Along these lines, see Aquinas, *Summa Theologiae* I, quaest. 1, art. 6, ad. 3, where he distinguishes between knowledge of and possession of virtue.

76. Bok, *Lying*, 32–46.

77. On this obligation, see Denery, *Seeing and Being Seen*, 22–30.

78. David of Augsburg, *De institutione novitiorum*, in Bonaventure, *Opera Omnia*, vol. 12 (Paris: Vivès, 1868), 294.

79. On hypocrisy, see Frederic Amory, "Whited Sepulchres: The Semantic History of Hypocrisy to the High Middle Ages," *Recherches de Théologie ancienne et médiévale* 53 (1986): 5–39.

80. Humbert of Romans, *De eruditione praedicatorum*, in *De vita regulari*, 2 vols., vol. II, ed. Joachim Joseph Berthier (Rome, 1889), 373–484. On Humbert's treatise and mendicant tensions between public performance and inner intention, see Denery, *Seeing and Being Seen*, 19–38, and Claire Waters, *Angels and Earthly Creatures; Preaching, Performance and Gender in the Later Middle Ages* (Philadelphia: University of Pennsylvania Press, 2004), 31–56.

81. Johannes Nider, *Praeceptorium: sive orthodoxea et accurata decalogi explicatio* (Douay: Ioannis Bogardi, 1611), 126.

82. The seventeenth-century Catholic theologian Juan Caramuel writes as much in his *Haplotes de restrictionibus mentalibus* (Lyons, 1672), sig. OO 2: "The discussion here is not concerned with what the truth is, but with the grounds on which the truth rests. The question is not *whether* Peter is lying if he states that he does not know something that was confided to him under a seal of secrecy. For we are all bound to declare that in making such a denial he does not lie. But since *Ipse dixit* does not satisfy the fervour of intellects nowadays, we proceed further and wish to know, *why* Peter is not lying if he asserts that he does not know something that we presume he does know." Cited and translated in A. E. Malloch, "Equivocation: A Circuit of Reasons," in *Familiar Colloquy: Essays Presented to Arthur Edward Barker*, ed. Patricia Bruckmann (Ottawa: Oberon Press, 1978), 132–43, here, 132.

83. Stefania Tutino, "Nothing but the Truth? Hermeneutics and Morality in the Doctrines of Equivocation and Mental Reservation in Early Modern

Europe," *Renaissance Quarterly* 64:1 (Spring 2011): 115–55, frames the early modern discussion about lies in terms of these two historical moments. Zagorin, *Ways of Lying*, examines the question of lying in connection with religious belief.

84. Antoninus of Florence, *Summae Sacra Theologiae* (Venice: Bernardus Iuntus & Socios., 1571), pars secunda, titulus 10, cap. 1, 330r.

85. Nider, *Praeceptorium*, "Praeceptum Primum," cap. 15, 124.

86. Antoninus, *Summae*, pars secunda, titulus 10, cap. 1, 330v. The story of Samuel and the calf can be found at 1 Samuel 16:1–5.

87. Antoninus, *Summae*, pars secunda, titulus 10, cap. 1, p. 330v. I follow Martin Stone's translation of *gabella* in a now-retracted article. The story of Tobit and the angel can be found at Tobit 5: 5–18.

88. Antoninus, *Summae*, pars secunda, titulus 10, cap. 1, 330r.

89. Antoninus, *Summae*, pars secunda, titulus 10, cap. 1, 330v.

90. Sylvester Prierias, *Sylvestrinae Summae*, pars secunda, "De Mendacio & Mendace," cols. 227–28.

91. Zagorin, *Ways of Lying*, 163–85, for an overview of Navarrus's life and theory of amphibology.

92. Martin Azpilcueta, *Commentarius in Cap. Humanae Aures XXII. Q.V. De Veritate responsi, Partim verbo, partim mente concepti, & de arte bona, & mala simulandi* (Rome, 1584), 2. Zagorin, *Ways of Lying*, 169–70, briefly explains the nature of this, admittedly rare, type of marriage vow.

93. Azpilcueta, *Commentarius*, quaest. 1, sect. 1, 2, 4, and 5, 3–5.

94. Martin Azpilcueta, *Enchiridion, sive Manuale Confessariorum et Poenitentium*, "De octavo praecepto Decalogi, Non fis falsus testis," cap. XVIII, sect. 1–3 (Venice, 1594), 165r–v.

95. Azpilcueta, *Commentarius*, quaest. III, sect. 8–10, 22–23. The crucial insight that Navarrus is offering a theory of language, not simply another refinement of moral theology, can be found in Tutino, "Nothing but the Truth," 127–34. This account, obviously, depends upon her analysis.

96. Azpilcueta, *Commentarius*, quaest. II, sect. 12, 15, offers examples of acting with just cause and quaest. III, sect. 3, 19, with evil intent.

97. Azpilcueta, *Commentarius*, quaest. III, sect. 13–15, 25.

98. Juan Azor, *Institutionum moralium*, pt. III, bk. XIII, "De Octavo Decalogi Praecepto," cap. III (Cologne: Hierat, 1612), col. 1132.

99. On these developments, Tutino, "Nothing but the Truth," 134–52, and Sommerville, "The 'New Art of Lying,'" 170–73.

100. Jan Miel, *Pascal and Theology* (Baltimore: Johns Hopkins Press, 1969), 125.

101. Pascal, *Provincial Letters*, "Letter VII," 241–42. Miel, *Pascal and Theology*, 132.

102. Pascal, *Pensées*, ed. and trans. Roger Ariew (Indianapolis: Hackett Publishing Company, 2005), S78/L45, 16. References to the *Pensées* indicate both Philippe Sellier's ("S") and Louis Lafuma's (L) reconstruction of the text. On the disorienting aspects of pride, see Philippe Sellier, *Pascal et Saint Augustin* (Paris: Librairie Armand Colin, 1970), 182–90, and William D. Wood, "Axiology, Self-Deception and Moral Wrongdoing in Blaise Pascal's *Pensées*," *Journal of Religious Ethics* 37:2 (June 2009): 355–84, here 372–79.

103. Pascal, *Provincial Letters,* "Letter V," 197.

104. Pascal, *Les écrits des curés de Paris,* in *Oeuvres Complètes,* ed. Louis Lafuma (Paris: Éditions du Seuil, 1963), "Sixième écrit," 488.

105. Pascal, *Pensées,* S743/L978, 268. Pierre Cariou, *Pascal et la casuistique* (Paris: Presses Universitaire de France, 1993), p. 138, "La duplicité est le vice de qui n'aime ni la verité ni l'erreur, et qui demeure en suspens, mais dans la pensée que l'une et l'autre, selon les circonstances, seront utiles."

106. Pascal, *Pensées,* S164/L131, 37. On Pascal and original sin, Michael Moriarty, *Fallen Nature, Fallen Selves: Early Modern French Thought II* (Oxford: Oxford University Press, 2006), 125–32.

107. Pierre Force, *Le problème herméneutique chez Pascal* (Paris: Librairie Philosophique J. Vrin, 1989), 173–84.

108. Pascal, "Comparaison des Chrétiens des premiers temps avec ceux d'aujourd'hui," in *Oeuvres Complèts,* 360–62, here, 360 [4].

109. Pascal, "Comparaison," 360–61.

110. Pascal, *Pensées,* S245/L212, 66.

111. Pascal, "Comparaison," 360 [3].

112. Pascal, *Pensées,* S680/L418, 211–14. On the possibility of self-interest and hypocrisy in the wager, Michael Moriarty, *Disguised Vices: Theories of Virtues in Early Modern French Thought* (Oxford: Oxford University Press, 2011), 249–50, and Jennifer A. Herdt, *Putting on Virtue: The Legacy of the Splendid Vices* (Chicago: University of Chicago Press, 2008), 242–43.

CHAPTER FOUR. COURTIERS

1. John of Salisbury, *Frivolities of the Courtiers and Footprints of the Philosophers: Being a Translation of the First, Second, and Third Books and Selections from the Seventh and Eighth Books of the Policraticus of John of Salisbury,* bk. III, ch. 4, trans. Joseph B. Pike (Minneapolis: University of Minnesota Press, 1938), 159.

2. John of Salisbury, *Policraticus,* bk. III, ch. 6, 166. John was hardly alone in thinking he lived in an age of decline. See C. Stephen Jaeger, "Pessimism in the Twelfth-Century Renaissance," *Speculum* 78:4 (October 2003): 1151–83. For more on medieval flattery, see Douglas Wurtele, "The Bane of Flattery in the World of Langland," *Florigelium* 19 (2002): 1–25.

3. Baldassare Castiglione, *The Book of the Courtier,* trans. George Bull (London: Penguin Books, 1976 rev.), 107.

4. For an overview of John's life, see Cary Nederman, *John of Salisbury* (Tempe: Arizona Center for Medieval and Renaissance Studies, 2005), 1–39.

5. John of Salisbury, *Policraticus,* bk. I, ch. 1, 11.

6. Alain Chartier, *Le Curial,* in *Les Oeuvres Latins d'Alain Chartier,* ed. Pascale Bourgain-Hemeryck (Paris: Éditions du Centre National de la Recherche Scientifique, 1977), 347–48. The edition contains both Latin and old French versions of the letter. I cite the French version because it is a bit more colorful. For an early English translation, see William Caxton, *The Curial made*

by *maystere Alain Charretier* (1484), ed. Fredrick J. Furnival (London: Early English Text Society, 1888), 2–16.

7. Chartier, *Le Curial*, 351.
8. Chartier, *Le Curial*, 369.
9. Chartier, *Le Curial*, 365–67.
10. Chartier, *Le Curial*, 369.
11. Chartier, *Le Curial*, 373.
12. Genesis 3:7.
13. Isidore of Seville in *Glossa Ordinaria*, vol. 1, col. 94, commenting on Genesis 3:6–7.
14. Peter Damian, "NR. 69," in *Die Briefe des Petrus Damiani*, vol. 2, NR. 41–90, ed. Kurt Reindel (Munich: Monumenta Germaniae Historica, 1988), 300.
15. Peter of Blois, "Epistle 14b," 6.1 and 3, in *The Letter Collections of Peter of Blois*, ed. Lena Wahlgren (Göteburg: Acta Universitatis Gothoburgensis, 1993), 153. For a very nice analysis of Peter's hot and cold love affair with the court, see John D. Cotts, *The Clerical Dilemma: Peter of Blois and Literate Culture in the Twelfth Century* (Washington, D.C.: Catholic University of America Press, 2009), 131–75, and, specifically on *Epistle 14a/b*, 151–58. C. Stephen Jaeger, "The Court Criticism of MGH Didactic Poets: Social Structures and Literary Conventions," *Monatshefte* 74:4 (Winter 1982): 398–409, provides a brief overview of the medieval genre of court carping.
16. Peter of Blois, "Epistle 14b," 16.4, 158.
17. Quoted in Cotts, *The Clerical Dilemma*, 154.
18. Studies concerning the response of sixteenth- and seventeenth-century European thinkers and writers to uncertainty are too numerous to list in full. Theodore Rabb's *The Struggle for Stability in Early Modern Europe* (New York: Oxford University Press, 1975) is still a valuable entry point. Among recent works I have found helpful are Michael Allen Gillespie, *The Theological Origins of Modernity* (Chicago: University of Chicago Press, 2008), Stuart Clark, *Vanities of the Eye*, John Farrell, *Paranoia and Modernity*, and Karsten Harries, *Infinity and Perspective* (Cambridge: MIT Press, 2001). The classic work on early modern skepticism remains Richard Popkin, *The History of Skepticism: From Savanarola to Bayle* (New York: Oxford University Press, 2003 rev.), although he undervalues the importance of earlier medieval debates. For correctives, see *Rethinking the History of Skepticism: The Missing Medieval Background*, ed. H. Lagerlund (Leiden: E. J. Brill, 2010), and Dominik Perler, *Zweifel und Gewissheit. Skeptische Debatten im Mittelalter* (Frankfurt a.M.: Klostermann, 2006).
19. Daniel Javitch, "*Il Cortegiano* and the Constraints of Despotism," in *Castiglione: The Ideal and Real in Renaissance Culture*, ed. Robert W. Hanning and David Rosand (New Haven: Yale University Press, 1983), 17–28. For the intensification of these pressures in France during the seventeenth century, see Henry C. Clark, *La Rochefoucauld and the Language of Unmasking in Seventeenth-Century France* (Geneva: Librairie Droz, 1994).

20. Eugene Garver, *Machiavelli and the History of Prudence* (Madison: University of Wisconsin Press, 1987), 3–5. Quentin Skinner, *Reason and Rhetoric in the Philosophy of Hobbes* (Cambridge: Cambridge University Press, 1996), 426–37, depicts Hobbes as the thinker who is most torn between these two approaches.

21. René Descartes, *Discourse on Method*, pt. 1, in *The Philosophical Writings of Descartes*, vol. 1, trans. John Cottingham et al. (Cambridge: Cambridge University Press, 1985), 111–16.

22. Descartes, *Meditations on First Philosophy*, "1st Meditation," in *The Philosophical Writings of Descartes*, vol. II, 12–15. On the connections between certainty and doubt in Descartes's philosophy, see Janet Broughton, *Descartes's Method of Doubt* (Princeton: Princeton University Press, 2002).

23. Victoria Kahn, *Rhetoric, Prudence and Skepticism in the Renaissance* (Ithaca: Cornell University Press, 1985), 19–28.

24. *John Rainolds's Oxford Lectures on Aristotle's* Rhetoric, ed. and trans. Lawrence D. Green (Newark: University of Delaware Press, 1986), 205.

25. *John Rainolds's Oxford Lectures*, 161.

26. Cited in Stephen Pender, "The Open Use of Living: Prudence, Decorum and the 'Square Man,'" *Rhetorica* 23:4 (April 2005): 363–400, here, 384. Pender also discusses John Rainolds. The quoted passage can be found in Pierre Charon, *Of Wisdom: The Second and Third Books*, 2nd ed., trans. George Stanhope (London, 1707), bk. III, ch. 1, 2. I have silently modernized the spelling.

27. Charron, *Of Wisdom*, bk. III, ch. 2, 21.

28. Charron, *Of Wisdom*, bk. III, ch. 1, 7–8.

29. Castiglione, *The Book of the Courtier*, bk. 1, 53. On Castiglione's skepticism and debt to Cicero, see Stephen Kolsky, "The Limits of Knowledge: Scholasticism and Scepticism in *The Book of the Courtier*," *Parergon* 25:2 (2008): 17–32, who notes the skeptical basis of Ludovico's comments. Commenting on the value of a skeptical attitude for the courtier, Kolsky writes, 30, "The courtier cannot depend upon absolutes in the theatre of the court where change and mutability are key factors in determining behaviour." See also Jennifer Richards, "Assumed Simplicity and the Critique of Nobility: Or, How Castiglione Read Cicero," *Renaissance Quarterly* 54:2 (Summer 2001): 460–86.

30. Castiglione, *Book of the Courtier*, bk. II, 115. Peter Burke, *The Fortunes of the Courtier* (University Park: Pennsylvania State University Press, 1996), discusses the immense influence of Castiglione's work.

31. Recent discussions of this transformation in prudence include Pender, "The Open Use of Living," 379–80, and John Martin, "Inventing Sincerity, Refashioning Prudence: The Discovery of the Individual in Renaissance Europe," *American Historical Review* 102:5 (December 1997): 1309–42, here, 1323–26.

32. Niccolò Machiavelli, *The Prince*, ch. 17, 56.

33. Castiglione, *Book of the Courtier*, bk. II, 149–50. The literature on Renaissance conceptions of prudence and dissimulation is enormous. Some particu-

larly useful recent works include Snyder, *Dissimulation*, Martin, *Myths*, and Cavaillé, *Dis/simulations*.

34. Christine de Pizan, *The Treasure of the City of Ladies or The Book of the Three Virtues*, trans. Sarah Lawson (London: Penguin Books, 2003, rev.), pt. 1.3, 6–7.

35. John of Salisbury, *Policraticus*, bk. I, ch. 1, 11.

36. On Christine's awareness of Latin sources and Scholastic theology, see Constant J. Mews, "Latin Learning in Christine de Pizan's *Livre de Paix*," in *Healing the Body Politic: The Political Thought of Christine de Pizan*, ed. Karen Green and Constant J. Mews (Turnhout: Brepols, 2005), 61–75, and Earl Jeffrey Richards, "Somewhere between Destructive Glosses and Chaos: Christine de Pizan and Medieval Theology," in *Christine de Pizan: A Casebook*, ed. Barbara K. Altman and Deborah L. McGrady (New York: Routledge, 2003), 43–55.

37. Plato, *Phaedo*, in *The Collected Dialogues of Plato*, ed. Edith Hamilton and Huntington Cairns, trans. Hugh Tredennick (Princeton: Princeton University Press, 1961), 83d.

38. John of Salisbury, *Policraticus*, bk. III, ch. 4, 161.

39. Christine de Pizan, *The Treasure*, pt. 1.16, 44.

40. John of Salisbury, *Policraticus*, bk. 1, prologue, 10. On John's skepticism, Cary Nederman, "Beyond Stoicism and Aristotelianism: John of Salisbury's Skepticism and Twelfth-Century Moral Philosophy," in *Virtue and Ethics in the Twelfth Century*, ed. Istvan Bejczy (Leiden: E. J. Brill, 2005): 177–84, and Christophe Grellard, *Jean de Salisbury et la renaissance médiévale du scepticisme* (Paris: Les Belles Lettres, 2013).

41. John of Salisbury, *The Metalogicon of John of Salisbury: A Twelfth-Century Defense of the Verbal and Logical Arts of the Trivium*, trans. Daniel D. McGarry (Berkeley: University of California Press, 1955), bk. IV, ch. 31, 251.

42. John of Salisbury, *Entheticus Maior and Minor*, 3 vols., ed. Jan van Laarhoven (Leiden: E. J. Brill, 1987), vol. I, 180.

43. John of Salisbury, *Policraticus*, bk. VII, ch. 2, 221.

44. John of Salisbury, *Metalogicon*, bk. II, ch. 3, 78.

45. John of Salisbury, *Metalogicon*, bk. II, ch. 3, 79.

46. John of Salisbury, *Metalogicon*, bk. II, ch. 12, 102.

47. John of Salisbury, *Metalogicon*, bk. II, ch. 13, 105.

48. John of Salisbury, *Metalogicon*, bk. II, ch. 12, 101–2.

49. John of Salisbury, *Metalogicon*, bk. IV, ch. 40, 269.

50. John of Salisbury, *Policraticus*, bk. VII, ch. 1, 217–18.

51. John of Salisbury, *Metalogicon*, bk. IV, ch. 40, 269–70. On medieval attitudes toward curiosity, see Richard Newhauser, "Towards a History of Human Curiosity: A Prolegomenon to Its Medieval Phase," *Deutsche Vierteljahrsschrift* 56 (1982): 559–75.

52. John of Salisbury, *Metalogicon*, prologue, 3.

53. John of Salisbury, *Metalogicon*, prologue, 6.

54. Denis Foulechat, *Le policratique de Jean de Salisbury*, livres I–III, ed. Charles

Brucker (Geneva: Librairie Droz , 1994), 82. For Boethius's Latin translation see Boethius, *De sophisticis elenchis*, ed. Bernardus G. Dod, in *Aristoteles latinus* VI, 1–3 (Leiden: E. J. Brill, 1975), 6.

55. Foulechat, *Le policratique*, 82.
56. Foulechat, *Le policratique*, 86.
57. John of Salisbury, *Metalogicon*, bk. II, ch. 1, 74–75.
58. John of Salisbury, *Metalogicon*, bk. I, ch. 4, 19–20. Limiting his discussion to the *Metalogicon*, Jerrold Seigel, *Rhetoric and Philosophy in Renaissance Humanism* (Princeton: Princeton University Press, 1968), 183–89, overlooks John's rhetorical turn in the *Policraticus*.
59. Boethius, *De topicis differentiis*, trans. Eleonore Stump (Ithaca: Cornell University Press, 1978), bk. IV, 1205C: "The dialectical discipline examines the thesis only; a thesis is a question not involved in circumstances. The rhetorical discipline, on the other hand, investigates and discusses hypotheses, that is, questions hedged in by a multitude of circumstances. Circumstances are who, what, where, when, why, how and by what means."
60. Cicero, *On Duties*, ed. M. T. Griffin and E. M. Adams, trans. Margaret Atkins (Cambridge: Cambridge University Press, 1991), bk. I, ch. 107, 42, and, more generally, the entire first book for this conception of the honorable man. Albert R. Jonsen and Stephen Toulmin, *The Abuse of Casuistry*, 75–88, offer a concise summary of what these calculations would look like. On prudence and decorum in Cicero, Robert W. Cape, Jr., "Cicero and the Development of Prudential Practice at Rome," in *Prudence: Classical Virtue, Postmodern Practice*, ed. Robert Harriman (University Park: Pennsylvania State University Press, 2003), 35–65. Cary Nederman, "Nature, Sin and the Origins of Society: The Ciceronian Tradition in Medieval Political Thought," *Journal of the History of Ideas* 49:1 (January–March 1988): 3–26, surveys Cicero's influence from the twelfth through the fourteenth centuries.
61. Cicero, *On Duties*, bk. I (101), 40. Gary Remer, "Rhetoric as a Balancing of Ends: Cicero and Machiavelli," *Philosophy and Rhetoric* 42:1 (2009): 1–29, discusses the connections and tensions between decorum, usefulness, and the demands of circumstance in Cicero's writings.
62. Cicero, *On Duties*, bk. I (59), 24. For the original Latin, Cicero, *De officiis* (Cambridge: Harvard University Press, 1913), bk. I, ch. xviii, 62: "Haec igitur et talia circumspicienda sunt in omni officio [et consuetudo exercitatioque capienda], ut boni ratiocinatores officiorum esse possimus et addendo deducendoque videre, quae reliqui summa fiat, ex quo, quantum cuique debeatur, intellegas."
63. John of Salisbury, *Policraticus*, bk. I, ch. 2, 12.
64. John of Salisbury, *Policraticus*, bk. III, ch. 2, 155.
65. John of Salisbury, *Policraticus*, bk. III, ch. 1, 155.
66. John of Salisbury, *Policraticus*, bk. VII, ch. 2, p. 221–22.
67. John of Salisbury, *Policraticus*, bk. I, ch. 4, 23. Nederman, "Beyond Stoicism and Aristotelianism," 187, makes this observation in somewhat different terms when he links John's skepticism to his "praise of liberty of thought and speech."

68. John of Salisbury, *Policraticus*, bk. I, ch. 5, 27.
69. John of Salisbury, *Policraticus*, bk. I, ch. 5, 28. Compare this with Michael Wilks's very interesting essay "John of Salisbury and the Tyranny of Nonsense," in *The World of John of Salisbury*, ed. Michael Wilks (Oxford: Blackwell, 1984), 263–86, here, 275–77, where he suggests the principle of the middle way guides John's ethics, while making no reference to John's skeptical and rhetorical leanings.
70. John of Salisbury, *Policraticus*, bk. III, ch. 15, 211.
71. John of Salisbury, *Policraticus*, bk. III, ch. 11, 186.
72. John of Salisbury, *Policraticus*, bk. III, ch. 12, 190–91.
73. Both Garver, *Machiavelli*, 3–25, and Robert Harriman, "Theory without Modernity," in *Prudence*, 1–32, here, 14–20, stress that prudence must never be reduced to a mere reactive, ends-justify-the-means form of reasoning.
74. John of Salisbury, *Policraticus*, bk. III, ch. 12, 192.
75. John of Salisbury, *Policraticus*, bk. VIII, ch. 14, 389–90, also bk. III, ch. 8, 172.
76. Gratian, *The Treaty on Laws with the Ordinary Gloss*, trans. Augustine Thompson and James Gordley (Washington, D.C.: Catholic University of America Press, 1993), dist. 13, pt. 1, 49. For a recent discussion of Gratian, the glossators, and moral dilemmas, see M. V. Dougherty, *Moral Dilemmas in Medieval Thought from Gratian to Thomas Aquinas* (Cambridge: Cambridge University Press, 2011). Anders Winroth, *The Making of Gratian's* Decretum (Cambridge: Cambridge University Press, 2000), suggests the *Decretum* as we know it is an expansion subsequent lawyers made to Gratian's initially much smaller treatise. I will simply refer to the work as Gratian's for the sake of convenience.
77. Gratian, *Treaty on Laws*, dist. 13, pt. 1, c. 2.1, 50. Early thirteenth-century Scholastic thinkers, such as William of Auxerre and Alexander of Hales, seem to have agreed with Gratian. See Doughtery, *Moral Dilemmas*, 41–84.
78. Gratian, *Treaty on Laws*, dist. 13, pt. 1, gloss, 49.
79. Gratian, *Treaty on Laws*, dist. 13, pt. 1, c. 2.3, 51. Dougherty, *Moral Dilemmas*, 6–8, notes that the difference between Gratian and the glossators can be captured in the different definitions of the word *perplexitas* itself, which has both epistemological and ontological connotations.
80. Dougherty, *Moral Dilemmas*, 22–25.
81. John of Salisbury, *Policraticus*, bk. I, introduction, 9.
82. John of Salisbury, *Policraticus*, bk. I, introduction, 9–10. On Augustine's prohibition against lying, see chapter 4.
83. John of Salisbury, *Entheticus*, 97–99. On John and the permissibility of lying, see Dallas G. Denery II, "Christine de Pizan against the Theologians: The Virtue of Lies in *The Book of Three Virtues*," *Viator* 39:1 (2008): 229–47, Marcia Colish, "Rethinking Lying in the Twelfth Century," in *Virtue and Ethics in the Twelfth Century*, ed. István P. Bejczy and Richard G. Newhauser (Leiden: E. J. Brill, 2005), 155–74, and, especially, Cary J. Nederman and Tsae Lan Lee Dow, "The Road to Heaven Is Paved with Pious Deception: Medieval Speech Ethics and Deliberative Democracy," in Benedetto Fontana,

ed., *Talking Democracy: Historical Perspectives on Rhetoric and Democracy* (University Park: Pennsylvania State University Press, 2005), 187–212, who were the first to identify and stress this aspect of both John's and Christine de Pizan's ethics.

84. Christine de Pizan, *The Treasure*, 14–15.
85. Christine de Pizan, *The Treasure*, 28.
86. Christine de Pizan, *The Treasure*, 28. Karen Green, "On Translating Christine as a Philosopher," in *Healing the Body Politic*, 117–37, here, 119, warns against anachronistic interpretations of prudence in Christine's writings that equate it with something like "intelligent self-interest" and contrast it with morality. For a more purely pragmatic interpretation of prudence in Christine's work, see Kate L. Forhan, *The Political Theory of Christine de Pizan* (Aldershot: Ashgate Publishing, 2002), 100–108.
87. Christine de Pizan, *The Treasure*, 29.
88. Christine de Pizan, *The Treasure*, 35.
89. Christine de Pizan, *The Treasure*, 30.
90. Christine de Pizan, *The Treasure*, 36.
91. Christine de Pizan, *The Treasure*, 38.
92. Christine de Pizan, *The Treasure*, 55.
93. Christine de Pizan, *The Treasure*, 4445.
94. Christine de Pizan, *The Treasure*, 45. On Christine's advice concerning lies and deception, Sharon C. Mitchell, "Moral Posturing: Virtue in Christine de Pisan's *Livre de Trois Vertus*," in *The Inner Life of Women in Medieval Romance Literature: Grief, Guilt and Hypocrisy*, ed. Jeff Rider and Jamie Friedman (New York: Palgrave Macmillan, 2011), 85–106, Tracy Adams, "Appearing Virtuous: Christine de Pizan's *Le Livre des trois vertus* and Anne de France's *Les Enseignements d'Anne de France*," in *Virtue Ethics for Women, 1250–1500*, ed. K. Green and C. J. Mews (Dordrecht: Springer, 2011), 115–31, and Linda Rouillard, "Faux semblant ou faire semblant? Christine de Pizan and Virtuous Artifice," *Forum for Modern Language Studies* 46:1 (2009): 1–13.
95. Christine de Pizan, *The Treasure*, 41.
96. Christine de Pizan, *The Treasure*, 39.
97. Christine de Pizan, *The Treasure*, 39.
98. Christine de Pizan, *The Treasure*, 43.
99. Christine de Pizan, *The Treasure*, 23.
100. Christine de Pizan, *The Treasure*, 23–24. Liliane Dulac, "The Representation and Functions of Feminine Speech in Christine de Pizan's *Livre des Trois Virtus*," in *Reinterpreting Christine de Pizan*, ed. Earl Jeffrey Richards (Athens: University of Georgia Press, 1990), 13–22, stresses the "premeditated and cunning" nature of Christine's advice.
101. Christine de Pizan, *The Treasure*, 46.
102. As Tracy Adams notes, "*Moyennerresse de traictié de paix*: Christine de Pizan's Mediators," in *Healing the Body Politic*, 186–88 and 198–99, Christine herself recognizes the princess will almost inevitably fail as an intermediary, hence her advice on how to deal with adversity. "Christine's motive," Adams

adds, 188, "in exposing the limitations of female intervention seems to be to make a moral point: that the problems of the world . . . are the fault of men. On the other hand, even if they are deprived of political authority, women possess tremendous moral authority." Also, Forhan, *The Political Theory*, 62–64.

103. Christine de Pizan, *The Treasure*, 47.

104. Christine de Pizan, *The Treasure*, 48.

105. Scotus, *In librum tertium sententiarum*, dist. 38, quaest. 1.

106. Christine de Pizan, *The Treasure*, 48.

107. Christine, de Pizan, *The Treasure*, 48. Barry Collett, "The Three Mirrors of Christine de Pizan," in *Healing the Body Politic*, 1–18, here, 13, places Christine's union of moral, practical, and political advice as part of a larger fourteenth-century transformation in the style and content of mirrors for princes.

108. Philibert de Vienne, *Le Philosophe de court*, ed. Pauline M. Smith (Geneva: Librairie Droz, 1990), 81–82. On sixteenth-century critiques of the court, see Pauline M. Smith, *The Anti-courtier Trend in Sixteenth Century French Literature* (Geneva: Librairie Droz, 1966).

109. Philibert, *Le Philosophe*, 86–87.

110. For a notable precursor to Philibert's discussion of courtly musical ability, Gottfried von Strassburg, *Tristan: With the Tristan of Thomas*, trans. A. T. Hatto (London: Penguin Books, 1967, rev.), 89–91.

111. Philibert, *Le Philosophe*, 168–70.

112. Daniel Javitch, "The Philosopher of the Court: A French Satire Misunderstood," *Comparative Literature* 23:2 (Spring 1971): 97–124.

113. Nathaniel Walker, *The Refin'd Courtier or, A Correction of Several Indecencies crept in Civil Conversation: Written originally in Italian by John Casa, from thence in Latin by Nathan Chytroeus, and from both by way of Paraphrase, made English, by N.W.* (London: Matthew Gilliflower, 1681), 2. On the English reception of della Casa's treatise, see John R. Woodhouse, "The Tradition of Della Casa's *Galateo* in English," in *The Crisis of Courtesy: Studies in the Conduct-Book in Britain, 1600–1900*, ed. Jacques Carré (Leiden: E. J. Brill, 1994), 11–26, on Walker in particular, 18. Woodhouse contends, 11–12, that while clearly a conduct manual, della Casa's treatise was also satirical, though none of his English readers, nor anyone else for that matter, seems to have recognized it.

114. Walker, *The Refin'd Courtier*, 7.

115. Walker, *The Refin'd Courtier*, 126.

116. Stephano Guazzo, *The Art of Conversation* (London: J. Brett, 1738), 59.

117. Guazzo, *The Art of Conversation*, 64. Javitch, "Rival Arts of Conduct in Elizabethan England: Guazzo's *Civile Conversation* and Castiglione's *Courtier*," *Yearbook of Italian Studies* 1 (1971): 171–98, stresses the differences between Guazzo's and Castiglione's depiction of the ideal courtier and how the English overlooked them.

118. Torquato Accetto, *De l'honnête dissimulation*, ed. Salvatore S. Nigro and trans. Mireille Blanc-Sanchez (Paris: Éditions Verdier, 1990), 31. On the courtly practice of dissimulation, see Snyder, *Dissimulation*, 68–105.

119. Accetto, *De l'honnête dissimulation*, 41–42. Cavaillé, *Dis/simulations*, 333–39, offers helpful context for Accetto's treatise.
120. Accetto, *De l'honnête dissimulation*, 51.
121. On Thomas see chapter 4, and on Christ and the Devil see chapter 1. Francis Bacon, "Of Simulation and Dissimulation," in *The Major Works*, ed. Brian Vickers (Oxford: Oxford University Press, 1996), 349–51, here, 350, offers a more or less standard definition: "There be three degrees of this hiding and veiling of a man's self. The first, closeness, reservation, and secrecy; when a man leaveth himself without observation, or without hold to be taken, what he is. The second, dissimulation, in the negative; when a man lets fall signs and arguments, that he is not, that he is. And the third, simulation, in the affirmative; when a man industriously and expressly feigns and pretends to be, that he is not." On the various distinctions between simulation and dissimulation, see Cavaillé, *Dis/simulations*, 11–31.
122. Accetto, *De l'honnête dissimulation*, 51–55.
123. Accetto, *De l'honnête dissimulation*, 26–27.
124. Jean de Sponde, *Homeri quae extant omnia: Ilias, Odyssea, Batrachomyomachia, Hymni, Poematia aliquot* (Basil: E. Episcopii, 1583), 275: "Dixit, mendacia multa dicens veris similia." In his commentary to Accetto's *De l'honnête dissimulation*, 54, n. 6, Nigro suggests that Accetto used Sponde's translation of Homer. On scars in Accetto, Cavaillé, *Dis/simulations*, 340–44, although he does not discuss this particular scar.
125. Accetto, *De l'honnête dissimulation*, 41. Here I agree with Cavaillé, *Dis/simulations*, 351–54, who argues for the dependence of dissimulation on simulation. Contrast this reading with Snyder, *Dissimulation*, 59–67, who argues that Accetto clearly distinguishes "honest dissimulation" from all forms of deceit and lying.
126. Guazzo, *The Art of Conversation*, 48. Snyder, *Dissimulation*, 33–36, discusses these passages.
127. Guazzo, *The Art of Conversation*, 57.
128. Guazzo, *The Art of Conversation*, 67.
129. Guazzo, *The Art of Conversation*, 74–75.
130. Walker, *The Refin'd Courtier*, 90.
131. Walker, *The Refin'd Courtier*, 95.
132. Walker, *The Refin'd Courtier*, 8.
133. Guazzo, *The Art of Conversation*, 38.
134. Walker, *The Refin'd Courtier*, 234.
135. François duc de La Rochefoucauld, *Maxims*, trans. Leonard Tancock (London: Penguin Books, 1959), maxim 206, 63.
136. La Rochefoucauld, *Maxims*, maxim 87, 48.
137. Walker, *The Refin'd Courtier*, 106.
138. Guazzo, *The Art of Conversation*, 62. Ruth Grant, *Hypocrisy and Integrity: Machiavelli, Rousseau and the Ethics of Politics* (Chicago: University of Chicago Press, 1997), 30–31, on the relation between manners, lying, and hypocrisy, writes: "There is a kinship between social manners and more serious hypocritical behavior that lies in the pretense of sympathetic concern

or respect for others—a kind of pretense of virtue—that manners express. Manners are insincere or 'phony.' People are not treated according to their individual merits or their just deserts, not according to one's true feeling toward them as individuals, but according to conventional forms. This is precisely the advantage of manners: they are formalities. They allow civil public relations between people who are not friends, and delineate the boundary between public and private."

139. Guazzo, *The Art of Conversation*, 64–65. Jennifer Richards, *Rhetoric and Courtliness in Early Modern Literature* (Cambridge: Cambridge University Press, 2003), 30–32, discusses the variety of definitions of the term *honestas* in Guazzo's dialogue, including the notion of honest lies.

140. Republished in J. Martin Stafford, *Private Vices, Publick Benefits? The Contemporary Reception of Bernard Mandeville* (Solihull: Ismeron, 1997), 10–12. On the English and Dutch contexts for Mandeville's ideas, see Laurence Dickey, "Pride, Hypocrisy and Civility in Mandeville's Social and Historical Theory," *Critical Review* 4:3 (Summer 1990): 387–431, and Harold J. Cook, "Bernard Mandeville and the Therapy of the 'Clever Politician,' " *Journal of the History of Ideas* 60:1 (January 1999): 101–24.

141. Bernard Mandeville, *The Fable of the Bees: Or, Private Vices, Publick Benefits*, 2 vols. (Oxford: Clarendon Press, 1924) I, 348–49.

142. Mandeville, *The Fable of the Bees* II, 109–11.

143. Mandeville, *The Fable of the Bees* I, 51. For more on the connections among moral virtue, civility, and self-love, see Dickey, "Pride, Hypocrisy and Civility," 397–401, and Herdt, *Putting on Virtue*, 272–75.

144. Mandeville, *The Fable of the Bees* I, 51–53.

145. Mandeville, *The Fable of the Bees* I, 24.

146. Baltasar Gracián, *The Pocket Oracle and Art of Prudence*, trans. Jeremy Robbins (London: Penguin Books, 2011), #120, 44–45.

147. Quoted in Richard G. Hodgson, *Falsehood Disguised: Unmasking the Truth in La Rochefoucauld* (West Lafayette: Purdue University Press, 1995), 48 and 137.

148. Madeleine de Souvré [Marquise de Sablé], *Maximes* (Paris: Librairie des Bibliophiles, 1678), #20, 21.

149. Gracián, *The Pocket Oracle*, #99, 37. On concern for this gap between appearance and reality, see Domna C. Stanton, *The Aristocrat as Art: A Study of the Honnête Homme and the Dandy in Seventeenth- and Nineteenth-Century Literature* (New York: Columbia University Press, 1989), 184–89.

150. Pierre Nicole, *Moral Essays, Contain'd in Several Treatises on Many Important Duties . . . Done into English by a Person of Quality*, vol. III (London: Sam Manship, 1696), 79. For a brief summary of Nicole's conception of self-love, see Nannerl O. Keohane, *Philosophy and the State in France: The Renaissance to the Enlightenment* (Princeton: Princeton University Press, 1980), 293–303, and Herdt, *Putting on Virtue*, 248–61.

151. Nicole, *Moral Essays*, 83–84.

152. Nicole, *Moral Essays*, 85.

153. Nicole, *Moral Essays*, 87. La Rochefoucauld, *Maxims*, maxim 236, 68,

makes much the same point: "When we work for the benefit of others it would appear that our self-love is tricked by kindness and forgets itself; and yet this is the most certain way to achieve our ends, for it is lending at interest while pretending to give, in fact a way of getting everybody on our own side by subtle and delicate means."

154. La Rochefoucauld, *Maxims*, maxim 119, 52.

155. Nicole, *Moral Essays*, 107–8. On deception and self-deception in La Rochefoucauld, see Hodgson, *Falsehood Disguised*, 39–55.

156. Nicole, *Moral Essays*, 109–10.

157. Gracián, *The Pocket Oracle*, #300, 112.

158. Nicole, *Moral Essays*, 103–4.

159. Nicole, *Moral Essays*, 105. Keohane, *Philosophy and the State*, 297: "Our motives are less important to Nicole in this analysis than the outcomes of our behavior." Also, Herdt, *Putting on Virtue*, 256, on how suspicion of virtue's efficacy, combined with an emphasis on self-love, set the stage for "the outright denial of the existence of true virtue."

160. Mandeville, *The Fable of the Bees* II, 12–13. Herdt, *Putting on Virtue*, 280.

161. Mandeville, *The Fable of the Bees* II, 110.

162. On the coherence of Mandeville's hidden-hand theory of social evolution, see Eugene Heath, "Mandeville's Bewitching Engine of Praise," *History of Philosophy Quarterly* 15:2 (April 1998): 205–26.

163. William Law, *Remarks Upon a Late Book Entitled* The Fable of the Bees, or Private Vices, Publick Benefits, *in a Letter to the Author* (London: William and John Innys, 1724), 57, republished in Stafford, *Private Vices, Publick Benefits?* 74.

CHAPTER FIVE. WOMEN

1. Christine de Pizan, *The Book of the City of Ladies*, trans. Earl Jeffrey Richards (New York: Persea Books, 1982) I.1.1, 3.

2. Christine de Pizan, *The Book* I.1.1, 3–5.

3. Jehan le Fèvre, *Les Lamentations de Matheolus et le Livre de Leesce*, vol. 1, ed. A.-G. van Hamel (Paris: Émile Bouillon, 1892), ln. 5–6, 2. Matthew's Latin version of the poem runs along the bottom of each page.

4. Karen Pratt, "Translating Misogamy: The Authority of the Intertext in the *Lamentationes Matheoluli* and Its Middle French Translation," *Forum for Modern Language Studies*, 35:4 (1999): 421–35, here, 423.

5. Jehan le Fèvre, *Les Lamentations* I:299–310, 9.

6. Jehan le Fèvre, *Les Lamentations* II:4120–32, 158–59. A translation of this section and some others can be found in *Woman Defamed and Woman Defended: An Anthology of Medieval Texts*, ed. Alcuin Blamires, Karen Pratt, and C. W. Marx (Oxford: Clarendon Press, 1992), 195–96.

7. Jehan le Fèvre, *Les Lamentations*, in *Woman Defamed*, 179–80.

8. Jehan le Fèvre, *Les Lamentations*, in *Woman Defamed*, 184. Pratt, "Translating Misogamy," 421–35, argues that Matthew's reputation as a great misogynist has much to do with Jehan's decision to add additional antifem-

inist exempla (borrowed mostly from the *Romance of the Rose*) and to excise almost all of Matthew's satire and critique of the mendicant orders. Renate Blumenfeld-Kosinski, "Jean le Fèvre's *Livre de Leesce*: Praise of Blame of Women?" *Speculum* 69:3 (July 1994): 705–25, reconsiders the sincerity of Jehan's misogyny in light of his subsequent work in praise of women, *Le Livre de Leesce*, presented as an apology for his translation of the *Lamentations*. Regardless of either man's intent, subsequent readers certainly understood them as true representatives of the misogynist tradition.

9. *Fifteen Joys of Marriage*, trans. Brent A. Pitts (New York: Peter Lang, 1985), 119–25.

10. *The Vices of Women*, in *Three Medieval Views of Women*, ed. and trans. Gloria K. Fiero, Wendy Pfeffer, and Mathé Allain (New Haven: Yale University Press, 1989), 123.

11. Guillaume de Lorris and Jean de Meun, *The Romance of the Rose*, trans. Charles Dahlberg (Princeton: Princeton University Press, 1971), 276.

12. Guillaume de Lorris and Jean de Meun, *The Romance of the Rose*, 259.

13. Jehan le Fèvre, *Les Lamentations*, in *Woman Defamed*, 184–85.

14. Ambrose, *Paradise*, ch. 12 (54), 333. See above, chapter 1.

15. Tertullian, *The Apparel of Women*, in *Disciplinary, Moral and Ascetical Works*, trans. Edwin A. Quain (Washington, D.C.: Catholic University of America Press, 1959), bk. 1, ch. 1 (1–2), 117–49, here, 117–18.

16. *The Hammer of Witches: A Complete Translation of the* Malleus Maleficarum, by Heinrich Kramer and James Sprenger, trans. Christopher S. MacKay (Cambridge: Cambridge University Press, 2009), 160–71. On the debate concerning the true author(s) of the text, see MacKay's introduction, 2–6.

17. Christine de Pizan, *The Book* I.8.3, 16–17. Put differently, Christine would have understood the misogynist discourse she confronted and critiqued to conform to one the various definitions of "ideology" that Terry Eagleton, *Ideology: An Introduction* (London: Verso, 1991), 30, offers. "[I]deology," he writes, "signifies ideas and beliefs which help to legitimate the interests of a ruling group or class specifically by distortion and dissimulation." At different moments, as we will see, Christine suggests that men realize the misogynist discourse is false but promote it anyway, while at other moments she seems to think it deceives men as well.

18. Rupert of Deutz, *In Genesim*, lib. III, cap. V, 38. George Duby, *Dames du XIIIe siècle*, tom. III, *Ève et les prêtres* (Paris: Éditions Gallimard, 1996), 69–73, commenting on these passages, stresses Rupert's exegetical debt to Augustine. On Rupert's life and work, see John H. Van Engen, *Rupert of Deutz* (Berkeley: University of California Press, 1983).

19. Rupert of Deutz, *In Genesim*, lib. III, cap. V, 38, quoting Revelation 22:18–19.

20. Rupert of Deutz, *In Genesim*, lib. III, cap. IX, 39, quoting 1 Timothy 2:14.

21. Avitus, *The Poems*, 83–84.

22. Jacobus de Voragine, *Legenda Aurea*, trans. William Caxton (London: Wynkyn the Worde, 1512), 2r.

23. Vincent of Beauvais, *Speculum historiale* (Venice: Dominic Nicolini, 1591),

lib. I, cap. XLI, 6v. Philippe Buc, *L'Amiguïté du livre: Prince, pouvoir, et peuple dans les commentaires de la bible au moyen age* (Paris: Beauchesne Éditeur, 1994), 71–122, discusses thirteenth-century debates concerning hierarchy in the garden.

24. 1 Timothy 2:11–12. Elizabeth A. Clark, "Ideology, History, and the Construction of 'Woman' in Late Ancient Christianity," *Journal of Early Christian Studies* 2:2 (1994): 155–84, especially 166–69, on the "universalizing tendency of ideology."

25. *Glossa Ordinaria* vol. 6, col. 699–700. Despite this expressed ideal of submission, in fact, the exclusion of women from active roles in the church and their total submission to men was never total, at least until the late twelfth century. See Gary Macy, *The Hidden History of Women's Ordination: Female Clergy in the Medieval West* (Oxford: Oxford University Press, 2008).

26. Tertullian, *The Apparel of Women*, bk. II, ch. 5 (4), 136. This reading of Tertullian is heavily indebted to R. Howard Bloch, *Medieval Misogyny and the Invention of Western Romantic Love* (Chicago: University of Chicago Press, 1991), 39–47.

27. Tertullian, *The Apparel of Women*, bk. I, ch. 4 (1),122.

28. Tertullian, *The Apparel of Women*, bk. II, ch. 2 (5), 133.

29. Tertullian, *The Apparel of Women*, bk. II, ch. 2 (4–5), 132.

30. Philo of Alexandria, *On the Creation of the Cosmos*, ch. 21, 87.

31. Philo of Alexandria, *On the Creation of the Cosmos*, ch. 23, 89–91. On Philo's exegesis of Adam and the Woman, see Annewies van den Hoek, "Endowed with Reason or Glued to the Senses: Philo's Thoughts on Adam and Eve," in *The Creation of Man and Woman: Interpretations of the Biblical Narratives in Jewish and Christian Traditions*, ed. Gerard P. Luttikhuizen (Leiden: E. J. Brill, 2000), 63–75, and Bloch, *Medieval Misogyny*, 29–35.

32. Philo of Alexandria, *On the Creation of the Cosmos*.

33. Both Jerome and Chrysostom quoted in Clark, "Ideology," 166–67.

34. Duby, *Dames du XIIe siècle*, 68. These ideas would continue into the Renaissance, more or less unchanged. See Ian Maclean, *The Renaissance Notion of Woman: A Study in the Fortunes of Scholasticism and Medical Science in European Intellectual Life* (Cambridge: Cambridge University Press, 1980).

35. Aristotle, *On the Generation of Animals*, 2.3.737a, ln. 19–34, in *The Complete Works of Aristotle*, vol. 1, ed. Jonathan Barnes (Princeton: Princeton University Press, 1984), 1111–218, here, 1144. For a general overview of Aristotle's biological misogyny, see Maryanne Cline Horowitz, "Aristotle and Woman," *Journal of History of Biology* 9:2 (Autumn 1976): 183–213.

36. Galen, *On the Usefulness of the Bodies Parts*, vol. II, trans. Margaret Tallmadge May (Ithaca: Cornell University Press, 1968), 628–30.

37. For a discussion of complexion theory, see Nancy Siraisi, *Medieval and Early Renaissance Medicine: An Introduction to Knowledge and Practice* (Chicago: University of Chicago Press, 1990), 101–4. On the transmission and medieval adoption of these ideas, Roger French, *Medicine before Science: The Rational and Learned Doctor from the Middle Ages to the Enlightenment* (Cambridge: Cambridge University Press, 2003), 59–126.

38. Both John Buridan and John of Paris, cited in Lynn Thorndike, "De Complexionibus," *Isis* 49:4 (December 1958): 398–408, here, 398.

39. Bartholomew of England, *De proprietatibus rerum*, bk. XV, cap. 13 (London: Thomas East, 1582), 74v. Cited in Joan Cadden, *Meanings of Sex Difference in the Middle Ages: Medicine, Science, Culture* (Cambridge: Cambridge University Press, 1993), 183–84 and, on complexion more generally, 183–88.

40. Bartholomew of England, *De proprietatibus rerum*, bk. XV, cap. 13, 74v.

41. John Buridan, *Quaestiones super octo libros politicorum Aristotelis*, lib. III, quaest. XXVI (Paris, 1513, rprt Frankfurt: Minerva G.M.B.H., 1969), XLIXr. On ideas about female counsel in the Middle Ages, Misty Schieberle, *Feminized Counsel: Women Counselors in Late Medieval Advice Literature, 1380–1500* (Turnhout: Brepols Publishers, n.v., 2014).

42. Buridan, *Quaestiones*, lib. III, quaest. XXVI, XLVIIIv, where he introduces the possibility of feminine prudence at "Arguitur primo," and XLIXv.

43. Nicole Oresme, "Le livre des politiques d'Aristote de Nicole Oresme," ed. Albert Douglas Menut, *Transactions of the American Philosophical Society*, n.s., 60:6 (1970): 123.

44. Aquinas, *Summa of Theology* II-II, quest. 55, art. 3, sed contra, 1423. The passage from Paul's letter is found at 2 Corinthians 4:2.

45. See above, chapter 2.

46. Albert the Great, *Quaestiones super de animalibus*, ed. Ephrem Filthaut, lib. XV, quaest. 11, in *Opera Omnia*, vol. XII (Münster: Aschendorff, 1955), 265. For discussions of this question, Alcuin Blamires, "Women and Creative Intelligence in Medieval Thought," in *Voices in Dialogue: Reading Women in the Middle Ages*, ed. Linda Olson and Kathryn Kerby-Fulton (Notre Dame: University of Notre Dame Press, 2005), 213–30, here 215, Cadden, *Meanings of Sex Difference*, 185, and J. D. Burnley, "Criseyde's Heart and the Weakness of Women: An Essay in Lexical Interpretation," *Studia Neophilologica* 54:1 (1982): 25–38, here, 33–35.

47. Albert the Great, *Super de animalibus*, lib. XV, quaest. 11, 265–66.

48. pseudo–Albert the Great, *Women's Secrets*, trans. Helen Rodnite Lemay (Albany: State University of New York Press, 1992), 59–60. On the work's influence on *The Hammer of Witches*, see Lemay's introduction, 49–58. Sarah Alison Miller, *Medieval Monstrosity and the Female Body* (New York: Routledge, 2010), 55–89, on "secrets" in *Women's Secrets*.

49. *The Hammer of Witches*, 169.

50. Christine de Pizan, *The Book* I.1.2, 5.

51. Christine de Pizan, *The Treasure*, and see above, chapter 3, "Institutional Transformations."

52. Christine de Pizan, *The Book* I.2.1–2.2, 6.

53. Christine de Pizan, *The Book* I.8.3–8.7, 17–19. On Christine's argumentative strategies, see Renate Blumenfeld-Kosinski, "Christine de Pizan and the Misogynistic Tradition," *Romanic Review* 81:3 (May 1990): 279–92, and Sarah Gwyneth Ross, *The Birth of Feminism: Woman as Intellect in Renaissance Italy and England* (Cambridge: Harvard University Press, 2009), 133–43.

54. Christine de Pizan, *The Book* I 1.8.9, 20.

55. Christine de Pizan, *The Letter to the God of Love*, in *The Selected Writings of Christine de Pizan*, ed. Renate Blumenfeld-Kosinski and trans. Renate Blumenfeld-Kosinski and Kevin Brownlee (New York: W.W. Norton & Company, 1997), ln. 267–72, 20.

56. Christine de Pizan, *The Book* II.47.1, 165.

57. Christine de Pizan, *The Book* I.10.1, 25.

58. Christine de Pizan, *The Book* I.9.3, 24.

59. Christine de Pizan, *The Book* I.11.1, 30–32.

60. Christine de Pizan, *The Book* II.13.1, 118 and *The Letter to the God of Love*, ln. 417–19, 71. Alcuin Blamires, *The Case for Women in Medieval Culture* (Oxford: Clarendon Press, 1997), takes up this challenge.

61. Christine de Pizan, *The Book* I.9.2, 22–23, and II.31.1, 119.

62. Ruth Morse, *Truth and Convention: Rhetoric, Representation and Reality* (Cambridge: Cambridge University Press, 1991), 6, stressing the importance of rhetorical invention to the medieval practice of history, writes, "In the different conceptual space of the Middle Ages, true might mean in the main or for the most part, or even, it could have happened like this." There was, in short, nothing untoward in Christine's rewriting of history. For an excellent and comprehensive overview of medieval historical practice, see Matthew Kempshall, *Rhetoric and the Writing of History: 400–1500* (Manchester: Manchester University Press, 2011).

63. Giovanni Boccaccio, *Famous Women*, trans. and ed. Virginia Brown (Cambridge: Harvard University Press, 2001), ch. LXXIV, 310–15. On Boccaccio's *Famous Women*, see Glenda McLeod, *Virtue and Venom: Catalogs of Women from Antiquity to the Renaissance* (Ann Arbor: University of Michigan Press, 1991), 59–80, who notes, 66, that for all Boccaccio's praise of certain women, "Such women do nothing to refute long standing debasement of femininity; no matter how great their numbers or how impressive their achievement, they do not speak for their gender." On Christine and Boccaccio, see Patricia A. Phillippy, "Establishing Authority: Boccaccio's *De claris mulieribus* and Christine de Pizan's *Livre de la cité des dames*," *Romanic Review* 77 (1986): 167–94.

64. Christine de Pizan, *The Book* II.20.1–20.2, 129–30.

65. Christine de Pizan, *The Book* I.9.2, 23–24.

66. Christine de Pizan, *The Letter to the God of Love*, ln. 600–16, 81. Christine was far from the only person to defend Eve in the Middle Ages. See Blamires, *The Case for Women*, 96–125.

67. Boccaccio, *Famous Women*, 16–25. Liliane Dulac, "Un mythe didactique chez Christine de Pizan: Sémiramis ou la Veuve héroïque," in *Mélanges de Philologie Romane offerts à Charles Camproux*, tom. I (Montpellier: C.E.O, 1978), 315–31.

68. Christine de Pizan, *The Book* I.15.2, 40. See Maureen Quilligan, *The Allegory of Female Authority: Christine de Pizan's Cité des dames* (Ithaca: Cornell University Press, 1991), 69–85, for an extended analysis of Christine's claim in terms of oral and written authority.

69. Vincent of Beauvais, *Speculum Doctrinale* (Venice: Dominic Nicolini, 1591),

lib. X, cap. XXXVIII, "Qualiter antiqui patres excusantur a culpa adulterii," 168r. This sort of argument has a long history and can already be found in the early fourth century, for example, Methodius, *The Symposium: A Treatise on Chastity*, trans. Herbert Musurillo (Westminster: Newman Press, 1958), Logos I:2–3, 41–45.

70. Christine de Pizan, *The Book* I.43.1, 86–87.

71. Christine de Pizan, *The Book* I.48.1, 96–97.

72. For each of these stories in order, see Christine de Pizan, *The Book* II.9.1, 113–14 (Hypsipyle), II.26.1, 135–36 (Lady Curia), 129 (Tertia Aemillia). On Christine and prudence, Karen Green, "*Phronesis* Feminised: Prudence from Christine de Pizan to Elizabeth I," in *Virtue, Liberty and Toleration: Political Ideas of European Women*, ed. Jacqueline Broad and Karen Green (Dordrecht: Springer, 2007), 24–29.

73. Moderata Fonte, *The Worth of Women: Wherein Is Clearly Revealed Their Nobility and Their Superiority to Men*, ed. and trans. Virginia Cox (Chicago: University of Chicago Press, 1997), 29. Despite Pietro's assertions concerning the purpose of his mother's book, Patricia H. Labalme, "Venetian Women on Women: Three Early Modern Feminists," *Archivo Veneto*, ser. 5, 3 (1981): 81–109, here 90, argues: "the main purpose of the work is not the condemnation of the male sex with old and new arguments. The dialogue is a vehicle for the display of Modesta's and Corinna's encyclopedic, if superficial learning." It is certainly this, but display needn't prohibit critique as well.

74. Lucrezia Marinella, *The Nobility and Excellence of Women and the Defects and Vices of Men*, ed. and trans. Anne Dunhill (Chicago: University of Chicago Press, 1999), 39. On the social context for both these works, especially the collapse of the Venetian marriage market and a related increase in enforced female claustration, see Virginia Cox, "The Single Self: Feminist Thought and the Marriage Market in Early Modern Venice," *Renaissance Quarterly* 48:3 (Autumn 1995): 513–581. See also Stephen Kolsky, "Moderate Fonte, Lucrezia Marinella, Giuseppe Passi: An Early Seventeenth-Century Feminist Controversy," *Modern Language Review* 96:4 (October 2001): 973–89. Ross, *Birth of Feminism*, 195–212, offers biographies for both women and places their work in context.

75. I take this from Labalme, "Venetian Women," 109, who, making this argument using these examples, writes: "Venetian women, for all that they were confined and cloistered, were also, in the seventeenth century, made self-aware by law, by political legend and ritual, by social custom, by artistic and literary culture, by the reputations of foreign women and the exhibitionism of less private females than themselves. Is it not possible that this dichotomy, the very variety of experience, encouraged them to begin to measure themselves against each other and against men, impelled them to challenge old theories of inadequacy and subjugation, to come to their own defense, to produce a triad of female feminists, among the earliest in European history."

76. Ross, *Birth of Feminism*, 206, notes that even the way in which both Fonte and Marinella present themselves in their writings differs from their female

predecessors, adopting a more "'masculine' mode, using only the sparest form of political rhetoric to flatter patrons."

77. Fonte, *The Worth of Women*, 53.
78. Fonte, *The Worth of Women*, 46–47.
79. Fonte, *The Worth of Women*, 54–55.
80. Fonte, *The Worth of Women*, 57.
81. Fonte, *The Worth of Women*, 72.
82. Fonte, *The Worth of Women*, 73.
83. Fonte, *The Worth of Women*, 73–78.
84. Fonte, *The Worth of Women*, 226–230. Suzanne Magnanini, "Una selva luminosa: The Second Day of Moderata Fonte's *Il merito delle donne*," *Modern Philology* 101:2 (November 2003): 278–96, stresses the connections between much of the second day's conversation and the genre of the *selva*.
85. Fonte, *The Worth of Women*, 232–33.
86. Fonte, *The Worth of Women*, 233.
87. Fonte, *The Worth of Women*, 226.
88. Fonte, *The Worth of Women*, 237. For a recent overview on the rise of fashion in early modern Europe, see Carlo Marco Belfanti, "The Civilization of Fashion: At the Origins of a Western Social Institution," *Journal of Social History* 43:2 (Winter 2009): 261–83. On Venice in particular, see Jennifer Haraguchi, "Debating Women's Fashion in Renaissance Venice," in Elizabeth Rodini and Elissa B. Weaver, *A Well-Fashioned Image: Clothing and Costume in European Art, 1500–1850* (Chicago: David and Alfred Smart Museum of Art, 2002), 23–34, on Fonte and Marinella, 31–32.
89. Fonte, *The Worth of Women*, 235.
90. Marinella, *The Nobility and Excellence of Women*, 166.
91. Marinella, *The Nobility and Excellence of Women*, 166–67.
92. Marinella, *The Nobility and Excellence of Women*, 167–68.
93. Giovanni Pico della Mirandola, "Letter to Ermalao Barbaro, June 1485," in Quirinus Breem, "Document: Giovanni Pico della Mirandola on the Conflict of Philosophy and Rhetoric," *Journal of the History of Ideas* 13:3 (June 1952): 384–412, here, 395. On rhetoric and masculine effeminacy in Pico's letter, see Wayne A. Rebhorn, *The Emperor of Men's Minds: Literature and the Renaissance Discourse of Reason* (Ithaca: Cornell University Press, 1995), 133–47. "Although Renaissance critics of rhetoric generally refrain from joining Pico in denouncing the negative version of the art as *cinaedus*, or *sodomitical*," Rebhorn explains at 143, "their presentation of it as a Siren has much the same effect, since they wind up identifying rhetors with women."
94. Patricia Parker, "Virile Style," in *Premodern Sexualities*, ed. Louise Fradenburg and Carla Freccero (New York: Routledge, 1996), 201–22, here 203, for the quotation from Quintillian.
95. Quoted in Catherine R. Eskin, "The Re(i)gning of Women's Tongues in English Books of Instruction and Rhetorics," in *Women's Education in Early Modern Europe: A History, 1500–1800*, ed. Barbara Whitehead (New York: Routledge, 1999), 101–30, here, 104.

96. Karl E. Scheibe, "In Defense of Lying: On the Moral Neutrality of Misrep-resentation," *Berkshire Review* 15 (1980): 15–24, makes a similar point, 19: "Let it not be protested that cosmetics and attractive clothing are distorting lies, making fictions of our real selves. For we, in our real selves, are inescap-ably fictions. . . . Human reality is always clothes, and should the clothes be removed, underclothes will be discovered."

97. On Fonte's use of the genre of dialogue, see Janet Levarie Smarr, "The Uses of Conversation: Moderata Fonte and Edmund Tilney," *Comparative Litera-ture Studies* 32:1 (1995): 1–25.

98. For example, Fonte, *The Worth of Women*, 223–24.

99. Fonte, *The Worth of Women*, 201.

100. Fonte, *The Worth of Women*, 61. Immediately after Leonora makes this observation, Virginia asks if men do these things through ignorance. Cornelia responds, "Now you really sound like the naïve little creature you are. Igno-rance does not excuse sin and, besides, their ignorance is willful vice and they are all too aware of the evil they are doing."

101. Kolsky, "An Early Seventeenth-Century Feminist Controversy," 980, stresses that here it is Adriana, "the mother who is instrumentalized by male coercive practice."

102. Fonte, *The Worth of Women*, 82. Marguerite de Navarre, *The Heptameron*, trans. P. A. Chilton (London: Penguin Books, 1984), story 21, 236–54, tells just such a tale, about Rolandine's love for the unnamed "bastard son of a good and noble family," who conceals his duplicity for years. Joanne M. Ferraro, "The Power to Decide: Battered Wives in Early Modern Venice," *Renaissance Quarterly* 48:3 (Autumn 1995): 492–512, at 509–10, argues that Venetian women in abusive marriages had some means of redress: "Mar-riage was not a private matter in Venetian neighborhoods. Thus kinsmen and community had a decisive relationship with the married couple as well: the Venetian case demonstrates that they were, in effect, institutions of public life that protected women and disciplined men. Women in bad marriages had some powers of decision, and they were not alone."

103. Madeleine de Scudéry, "De la Conversation," in *Conversations sur divers su-jets*, 2 tom. (Paris: Thomas Amaulry, 1680), tom. 1, 2–3. On Scudéry and her place in seventeenth-century French society, Elisa Biancardi, "Madeleine de Scudéry et son cercle: spécificité socioculterelle et créativité littéraire," *Papers on French Seventeenth-Century Literature* 22:43 (1995): 415–29.

104. Scudéry, "De la Conversation," in *Conversations*, tom. 1, 1. For an overview of seventeenth-century accounts of what constitutes good conversation, see Alain Montandon, "Les bienséances de la conversation," in *Art de la lettre, Art de la conversation*, ed. Bernard Bray and Christophe Strosetzki (Paris : Klincksieck, 1995), 61–79.

105. Christine de Pizan, *The Treasure*, 45–46, already recognizes this when she notes that one of the noble woman's chief goals is the maintenance of har-mony and peace at the court. On this topic, see Antoine Lilti, "The Kingdom of *Politesse*: Salons and the Republic of Letters in Eighteenth-Century Paris," *Republic of Letters: A Journal for the Study of Knowledge, Politics and the*

Arts 1:1 (2009): 1–11. On the continuity of the salon from the early sixteenth century forward, Steven D. Kale, "Women, the Public Sphere, and the
Persistence of Salons," *French Historical Studies* 25:1 (Winter 2002): 115–
148, here 147, writes: "Modern noble attitudes towards women reflected the
courtly traditions of the Renaissance and the codes of gallantry elaborated
before and during the decline of feudal institutions, in which 'polite, civilized
attention to the ladies' required magnanimity between both sexes by ascrib-
ing to women the role of teaching men how to act toward 'the fairer sex.'
Pleasing women, therefore, became not only the font of *mondain* civility but
an ethical cornerstone that complemented the importance of patrimony and
lineage in noble society. The counterpart of *la galanterie* was the notion of
women as civilizers."

106. Scudéry, "De la Conversation," in *Conversations*, tom. 1, 3–6.
107. Scudéry, "De la Conversation," in *Conversations*, tom. 1, 10–12.
108. Scudéry, "De parler trop, ou trop peu," in *Conversations*, tom. 1, 94.
109. Scudéry, "De la Conversation," in *Conversations*, tom. 1, 30.
110. Scudéry, "De la Conversation," in *Conversations*, tom. 1, 31.
111. Madeleine Scudéry, *Les Femmes Illustrés ou Les Harangues Heroïques* (Paris:
     Antoine de Sommaville & Augustin Courbe, 1642), unpaginated prefatory
     material. The nature of seventeenth-century female rhetorical education
     was designed to facilitate this concealed rhetorical prowess, Stina Hansson,
     "Rhetoric for Seventeenth-Century Salons: Beata Rosenhane's Exercise
     Books and Classical Rhetoric," *Rhetorica: A Journal of the History of
     Rhetoric* 12:1 (Winter 1994): 43–65. Describing the ideal of naturalness in
     seventeenth-century French conversation, Marc Fumaroli, "De l'Age de l'élo-
     quence à l'Age de la conversation: la conversion de la rhétorique humaniste
     dans la France du XVIIe siècle," in *Art de la lettre*, 25–45, here 42–43, writes,
     "Le loisir et le naturel de la conversation française sont les degrés supérieurs
     d'un ordre harmonique qui, loin de dissocier ou opposer nature et culture
     aspirent à les restituer l'une à l'autre, à les revéler l'une a l'autre."
112. Scudéry, "De la Conversation," in *Conversations*, tom. 1, 1–2.
113. Jane Donawerth, "As Becomes a Rational Woman to Speak," in *Listening
     to Their Voices: The Rhetorical Activities of Historical Women*, ed. Molly
     Meijer Wertheimer (Columbia: University of South Carolina Press, 1997),
     305–19, makes this point while discussing these same texts by Scudéry, here
     309. Antoine Lilti, *Le Monde des salons: Sociabilité et mondanité à Paris
     au XVIIIe siècle* (Paris: Librairie Arthème Fayard, 2005), 155–58, stresses
     that aristocratic claims to social equality in the salon need be taken with
     more than a grain of salt. For a contrasting interpretation, see Elizabeth C.
     Goldsmith, *Exclusive Conversations: The Art of Interaction in Seventeenth-
     Century France* (Philadelphia: University of Pennsylvania Press, 1988), 47–
     48.
114. Scudéry, "De la complaisance," in *Conversations*, tom. 1, 275.
115. Scudéry, "De la complaisance," in *Conversations*, tom. 1, 279.
116. Scudéry, "De la complaisance," in *Conversations*, tom. 1, 267. Later in the
     same conversation, 278–79, Plotina suggests that Amilcar does not hide his

own complaisance so well: "I am persuaded that when he seems most complaisant towards others, that is when he is most interested in himself."

117. Scudéry, "De la complaisance," in *Conversations*, tom. 1, 262–63.
118. Scudéry, "De la connoissance d'autruy et de soy-mesme," in *Conversations*, tom. 1, 71.
119. Scudéry, "De la connoissance d'autruy et de soy-mesme," in *Conversations*, tom. 1, 72.
120. Scudéry, "De la connoissance d'autruy et de soy-mesme," in *Conversations*, tom. 1, 104.
121. Scudéry, "De la connoissance d'autruy et de soy-mesme," in *Conversations*, tom. 1, 105.
122. Scudéry, "De la connoissance d'autruy et de soy-mesme," in *Conversations*, tom. 1, 76.
123. Scudéry, "De la connoissance d'autruy et de soy-mesme," in *Conversations*, tom. 1, 133–34.
124. Scudéry, "De la connoissance d'autruy et de soy-mesme," in *Conversations*, tom. 1, 84.
125. Scudéry, "De la complaisance," in *Conversations*, tom. 1, 264.
126. Scudéry, "De la complaisance," in *Conversations*, tom. 1, 272–73.
127. Scudéry, "De la complaisance," in *Conversations*, tom. 1, 267–68. Stanton, *The Aristocrat as Art*, 134: "[H]onnête complaisance demands deft, unceasing negotiation between ever changing alternatives that manages life as it were the stuff of art."
128. Scudéry, "De la difference du flateur et du complaisant," in *Conversations*, tom. 1, 296.
129. Scudéry, "De la difference du flateur et du complaisant," in *Conversations*, tom. 1, 294.
130. Scudéry, "De la dissimulation et de la sincerité," in *Conversations*, tom. 1, 303–4.
131. Scudéry, "De la dissimulation et de la sincerité," in *Conversations*, tom. 1, 305–6.
132. Scudéry, "De la dissimulation et de la sincerité," in *Conversations*, tom. 1, 321.
133. Scudéry, "De la dissimulation et de la sincerité," in *Conversations*, tom. 1, 311.

CONCLUSION: THE LIE BECOMES MODERN

1. Jean–Jacques Rousseau, *Discourse on the Origins of Inequality*, in *The Collected Writings of Rousseau*, vol. 3, ed. Roger D. Masters and Christopher Kelly, trans. Judith R. Bush, Roger D. Masters, Christopher Kelly, and Terrence Marshall (Hanover: University Press of New England, 1992), pt. 2, 50. On the *Discourse on Inequality* as a secularization of Genesis, see Jean Starobinski, *Jean-Jacques Rousseau: Transparency and Obstruction*, trans. Arthur Goldhammer (Chicago: University of Chicago Press, 1988), 290.
2. Rousseau, *Discourse on Inequality*, pt. 2, 51.

3. Rousseau, *Discourse on the Sciences and Arts (Second Discourse)*, in *Collected Writings*, vol. 2, pt. 1, 6.

4. Rousseau, *Letter to Beaumont*, in *Letter to Beaumont, Letters Written from the Mountain, and Related Writings*, in *Collected Writings*, vol. 9, 30.

5. Rousseau, *Letter to Beaumont*, 31: "The cause of evil, according to you, is corrupted nature, and this corruption itself is an evil whose cause has to be sought. Man was created good. We both agree on that, I believe. But you say he is wicked because he was wicked. And I show how he was wicked. Which of us, in your opinion, better ascends to the principle?" See Jeremiah L. Alberg's perceptive essay, "Rousseau and the Original Sin," in *Revista Portuguesa de Filosofia* 57:4 (October–December 2001): 773–90, and, on transformations in the understanding of original sin in the centuries leading up to Rousseau, *Die verlorene Einheit: Die Suche nach einer philosophischen Alternative zu der Erbsündenlehre von Rousseau bis Schelling* (Frankfurt am Main: Peter Lang, 1996), 31–43.

6. Rousseau, *Discourse on Inequality*, pt. 2, 47.

7. Rousseau, *Discourse on the Sciences and Arts*, pt. 1, p. 6.

8. Quoted in Grant, *Hypocrisy and Integrity*, 87, and, more generally, 75–88.

9. Rousseau, *The Reveries of the Solitary Walker, Botanical Writings, and Letter to Franquières*, in *Collected Writings*, vol. 8, "Fourth Walk," 29. On the motto's background, see 283–84, ft. 2.

10. Jean Starobinski, "The Motto *Vitam impendere vero* and the Question of Lying," in *The Cambridge Companion to Rousseau*, ed. Patrick Riley (Cambridge: Cambridge University Press, 2001), 365–96, at 381–85, traces this definition to Hugo Grotius and Samuel Pufendorf.

11. Rousseau, *Reveries*, "Fourth Walk," 29. Lester Gilbert Crocker, "The Problem of Truth and Falsehood in the Age of the Enlightenment," *Journal of the History of Ideas* 14:4 (October 1953): 573–603, surveys the attitudes of Enlightenment writers about lying.

12. Rousseau, *Reveries*, "Fourth Walk," 30.

13. Rousseau, *Reveries*, "Fourth Walk," 39.

14. Augustine, *City of God*, bk. XIV, ch. 3, 586.

15. Rousseau, *Reveries*, "Fourth Walk," 39. Charles Taylor, *Sources of the Self* (Cambridge: Harvard University Press, 1989), 361, makes this point: "For [with Rousseau] the distinction of vice and virtue, of good and depraved will, has been aligned with the distinction between dependence on self and dependence on others. Goodness is identified with freedom, with finding the motives for one's actions within oneself. Although drawing on ancient sources, Rousseau is actually pushing this subjectivism of modern moral understanding a stage further." Although his literary sources may well have been ancient, the culture of the salon clearly animates his critique.

16. Rousseau, *Reveries*, "Fourth Walk," 39.

17. Rousseau, *Reveries*, "Fourth Walk," 34.

18. Following Victor Gourevitch, "Rousseau on Lying: A Provisional Reading of the Fourth *Rêverie*, *Berkshire Review* 15 (1980): 93–107, here, 100–103. Compare with Starobinski, "*Vitam impendere vero*," 386–90.

19. Arthur M. Melzer, "Rousseau and the Modern Cult of Sincerity," *Harvard Review of Philosophy* (Spring 1995): 4–21, writes, 14: "In Shakespeare and Molière we find much emphasis on the falseness of men's claims to virtue and nobility, but the opposite of hypocritical nobility is still taken to be genuine nobility—not sincerity as such. Thus, Rousseau (and we after him) is doing something fundamentally new when he makes the seemingly obvious move from blaming hypocrisy to praising sincerity—that is, not praising sincere piety, or sincere righteousness, but sincerity itself and by itself. In other words, Rousseau is the first to define the good as being oneself regardless of what one may be. And that is a radically new position—a position which is at the core of his and our unique obsession with sincerity."

20. Karl Barth, *Protestant Thought from Rousseau to Ritschl* (New York: Harper & Brothers, 1959), 105–8: "In common with the whole of the eighteenth century Rousseau was a confirmed Pelagian, a declared opponent of the Church doctrine of original sin . . . [but] . . . Rousseau was so energetic in pursuing this idea, so naïve in taking it as his constant premise even in his own Pelagian century, [he] became a kind of martyr to Pelagianism. . . . Be that as it may, the church doctrine of original sin has seldom, I believe, been denied with such disconcerting candour and in so directly personal a way." This is partially cited and the general argument reaffirmed in Arthur M. Melzer, *The Natural Goodness of Man: On the System of Rousseau's Thought* (Chicago: University of Chicago Press, 1990), 18.

21. Immanuel Kant, *The Metaphysics of Morals: Part II, Metaphysical First Principles of the Doctrine of Virtue*, in *Practical Philosophy*, ed. and trans. Mary J. Gregor (Cambridge: Cambridge University Press, 1996), 552–53. Useful starting points into the literature on Kant's analysis of lies are James Mahon, "The Truth about Lies in Kant," in *The Philosophy of Deception*, ed. Clancy Martin (Oxford: Oxford University Press, 2009), 201–24, Alasdaire MacIntyre, *Truthfulness, Lies and Moral Philosophers: What Can We Learn from Mill and Kant*, in *The Tanner Lectures on Human Values*, vol. 15 (Salt Lakes City: University of Utah Press, 1994), 309–69, and Christine M. Korsgaard, "The Right to Lie: Kant on Dealing with Evil," *Philosophy and Public Affairs* 15:4 (Autumn 1986): 325–49.

22. Immanuel Kant, "On a Supposed Right to Lie from Philanthropy," in *Practical Philosophy*, 613.

23. Kant, *Metaphysics of Morals*, 554.

24. Immanuel Kant, *Conjectures on the Beginning of Human History*, in *Political Writings*, ed. Hans Reiss (Cambridge: Cambridge University Press, 1992), 221–34, here, 221.

Bibliography

PRIMARY SOURCES

The Aberdeen Bestiary. Aberdeen University Library MS 24, http://www.abdn. ac.uk/bestiary/intro.hti.

Accetto, Torquato. *De l'honnête dissimulation.* Edited by Salvatore S. Nigro, translated by Mireille Blanc-Sanchez. Paris: Éditions Verdier, 1990.

Acontius, Jacobus. *Satans Strategems or the Devils Cabinet-Council Discovered.* London: John Macock, 1648.

Alan of Lille. *Liber poenitentialis.* Edited by Jean Longère. Louvain: Editions Nauwelaerts, 1965.

Albert the Great. *Quaestiones super de animalibus. Alberti Magni Opera Omnia edenda curavit Institutum Alberti Magni Coloniense Bernhardo Geyer praeside,* vol. XII. Edited by Ephrem Filthaut. Münster: Aschendorff, 1955.

———. *Super Ethica.* In *Alberti Magni Opera Omnia edenda curavit Institutum Alberti Magni Coloniense Bernhardo Geyer praeside,* vol. XIV. Edited by W. Kübel. Münster: Aschendorff, 1968.

Albert the Great, pseudo-. *Women's Secrets.* Translated by Helen Rodnite Lemay. Albany: State University of New York Press, 1992.

Alexander of Hales. *Summa theologica,* 4 vols. Quaracchi: Rome, 1924–79.

Ambrose. *Expositio evangelii secundum Lucam.* In *Corpus Christianorum Series Latina,* vol. XIV. Edited by M. Adriaen. Turnholt: Brepols, 1957.

———. *Hexameron, Paradise, and Cain and Abel.* Translated by John J. Savage. New York: Fathers of the Church, 1961.

Anselm of Canterbury. *Opera Omnia.* Edited by Salesius Schmidt. Stuttgart: F. Frommann, 1968.

———. *Anselm of Canterbury,* 4 vols. Edited and translated by Jasper Hopkins and Herbert Richardson. Toronto: Edwin Mellen Press, 1974–76.

Antoninus of Florence. *Summae Sacra Theologiae.* Venice: Bernardus Iuntus & Socios., 1571.

Aquinas, Thomas. *Summa Theologiae,* 9 vols. In *Opera Omnia* IV–XII. Rome, 1888–1906.

———. *Summa Contra Gentiles,* 3 vols. In *Opera Omnia* XIII–XV. Rome, 1918–30.

———. *Summa of Theology.* Translated by the Fathers of the English Dominican Province. New York: Benziger Brothers, 1947.

———. *Quaestiones disputatae de veritate*. In *Opera Omnia* XXII, vol. I. Rome, 1975.

———. *Summa Contra Gentiles* III. Translated by Vernon J. Bourke. Notre Dame: University of Notre Dame Press, 1975.

Aristotle. *On the Generation of Animals*. In *The Complete Works of Aristotle*, vol. 1. Edited by Jonathan Barnes. Princeton: Princeton University Press, 1984, 1111–218.

Augustine. *Soliloquies*. Translated by Thomas F. Gilligan. New York: CIMA Publishing Co., 1948.

———. *Saint Augustine: Letters*, vol. 1 (1–82). Translated by Wilifrid Parsons. Washington, D.C.: Catholic University of America Press, 1951.

———. *Against Lying*. Translated by Harold B. Jaffee. In Augustine, *Treatises on Various Subjects* (1952), 112–75.

———. *Treatises on Various Subjects*. Edited by Roy J. Deferrari. Washington, D.C.: Catholic University of America Press, 1952.

———. *De civitate dei*, 2 vols. In *Corpus Christianorum Series Latina*, vols. XLVII–XLVIII. Edited by Bernardus Dombart and Alphonsus Kalb. Turnholt: Brepols, 1955.

———. *De symbol ad catechumenos*. In *Corpus Christianorum Series Latina*, vol. XLVI. Edited by R. Vander Plaetse. Turnholt: Brepols, 1959: 179–99.

———. *The Fathers of the Church: Saint Augustine, Sermons on the Liturgical Seasons*. Translated by Mary Sarah Muldowney. Washington, D.C.: Catholic University of America Press, 1959.

———. *On Free Choice of the Will*. Translated by Anna S. Benjamin and L. H. Hackstaff. Indianapolis: Bobbs-Merrill Company, 1964.

———. *De trinitate*, 2 vols. In *Corpus Christianorum Series Latina*, vols. L–La. Edited by W. J. Mountain. Turnholt: Brepols, 1968.

———. *The Literal Meaning of Genesis*. Translated by John Hammond Taylor. New York: Newman Press, 1982.

———. *De doctrina christiana*. Edited and translated by R.P.H. Green. Oxford: Oxford University Press, 1995.

———. *The City of God*. Edited and translated by R. W. Dyson. Cambridge: Cambridge University Press, 1998.

———. *On the Trinity*. Edited by Gareth B. Matthews and translated by Stephen McKenna. Cambridge: Cambridge University Press, 2002.

Avitus, Alcimus Ecdicius. *The Poems of Alcimus Ecdicius Avitus*. Translated by George W. Shea. Tempe: Medieval & Renaissance Texts & Studies, 1997.

Azor, Juan. *Institutionum moralium*. Cologne: Hierat, 1612.

Azpilcueta, Martin. *See* Navarrus.

Bacon, Francis. "Of Simulation and Dissimulation," In *The Major Works*. Edited by Brian Vickers. Oxford: Oxford University Press, 1996, 349–51.

Bartholomew of England. *De proprietatibus rerum*. London: Thomas East, 1582.

Bayle, Pierre. *Dictionaire [sic] Historique et Critique*, 4th ed. Amsterdam: P. Brunel et al., 1730.

———. *Ce que c'est que la France toute Catholique sous le règne de Louis le Grand*. Edited by Elisabeth Labrousse. Paris: J. Vrin, 1973.

Bernard of Clairvaux. *Bernard of Clairvaux: Selected Works*. Translated by G. R. Evans. New York: Paulist Press, 1987.

Boccaccio, Giovanni. *Famous Women*. Translated and edited by Virginia Brown. Cambridge: Harvard University Press, 2001.

Boethius. *De sophisticis elenchis*. In *Aristoteles latinus* VI1-3. Edited by Bernardus G. Dod. Leiden: E. J. Brill, 1975.

———. *De topicis differentiis*. Translated by Eleonore Stump. Ithaca: Cornell University Press, 1978.

Bonaventure. *Commentaria in quatuor libros sententiarum Magistri Petri Lombardi*, 4 vols. In *Opera Omnia*, vols. I–IV. Quaracchi: Collegii S. Bonaventurae, 1882–89.

———. *Commentarius in Evangelium S. Ioannis*. In *Opera Omnia*, vol. VI. Quaracchi: Collegii S. Bonaventurae, 1893.

———. *Tractatus de praeparatione ad missam*. In *Opera Omnia*, vol. VIII. Rome: Quaracchi, 1898: 99–106.

———. *Collations on the Six Days*. In *The Works of Bonaventure*, vol. 5. Translated by José de Vinck. Patterson: St. Anthony Guild Press, 1970.

Buridan, John. *Super decem libros ethicorum*. Paris, 1513, rprt. Frankfurt: Minerva G.M.B.H., 1968.

———. *Quaestiones super octo libros politicorum Aristotelis*. Paris, 1513, rprt. Frankfurt: Minerva G.M.B.H., 1969.

Caesarius of Heisterbach. *The Dialogue on Miracles*, 2 vols. Translated by H. Von E. Scott and C. C. Swinton Bland. London: George Routledge & Sons, 1929.

Calvin, John. *Commentaries on the First Book of Moses Called Genesis*, vol. 1. Translated by John King. Edinburgh: The Calvin Translation Society, 1847.

———. *Commentary on Corinthians*, vol. 2. Translated by John Pringle. Edinburgh: Calvin Translation Society, 1849.

———. *Commentaries on the Prophet Ezekiel*, vol. II. Translated by Thomas Myers. Edinburgh: Calvin Translation Society, 1881.

———. *Institutes of the Christian Religion*. Translated by Ford Lewis Battles. Philadelphia: Westminster Press, 1960.

Caramuel, Juan. *Haplotes de restrictionibus mentalibus*. Lyons, 1672.

Castiglione, Baldassare. *The Book of the Courtier*. Translated by George Bull. London: Penguin Books, 1976.

Caxton, William. *The Curial made by maystere Alain Charretier* (1484). Edited by Fredrick J. Furnival. London: Early English Text Society, 1888.

Charon, Pierre. *Of Wisdom: The Second and Third Books*, 2nd. ed. Edited and translated by George Stanhope. London, 1707.

Chartier, Alain. *Les Oeuvres Latins d'Alain Chartier*. Edited by Pascale Bourgain-Hemeryck. Paris: Éditions du Centre National de la Recherche Scientifique, 1977.

Chobham, Thomas. *Summa Confessorum*. Edited by F. Broomfield. Louvain: Editions Nauwelaerts, 1968.

Christine de Pizan. *The Book of the City of Ladies*. Translated by Earl Jeffrey Richards. New York: Persea Books, 1982.

———. *The Selected Writings of Christine de Pizan*. Edited by Renate Blumenfeld-

Kosinski. Translated by Renate Blumenfeld-Kosinski and Kevin Brownlee. New York: W.W. Norton & Company, 1997.

———. *The Treasure of the City of Ladies or The Book of the Three Virtues.* Translated by Sarah Lawson. London: Penguin Books, 2003.

Chrysostom, John. *Homilies on Genesis: 1–17.* Translated by Robert C. Hill. Washington, D.C.: Catholic University of America Press, 1985.

Cicero. *De officiis.* Cambridge: Harvard University Press, 1913.

———. *On Duties.* Edited by M. T. Griffin and E. M. Adams and translated by Margaret Atkins. Cambridge: Cambridge University Press, 1991.

Cyril of Alexandria. *A Commentary on the Gospel According to S. Luke.* Translated by R. Payne Smith. Oxford: Oxford University Press, 1859.

Damian, Peter. *Die Briefe des Petrus Damiani,* vol. 2, *NR. 41–90.* Edited by Kurt Reindel. Munich: Monumenta Germaniae Historica, 1988.

Dante Alighieri. *Dante's Inferno: The Indiana Critical Edition.* Translated by Mark Musa. Bloomington: Indiana University Press, 1995.

David of Augsburg. *De institutione novitiorum.* In Bonaventure, *Opera Omnia,* vol. XII. Paris: Vivès, 1868, 292–312.

Descartes, René. *The Philosophical Writings of Descartes,* 2 vols. Translated by John Cottingham, Robert Stoothoff, and Dugald Murdoch. Cambridge: Cambridge University Press, 1985.

Downame, John. *A Treatise Against Lying.* London, 1636.

Fasciculus Morum. Edited by Siegfried Wenzel. University Park: Pennsylvania State University Press, 1989.

Fifteen Joys of Marriage. Translated by Brent A. Pitts. New York: Peter Lang, 1985.

Fonte, Moderata. *The Worth of Women: Wherein Is Clearly Revealed Their Nobility and Their Superiority to Men.* Edited and translated by Virginia Cox. Chicago: University of Chicago Press, 1997.

Foulechat, Denis. *Le policratique de Jean de Salisbury,* livres I–III. Edited by Charles Brucker. Geneva: Librairie Droz, 1994.

Galen. *On the Usefulness of the Bodies Parts.* Translated by Margaret Tallmadge May. Ithaca: Cornell University Press, 1968.

Gerson, Jean. *Considérations sur Saint Joseph.* In *Oeuvres Complètes, VII: L'oeuvre Française.* Edited by Palemon Glorieux. Paris: Desclée & Cii, 1966.

Gracián, Baltasar. *The Pocket Oracle and Art of Prudence.* Translated by Jeremy Robbins. London: Penguin Books, 2011.

Gratian. *The Treaty on Laws with the Ordinary Gloss.* Translated by Augustine Thompson and James Gordley. Washington, D.C.: Catholic University of America Press, 1993.

Gregory of Rimini. *Lectura super primum et secundum Sententiarum,* vol. 3. Edited by A. Damasus Trapp and Venicio Marcolino. Berlin: Walter de Gruyter, 1979.

Guazzo, Stephano. *The Art of Conversation.* London: J. Brett, 1738.

Guido de Monte Rocherii. *Manipulus curatorum.* Strassburg, 1490.

Gyfford, George. *A Discourse on the Subtill Practices of Devilles by Witches and Sorcerers.* London: Toby Cooke, 1587.

The Hammer of Witches: A Complete Translation of the Malleus Maleficarum, by Heinrich Kramer and James Sprenger. Translated by Christopher S. MacKay. Cambridge: Cambridge University Press, 2009.

Holkot, Robert. *Super sententias*. Lugduni, 1518, rprt. Frankfurt: Minerva G.M.B.H., 1967.

———. *Seeing the Future Clearly: Questions on Future Contingents*. Edited by Paul A. Streveler and Katherine H. Tachau. Toronto: Pontifical Institute of Mediaeval Studies, 1995.

Hugh of St. Victor. *De sacramentis christiane fidei*. In *Patrologiae Latina*, vol. CLXXVI. Paris: J. P. Migne, 1854: 174–613.

———. *On the Sacraments of the Christian Faith (De Sacramentis)*. Translated by Roy J. Deferrari. Cambridge: Mediaeval Academy of America, 1951.

Humbert of Romans. *De eruditione praedicatorum*. In *De vita regulari*, vol. II. Edited by Joachim Joseph Berthier. Rome, 1889, 373–484.

Isidore of Seville. *The Etymologies of Isidore of Seville*. Translated by Stephen A. Barney. Cambridge: Cambridge University Press, 2006.

Jacobus de Voragine. *Legenda Aurea*. Translated by William Caxton. London: Wynkyn the Worde, 1512.

———. *The Golden Legend: Readings on the Saints*, 2 vols. Translated by William Granger Ryan. Princeton: Princeton University Press, 1993.

John of Salisbury. *Frivolities of the Courtiers and Footprints of the Philosophers: Being a Translation of the First, Second, and Third Books and Selections from the Seventh and Eighth Books of the Policraticus of John of Salisbury*. Translated by Joseph B. Pike. Minneapolis: University of Minnesota Press, 1938.

———. *The Metalogicon of John of Salisbury: A Twelfth-Century Defense of the Verbal and Logical Arts of the Trivium*. Translated by Daniel D. McGarry. Berkeley: University of California Press, 1955.

———. *Entheticus Maior and Minor*, 3 vols. Edited by Jan van Laarhoven. Leiden: E. J. Brill, 1987.

———. *Metalogicon*. In *Corpus Christianorum Continuatio Mediaevalis* 98. Edited by J. B. Hall. Turnholt: Brepols, 1991.

———. *Policraticus I–IV*. In Corpus Christianorum Continuatio Mediaevalis 118. Edited by K.S.B. Keats-Rohan. Turnholt: Brepols, 1993.

Kant, Immanuel. *Conjectures on the Beginning of Human History*. In *Political Writings*. Edited by Hans Reiss. Cambridge: Cambridge University Press, 1992, 221–34.

———. *The Metaphysics of Morals: Part II, Metaphysical First Principles of the Doctrine of Virtue*. In *Practical Philosophy*. Edited and translated by Mary J. Gregor. Cambridge: Cambridge University Press, 1996.

La Rochefoucauld, François. *Maxims*. Translated by Leonard Tancock. London: Penguin Books, 1959.

Langland, William. *Piers Plowman: A New Annotated Edition of the C-Text*. Edited by Derek Pearsall. Exeter: University of Exeter Press, 2008.

The Later Christian Fathers: A Selection from the Writings of the Fathers from St. Cyril of Jerusalem to St. Leo the Great. Edited and translated by Henry Bettenson. London: Oxford University Press, 1970.

le Fèvre, Jehan. *Les Lamentations de Matheolus et le Livre de Leesce*. Edited by A. G. van Hamel. Paris: Émile Bouillon, 1892.

Leo the Great. *Letters and Sermons of Leo the Great*. In *Nicene and Post-Nicene Fathers*, 2nd series, vol. 12. New York: Christian Literature Co., 1895.

Lombard, Peter. *The Sentences*, 4 vols. Translated by Giulio Silano. Toronto: Pontifical Institute of Mediaeval Studies, 2008.

Lorris, Guillaume de, and Jean de Meun, *The Romance of the Rose*. Translated by Charles Dahlberg. Princeton: Princeton University Press, 1971.

Luther, Martin. *The Sermon on the Mount*. In *Luther's Works*, vol. 21. Edited and translated by Jaroslav Pelikan. Saint Louis: Concordia Publishing House, 1956.

———. *Lectures on Genesis, Chapters 1–5*. In *Luther's Works*, vol. 1. Edited by Jaroslav Pelikan and translated by George V. Schick. St. Louis: Concordia Publishing House, 1958.

———. *Selected Psalms III*. In *Luther's Works*, vol. 14. Edited by Jaroslav Pelikan and translated by Edward Sittler. Philadelphia: Fortress Press, 1958.

———. *Catholic Epistles*. In *Luther's Works*, vol. 30. Edited by Jaroslav Pelikan and translated by Walter A. Hansen. Saint Louis: Concordia Publishing House, 1967.

———. *The Bondage of the Will*. In *Luther's Works*, vol. 33. Edited and translated by Philip S. Watson. Philadelphia: Fortress Press, 1972.

Machiavelli, Niccolò. *The Letters of Machiavelli: A Selection of His Letters*. Edited and translated by Allan Gilbert. New York: Capricorn Books, 1961.

———. *The Prince*. Translated by Peter Bonadanella. Oxford: Oxford University Press, 1979.

Mandeville, Bernard. *The Fable of the Bees: Or, Private Vices, Publick Benefits*, 2 vols. Oxford: Clarendon Press, 1924.

Marguerite de Navarre. *The Heptameron*. Translated by P. A. Chilton. London: Penguin Books, 1984.

Marinella, Lucrezia. *The Nobility and Excellence of Women and the Defects and Vices of Men*. Edited and translated by Anne Dunhill. Chicago: University of Chicago Press, 1999.

Methodius. *The Symposium: A Treatise on Chastity*. Translated by Herbert Musurillo. Westminster: Newman Press, 1958.

Milton, John. *Paradise Lost*. Edited by Merritt Y. Hughes. New York: Odyssey Press, 1935.

Navarrus [Martin de Azpilcueta]. *Commentarius in Cap. Humanae Aures XXII. Q.V. De Veritate responsi, Partim verbo, partim mente concepti, & de arte bona, & mala simulandi*. Rome, 1584.

———. *Enchiridion, sive Manuale Confessariorum et Poenitentium*. Venice, 1594.

The New Oxford Annotated Bible, with Apocrypha. New Standard Revised Version. Oxford: Oxford University Press, 1995.

Nicholas of Lyra. *Bibliorum Sacrorum cum Glossa Ordinaria . . . et Postilla Nicolai Lyrani*. Venice, 1603.

Nicole, Pierre. *Moral Essays, Contain'd in Several Treatises on Many Important*

Duties . . . Done into English by a Person of Quality, vol. III. London: Sam Manship, 1696.

Nider, Johannes. *Praeceptorium: sive orthodoxea et accurata decalogi explicatio*. Douay: Ioannis Bogardi, 1611.

Ockham, William. *Quodlibeta* VI. In *Opera philosophica et theologica*, vol. IX. Edited by Gedeon Gál et al. St. Bonaventure: Franciscan Institute, 1980.

———. *De corpore christi in eucharistia*. In *Opera Theologica*, vol. X. Edited by Carolus A. Grassi. St. Bonaventure: Franciscan Institute, 1986.

Oresme, Nicole. "*Le livre des politiques d'Aristote de Nicole Oresme*." Edited by Albert Douglas Menut. *Transactions of the American Philosophical Society*, n.s., 60:6 (1970).

Origen. *Contra Celsum*. Translated by Henry Chadwick. Cambridge: Cambridge University Press, 1965.

Pascal, Blaise. *Les Provinciales, or, The Mystery of Jesuitisme*, 2nd ed. Translated by Henry Hammond. London: Richard Royston, 1658.

———. *The Provincial Letters*. Translated by Thomas M'Crie. Boston: Houghton, Osgood and Company, 1880.

———. *Les Provinciales*, in *Pascal: Edition definitive des Oeuvres Complètes*, vol. II. Edited by Fortunat Strowski. Paris: Libraire Ollendorff, 1926.

———. *Oeuvres Complètes*. Edited by Louis Lafuma. Paris: Éditions du Seuil, 1963.

———. *Pensées*. Edited and translated by Roger Ariew. Indianapolis: Hackett Publishing Company, 2005.

Pecham, John. *Quodlibeta Quatuor*. Edited by F. Delorme and G. J. Etzkorn. Grottaferrata: Quaracchi, 1989.

Peter of Blois. *The Letter Collections of Peter of Blois*. Edited by Lena Wahlgren. Göteburg: Acta Universitatis Gothoburgensis, 1993.

Philibert de Vienne. *Le Philosophe de court*. Edited by Pauline M. Smith. Geneva: Librairie Droz, 1990.

Philo of Alexandria. *On the Creation of the Cosmos according to Moses*. Translated by David T. Runia. Leiden: E. J. Brill, 2001.

Physiologus. Translated by Robert Curley. Austin: University of Texas Press, 1979.

Pico della Mirandola, Giovanni. "Letter to Ermalao Barbaro, June 1485." In Quirinus Breem, "Document: Giovanni Pico della Mirandola on the Conflict of Philosophy and Rhetoric." *Journal of the History of Ideas* 13:3 (June 1952): 384–412.

Plato. *Phaedo*. In *The Collected Dialogues of Plato*. Edited by Edith Hamilton and Huntington Cairns and translated by Hugh Tredennick. Princeton: Princeton University Press, 1961.

Prierias, Sylvester. *Sylvestrinae Summae*. Lyons: Mauricius Roy & Ludovicus Pesnot, 1555.

Rainolds, John. *John Rainolds's Oxford Lectures on Aristotle's Rhetoric*. Edited and translated by Lawrence D. Green. Newark: University of Delaware Press, 1986.

Régis, Pierre Sylvain. *Systême de Philosophie Contenant La Logique. La Métaphy-sique. La Physique et La Morale*, vol. 1. Paris: Denys Thierry, 1690.

Rousseau, Jean-Jacques. *Discourse on the Origins of Inequality*. In *The Collected Writings of Rousseau*, vol. 3. Edited by Roger D. Masters and Christopher Kelly and translated by Judith R. Bush, Roger D. Masters, Christopher Kelly, and Terrence Marshall. Hanover: University Press of New England, 1992, 3–67.

———. *Discourse on the Sciences and Arts (Second Discourse)*. In *The Collected Writings of Rousseau*, vol. 2. Edited by Roger D. Masters and Christopher Kelly and translated by Judith R. Bush, Roger D. Masters, and Christopher Kelly. Hanover: University Press of New England, 1992, 3–22.

———. *The Reveries of the Solitary Walker*. In *Collected Writings*, vol. 8. Edited by Christopher Kelly and translated by Charles E. Butterworth, Alexandra Cook, and Terrence E. Marshall. Hanover: University Press of New England, 2000, 3–90.

———. *Letter to Beaumont*. In *The Collected Writings of Rousseau*, vol. 9. Edited by Christopher Kelly and Eve Grace and translated by Christopher Kelly and Judith R. Bush. Hanover: University Press of New England, 2001, 3–83.

Rufinus, Tyrannius. *Expositio symboli*. In *Corpus Christianorum Series Latina*, vol. XX. Edited by M. Simonetti. Turnholt: Brepols, 1961.

Rupert of Deutz. *In Genesim*. In *Opera*. Paris: Caroli Chastellain, 1638.

Saluste, Guillaume de, Sieur du Bartas. *The Divine Weeks and Works of Guil-laume de Saluste Sieur du Bartas*. Edited by Susan Snyder and translated by Joshua Sylvester. Oxford: Clarendon Press, 1979.

Scotus, John Duns. *Duns Scotus on the Will and Morality*. Edited and translated by Allan B. Wolter. Washington, D.C.: Catholic University of America Press, 1986.

Scudéry, Madeleine de. *Les Femmes Illustrés ou Les Harangues Heroïques*. Paris: Antoine de Sommaville & Augustin Courbe, 1642.

———. *Conversations sur divers sujets*, 2 tom. Paris: Thomas Amaulry, 1680.

Souvré, Madeleine de [Marquise de Sablé]. *Maximes*. Paris: Librairie des Biblio-philes, 1678.

Sponde, Jean de. *Homeri quae extant omnia: Ilias, Odyssea, Batrachomyomachia, Hymni, Poematia aliquot*. Basil: E. Episcopii, 1583.

Stafford, J. Martin. *Private Vices, Publick Benefits? The Contemporary Reception of Bernard Mandeville*. Solihull: Ismeron, 1997.

Tertullian. *The Apparel of Women*. In *Disciplinary, Moral and Ascetical Works*. Translated by Edwin A. Quain. Washington, D.C.: Catholic University of America Press, 1959, 117–49.

Three Medieval Views of Women. Edited and translated by Gloria K. Fiero, Wendy Pfeffer, and Mathé Allain. New Haven: Yale University Press, 1989.

Vincent of Beauvais. *Speculum Doctrinale*. Venice: Dominic Nicolini, 1591.

_____. Speculum Historiale. Venice: Dominic Nicolini, 1591.

———. *Speculum Morale*. Venice: Dominic Nicolini, 1591.

von Strassburg, Gottfried. *Tristan: With the Tristan of Thomas*. Translated by A. T. Hatto. London: Penguin Books, 1967.

Walker, Nathaniel. *The Refin'd Courtier or, A Correction of Several Indecencies crept in Civil Conversation: Written originally in Italian by John Casa, from thence in Latin by Nathan Chytroeus, and from both by way of Paraphrase, made English, by N. W.* London: Matthew Gilliflower, 1681.

William of Auxerre. *Summa Aurea.* Edited by J. Ribaillier. Rome: Collegii S. Bonaventurae ad Claras Aquas, 1980.

Woman Defamed and Woman Defended: An Anthology of Medieval Texts. Edited and translated by Alcuin Blamires, Karen Pratt, and C. W. Marx. Oxford: Clarendon Press, 1992.

Wyclif, John. *De benedicta incarnacione.* Edited by Edward Harris. London: Wyclif Society, 1886.

———. *Sermones.* Edited by Iohann Loserth. London: Wyclif Society, 1889.

———. *De eucharistia.* Edited by Iohann Loserth. London: Wyclif Society, 1892.

SECONDARY SOURCES

Adams, Tracy. "*Moyennerresse de traictié de paix*: Christine de Pizan's Mediators." In *Healing the Body Politic*, 177–200.

———. "Appearing Virtuous: Christine de Pizan's *Le Livre des trois* and Anne de France's *Les Enseignements d'Anne de France*." In *Virtue Ethics for Women, 1250–1500*. Edited by K. Green and C. J. Mews. Dordrecht: Springer, 2011, 115–31.

Alberg, Jeremiah L. *Die verlorene Einheit: Die Suche nach einer philosophischen Alternative zu der Erbsündenlehre von Rousseau bis Schelling.* Frankfurt am Main: Peter Lang, 1996.

———. "Rousseau and the Original Sin." *Revista Portuguesa de Filosofia* 57:4 (October–December 2001): 773–90.

Almond, Philip C. *Adam & Eve in Seventeenth-Century Thought.* Cambridge: Cambridge University Press, 1999.

Amory, Frederic. "Whited Sepulchres: The Semantic History of Hypocrisy to the High Middle Ages." *Recherches de Théologie ancienne et médiévale* 53 (1986): 5–39.

Angier, Natalie. "The Art of Deception: Sometimes Survival Means Lying, Stealing or Vanishing in Place." *National Geographic*, August 2009, 70–87.

Arbel, Vita Daphna. *Forming Femininity in Antiquity: Eve, Gender and Ideologies in the Greek "Life of Adam and Eve."* Oxford: Oxford University Press, 2012.

Art de la lettre, Art de la conversation. Edited by Bernard Bray and Christophe Strosetzki. Paris: Klincksieck, 1995.

Aulén, Gustaf. *Christus Victor: An Historical Study of the Three Main Types of the Idea of Atonement.* Translated by A. G. Herbert. New York: Macmillan, 1954.

Babcock, William S. "The Human and Angelic Fall: Will and Moral Agency in Augustine's *City of God*." In *Augustine: From Rhetor to Theologian*. Edited by Timothy D. Barnes. Waterloo: Wilfrid Laurier University Press, 1992, 133–49.

Barnes, J. A. *A Pack of Lies: Towards a Sociology of Lying.* Cambridge: Cambridge University Press, 1994.

Barth, Karl. *Protestant Thought from Rousseau to Ritschl.* New York: Harper & Brothers, 1959.

Bartlett, Robert C. "On the Politics of Faith and Reason: The Project of Enlightenment in Pierre Bayle and Montesquieu." *Journal of Politics* 63:1 (February 2001): 1–28.

BeDuhn, Jason David. *Augustine's Manichaean Dilemma, I: Conversion and Apostasy, 373–388 C.E.* Philadelphia: University of Pennsylvania Press, 2009.

Belfanti, Carlo Marco. "The Civilization of Fashion: At the Origins of a Western Social Institution." *Journal of Social History* 43:2 (Winter 2009): 261–83.

Bell, Millicent. "The Fallacy of the Fall in *Paradise Lost*." *PMLA* 68:4 (September 1953): 863–83.

Bevir, Mark. "Are There Perennial Problems in Political Theory?" *Political Studies* 42 (1994): 662–75.

———. *The Logic of the History of Ideas.* Cambridge: Cambridge University Press, 1999.

Beyssade, Jean-Marie. "The Idea of God and the Proofs of His Existence." In *The Cambridge Companion to Descartes*, 174–199.

Biancardi, Elisa. "*Madeleine de Scudéry et son cercle: spécificité socioculterelle et créativité littéraire.*" *Papers on French Seventeenth-Century Literature* 23:43 (1995): 415–29.

Blamires, Alcuin. *The Case for Women in Medieval Culture.* Oxford: Clarendon Press, 1997.

———. "Women and Creative Intelligence in Medieval Thought." In *Voices in Dialogue: Reading Women in the Middle Ages.* Edited by Linda Olson and Kathryn Kerby-Fulton. Notre Dame: University of Notre Dame Press, 2005, 213–30.

Blenkinsopp, Joseph. *The Pentateuch: An Introduction to the First Five Books of the Bible.* New York: Doubleday, 1992.

Bloch, R. Howard. *Medieval Misogyny and the Invention of Western Romantic Love.* Chicago: University of Chicago Press, 1991.

Blumenfeld-Kosinski, Renate. "Christine de Pizan and the Misogynistic Tradition." *Romanic Review* 81:3 (May 1990): 279–92.

———. "Jean le Fèvre's *Livre de Leesce*: Praise of Blame of Women?" *Speculum* 69:3 (July 1994).

Boehner, Philotheus. "The Notitia Intuitiva of Non-Existents According to William Ockham." In *Collected Articles on Ockham.* Edited by Eligius Buytaert. St. Bonaventure: Franciscan Institute, 1958, 274–87.

Bok, Sissela. *Lying: Moral Choice in Public and Private Life*, 2nd ed. New York: Vintage Books, 1999.

Bouwsma, William. *John Calvin.* New York: Oxford University Press, 1988.

Broughton, Janet. *Descartes's Method of Doubt.* Princeton: Princeton University Press, 2002.

Bruckmann, Patricia, ed. *Familiar Colloquy: Essays Presented to Arthur Edward Barker.* Ottawa: Oberon Press, 1978.

Bruns, Gerald L. *Inventions: Writing, Textuality, and Understanding in Literary History.* New Haven: Yale University Press, 1982.

Buc, Philippe. *L'Amiguïté du livre: Prince, pouvoir, et peuple dans les commentaires de la bible au moyen age*. Paris: Beauchesne Éditeur, 1994.

Buescher, Gabriel N. *The Eucharistic Teaching of William Ockham*. Washington D.C.: Catholic University of America Press, 1950.

Burke, Peter. *The Fortunes of the Courtier*. University Park: Pennsylvania State University Press, 1996.

Burnley, J. D. "Criseyde's Heart and the Weakness of Women: An Essay in Lexical Interpretation." *Studia Neophilologica* 54:1 (1982): 25–38.

Burns, J. Patout. "Creation and Fall According to Ambrose of Milan." In *Augustine: Biblical Exegete*. Edited by Frederick Van Fleteren and Joseph C. Schnaubelt. New York: Peter Lang, 2001.

Burrus, Virginia. *The Making of a Heretic: Gender, Authority and the Priscillianist Controversy*. Berkeley: University of California Press, 1995.

Cadden, Joan. *Meanings of Sex Difference in the Middle Ages: Medicine, Science, Culture*. Cambridge: Cambridge University Press, 1993.

The Cambridge Companion to Augustine. Edited by Elenore Stump and Norman Kretzman. Cambridge: Cambridge University Press, 2001.

The Cambridge Companion to Descartes. Edited by John Cottingham. Cambridge: Cambridge University Press, 1992.

Cape, Robert W., Jr. "Cicero and the Development of Prudential Practice at Rome." In *Prudence*, 35–65.

Cariou, Pierre. *Pascal et la casuistique*. Paris: Presses Universitaire de France, 1993.

Casagrande, Carla, and Silvana Vecchio. *Les péchés de la langue: Discipline et éthique de la parole dans la culture médiévale*. Translated by Philippe Baillet. Paris: Les Éditions du Cerf, 1991.

Catto, J. I. "John Wyclif and the Cult of the Eucharist." In *The Bible in the Medieval World: Essays in Memory of Beryl Smalley*. Edited by Katherine Walsh and Diana Wood. Oxford: Blackwell, 1985, 269–86.

Cavaillé, Jean-Pierre. *Dis/simulations. Jules-César Vanini, François La Mothe Le Vayer, Gabriel Naudé, Louis Machon et Torquato Accetto. Religion, morale et politique au XVIIe siècle*. Paris: Honoré Champion, 2002.

Celano, Anthony J. "The End of Practical Wisdom: Ethics as Science in the Thirteenth Century." *Journal of the History of Philosophy* 33:2 (April 1995): 225–43.

Chenu, Marie Dominique. *Toward Understanding Saint Thomas*. Translated and corrected by A. M. Landry and D. Hughes. Chicago: Regnery Publishing, 1964.

Clark, Elizabeth A. "Heresy, Asceticism, Adam and Eve: Interpretations of Genesis 1–3 in the Later Latin Fathers." In *Genesis 1–3 in the History of Exegesis: Intrigue in the Garden*. Edited by Gregory Allen Robbins. Lewiston: Edwin Mellen Press, 1988, 99–133.

———. "Ideology, History, and the Construction of 'Woman' in Late Ancient Christianity." *Journal of Early Christian Studies* 2:2 (1994): 155–84.

Clark, Henry C. *La Rochefoucauld and the Language of Unmasking in Seventeenth-Century France*. Geneva: Librairie Droz, 1994.

Clark, Stuart. *Vanities of the Eye: Vision in Early Modern European Culture*. Oxford: Oxford University Press, 2007.

Cogan, Marc. *The Design in the Wax: The Structure of the Divine Comedy and Its Meaning*. Notre Dame: University of Notre Dame Press, 1999.

Colish, Marcia. "The Stoic Theory of Verbal Signification." In *Archéologie de signe*. Edited by Lucie Brind'Amour and Eugene Vance. Toronto: Pontifical Institute of Mediaeval Studies Press, 1982, 17–43.

———. "Systematic Theology and Theological Renewal in the Twelfth Century." *Journal of Medieval and Renaissance Studies* 18:2 (1988): 135–56.

———. "Rethinking Lying in the Twelfth Century." In *Virtue and Ethics in the Twelfth Century*. Edited by István P. Bejczy and Richard G. Newhauser. Leiden: E. J. Brill, 2005: 155–74.

Collett, Barry. "The Three Mirrors of Christine de Pizan." In *Healing the Body Politic*, 1–18.

Constas, Nicholas P. "The Last Temptation of Satan: Divine Deception in Greek Patristic Interpretations of the Passion Narrative." *Harvard Theological Review* 97:2 (April 2004): 139–63.

Cook, Harold J. "Bernard Mandeville and the Therapy of the 'Clever Politician.'" *Journal of the History of Ideas* 60:1 (January 1999): 101–24.

Corran, Emily. "Hiding the Truth: Exegetical Discussions of Abraham's Lies from Hugh of Saint Victor to Stephen Langton." *Historical Research* 87:235 (December, 2013): 1–17.

Cotts, John D. *The Clerical Dilemma: Peter of Blois and Literate Culture in the Twelfth Century*. Washington, D.C.: Catholic University of America Press, 2009.

Cox, Virginia. "The Single Self: Feminist Thought and the Marriage Market in Early Modern Venice." *Renaissance Quarterly* 48:3 (Autumn 1995): 513–81.

Craun, Edwin D. *Lies, Slander, and Obscenity in Medieval English Literature*. Cambridge: Cambridge University Press, 1997.

Crocker, Lester Gilbert. "The Problem of Truth and Falsehood in the Age of the Enlightenment." *Journal of the History of Ideas* 14:4 (October,1953): 573–603.

Cross, Richard. "Duns Scotus on Goodness, Justice, and What God Can Do." *Journal of Theological Studies* 48 (1997): 48–76.

———. *Duns Scotus*. Oxford: Oxford University Press, 1999.

Crowther, Kathleen M. *Adam and Eve in the Protestant Reformation*. Cambridge: Cambridge University Press, 2010.

Cullen, Christopher M. *Bonaventure*. Oxford: Oxford University Press, 2006.

Cunning, David. "Descartes on the Immutability of the Divine Will." *Religious Studies* 39 (2003): 79–92.

———. *Argument and Persuasion in Descartes' Meditations*. Oxford: Oxford University Press, 2010.

de Groot, Art. "Acontius's Plea for Tolerance." In *From Strangers to Citizens: The Integration of Immigrant Communities in Britain, Ireland and Colonial America, 1550–1750*. Edited by Randolph Vigne and Charles Littleton. Brighton: Sussex Academic Press, 2001, 48–54.

Denery, Dallas G., II. "From Sacred Mystery to Divine Deception: Robert Holkot,

John Wyclif and the Transformation of Fourteenth-Century Eucharistic Discourse." *Journal of Religious History* (June 2005): 129–44.

———. *Seeing and Being Seen in the Later Middle Ages: Optics, Theology and Religious Life.* Cambridge: Cambridge University Press, 2005.

———. "Biblical Liars and Medieval Theologians." In *The Seven Deadly Sins: From Individuals to Communities.* Edited by Richard Newhauser. Leiden: E. J. Brill, 2007, 111–28.

———. "Christine de Pizan against the Theologians: The Virtue of Lies in *The Book of Three Virtues.*" *Viator* 39:1 (2008): 229–47.

———. "Christine de Pizan on Misogyny, Gossip and Possibility." In *The Middle Ages in Texts and Texture.* Edited by Jason Glenn. Toronto: University of Toronto Press, 2011, 309–21.

———. "Uncertainty and Deception in the Medieval and Early Modern Court." In *Uncertain Knowledge: Scepticism, Relativism and Doubt in the Middle Ages.* Edited by Dallas G. Denery II, Kantik Ghosh and Nicolette Zeeman (Turnhout: Brepols, 2014), 13–36.

Dickey, Laurence. "Pride, Hypocrisy and Civility in Mandeville's Social and Historical Theory." *Critical Review* 4:3 (Summer,1990): 387–431.

Diggins, John Patrick. "The Oyster and the Pearl: The Problem of Contextualism in Intellectual History." *History and Theory* 23:2 (May 1984): 151–69.

Donawerth, Jane. "As Becomes a Rational Woman to Speak." In *Listening to Their Voices: The Rhetorical Activities of Historical Women.* Edited by Molly Meijer Wertheimer. Columbia: University of South Carolina Press, 1997, 305–19.

Dougherty, M. V. *Moral Dilemmas in Medieval Thought from Gratian to Thomas Aquinas.* Cambridge: Cambridge University Press, 2011.

Duby, Georges. *Dames du XIIe siècle*, tom. III, *Ève et les prêtres.* Paris: Éditions Gallimard, 1996.

Dulac, Liliane. "Un mythe didactique chez Christine de Pizan: Sémiramis ou la Veuve héroïque." In *Mélanges de Philologie Romane offerts à Charles Camproux*, tom. I. Montpellier: C.E.O., 1978, 315–31.

———. "The Representation and Functions of Feminine Speech in Christine de Pizan's *Livre des Trois Virtus.*" In *Reinterpreting Christine de Pizan.* Edited by Earl Jeffrey Richards. Athens: University of Georgia Press, 1990, 13–22.

Dumoutet, E. *Le Désir de voir l'hostie et les origins de la dévotion au saint-sacrament.* Paris: Beauchesne, 1926.

Duriez, George. *Le théologie dans le drame religieux en Allemagne au moyen âge.* Lille: René Girard, 1914.

Eagleton, Terry. *Ideology: An Introduction.* London: Verso, 1991.

Eskin, Catherine R. "The Re(i)gning of Women's Tongues in English Books of Instruction and Rhetorics." In *Women's Education in Early Modern Europe: A History, 1500–1800.* Edited by Barbara Whitehead. New York: Routledge, 1999, 101–30.

Evans, G. R. *Old Arts and New Theology: The Beginning of Theology as an Academic Discipline.* Oxford: Clarendon Press, 1980.

Evans, J. M. *'Paradise Lost' and the Genesis Tradition*. Oxford: Clarendon Press, 1968.

Farrell, John. *Paranoia and Modernity: Cervantes to Rousseau*. Ithaca: Cornell University Press, 2007.

Feehan, Thomas. "Augustine on Lying and Deception." *Augustinian Studies* 19 (1988): 131–39.

————. "The Morality of Lying in St. Augustine." *Augustinian Studies* 21 (1990): 67–81.

Feldman, Robert. *The Liar in Your Life: The Way to a Truthful Relationship*. New York: Twelve, 2009.

Ferrante, Joan. "The Relation of Speech to Sin in the Inferno." *Dante Studies* 87 (1969): 33–46.

Ferraro, Joanne M. "The Power to Decide: Battered Wives in Early Modern Venice." *Renaissance Quarterly* 48:3 (Autumn 1995): 492–512.

Finnis, John. *Aquinas: Moral, Political, and Legal Theory*. Oxford: Oxford University Press, 1998.

Force, Pierre. *Le problème herméneutique chez Pascal*. Paris: Librairie Philosophique J. Vrin, 1989.

Forhan, Kate L. *The Political Theory of Christine de Pizan*. Aldershot: Ashgate Publishing, 2002.

Forsyth, Neil. *The Old Enemy: Satan and the Combat Myth*. Princeton: Princeton University Press, 1987.

————. *The Satanic Epic*. Princeton: Princeton University Press, 2003.

French, Roger. *Medicine before Science: The Rational and Learned Doctor from the Middle Ages to the Enlightenment*. Cambridge: Cambridge University Press, 2003.

Fumaroli, Marc. "*De l'Age de l'éloquence à l'Age de la conversation: la conversion de la rhétorique humaniste dans la France du XVIIe siècle.*" In *Art de la lettre*, 25–45.

Funkenstein, Amos. *Theology and the Scientific Imagination from the Middle Ages to the Seventeenth Century*. Princeton: Princeton University Press, 1986.

Garber, Daniel. "Descartes' Physics." In *The Cambridge Companion to Descartes*, 286–334.

Garver, Eugene. *Machiavelli and the History of Prudence*. Madison: University of Wisconsin Press, 1987.

Gehl, Paul F. "Mystical Language Models in Monastic Educational Psychology." *Journal of Medieval and Renaissance Studies* 14:2 (1984): 219–43.

————. "Competens Silentium: Varieties of Monastic Silence in the Medieval West." *Viator* 18 (1987).

Gelber, Hester Goodenough. *It Could Have Been Otherwise*. Leiden: E. J. Brill, 2004.

Gibert, Pierre. "De l'intuition à l'évidence: la multiplicité documentaire dans la Genèse chez H. B. Witter et Jean Astruc." In *Sacred Conjectures: The Context and Legacy of Robert Lowth and Jean Astruc*. Edited by John Jarick. New York: T&T Clark, 2007, 174–89.

Gillespie, Michael Allen. *The Theological Origins of Modernity*. Chicago: University of Chicago Press, 2008.

Goldsmith, Elizabeth C. *Exclusive Conversations: The Art of Interaction in Seventeenth-Century France*. Philadelphia: University of Pennsylvania Press, 1988.

Gourevitch, Victor. "Rousseau on Lying: A Provisional Reading of the Fourth Rêverie." *Berkshire Review* 15 (1980): 93–107.

Grant, Ruth W. *Hypocrisy and Integrity: Machiavelli, Rousseau and the Ethics of Politics*. Chicago: University of Chicago Press, 1997.

Gray, Douglas. *Themes and Images in the Medieval English Lyric*. London/Boston: Routledge and Keegan Paul, 1972.

Green, Karen. "On Translating Christine as a Philosopher." In *Healing the Body Politic*, 117–37.

———. "*Phronesis* Feminised: Prudence from Christine de Pizan to Elizabeth I." In *Virtue, Liberty and Toleration: Political Ideas of European Women*. Edited by Jacqueline Broad and Karen Green. Dordrecht: Springer, 2007, 24–29.

Grellard, Christophe. *Jean de Salisbury et la renaissance médiévale du scepticisme*. Paris: Les Belles Lettres, 2013.

Griffiths, Paul J. *Lying: An Augustinian Theology of Duplicity*. Grand Rapids: Brazos, 2004.

Hamilton, Victor P. *The Book of Genesis: Chapters 1–17*. Grand Rapids: William B. Eerdmans Publishing Company, 1990.

Hansson, Stina. "Rhetoric for Seventeenth-Century Salons: Beata Rosenhane's Exercise Books and Classical Rhetoric." *Rhetorica: A Journal of the History of Rhetoric* 12:1 (Winter 1994): 43–65.

Haraguchi, Jennifer. "Debating Women's Fashion in Renaissance Venice." In *A Well-Fashioned Image: Clothing and Costume in European Art, 1500–1850*. Edited by Elizabeth Rodini and Elissa B. Weaver. Chicago: David and Alfred Smart Museum of Art, 2002, 23–34.

Harries, Karsten. *Infinity and Perspective*. Cambridge: MIT Press, 2001.

Harriman, Robert. "Theory without Modernity." In *Prudence*, 1–32.

Haulotte, Edgar. *Symbolique du vêtement selon la Bible*. Paris: Aubier, 1966.

Healing the Body Politic: The Political Thought of Christine de Pizan. Edited by K. Green and C. J. Mews. Turnhout: Brepols, 2005.

Heath, Eugene. "Mandeville's Bewitching Engine of Praise." *History of Philosophy Quarterly* 15:2 (April 1998): 205–26.

Henry, John. "Metaphysics and the Origins of Modern Science: Descartes and the Importance of Laws of Nature." *Early Science and Medicine* 9:2 (2004): 73–114.

Herdt, Jennifer A. *Putting on Virtue: The Legacy of the Splendid Vices*. Chicago: University of Chicago Press, 2008.

Hodgson, Richard G. *Falsehood Disguised: Unmasking the Truth in La Rochefoucauld*. West Lafayette: Purdue University Press, 1995.

Horowitz, Maryanne Cline. "Aristotle and Woman." *Journal of History of Biology* 9:2 (Autumn 1976): 183–213.

Jaeger, C. Stephen. "The Court Criticism of MGH Didactic Poets: Social Structures and Literary Conventions." *Monatshefte* 74:4 (Winter 1982): 398–409.

———. "Pessimism in the Twelfth-Century Renaissance." *Speculum* 78:4 (October 2003): 1151–83.

Jager, Eric. *The Tempter's Voice: Language and the Fall in Medieval Literature.* Ithaca: Cornell University Press, 1993.

Javitch, Daniel. "The Philosopher of the Court: A French Satire Misunderstood." *Comparative Literature* 23:2 (Spring 1971): 97–124.

———. "Rival Arts of Conduct in Elizabethan England: Guazzo's *Civile Conversation* and Castiglione's *Courtier.*" *Yearbook of Italian Studies* 1 (1971): 171–98.

———. "*Il Cortegiano* and the Constraints of Despotism." In *Castiglione: The Ideal and Real in Renaissance Culture.* Edited by Robert W. Hanning and David Rosand. New Haven: Yale University Press, 1983.

Jay, Martin. *The Virtues of Mendacity: On Lying in Politics.* Charlottesville: University of Virginia Press, 2010.

Jonsen, Albert, and Stephen Toulmin. *The Abuse of Casuistry: A History of Moral Reasoning.* Berkeley: University of California Press, 1988.

Jordan, Mark D. "Words and Word: Incarnation and Signification in Augustine's *De Doctrina Christiana.*" *Augustinian Studies* 11 (1980): 177–96.

Jordan, W. K. *The Development of Religious Toleration in England: From the Beginning of the English Reformation to the Death of Queen Elizabeth.* Cambridge: Harvard University Press, 1932.

Justice, Steven. "Eucharistic Miracle and Eucharistic Doubt." *Journal of Medieval and Early Modern Studies* 42:2 (2012): 307–32.

Kahn, Victoria. *Rhetoric, Prudence and Skepticism in the Renaissance.* Ithaca: Cornell University Press, 1985.

Kale, Steven D. "Women, the Public Sphere, and the Persistence of Salons." *French Historical Studies* 25:1 (Winter 2002): 115–48.

Keen, Maurice. "Wyclif, the Bible and Transubstantiation." In *Wyclif in His Times.* Edited by Anthony Kenny. Oxford: Clarendon Press, 1986, 11–30.

Kelly, Henry Angsar. *Satan: A Biography.* Cambridge: Cambridge University Press, 2006.

Kempshall, Matthew S. *The Common Good in Late Medieval Political Thought.* Oxford: Oxford University Press, 1999.

———. *Rhetoric and the Writing of History: 400–1500.* Manchester: Manchester University Press, 2011.

Kent, Bonnie. *Virtues of the Will: The Transformation of Ethics in the Late Thirteenth Century.* Washington, D.C.: Catholic University of America Press, 1995.

Keohane, Nannerl O. *Philosophy and the State in France: The Renaissance to the Enlightenment.* Princeton: Princeton University Press, 1980.

Kirwan, Christopher. "Augustine's Philosophy of Language." In *The Cambridge Companion to Augustine,* 186–204.

Klepper, Deeana Copeland. *The Insight of Unbelievers: Nicholas of Lyra and Christian Readings of Jewish Text in the Later Middle Ages.* Philadelphia: University of Pennsylvania Press, 2007.

Kolsky, Stephen. "Moderate Fonte, Lucrezia Marinella, Giuseppe Passi: An Early Seventeenth-Century Feminist Controversy." *Modern Language Review* 96:4 (October 2001): 973–89.

———. "The Limits of Knowledge: Scholasticism and Scepticism in *The Book of the Courtier.*" *Parergon* 25:2 (2008): 17–32.

Korsgaard, Christine M. "The Right to Lie: Kant on Dealing with Evil." *Philosophy and Public Affairs* 15:4 (Autumn 1986): 325–49.

Kugel, James L. *The Bible as It Was.* Cambridge: Harvard University Press, 1997.

Labalme, Patricia H. "Venetian Women on Women: Three Early Modern Feminists." *Archivo Veneto,* ser. 5, 3 (1981): 81–109.

Lahey, Steven. *John Wyclif.* Oxford: Oxford University Press, 2009.

Landgraf, Arthur. "Definition und Sündhaftigkeit der Lüge nach der Lehre der Frühscholastik." *Zeitschrift für Katholische Theologie* 63 (1939): 50–85.

Leclercq, Jean. *The Love of Learning and the Desire for God.* Translated by Catherine Mishari. New York: Fordham University Press, 1961.

Leff, Gordon. *Heresy in the Later Middle Ages: The Relation of Heterodoxy to Dissent, 1250–1450.* Manchester: Manchester University Press, 1967.

LeGoff, Jacques. *Intellectuals in the Middle Ages.* Translated by Teresa Lavendar Fagan. Oxford: Blackwell, 1992.

Levy, Ian Christopher. "*Christus qui mentiri non potest*: John Wyclif's Rejection of Transubstantiation." *Recherches de Théologie et Philosophie* 66:2 (1999): 316–34.

———. *John Wyclif: Scriptural Logic, Real Presence and the Parameters of Orthodoxy.* Milwaukee: Marquette University Press, 2003.

Lilti, Antoine. *Le Monde des salons: Sociabilité et mondanité à Paris au XVIIIe siècle.* Paris: Librairie Arthème Fayard, 2005.

———. "The Kingdom of *Politesse*: Salons and the Republic of Letters in Eighteenth-Century Paris." *Republic of Letters: A Journal for the Study of Knowledge, Politics and the Arts* 1:1 (2009): 1–11.

Lubac, Henri de. *Augustinianism and Modern Theology.* Translated by Lancelot Sheppard. New York: Herder and Herder, 1969.

Lunn-Rockliffe, Sophie. "The Diabolical Problem of Satan's First Sin: Self-Moved Pride or a Response to the Goads of Envy." *Studia Patristica Studia Patristica* 43:11 (2013): 121–40.

MacIntyre, Alasdair. *Truthfulness, Lies and Moral Philosophers: What Can We Learn from Mill and Kant.* In *The Tanner Lectures on Human Values,* vol. 15. Salt Lake City: University of Utah Press, 1994: 309–69.

Maclean, Ian. *The Renaissance Notion of Woman: A Study in the Fortunes of Scholasticism and Medical Science in European Intellectual Life.* Cambridge: Cambridge University Press, 1980.

Macy, Gary. *The Banquet's Wisdom: A Short History of the Lord's Supper.* Mahway: Paulist Press, 1992.

———. *The Hidden History of Women's Ordination: Female Clergy in the Medieval West.* Oxford: Oxford University Press, 2008.

Magnanini, Suzanne. "Una selva luminosa: The Second Day of Moderata Fonte's *Il merito delle donne.*" *Modern Philology* 101:2 (November 2003): 278–96.

Mahon, James. "The Truth about Lies in Kant." In *The Philosophy of Deception*. Edited by Clancy Martin. Oxford: Oxford University Press, 2009, 201–24.

Malloch, A. E. "Equivocation: A Circuit of Reasons." In *Familiar Colloquy: Essays Presented to Arthur Edward Barker*. Edited by Patricia Bruckmann. Ottawa: Oberon Press, 1978, 132–43.

Marion, Jean-Luc. "Outline of a History of Definitions of God in the Cartesian Epoch." In *On the Ego and God: Further Cartesian Questions*. Translated by Christina M. Geshwandtner. New York: Fordham University Press, 2007, 161–92.

Markus, R. A. "St. Augustine on Signs." *Phronesis* 2:1 (1957): 60–83.

Martin, John Jeffries. "Inventing Sincerity, Refashioning Prudence: The Discovery of the Individual in Renaissance Europe." *American Historical Review* 102:5 (December 1997): 1309–42.

———. *Myths of Renaissance Individualism*. New York: Palgrave MacMillan, 2004.

Marx, C. W. *The Devil's Rights and Redemption in the Literature of Medieval England*. Cambridge: D. S. Brewer, 1995.

McGrath, Alister E. *Luther's Theology of the Cross: Martin Luther's Theological Breakthrough*. Oxford: Basil Blackwell, 1985.

McHugh, Michael P. "Satan and Saint Ambrose." *Classical Folia* 26:1 (1972): 94–106.

McLeod, Glenda. *Virtue and Venom: Catalogs of Women from Antiquity to the Renaissance*. Ann Arbor: University of Michigan Press, 1991.

Melzer, Arthur M. *The Natural Goodness of Man: On the System of Rousseau's Thought*. Chicago: University of Chicago Press, 1990.

———. "Rousseau and the Modern Cult of Sincerity." *Harvard Review of Philosophy* (Spring 1995): 4–21.

Menn, Stephen. *Augustine and Descartes*. Cambridge: Cambridge University Press, 1998.

Mews, Constant J. "Latin Learning in Christine de Pizan's *Livre de Paix*." In *Healing the Body Politic*, 61–75.

Miel, Jan. *Pascal and Theology*. Baltimore: Johns Hopkins Press, 1969.

Miles, Margaret. "Vision: The Eye of the Body and the Eye of the Mind in Saint Augustine's *De trinitate*." *Journal of Religion* 63:2 (April 1983): 125–42.

Miller, Sarah Alison. *Medieval Monstrosity and the Female Body*. New York: Routledge, 2010.

Mitchell, Sharon C. "Moral Posturing: Virtue in Christine de Pisan's *Livre de Trois Vertus*." In *The Inner Life of Women in Medieval Romance Literature: Grief, Guilt and Hypocrisy*. Edited by Jeff Rider and Jamie Friedman. New York: Palgrave Macmillan, 2011, 85–106.

Montandon, Alain. "Les bienséances de la conversation." In *Art de la lettre*, 61–79.

Moriarty, Michael. *Fallen Nature, Fallen Selves: Early Modern French Thought II*. Oxford: Oxford University Press, 2006.

———. *Disguised Vices: Theories of Virtues in Early Modern French Thought*. Oxford: Oxford University Press, 2011.

Morse, Ruth. *Truth and Convention: Rhetoric, Representation and Reality*. Cambridge: Cambridge University Press, 1991.

Nederman, Cary. "Nature, Sin and the Origins of Society: The Ciceronian Tradition in Medieval Political Thought." *Journal of the History of Ideas* 49:1 (January–March 1988): 3–26.

———. "Beyond Stoicism and Aristotelianism: John of Salisbury's Skepticism and Twelfth-Century Moral Philosophy." In *Virtue and Ethics in the Twelfth Century*. Edited by Istvan Bejczy and Richard G. Newhauser. Leiden: E. J. Brill, 2005, 177–84.

———. *John of Salisbury*. Tempe: Arizona Center for Medieval and Renaissance Studies, 2005.

Nederman, Cary J., and Tsae Lan Lee Dow. "The Road to Heaven Is Paved with Pious Deception: Medieval Speech Ethics and Deliberative Democracy." In *Talking Democracy: Historical Perspectives on Rhetoric and Democracy*. Edited by Benedetto Fontana. University Park: Pennsylvania State University Press, 2005, 187–212.

Nelson, Alan H. "The Temptation of Christ; or, The Temptation of Satan." In *Medieval English Drama: Essays Critical and Contextual*. Edited by Jerome Taylor and Alan H. Nelson. Chicago: University of Chicago Press, 1972, 218–29.

Newhauser, Richard. "Towards a History of Human Curiosity: A Prolegomenon to Its Medieval Phase." *Deutsche Vierteljahrsschrift* 56 (1982): 559–75.

Nyberg, David. *The Varnished Truth: Truth Telling and Deceiving in Ordinary Life*. Chicago: University of Chicago Press, 1993.

Oberman, Heiko. "*Facientibus quod in se est deus non denegat gratiam*: Robert Holcot, O.P. and the Beginnings of Luther's Theology." In *The Dawn of the Reformation*. Edinburgh: T&T Clark, 1986, 84–103.

———. *Luther: Man between God and the Devil*. Translated by Eileen Walliser-Schwarzbart. New Haven: Yale University Press, 1989.

Parker, Patricia. "Virile Style." In *Premodern Sexualities*. Edited by Louise Fradenburg and Carla Freccero. New York: Routledge, 1996, 201–22.

Pelikan, Jaroslav. *The Emergence of the Catholic Tradition (100–600)*. Chicago: University of Chicago Press, 1971.

———. *The Reformation of Church and Dogma (1300–1700)*. Chicago: University of Chicago Press, 1984.

Pender, Stephen. "The Open Use of Living: Prudence, Decorum and the 'Square Man.'" *Rhetorica* 23:4 (April 2005): 363–400.

Perler, Dominik. *Zweifel und Gewissheit. Skeptische Debatten im Mittelalter*. Frankfurt a.M.: Klostermann, 2006.

———. "Does God Deceive Us? Skeptical Hypotheses in Late Medieval Epistemology." In *Rethinking the History of Skepticism*, 171–92.

Pessin, Andrew. "Malebranche's Distinction between General and Particular Volitions." *Journal of the History of Philosophy* 39:1 (January 2001): 77–99.

Phillippy, Patricia. "Establishing Authority: Boccaccio's *De claris mulieribus* and Christine de Pizan's *Livre de la cité des dames*." *Romantic Review* 77 (1986): 167–94.

Phillips, Heather. "John Wyclif and the Religion of the People." In *A Distinct*

Voice: Medieval Studies in Honor of Leonard E. Boyle, O.P. Edited by Jacqueline Brown and William P. Stoneman. Notre Dame: University of Notre Dame Press, 1997, 561–90.

Popkin, Richard. *The History of Skepticism: From Savanarola to Bayle.* New York: Oxford University Press, 2003.

Pratt, Karen. "Translating Misogamy: The Authority of the Intertext in the *Lamentationes Matheoluli* and Its Middle French Translation." *Forum for Modern Language Studies* 35:4 (1999): 421–35.

Prudence: Classical Virtue, Postmodern Practice. Edited by Robert Harriman. University Park: Pennsylvania State University Press, 2003.

Quilligan, Maureen. *The Allegory of Female Authority: Christine de Pizan's Cité des dames.* Ithaca: Cornell University Press, 1991.

Quinn, John F. "Bonaventure on Our Natural Obligation to Confess Truth." *Franciscan Studies* 35 (1975): 194–211.

Rabb, Theodore. *The Struggle for Stability in Early Modern Europe.* New York: Oxford University Press, 1975.

Ramsey, Boniface. "Two Traditions on Lying and Deception in the Ancient Church." *Thomist* 49 (1985): 504–33.

Rebhorn, Wayne A. *The Emperor of Men's Minds: Literature and the Renaissance Discourse of Reason.* Ithaca: Cornell University Press, 1995.

Remer, Gary. "Hobbes, the Rhetorical Tradition, and Toleration." *Review of Politics* 54:1 (Winter 1992): 5–33.

———. *Humanism and the Rhetoric of Toleration.* University Park: Pennsylvania State University Press, 1996.

———. "Rhetoric as a Balancing of Ends: Cicero and Machiavelli." *Philosophy and Rhetoric* 42:1 (2009): 1–29.

Remly, Paul G. "*Muscipula Diaboli* and Medieval English Antifeminism." *English Studies* (1989): 1–14.

Rethinking the History of Skepticism: The Missing Medieval Background. Edited by H. Lagerlund. Leiden: E. J. Brill, 2010.

Richards, Earl Jeffrey. "Somewhere between Destructive Glosses and Chaos: Christine de Pizan and Medieval Theology." In *Christine de Pizan: A Casebook.* Edited by Barbara K. Altman and Deborah L. McGrady. New York: Routledge, 2003, 43–55.

Richards, Jennifer. "Assumed Simplicity and the Critique of Nobility: Or, How Castiglione Read Cicero." *Renaissance Quarterly* 54:2 (Summer 2001): 460–86.

———. *Rhetoric and Courtliness in Early Modern Literature.* Cambridge: Cambridge University Press, 2003.

Rodis-Lewis, Geneviève. *Descartes: His Life and Thought.* Translated by Jane Marie Todd. Ithaca: Cornell University Press, 1999.

Ross, Sarah Gwyneth. *The Birth of Feminism: Woman as Intellect in Renaissance Italy and England.* Cambridge: Harvard University Press, 2009.

Rouillard, Linda. "Faux semblant ou faire semblant?" Christine de Pizan and Virtuous Artifice." *Forum for Modern Language Studies* 46:1 (2009): 1–13.

Rubin, Miri. *Corpus Christi: The Eucharist in Late Medieval Culture.* Cambridge: Cambridge University Press, 1991.

Russell, Jeffrey Burton. *Lucifer: The Devil in the Middle Ages.* Ithaca: Cornell University Press, 1984.

———. *Mephistopheles: The Devil in the Modern World.* Ithaca: Cornell University Press, 1986.

———. *The Devil: Perceptions of Evil from Antiquity to Primitive Christianity.* Ithaca: Cornell University Press, 1987.

———. *The Prince of Darkness: Radical Evil and the Power of Good in History.* Ithaca: Cornell University Press, 1988.

Satran, David. "Deceiving the Deceiver: Variations on an Early Christian Theme." In *Things Revealed: Studies in Early Jewish and Christian Literature in Honor of Michael E. Stone.* Edited by E. G. Chazon, D. Satran and R. A. Clements (Leiden: E. J. Brill, 2004), 357–64.

Schapiro, Meyer. "*Muscipula Diaboli*: The Symbolism of the Mérode Altarpiece." *Art Bulletin* 27:3 (1945): 182–87.

Scheibe, Karl E. "In Defense of Lying: On the Moral Neutrality of Misrepresentation." *Berkshire Review* 15 (1980): 15–24.

Schieberle, Misty. *Feminized Counsel: Women Counselors in Late Medieval Advice Literature, 1380–1500.* Turnhout: Brepols, 2014.

Schreiner, Susan. *Are You Alone Wise? The Search for Certainty in the Early Modern Era.* Oxford: Oxford University Press, 2012.

Seigel, Jerrold. *Rhetoric and Philosophy in Renaissance Humanism.* Princeton: Princeton University Press, 1968.

Sellier, Philippe. *Pascal et Saint Augustin.* Paris: Librairie Armand Colin, 1970.

Shumaker, Wayne, and Millicent Bell. "The Fallacy of the Fall in *Paradise Lost.*" *PMLA* 70:5 (December 1955): 1185–203.

Skinner, Quentin. *Reason and Rhetoric in the Philosophy of Hobbes.* Cambridge: Cambridge University Press, 1996.

Simmons, Alison J. "Sensible Ends: Latent Teleology in Descartes' Account of Sensation." *Journal of History of Philosophy* 39:1 (January 2001): 49–75.

Simpson, James. *Burning to Read: English Fundamentalism and Its Reformation Opponents.* Cambridge: Belknap Press of Harvard University Press, 2007.

Siraisi, Nancy. *Medieval and Early Renaissance Medicine: An Introduction to Knowledge and Practice.* Chicago: University of Chicago Press, 1990.

Smarr, Janet Levarie. "The Uses of Conversation: Moderata Fonte and Edmund Tilney." *Comparative Literature Studies* 32:1 (1995): 1–25.

Smith, David Livingstone. *Why We Lie: The Evolutionary Roots of Deception and the Unconscious Mind.* New York: St. Martin's Press, 2004.

Smith, Euclid O. "Deception and Evolutionary Biology." *Cultural Anthropology* 2 (1987): 50–64.

Smith, Pauline M. *The Anti-courtier Trend in Sixteenth Century French Literature.* Geneva: Librairie Droz, 1966.

Snyder, Jon. *Dissimulation and the Culture of Secrecy in Early Modern Europe.* Berkeley: University of California Press, 2009.

Sommerville, John. "The New Art of Lying: Equivocation, Mental Reservation, and Casuistry." In *Conscience and Casuistry in Early Modern Europe*. Edited by Edmund Leites. Cambridge: Cambridge University Press, 1988, 159–84.

Spade, Paul Vincent. "The Semantics of Terms." In *The Cambridge History of Later Medieval Philosophy*. Edited by Norman Kretzman. Cambridge: Oxford University Press, 1982, 188–90.

Stanton, Domna C. *The Aristocrat as Art: A Study of the Honnête Homme and the Dandy in Seventeenth- and Nineteenth-Century Literature*. New York: Columbia University Press, 1989.

Starobinski, Jean. *Jean-Jacques Rousseau: Transparency and Obstruction*. Translated by Arthur Goldhammer. Chicago: University of Chicago Press, 1988.

———. "The Motto *Vitam impendere vero* and the Question of Lying." In *The Cambridge Companion to Rousseau*. Edited by Patrick Riley. Cambridge: Cambridge University Press, 2001, 365–96.

Steinmetz, David C. "Divided by a Common Past: The Reshaping of the Christian Exegetical Tradition in the Sixteenth Century." *Journal of Medieval and Early Modern Studies* 27:2 (Spring 1997): 245–64.

Strickland, Debra Higgs. *Medieval Bestiaries: Text, Image, Ideology*. Cambridge: Cambridge University Press, 1995.

Sweeney, Eileen. "Hugh of St. Victor: The Augustinian Tradition of Sacred and Secular Reading Revised." In *Reading and Wisdom: The* De Doctrina Christiana *of Augustine in the Middle Ages*. Edited by Edward D. English. Notre Dame: University of Notre Dame Press, 1995, 61–83.

———. *Anselm of Canterbury and the Desire for the World*. Washington, D.C.: Catholic University of America Press, 2012.

Synan, Edward. "Prayer, Proof and Anselm's *Proslogion*." In *Standing before God: Studies on Prayer in Scriptures and in Tradition with Essays in Honor of John M. Oesterreicher*. Edited by Asher Finkel and Lawrence Frizzell. New York: KTAV Publishing House, 1981, 267–88.

Tachau, Katherine. *Vision and Certitude in the Age of Ockham*. Leiden: E. J. Brill, 1988.

———. "Robert Holcot on Contingency and Divine Deception." In *Filosofia e teologia nel trecento: Studi in ricordo di Eugenio Randi*. Edited by L. Bianchi. Louvain-la Neuve: Fédération internationale des instituts d'études médiévales, 1994.

———. "Logic's God and the Natural Order in Late Medieval Oxford." *Annals of Science* 53 (1996): 235–67.

Taylor, Charles. *Sources of the Self*. Cambridge: Harvard University Press, 1989.

Teselle, Eugene. "The Cross as Ransom." *Journal of Early Christian Studies* 4:2 (1996): 147–70.

Thorndike, Lynn. "*De Complexionibus*." *Isis* 49:4 (December 1958): 398–408.

Trilling, Lionel. *Sincerity and Authenticity*. Cambridge: Harvard University Press, 1972.

Tutino, Stefania. "Nothing but the Truth? Hermeneutics and Morality in the Doctrines of Equivocation and Mental Reservation in Early Modern Europe." *Renaissance Quarterly* 64:1 (Spring 2011): 115–55.

van den Hoek, Annewies. "Endowed with Reason or Glued to the Senses: Philo's

Thoughts on Adam and Eve." In *The Creation of Man and Woman: Interpretations of the Biblical Narratives in Jewish and Christian Traditions*. Edited by Gerard P. Luttikhuizen. Leiden: E. J. Brill, 2000: 63–75.

Van Engen, John H. *Rupert of Deutz*. Berkeley: University of California Press, 1983.

Vechio, Silvana. "Mensonge, Simulation, Dissimulation." In *Vestigia, Imagines, Verba: Semiotics and Logic in Medieval Theological Texts (XIIth–XIVth century)*. Edited by Constantine Marmo. Turnhout: Brepols, 1997.

Vincent-Cassy, Mireille. "Recherches sur le mensonge au Moyen Âge." In *Études sur la sensibilité au Moyen Âge*. Congrès national des sociétés savantes, France 1977, 165–73.

Visser, Sandra, and Thomas Williams. *Anselm*. Oxford: Oxford University Press, 2009.

Wajeman, Lise. *La parole d'Adam, le corps d'Eve: le péché originel au XVI siècle*. Geneva: Droz, 2007.

Waters, Claire. *Angels and Earthly Creatures; Preaching, Performance and Gender in the Later Middle Ages*. Philadelphia: University of Pennsylvania Press, 2004.

Watson, Gerard. "St. Augustine and the Inner Word: The Philosophical Background." *Irish Theological Quarterly* 54 (1988): 81–92.

Wei, Ian P. *Intellectual Culture in Medieval Paris: Theologians and the University, c. 1100–1333*. Cambridge, Cambridge University Press, 2012, 52–71.

Weiland, George. "The Reception and Interpretation of Aristotle's *Ethics*." In *The Cambridge History of Later Medieval Philosophy*. Edited by Norman Kretzman et al. Cambridge: Cambridge University Press, 1982, 657–72.

Wilks, Michael. "John of Salisbury and the Tyranny of Nonsense." In *The World of John of Salisbury*. Edited by Michael Wilks. Oxford: Blackwell, 1984, 263–86.

Williams, Arnold. *The Common Expositor: An Account of the Commentaries on Genesis, 1527–1633*. Chapel Hill: University of North Carolina Press, 1948.

Williams, Thomas. "Biblical Interpretation." In *The Cambridge Companion to Augustine*: 59–70.

Winroth, Anders. *The Making of Gratian's Decretum*. Cambridge: Cambridge University Press, 2000.

Wippel, John F. *Medieval Reactions to the Encounter between Faith and Reason*. Milwaukee: Marquette University Press, 1995.

Wood, William. "Axiology, Self-Deception and Moral Wrongdoing in Blaise Pascal's *Pensées*." *Journal of Religious Ethics* 37:2 (June 2009): 355–84.

———. "Thomas Aquinas on the Claim That God Is Truth." *Journal of the History of Philosophy* 51:1 (2013): 21–47.

Woodhouse, John R. "The Tradition of Della Casa's *Galateo* in English." In *The Crisis of Courtesy: Studies in the Conduct-Book in Britain, 1600–1900*. Edited by Jacques Carré. Leiden: E. J. Brill, 1994, 11–26.

Wurtele, Douglas. "The Bane of Flattery in the World of Langland." *Florigelium* 19 (2002): 1–25.

Zagorin, Perez. *Ways of Lying: Dissimulation, Persecution, and Conformity in Early Modern Europe*. Cambridge: Harvard University Press, 1990.

Index